Bridging the Technological Divide

Bridging the Technological Divide

Technology Adoption by Firms in Developing Countries

Xavier Cirera, Diego Comin,
and Marcio Cruz

WORLD BANK GROUP

Contents

Boxes

Figures

Map

Photos

Tables

Foreword

Poverty reduction and shared prosperity can be achieved only with sustained growth. But the global economy is increasingly vulnerable to global shocks. The COVID-19 (coronavirus) pandemic and its devastating impact on livelihoods has shown how vulnerable economies are. Potential future pandemics, climate change shocks, and political tensions threaten a sustainable recovery and future economic growth prospects. In this context, technology is emerging as a critical lifeline to increase the resilience of economies and boost economic growth. The pandemic has led to an unprecedented demand for the use of digital technologies by businesses and therefore provides a renewed opportunity to accelerate technology upgrading.

Since Joseph Schumpeter's pathbreaking work, technology has been recognized to be at the center of economic growth and development. Technologies used by firms are central to the process of creative destruction. Yet, existing measures of technology use fall short of providing a comprehensive characterization of technologies across and within firms, particularly for developing countries. This volume builds on a large effort to collect novel data through the new Firm-level Adoption of Technology (FAT) survey, providing a breakthrough contribution to address this knowledge gap. The new methods and data presented allow practitioners and policy makers to look inside the "black box" of technology adoption by firms and identify the key obstacles that constrain job creation through digital transformation and upgrading of business functions.

The volume's key findings contribute to the literature in three major directions. First, new measures of technology use show that most firms in developing countries are quite far from the technology frontier, and they may not be aware of the extent to which they lag. Second, new evidence shows that technology adoption is a key driver of long-term growth through its positive impact on productivity, jobs, and economic resilience. Third, in bridging the technological divide, access to reliable and high-quality infrastructure is a necessary condition for technology upgrading, but not a sufficient one. Developing countries need to enhance their institutions to promote market competition while shifting the focus from access to technology to the effective use of technology by firms.

The research presented here is part of the World Bank's Productivity Project led by the Chief Economist's Office of the Equitable Growth, Finance, and Institutions Vice Presidency. We are confident that researchers and development practitioners alike will highly value the new findings on technology adoption and the directions for development policies this volume contains.

Indermit S. Gill
Vice President, Equitable Growth, Finance, and Institutions
The World Bank

Preface

Productivity accounts for half of the differences in gross domestic product per capita across countries. Identifying policies that stimulate productivity is thus critical to alleviating poverty and fulfilling the rising aspirations of global citizens. In recent decades, however, productivity growth has slowed globally, and the lagging productivity performance of developing countries is a major barrier to convergence with income levels in advanced economies. The World Bank Productivity Project seeks to bring frontier thinking to the measurement and determinants of productivity, grounded in the developing country context, to global policy makers. Each volume in the series explores a different aspect of the topic through dialogue with academics and policy makers and through sponsored empirical work in the World Bank's client countries.

Bridging the Technological Divide: Technology Adoption by Firms in Developing Countries, the seventh volume in the series, breaks new ground in the empirics of technology adoption. Like *The Innovation Paradox* before it, this volume stresses the importance to economic growth of the flow of ideas and new practices. Indeed, recent studies suggest that differences in the evolution of technology diffusion across countries drive a corresponding evolution of productivity (total factor productivity) that can account for the divergence in the world income distribution over the last 200 years.

The agent that in practice undertakes technology adoption and drives technology diffusion is the firm. The Productivity Project opens the "black box" of the firm for the first time in a comprehensive way by developing and fielding the detailed Firm-level Adoption of Technology (FAT) survey in 11 countries. *Bridging the Technological Divide* brings together the first wave of findings from that effort, documenting the patterns of adoption of different types of technologies within and across firms, and the factors that facilitate or impede diffusion. The hope is that the volume will stimulate interest in exploring this critical dimension of growth generally, and exploiting these surveys in particular.

This book is a product of the Equitable Growth, Finance, and Institutions Vice Presidency.

William F. Maloney
Chief Economist, Latin America and the Caribbean Region
Director, World Bank Productivity Project series
The World Bank

Other Titles in the World Bank Productivity Project

Place, Productivity, and Prosperity: Revisiting Spatially Targeted Policies for Regional Development. 2022. Arti Grover, Somik V. Lall, and William F. Maloney. Washington, DC: World Bank.

At Your Service? The Promise of Services-Led Development. 2021. Gaurav Nayyar, Mary Hallward-Driemeier, and Elwyn Davies. Washington, DC: World Bank.

Harvesting Prosperity: Technology and Productivity Growth in Agriculture. 2020. Keith Fuglie, Madhur Gautam, Aparajita Goyal, and William F. Maloney. Washington, DC: World Bank.

High-Growth Firms: Facts, Fiction, and Policy Options for Emerging Economies. 2019. Arti Grover Goswami, Denis Medvedev, and Ellen Olafsen. Washington, DC: World Bank.

Productivity Revisited: Shifting Paradigms in Analysis and Policy. 2018. Ana Paula Cusolito and William F. Maloney. Washington, DC: World Bank.

The Innovation Paradox: Developing-Country Capabilities and the Unrealized Promise of Technological Catch-Up. 2017. Xavier Cirera and William F. Maloney. Washington, DC: World Bank.

All books in the World Bank Productivity Project are available free of charge at https://openknowledge.worldbank.org/handle/10986/30560.

Acknowledgments

This book was written by Xavier Cirera (senior economist, Finance, Competitiveness, and Innovation Global Practice, World Bank), Diego Comin (professor of economics, Dartmouth College), and Marcio Cruz (senior economist, Finance, Competitiveness, and Innovation Global Practice, World Bank), with the collaboration of a core team from the World Bank working on the Firm-level Adoption of Technology (FAT) project. Kyung Min Lee provided key contributions across this project as a core team member, from survey design to data implementation, and coauthorship of key background papers. Other core team members who provided key contributions on survey implementation and data analysis include Pedro Jose Martinez Alanis, Antonio Soares Martins Neto, Caroline Nogueira, and Santiago Reyes. Enrico Berkes (Ohio State University) and Jesica Torres contributed with coauthorship of background papers. Additional inputs were provided by Edgar Avalos, Ana Paula Cusolito, Sara Nyman, and Juni Zhu. The work was carried out under the guidance of Mona Haddad (global director, Trade, Investment, and Competitiveness, World Bank), Martha Martinez Licetti (practice Manager, Markets and Technology, World Bank), William F. Maloney (director, World Bank Productivity Project and chief economist, Latin America and the Caribbean Region), and Denis Medvedev (director, Economic Policy Research Department, International Finance Corporation).

We thank Ayhan Kose (chief economist, Equitable Growth, Finance, and Institutions Practice Group) for support and helpful comments. We also thank Najy Benhassine, Paulo Correa, and Caroline Freund (University of California San Diego) for supporting the project and providing guidance at early stages in the role of managers or directors. We are very thankful to peer reviewers who provided key inputs during the concept note review, the quality enhancement review, and the decision meeting, including Rami Amin, Paulo Bastos, Mark Dutz, Ana Margarida Fernandes, Mary Hallward-Driemeier, Maurice Kugler (George Mason University), and Mark Williams. Alvaro Gonzalez provided detailed revision and feedback.

We are grateful for additional comments and feedback provided by Mark Aguiar (Princeton University), Asya Akhlaque, Pol Antras (Harvard University), David Baqaee (University of California Los Angeles), Mark Bils (University of Rochester), Paco Buera (Washington University), Andrew L. Dabalen, Maria Cristina DiNardi (University of Minnesota), Apoorv Gupta (Dartmouth College), John Haltiwanger (University of Maryland), Elhanan Helpman (Harvard University), Justin Hill, Leonardo Iacovone,

David Lagakos (Boston University), Marti Mestieri (Northwestern University), Gaurav Nayyar, Antonio Nucifora, Nina Pavnik (Dartmouth College), Richard Rogerson (Princeton University), Consolate K. Rusagara, Manu Garcia Santana (Universitat Pompeu Fabra), Jon Skinner (Dartmouth College), Chris Snyder (Dartmouth College), Doug Staiger (Dartmouth College), Jaume Ventura (Universitat Pompeu Fabra), Stephen Yeo, and Albert G. Zeufack, as well as participants in a seminar at Dartmouth College from the Central Bank of Chile, Harvard Business School, Oxford University, and Seoul University.

The preparation of the FAT survey questionnaire involved the contribution of several sector experts within and outside the World Bank. First, we would like to thank Silvia Muzi and Jorge Rodriguez Meza for sharing the expertise of the World Bank Enterprise Survey team, and Mark Dutz for contributing with the revision and pilot. Next, we thank several colleagues who contributed with the development of the sector-specific modules, including Victor A. Aragones, Correia Araujo, Arturo Ardila Gomez, Kazimir Luka Bacic, Brendan Michael Dack, Edson Emiliano Duch, Erick C. M. Fernandes, Erik Feyen, Madhur Gautam, Laurent Gonnet, Aparajita Goyal, Etienne Raffi Kechichian, Austin Kilroy, Holger A. Kray, Blair Edward Lapres, Michael Morris, Harish Natarajan, Irina A. Nikolic, Ashesh Prasann, Robert Townsend, and Justin Yap. Similarly, we would like to thank several external experts. From Embrapa (Brazil), we thank Alexandre Costa Varella, Flávio Dessaune Tardin, Alberto Duarte Vilarinhos, Carlos Estevão Leite Cardoso, Edison Ulisses Ramos Junior, Isabela Volpi Furtini, and other participants of the internal seminars to validate the sector-specific questionnaires for agriculture and livestock. For other sectors, we thank Sandra Aris, Justin Barnes, Chris Baughman, James M. Keding, Daren Samuels, Shelly Wolfram, and Steve Zebovitz, as well as Sudha Jayaraman (University of Utah), Christina Kozycki (National Institutes of Health), Elizabeth Krebs (Jefferson University), and Jon Skinner (Dartmouth College). We also thank Tanay Balantrapu, João Bevilaqua Basto, and Carmen Contreras for their excellent support through the preparation of the questionnaire and implementation of the surveys.

The implementation of data collection across 11 countries also benefited from key contributions from World Bank colleagues working in the regions and local institutions. We thank the following colleagues for their collaboration in implementing the FAT survey: for Bangladesh and India, Siddharth Sharma; for Burkina Faso, Jean Michel Marchat; for Ghana, Elwyn Davies, David Elmaleh, and Katherine Anne Stapleton; for Kenya, Utz Johann Pape and Zenaida Uriz; for the Republic of Korea, Anwar Aridi, Sameer Goyal, Soyoun Jun, and Hoon Soh; for Malawi, Efrem Zephnath Chilima; for Poland, Magda Malec and Lukasz Marc; for Senegal, Carlos Castelan and Mark Dutz; and for Vietnam, Brian Mtonya and Trang Thu Tran. We also thank the following local institutions for collaboration during the implementation of the survey: Guilherme Muchale de Araujo and the Federation of Industries of the state of Ceará (Brazil), Ghana Statistical Service, National Statistical Office of Malawi, Statistics Poland, and

Pham Dinh Thuy and the General Statistics Office of Vietnam. We thank the following institutions for the provision of sampling frames: Bangladesh Bureau of Statistics, Central Statistics Office of India, Kenya National Bureau of Statistics, Statistics Korea, and the Senegal National Agency for Statistics and Demography. For technical guidance on implementing the sampling design and weights, we thank Filip Jolevski, Talip Kilic, and especially Diego Zardetto for extended support in designing the sampling weights.

We thank our publishing team—Cindy Fisher, Patricia Katayama, and Mark McClure—for the design, production, and marketing of this book; Nancy Morrison for her excellent and timely editorial services; Gwenda Larsen for proofreading; and our communications team for its creative energy in promoting the book.

Financial support from the Korea–World Bank Group Partnership Facility (KWPF) made possible this volume and data collection, and it is gratefully acknowledged. We also thank the infoDev Multi-Donor Trust Fund, the Competitive Industries and Innovation Program (CIIP), and the Facility for Investment Climate Advisory Services (FIAS) for the financial support provided for the design of the survey and data collection.

About the Authors

Xavier Cirera is a senior economist in the Finance, Competitiveness, and Innovation Global Practice of the World Bank. His work focuses on innovation and technology. He has led the policy effectiveness reviews in science, technology, and innovation implemented in Brazil, Chile, Colombia, Ukraine, and Vietnam. He is the coauthor of *The Innovation Paradox: Developing-Country Capabilities and the Unrealized Promise of Technological Catch-Up* and *A Practitioner's Guide to Innovation Policy: Instruments to Build Firm Capabilities and Accelerate Technological Catch-Up in Developing Countries.* His most recent work focuses on the measurement and impact of technology adoption and diffusion and the impact of innovation on employment and firm dynamics. Before joining the World Bank, he was a research fellow at the Institute of Development Studies at the University of Sussex. He holds a PhD in economics from the University of Sussex.

Diego Comin is a professor of economics at Dartmouth College. He is also a research fellow at the Center for Economic Policy Research and faculty research fellow in the National Bureau of Economic Research's Economic Fluctuations and Growth Program. He has published multiple articles in top economic journals on the topics of business cycles, technology diffusion, economic growth, and firm volatility. He has also authored case studies published in the book *Drivers of Competitiveness.* He has consulted for the World Bank, the International Monetary Fund, the Federal Reserve Bank of New York, the European Central Bank, the Danish Science Ministry, the Economic and Social Research Institute of the government of Japan, the prime minister of Malaysia, Citibank, and Microsoft. Previously, he was an assistant professor of economics at New York University and associate professor of business administration at the Harvard Business School (HBS). He has also designed and led immersion programs in Peru and Malaysia, for which he received the Apgar Award for Innovation in Teaching from the HBS Dean. He holds a PhD in economics from Harvard University.

Marcio Cruz is a senior economist in the Finance, Competitiveness, and Innovation Global Practice of the World Bank. Previously, he worked in the Development Economics unit contributing to the World Bank's flagship publications *Global Economic Prospects* and *Global Monitoring Report.* Before joining the World Bank, Cruz worked as a tenured professor in the Department of Economics at the Federal University of Paraná and as an economist for the Secretary of Planning of the state of Paraná, Brazil.

His main research interests are firm dynamics, technology adoption, entrepreneurship, international trade, and impact evaluation. His research has been published in scholarly journals such as the *Journal of International Economics, World Development,* and the *Cambridge Journal of Regions, Economy and Society.* He received the World Bank's Research Academy Award for the best new research from across the World Bank in 2015. He holds a PhD in international economics from the Graduate Institute of International and Development Studies in Geneva.

Abbreviations

ABF	all business functions
AI	artificial intelligence
B2B	business to business
BAS	business advisory services
BPS	Business Pulse Survey
CEO	chief executive officer
COVID-19	coronavirus disease 2019
CRM	customer relationship management
ERP	enterprise resource planning
EXT	extensive margin technology index
FAT	Firm-level Adoption of Technology survey
GBF	general business function
GDP	gross domestic product
GPT	general-purpose technology
GVC	global value chain
HR	human resources
ICT	information and communication technology
INT	intensive margin technology index
IT	information technology
KOTEC	Korea Technology Finance Corporation
R&D	research and development
SBF	sector-specific business function
SMEs	small and medium enterprises
SRM	supplier relationship management
TC	technology center
TES	technology extension services

Introduction

Every body must be sensible how much labour is abridged and facilitated by the application of proper machinery. By means of the plough two men, with the assistance of three horses, will cultivate more ground than twenty could do with the spade. A miller and his servant, with a wind or water mill, will at their ease grind more corn than eight men could do, with the severest labour, by hand mills.

—Adam Smith, *An Inquiry into the Nature and Causes of the Wealth of Nations*, 1776

The Imperative of Technology in Developing Countries

Technology is at the heart of economic growth. From historical accounts of how technological change since the Industrial Revolution has shaped economic development in Europe, such as David Landes' *The Unbound Prometheus* (Landes 2003), to endogenous growth models (Romer 1990; Aghion and Howitt 1992), technology has been identified as a key ingredient of growth and economic transformation. Measuring the uses of technology and understanding the drivers of and barriers to the adoption of technology are, therefore, critical to designing policies that facilitate economic development. Until the nineteenth century, the main source of cross-country variation in technology was whether new technologies had arrived in a country (Comin, Easterly, and Gong 2010). While there has been a widespread reduction in the time needed to acquire and adopt a new technology, current technological differences across countries originate mostly from differences in how intensively new technologies are eventually used once they arrive in a country (Comin and Mestieri 2018).

Technological catch-up happens through firms. Firms are the prime source for adopting more sophisticated technologies to be applied in the production of goods and provision of services. These upgrades are key to promoting gains in productivity, the engine of economic growth and prosperity. While technology can improve economic welfare through different channels, it is primarily through the process of adoption by firms that most workers are affected. Workers can have access to higher-productivity jobs and countries can achieve higher prosperity through the adoption of more sophisticated technologies. With very few exceptions of countries that are rich in natural resources, there is no successful example of a developing country that graduated to become an advanced economy without improving the technological level of its production through its firms, in either agriculture, manufacturing, or services.

Yet around the world, there is a large technological divide across firms. This divide is reflected in low productivity levels and a lack of better-quality jobs—particularly in developing countries, where the number of enterprises per worker relatively close to the forefront of technology sophistication (the technology frontier) is quite low. But this divide is not restricted to developing economies. In high-income countries, the gap between frontier and laggard firms is also large and could potentially increase, which could, in turn, deepen challenges associated with income inequality across and within countries. The technological divide across firms also affects firms' varying ability to cope with and bounce back from economic shocks, given that more capable and technologically sophisticated firms are also more resilient.

Bridging the technological divide is thus an imperative for development policies. Understanding how technology is used and distributed across firms and identifying the main drivers of adoption are critical to unpack the "black box" of the firm, and, even more important, to design policies that can help accelerate adoption and convergence to the technology frontier. Addressing some of the most relevant development challenges, from eradicating global poverty to promoting environmentally sustainable economic growth, will require not only innovation, but also technology upgrading of firms across the globe. The fact that most firms, particularly in developing countries, are far from the technology frontier suggests that this is not an easy challenge, but it also suggests that there are many opportunities for enhancing productivity and generating high-quality jobs in developing countries. To better understand this challenge at the firm level, we need to improve existing measures of technology and the body of data that can better reveal how firms make decisions and actually use (or do not use) technology in their operations. This will help answer the question of why firms, particularly in developing countries, are not adopting and using technology that clearly could benefit them. Armed with this understanding, policy makers and practitioners can design better policies and interventions to help firms adopt better and more sophisticated technologies.

Recent global trends have increased the focus on technology as a source of growth. First, numerous studies have documented a productivity growth slowdown in advanced economies and some middle-income countries in recent decades (Andrews, Criscuolo, and Gal 2016; Gordon 2012), as well as a decrease in business dynamism (Akcigit and Ates 2019). An important culprit for this slowdown is the lack of innovation, and more important, the low diffusion of technology to laggard firms. Second, the spread of advanced digital technologies and the so-called fourth industrial revolution (Industry 4.0), along with changes in production processes and potential reshoring, threaten some of the production and development models based on exports and low wages, which were enormously successful in the East Asia region. These new developments call for more investments in technology upgrading. Third, the COVID-19 pandemic and related restrictions have increased the pressure for more flexible and automated production and management processes that can circumvent lockdown restrictions and potential structural changes in demand and point to the need to be technology-ready for future shocks. Finally, climate change and increasing concerns about the state of the global environment will continue intensifying the need to upgrade to more sophisticated and cleaner technologies.

The Technological Divide

Despite the economic relevance of the technology frontier, there is no comprehensive body of data across countries and sectors describing where the frontier is and how far firms in developing countries are from it. As a famous saying—usually attributed to Peter Drucker, a well-known management consultant—goes, *"You cannot improve what you don't measure."* This dictum describes a common challenge policy makers and practitioners face when thinking about the effectiveness of policies to promote technology upgrading. The World Bank Group has made important contributions to address similar challenges in other areas in the past, such as poverty and education. The poverty line and associated household data collection, for example, introduced in the 1990s, have facilitated designing, targeting, and monitoring public interventions aimed at eradicating global poverty, including projects funded by the World Bank. Yet, efforts to measure technology adoption by firms have been restricted to a few variables included in the World Bank Enterprise Survey, mostly related to access to general-purpose technologies (such as electricity, the internet, or websites) or to individual projects (such as those promoting technology upgrading for agriculture). Other institutions are furthering measurements of technology, particularly national statistical offices, but most of them are restricted to measuring information and communication technology, or advanced manufacturing technologies in high-income countries.

This volume advances these efforts by proposing a new approach and body of data to understand adoption and use of technology from the perspective of the firm, particularly in developing countries. Specifically, this volume addresses data shortcomings in existing surveys, and offers a new framework for collecting data on the adoption and use of technology by firms. This new approach facilitates exploration of the process of technology adoption by firms and its variation (heterogeneity) across firms, sectors, and countries with a high level of granularity. In the light of the new data collected, the volume examines some of the theories on technology adoption and presents new stylized facts that can improve the design of policies to facilitate technology adoption and diffusion. It also provides a detailed overview of the process of technology adoption with special emphasis on developing countries, and the important variations that characterize technology use across and within firms.

To do so, the volume introduces a new data collection instrument, the Firm-level Adoption of Technology (FAT) survey. The development of the FAT survey involved intensive research and interaction with more than 50 industry experts with experience in firms in advanced economies as well as in developing countries to identify the location of the technology frontier and the array of technologies (the technology grid) available for a firm to perform a task, including the most relevant technology options— from most basic to most sophisticated. More specifically, the methodology identifies the relevant business functions conducted by the firm. They are split between general business functions (GBFs) that are common to all firms, such as business administration and payment methods, and sector-specific business functions (SBFs) relevant to specific sectors, such as harvesting for agriculture, and sewing for wearing apparel. Then, for each of these business functions, the FAT survey identifies a grid of technologies available to perform that task, and with guidance from industry experts, it ranks them according to their level of sophistication.

While the FAT survey identifies where the technology frontier is, the data collected across several countries help determine how far from the frontier firms are. The data provide a very rich characterization of the technologies used by firms and offer new insights on the main drivers of and barriers to technology adoption. The survey was implemented in 11 countries, across a variety of regions and income levels. In addition, the analysis is complemented by a review of some of the main policy instruments that can be used to support technology adoption, with the aim of helping government and public agencies design more effective policies to support technology adoption.

The FAT survey captures the multidimensionality of technology in terms of types, use, drivers, barriers, and impacts. These multiple dimensions require identifying and measuring the different types of technologies that are covered by this volume. While firms adopt technologies to accomplish specific tasks, the characteristics of these technologies vary and affect their potential benefits, their main drivers, and the key obstacles to adoption.

The attempt described in this volume to measure and document the mechanisms of technology adoption can be seen as analogous to recent efforts in the realm of managerial quality.[1] Despite these similarities, there are also important differences in these approaches. While management practices refer to establishing routines to deal with decision processes, the technology measures presented in this volume reflect actions embodied in machines and software or represent processes that typically require certain equipment and technological knowledge to use them. The effort reported here measures a large number of technologies used and derives several indexes of technology sophistication. This provides a very granular perspective of general-purpose and sector-specific technologies used to produce and sell goods and services.

Improving the measures of the technological divide is critical for developing countries, where firms are often confined to more rudimentary and less automated technologies. The more accurate and granular the information on technology use is, the better equipped researchers, policy makers, and practitioners can be to identify the key bottleneck(s) to facilitate technology upgrading that can lead to expansion of firms and creation of better jobs. For this purpose, data with detailed measures of technology used by firms across different sectors are needed. This kind of measure can be aggregated by country, regions, sectors, or specific business functions to identify the distance from the technology frontier, and to understand the key drivers, obstacles, and policies that could improve these results. This is the main contribution that this volume aims to provide.

Perhaps the best way to illustrate the implications of the technological divide is with an example. Imagine a young worker starting a job in two different country contexts. The first worker starts working in a food-processing firm producing dairy products in the Republic of Korea. This firm has 150 workers and uses frontier technologies to perform most business functions, from administration to production. The second worker goes to a firm of similar size in Kenya, producing similar products. Despite performing similar functions using above-average technologies compared to other firms in Kenya, there is a significant gap in technologies this firm uses for production compared to its Korean peer. The estimated productivity per worker in the Korean firm is about 55 percent higher than the firm in Kenya, which allows the Korean firm to pay higher salaries to its workers. But this is only part of the reason why the economic prospect for a worker is expected to be higher in Korea.

Firms in more advanced economies are not only more technologically sophisticated on average, but there are also many more of them. A key economic challenge for most developing countries and emerging economies is not only that their average formal firm is distant from the technology frontier, but there are also very few of them, relative to the population.[2] Returning to the comparison between Kenya and Korea, both countries have a relatively similar population (around 50 million), but a very different number of firms. The Kenyan economy has less than 1 formal business with more than 10 employees for every thousand individuals, and about 2.1 for every thousand individuals of working age. Korea has about 6.5 formal businesses with 10 or more employees for every thousand people, and 9.2 businesses for every thousand individuals of working age. To move closer to the frontier, developing countries need not only to improve the technological capabilities of existing firms but also to build the conditions to optimize the reallocation of resources toward more capable firms, and attract more entrepreneurs to increase the entry of high-quality firms and induce the exit of low-productivity firms, as highlighted by the second volume of the World Bank Productivity Project series (Cusolito and Maloney 2018).

Road Map to the Volume

This volume focuses on the adoption and use of technology by firms. The firm is at the center of the analysis. This implies that we need to understand how technologies are applied to the main tasks that firms need to carry out to produce and sell goods and services. This requires opening the black box of the firm further (Rosenberg 1983) and documenting the types of technology and the processes used to perform firms' tasks. To this end, the volume presents a new method to measure technology at the level of business functions particular to the operations of that firm (for some key definitions about business functions and technology, see box I.1). This approach allows us to understand what technologies are used, how they are used, and why they were chosen by firms, which is a critical step to understand the process of technology diffusion and the overall technological progress of an economy.

BOX I.1

Defining Technology and Business Functions

Technology can be defined as a manner of accomplishing a task especially using technical processes, methods, or knowledge. This definition captures the broader perspective of the way this term is used by social scientists, but it also highlights the challenges associated with measuring it. Technology is not only the machinery or "hardware" but also often includes the process or method. The discussion that follows highlights some important distinctions among different types of technologies and the concept of business functions widely used across the volume.

Business functions. Business functions are specific tasks carried out by an enterprise with the purpose of supporting or performing production or service provision. The concept of the business function has been used by national statistical offices.[a] This volume follows a conceptual framework that categorizes business functions in two groups: general business functions and sector-specific business functions. *General business functions* are tasks that all firms conduct regardless of the sector in which they operate (such as tasks related to business administration, including human resources and finance; production or services operation planning; sourcing, procurement, and supply chain management; sales; and payment methods). *Sector-specific business functions* are usually more directly associated with core production processes or service provision and are relevant only for firms in a given sector (such as food refrigeration in food processing or sewing in wearing apparel).[b]

General-purpose technologies (GPTs). Historical accounts of technological change have emphasized the role of certain technologies that have had a disruptive impact, such as the steam engine, the combustion engine, electricity, computers, and the internet.[c] GPTs are widely used as inputs of other technologies. For example, computers are necessary to implement enterprise resource planning.[d] The adoption and diffusion of GPTs are critical elements of aggregate productivity and countries' technology convergence.[e] But at a more micro level, what matters for firms' productivity is the application of these GPTs in complementary technologies.[f] Thus, the study of firm technology adoption needs to go beyond the use of GPTs and document the use of applied technologies.

Digital technologies. A digital technology allows the representation of information in bits to generate, store, or process data, which can reduce several relevant economic costs. Digital technologies are characterized by cost reduction along five dimensions: (1) search costs; (2) replication costs; (3) transportation costs; (4) tracking costs; and (5) verification costs.[g] Digital technologies are applications of other GPTs (including computers, software development, and the internet) that overcome the limitation of communication and integration across computers. Recently, mobile communications and cloud technologies have been expanding the

(Box continues on the following page.)

Defining Technology and Business Functions *(continued)*

development of these technologies. As a result, the use of these technologies also depends on the provision of GPT infrastructure, mainly the internet and the mobile network. While many frontier technologies are digital these days, there is large variation in terms of sophistication of digital technologies applied to different tasks of the firm.

Technology adoption. Technology adoption refers to the acquisition and use of a new technology by individual units (such as a firm, a household, or an organization).

Technology diffusion. Technology diffusion is the dynamic consequence of adoption across firms and organizations. It measures the accumulation of technology across adopters and over time, which arises from decision units at the level of individuals, firms, and governments. While the concept of technology adoption centers on individual units (such as firms), the process of technology diffusion is centered on the technology itself (Stoneman and Battisti 2010). For example, the diffusion of tractors with global positioning systems (GPS) in a given country, over time, represents an aggregated behavior of several adopters (including firms in this country that started using this technology).

Network effects. Network effects occur when the value of a technology, such as computers or automated teller machines (ATMs), increases the more users it has. Network effects are often accompanied by a production scale effect that reduces the cost of the technology. A critical element for adoption is that decisions to adopt depend on the number of users.[h] Most technologies have some degree of network effects, given that the more users a technology has, the greater the availability of additional or complementary services that can be provided. Understanding how large these network effects are will determine the decision by a firm or other adopters to adopt the technology, and hence also affects its diffusion.

a. Eurostat (2000) defines the term "business function" as the activities carried out by an enterprise, which can be divided into core functions and support functions. According to this definition, core business functions are activities of an enterprise yielding income: the production of final goods or services intended for the market or for third parties. Support business functions are ancillary (supporting) activities carried out by the enterprise in order to permit or to facilitate the core business functions, its production activity.

b. Chapter 1 and appendix A provide further details on these concepts and how they are linked to the technology measures at the firm level.

c. See Landes (2003); Rosenberg (1983); and Comin (2000). Bresnahan and Trajtenberg (1995) characterize GPTs as a handful of technologies that become ubiquitous in their use, and as they diffuse they bring about general productivity improvements.

d. For example, electricity enabled a revolution in the way machinery operated and new technologies were developed. Computers and the internet allow firms to implement new management and sales technologies. The Internet of Things is enabling a revolution in technologies implemented in agriculture.

e. Bresnahan (2010) identifies three key features. These technologies are "i) widely used, ii) [are] capable of ongoing improvement, and iii) [enable] innovation in the sectors where these are applied."

f. See Comin and Hobijn (2004) for evidence across countries. An example of the relevance of this topic is the ever-expanding literature on the impact of computers and information and communication technology on aggregate productivity and the missing productivity gains, described as the "productivity paradox" (Solow 1987).

g. See Goldfarb and Tucker (2019) for more details.

h. An extensive literature has focused on the market structure of these technologies (Katz and Shapiro 1986) and the prevalence of standards (David 1985). A famous case is that of video cassette recorders (VCRs) in the 1980s, with two competing main technologies, VHS and Beta. In the case of ATMs, Saloner and Shepard (1995) show how delays in adoption decline with the increase in the number of branches and users.

The volume is organized in three parts aiming to address the following questions:

- Where is the technology frontier and how far from it are firms in developing countries?
- What are the implications of the technological divide for jobs, growth, and resilience?
- What can countries do to bridge the technological divide?

Part 1. Measuring the Technological Divide (Chapters 1, 2, and 3)

The first part of the volume focuses on the need for this new measurement framework and describes in detail the main characteristics of the FAT survey and key findings. It provides the foundation to understand the degree of firms' adoption of technology and the multiple dimensions of the use of technology in firms. The remainder of this part is based on the analysis of the new data collected, which allows new stylized facts about technology adoption by firms to be uncovered and presented.

Chapter 1 describes the methodology of the FAT survey as a new approach to measure firm-level adoption and use of technology. The chapter starts by reviewing the literature on measuring technology adoption from different perspectives, including the macro and micro levels. It then explains further how the FAT survey was elaborated and what technologies are covered for both general and sector-specific business functions, and how the information is converted into a technology sophistication index that can be aggregated by business function, firm, sector, region, and country. The chapter concludes with a discussion about how the new method and the FAT survey can address some of the limitations of standard measures of technology through different dimensions: first, by identifying the purpose for which a technology is used for a particular business function; and second, by differentiating adoption (whether the firm uses a technology or not) from intensive use (what technology a firm is using most frequently to perform a business function).

Chapter 2 presents some stylized facts on firm adoption of technology analyzing primary data collected by the FAT survey. This volume uses primary data collected across 11 countries, including Bangladesh, Brazil (only the state of Ceará), Burkina Faso, Ghana, India (only the states of Tamil Nadu and Uttar Pradesh), Kenya, the Republic of Korea, Malawi, Poland, Senegal, and Vietnam. These facts are organized by cross-country, cross-firm, and within-firm dimensions. The technology facts highlighted in this chapter summarize some of the key messages across the volume. The discussion starts by showing how far the average and the top 20 percent of firms are in terms of technology sophistication from the technology frontier in manufacturing, agriculture, and services. The top 20 percent of firms in Korea and Poland are used as a benchmark and an aspirational frontier for developing countries. The results show that the technology index used in the analysis is strongly correlated with regional productivity across countries. They suggest that comparing the technology sophistication of the average formal firm is not enough to understand the aggregate technology gap, and therefore the income gap, on a per capita basis. The density of firms with sophisticated technology and the number of workers they employ also matter. The chapter also analyzes the variation of technology sophistication across business functions within firms, the trends of technology adoption across firm size, and the potential behavioral bias from firms misjudging their low levels of technology.

Chapter 3 provides a deep dive into differences in production technologies adopted by firms in different sectors. It starts with a detailed description of the technology sophistication used in agriculture, food processing (manufacturing), wearing apparel (manufacturing), and retail (services). For agriculture, it shows how the technology index captures variations in technology sophistication, using practical examples from Senegal comparing irrigation and storage practices. This chapter also provides a discussion about variations in technology intensity across sectors from the perspective of advanced Industry 4.0 technologies. In particular, it uses one business function that is common across all manufacturing firms and shows that some of these advanced technologies (such as robots and 3D printers) are much more prevalent among firms in the motor vehicles sector than in other manufacturing sectors. This focus on sectors also highlights that the technology frontier in some sectors might be more sophisticated and capital intensive. Yet, robots and 3D printers may not capture the level of sophistication of the average firm in another sector, such as pharmaceuticals, that is also knowledge and capital intensive. The chapter also challenges the popular perception that firms can jump across levels of technology, and finds that such leapfrogging is rare in sector-specific technologies. The chapter ends with an analysis of the relationship between technology sophistication and the decision to outsource SBFs. As an example, it shows that, on average, firms that outsource the SBF of design in the wearing apparel sector tend to have lower levels of sophistication.

Part 2. The Implications of the Technological Divide for Long-Term Economic Growth (Chapters 4 and 5)

The second part of the volume analyzes the relationship between technology adoption and productivity, jobs, and economic resilience.

Chapter 4 traces the links between technology adoption and firm performance, with a focus on productivity and jobs. To start, it shows a positive and significant association between technology sophistication as measured by the FAT technology index and productivity at the firm level. It then discusses how this relationship between technology and productivity is also associated with structural change, emphasizing the larger technology gap between Korea and Senegal in agriculture than in manufacturing and services. This gap is mostly driven by informal firms. The discussion highlights the importance of facilitating technology adoption in agriculture as a driver of structural change. The second part of the chapter focuses on the relationship between technology adoption and jobs. First, it shows that most firms report that they do not change the number of workers when adopting more sophisticated technologies. Indeed, contrary to popular belief, the results from the FAT data comparing firms across countries suggest that firms that have adopted more sophisticated technologies have generated more jobs, on average. Moreover, these additional jobs do not necessarily reduce the share of unskilled workers on their payrolls. If anything, the negative significant correlation with SBFs suggests that for some technologies the share of unskilled workers increases. The chapter also combines the FAT data with administrative matched employer-employee data from Brazil and shows that there is a positive and significant wage premium associated with more sophisticated technologies, as well as higher wage inequality within firms.

Chapter 5 analyzes how the COVID-19 shock has increased firms' investments in digitalization, and how firms that were more "digital ready" before the pandemic have been more resilient. This finding has relevance for the slower-moving crisis of climate change shocks. This chapter starts with a discussion of patterns of digitalization, emphasizing the heterogeneity of digital technologies across general and sector-specific business functions. It examines how the market structure related to the supply of digital solutions is important for the diffusion of digital technologies. Then, the chapter assesses how the COVID-19 pandemic led to an unprecedented shock that propelled firms to adopt digital technologies. To do so, the chapter introduces data from the World Bank Business Pulse Survey (BPS), which included a few questions on digital adoption. The results, based on data for more than 60 countries, show that around 45 percent of firms started to use or increased their use of digital platforms in response to the pandemic and 28 percent invested in digital solutions. The chapter then presents the results of an analysis that combined data from the FAT survey and the BPS to tease out the direct and indirect effects of technology readiness on firm performance during the COVID-19 pandemic. The indirect effect stems from the fact that technology readiness before the COVID-19 pandemic has also helped firms adopt and increase their use of digital technology in response to the shock. The results suggest that technology readiness significantly contributed to firm performance, and the direct effect was about five times larger than the indirect effect. The chapter ends with preliminary results for the FAT survey in Georgia, which incorporates questions on green technology. It shows a positive association between technology sophistication and the adoption of green technologies, which suggests the existence of complementarities between "green" and "nongreen" technologies, as well as the possibility of common drivers of and barriers to their adoption.

Part 3. What Countries Can Do to Bridge the Technological Divide (Chapters 6 and 7)

The third part of the volume discusses the key factors that impede technology upgrading by firms and the policy instruments available to promote technological catch-up.

Chapter 6 focuses on the drivers of and barriers to technology adoption and use. This chapter starts by providing a conceptual framework, informed by a wide review of the literature emphasizing the factors that drive adoption, including those that are external to the firm (such as infrastructure, competition, demand, regulations, access to finance, and supply of knowledge and human capital) and those that are internal to the firm (such as information and behavioral biases, management quality and organization, and know-how and skills capabilities). It then follows the structure provided by this framework to analyze the association between technology sophistication and these factors, based on the FAT data. First, it focuses on firms' perceptions, and presents results based on what firms report as the most relevant drivers (competition) and obstacles for adoption (lack of demand, lack of capabilities, and lack of finance). It then uses factual data from the FAT survey to check the association between these variables and technology sophistication, for both the extensive margin (whether the firm uses a technology or not) and the intensive margin (the technology most frequently used by the firm). The discussion highlights the various factors that drive adoption, and emphasizes that the context and type of technology are important in understanding adoption.

Chapter 7 reviews the main policies and programs that can be most effective to reduce the technological divide. It starts by providing some general guidelines to design technology upgrading programs and emphasizes that public agencies have an important role to play to address coordination and information failures. The starting point should be to ensure that the enabling conditions to adopt technologies are in place in terms of access to infrastructure, information, and external knowledge, and the removal of regulatory bottlenecks. The chapter provides a checklist of actions for policy makers to minimize the risk of government failure, and highlights the importance of implementing good diagnostics to identify key technology gaps and better target firms. It provides some examples of how the FAT data can be used in this process to help policy makers and practitioners identify key bottlenecks and prioritize policy interventions. It also shows how the FAT survey can be used as a firm-level diagnostic to support business advisory interventions. Finally, the chapter describes a variety of policy instruments to support technology upgrading, and discusses some of the most important features for design and implementation. These instruments can play an important role in addressing some of the barriers highlighted in the previous chapter to promote technology diffusion and the digital transformation of businesses.

Contributions to the Literature

This seventh volume in the World Bank Productivity Project series contributes to the literature on technology adoption in several ways:

- It describes a new methodology for measuring technology adoption at the firm level.
- It presents new evidence of the firm-level technological divide across different dimensions, such as countries, regions, sectors, firms, and business functions, using a novel data set covering firms in agriculture, manufacturing, and services from 11 countries.
- It uncovers the richness of the variation for technology sophistication across sectors and the association with outsourcing some tasks.
- It provides new evidence on the effects of technology readiness on resilience.
- It offers novel findings regarding the limitations of improving access to digital infrastructure on technology adoption.
- It summarizes the tools available to policy makers aiming to promote technology upgrading.

The FAT data can serve as a benchmark for firms, regions, and countries to understand their distance from the technology frontier. The survey can also be used as a firm-level diagnostic, helping policy makers and practitioners set areas to be prioritized when designing and implementing measures to support technology adoption.

Main Messages from the Volume

The volume's findings and analytical insights draw on a set of background papers supported by the World Bank through this project. Cirera et al. (2020) provide key concepts on technology measures and findings that are used throughout this volume. These findings can be summarized in the nine main messages that follow.

There Is a Large Technological Divide across Firms

Message 1. Most firms in developing countries are quite far from the technology frontier, and they may not be aware of the extent to which they lag.

Evidence from the FAT data shows that most firms are far from the technology frontier, particularly in developing countries. This gap is present even for top firms with respect to technology sophistication across countries and is wider in developing countries, where few firms are relatively close to the technology frontier. Importantly, when firms are asked to assess themselves in terms of technology sophistication with respect to other similar firms in the country or globally, firms in the lower levels (quintiles) of technology sophistication tend to demonstrate overconfidence, reporting a ranking that is well above their actual level of sophistication. This behavioral bias may lead to an important market failure by reducing firms' willingness to pay for technology upgrading.

Message 2. Firms' levels of technology sophistication span multiple dimensions. The more disaggregated the unit of analysis—from country to region, to sector, to firm, to business functions within the firm—the larger the variation.

Firms use different technologies to perform a variety of tasks needed for different business functions. Some of these functions are common across firms (such as business administration, sales, and payment methods), while others are sector specific. A firm's level of technology sophistication, measured by their proximity to the technology frontier to perform a task, is not uniform across the business functions of the same establishment. Indeed, the more technologically advanced firms are, on average, the more variation there is in the level of sophistication across functions. From this perspective, significant improvements in digital infrastructure and access to general-purpose technologies are important enablers, but they have limited power to explain the large variation of adoption between and within firms.

Message 3. The transition from industrial revolutions is incomplete in developing countries.

The simultaneous rapid spread of information and communication technology (ICT) alongside the persistence of a large share of firms still struggling to access reliable electricity is one of the many paradoxes of technology in developing countries. First, it shows the power and the limits of technology disruptions associated with the digital revolution. Second, there is large variation in terms of the quality of supply and potential for network effects through the diffusion of knowledge and technology across firms and through different uses of digital technologies.[3] Thus, while the focus of the media and policy makers is on the latest technological transition (or industrial revolution), many firms in developing countries have yet to complete previous transitions.

Message 4. Leapfrogging is rare. Technology upgrading by firms is mostly a continuous process of learning.

Despite some perceived opportunities for leapfrogging, technological progress is, and should be seen as, a continuous and accumulative process: a process that requires firms to acquire the capabilities needed to increasingly adopt more sophisticated technologies. It takes a significant amount of knowledge to learn about frontier technologies in a given field, to identify which ones are the most relevant for production processes, and to learn how to integrate them in the business under different market conditions. Knowledge is also required to think about the types of products, services, and processes that can be produced with each new technology, and once a plan to upgrade technology has been made, to implement it and train the workforce to execute it. As a result, a key objective of innovation policies in developing countries must be to build these managerial, production, and technological capabilities.

Message 5. Technology adoption is important for productivity, jobs, and economic resilience.

The FAT data show that there is a significant and robust association between the level of sophistication of technologies adopted and used by firms and labor productivity. This association is also present when comparing the average technology sophistication and productivity across regions and countries. These findings are consistent with both the macroeconomic and microeconomic literature emphasizing the contribution of technology for productivity and long-term economic growth. Moreover, firms with higher levels of technology sophistication grow more and generate more and better jobs. While there is a positive wage premium for technology, evidence across countries for which FAT data are available suggests there is not a significant association between technology sophistication and changes in firms' skills composition over the same period that these firms grew faster. If anything, for sector-specific technologies, the results suggest that firms that have adopted better technology have increased employment, including for low-skilled jobs. Technology adoption also leads to more resilience. Previous research shows that firms with more diverse technologies were more resilient following natural disasters. The same may be true for the COVID-19 pandemic. The FAT survey provides evidence suggesting that those firms with higher levels of technology sophistication have been more likely to adjust and performed better in terms of sales.

Bridging the Technological Divide Is an Imperative for Development Policies

Message 6. Access to reliable and high-quality internet service and other infrastructure is a necessary condition for technology upgrading, but not a sufficient one.

For a given quality of infrastructure access, there is large variation in the use of technologies for particular business functions at the firm level. This message has important implications for investments supported by development agencies, including the World Bank Group, by emphasizing the complementarities between investment in infrastructure and the necessary firm capabilities to benefit from it.

Message 7. Market competition is an important driver of adoption.

When looking at adoption decisions, it is important to understand not only barriers but also drivers. One of the most important drivers is competition, which more than 40 percent of firms report is a main incentive to upgrade their technologies. Given the barriers and drivers identified by this volume and the literature, the first and most important role for the government is to create the enabling conditions for technology adoption by: (1) investing in infrastructure; (2) eliminating regulatory bottlenecks; and (3) solving coordination failures around the provision of technology and advisory services and information infrastructure jointly with the private sector.

Message 8. Technology upgrading policies should shift the focus from access to technology to use of technology.
Many firms, particularly in developing countries, do not intensively use technologies for which they already have access to perform relevant business functions. While in some cases this might be explained by network effects, such as the use of digital payments that depends on other actors, in others cases the constraint seems to be more related to lack of complementary capabilities of the firm, such as the intensive use of handwritten processes for business administration and planning, when the firm already has access to computers and the internet. This is also related to other complementary factors that the firm may need to make the best productive use of available technologies. In terms of direct support, for example, significant imperfections in financial markets in developing countries limit firms' access to finance for technology upgrading, especially for intangible assets. Working with the financial sector to address information asymmetries between lenders and potential borrowers is critical. Instruments such as grants and vouchers need to be linked to some measurable positive spillovers and externalities, accompanied by technical assistance, and monitored for their effects on the adoption and use of technologies, to avoid the risks of government failure.

Message 9. The COVID-19 shock has provided an opportunity for technology upgrading.
The COVID-19 pandemic has led to an unprecedented demand for the use of digital technologies by businesses. Building on this renewed interest in technology upgrading, governments and business-support organizations are intensifying the use of policy instruments to assist digital adoption and upgrading. While the surge in demand for solutions opens several opportunities for technology upgrading for firms in developing countries, there are also signs that the technology gap is increasing across firms, such as a larger concentration of online sales by digitally connected companies at the expense of brick-and-mortar retail businesses. New evidence presented in this volume shows that firms that had a higher level of technologies before the pandemic, particularly digital technologies, were significantly more likely to accelerate adoption after the COVID-19 crisis struck. These results reinforce the finding that existing barriers may be persistent. Mitigating the risks of this growing technology gap requires removing existing barriers to adoption, especially in laggard firms.

Notes

1. There is a long tradition in management and economics documenting and measuring specific management practices. Pathbreaking studies by Bloom and Van Reenen (2007) and Bloom et al. (2019) have extended the scope of this literature by conducting firm-level surveys in a large number of firms across countries to measure the quality of management practices along several dimensions connected to operations, planning, monitoring, and human resources. These surveys include the World Management Survey (WMS) and the Management and Organizational Practices Survey (MOPS). While the WMS is a telephone-based survey using double-blind methodologies, MOPS is an online and paper-based survey.

2. This challenge goes beyond having more big firms (Ciani et al. 2020), given that large firms in developing countries are also significantly behind the technology frontier.

3. Network effects occur when the value of a technology, such as computers or automated teller machines (ATMs), increases the more users it has. Network effects are often accompanied by a production scale effect that reduces the cost of the technology.

References

Aghion, P., and P. Howitt. 1992. "A Model of Growth through Creative Destruction." *Econometrica* 60 (2): 323–51.

Akcigit, U., and S. T. Ates. 2019. "What Happened to U.S. Business Dynamism?" NBER Working Paper 25756, National Bureau of Economic Research, Cambridge, MA.

Andrews, D., C. Criscuolo, and P. N. Gal. 2016. "The Best versus the Rest: The Global Productivity Slowdown, Divergence across Firms and the Role of Public Policy." OECD Productivity Working Paper 5, Organisation for Economic Co-operation and Development.

Bloom, N., E. Brynjolfsson, L. Foster, R. Jarmin, M. Patnaik, I. Saporta-Eksten, and J. Van Reenen. 2019. "What Drives Differences in Management Practices?" *American Economic Review* 109 (5): 1648–83.

Bloom, N., and J. Van Reenen. 2007. "Measuring and Explaining Management Practices across Firms and Countries." *Quarterly Journal of Economics* 122 (4): 1351–1408.

Bresnahan, T. 2010. "General Purpose Technologies." In *Handbook of the Economics of Innovation*, Vol. 2, 761–91. Amsterdam: Elsevier.

Bresnahan, T. F., and M. Trajtenberg. 1995. "General Purpose Technologies 'Engines of Growth'?" *Journal of Econometrics* 65 (1): 83–108.

Ciani, A., M. C. Hyland, N. Karalashvili, J. L. Keller, A. Ragoussis, and T. T. Tran. 2020. *Making It Big: Why Developing Countries Need More Large Firms*. Washington, DC: World Bank.

Cirera, X., D. Comin, M. Cruz, and K. M. Lee. 2020. "Technology within and across Firms." CEPR Discussion Paper 15427, Center for Economic and Policy Research, Washington, DC.

Comin, D. 2000. "An Uncertainty-Driven Theory of the Productivity Slowdown in Manufacturing." PhD thesis, Harvard University, Cambridge, MA.

Comin, D., W. Easterly, and E. Gong. 2010. "Was the Wealth of Nations Determined in 1000 B.C.?" NBER Working Paper 12657, National Bureau of Economic Research, Cambridge, MA.

Comin, D., and B. Hobijn. 2004. "Cross-Country Technology Adoption: Making the Theories Face the Facts." *Journal of Monetary Economics* 51 (1): 39–83.

Comin, D., and M. Mestieri. 2018. "If Technology Has Arrived Everywhere, Why Has Income Diverged?" *American Economic Journal: Macroeconomics* 10 (3):137–78.

Cusolito, A. P., and W. F. Maloney. 2018. *Productivity Revisited: Shifting Paradigms in Analysis and Policy*. World Bank Productivity Project series. Washington, DC: World Bank.

David, P. A. 1985. "Clio and the Economics of QWERTY." *American Economic Review* 75 (2): 332–37.

Eurostat. 2000. "Glossary: Business Functions."

Goldfarb, A., and C. Tucker. 2019. "Digital Economics." *Journal of Economic Literature* 57 (1): 3–43.

Gordon, R. J. 2012. "Is U.S. Economic Growth Over? Faltering Innovation Confronts the Six Headwinds." NBER Working Paper 18315, National Bureau of Economic Research, Cambridge, MA.

Katz, M. L., and C. Shapiro. 1986. "Technology Adoption in the Presence of Network Externalities." *Journal of Political Economy* 94 (4): 822–41.

Landes, D. S. 2003. *The Unbound Prometheus: Technological Change and Industrial Development in Western Europe from 1750 to the Present*. 2nd ed. Cambridge, UK: Cambridge University Press.

Romer, P. M. 1990. "Endogenous Technological Change." *Journal of Political Economy* 98 (5, Part 2): S71–S102.

Rosenberg, N. 1983. *Inside the Black Box: Technology and Economics.* Cambridge, UK: Cambridge University Press.

Saloner, G., and A. Shepard. 1995. "Adoption of Technologies with Network Effects: An Empirical Examination of the Adoption of Automated Teller Machines." *RAND Journal of Economics* 26 (3): 479–501.

Smith, A. 1776. *An Inquiry into the Nature and Causes of the Wealth of Nations.* London: W. Strahan and T. Cadell.

Solow, R. 1987. "We'd Better Watch Out." *New York Times Book Review* (July 12): 36.

Stoneman, P., and G. Battisti. 2010. "The Diffusion of New Technology." In *Handbook of the Economics of Innovation*, Vol. 2, 733–60. Amsterdam: Elsevier.

PART 1

Measuring the Technological Divide

1. A New Approach to Measure Technology Adoption by Firms

Introduction

When firms adopt more sophisticated technology, it can boost productivity and enhance opportunities for good-quality jobs. But technology is not a unique and narrow set of equipment or processes. Firms use various technologies to perform a variety of productive tasks, from administration to production, to delivery of their products or services. The effects and limitations of different types of technologies utilized by firms are still unknown. Thus, understanding firms' process of deciding *why* to apply a technology, *what* given technology they apply to perform specific tasks, and *how* they apply it is fundamental to comprehending firms' performance and improving evidence-based policies that aim to boost technological progress.

Measuring "what" and "how" technologies are used by firms across a range of sectors and levels of development is a challenge. Going back to the seminal works by Ryan and Gross (1943) and Griliches (1957) on the diffusion of hybrid varieties of corn, the dominant approach to measuring technology has focused on whether a potential adopter uses an advanced technology. In addition to studying technology diffusion and the drivers of adoption, this approach has facilitated the study of the effect of technology on productivity or wages.[1] Most of these studies, however, have looked at the impact of one specific technology, typically an advanced one. Although these measures have significantly contributed to our understanding of "why" firms adopt a given technology, they do not provide a comprehensive perspective for understanding "what" different kinds of technologies firms are using and "how" they are using them for different tasks that could complement one another.

This chapter reviews some of the existing approaches to measuring technology at the firm level and proposes a new method to capture the multiple dimensions of the use of technology from the perspective of the firm. The chapter addresses the following questions:

- What are the main limitations of the current approaches measuring "what" and "how" technologies are used by firms?
- What more granular measures can be devised to better ascertain "what" and "how" technologies are being adopted and used by firms?
- How can more granular measures of the use of technology within the firm help us understand the importance of complementary factors—beyond

infrastructure and the diffusion of general-purpose technologies (GPTs) such as computers—to explain the technological progress of firms and inform policy design tailored to different firms in different contexts?

Measuring Adoption and Use of Technology by Firms

Moving from Macro to Micro Analysis

The importance of technology adoption has been emphasized by macro, sectoral, and micro studies, but the measures used at each level are difficult to reconcile. Macro-level studies tend to be based on cross-country analysis mostly focusing on GPTs, such as electricity, the internet, or computers, using information on adoption by individuals or firms that is aggregated at the country level. Sectoral studies tend to rely on firm-level or household-level data, with a focus on the diffusion and impact of sector-specific technologies at a very granular level (such as the diffusion of varieties of seeds in agriculture). Other firm-level studies tend to be broader in terms of sector and focus on the use of GPTs (such as cloud computing) without identifying the specific purpose for which technologies are being used, or examine very specific technologies that can be used by any firm (such as enterprise resource planning [ERP] systems). Despite different approaches and measures, studies at different levels of aggregation tend to converge on the importance of technology for firm performance and the overall economic development of countries.

Recent findings from the macro literature support the need for better measures of the adoption and intensity of use of technologies by firms. A recent important finding is that while the lag between lower-income and high-income countries in the adoption of technology has narrowed, the gap in the intensity of use of adopted technologies has increased (Comin and Mestieri 2018). Thus, although the pace of technology diffusion has accelerated, diffusion is uneven, resulting in an increasing *technology gap* across firms and countries. A comparison of the diffusion of 25 GPTs in the past 200 years, as shown in figure 1.1, suggests that newer technologies, such as personal computers and the internet, are arriving more quickly in developing countries than older technologies, such as the telegraph and tractors (panel a). Yet, despite their earlier arrival in developing countries, the gap in the intensity of their use between developing countries and advanced economies is widening (panel b).[2]

At the sector level, agriculture is likely the most well covered in terms of studies measuring and assessing the diffusion of sector-specific technologies.[3] There are several reasons for the predominance of technology adoption studies focusing on agriculture, including data availability, the large share of workers in low-income countries who are still in agriculture, and the increasing importance of total factor productivity (TFP) as a source of agricultural growth in the past few decades, as highlighted in Foster and Rosenzweig (2010) and the fourth volume in the World Bank Productivity Project series (Fuglie et al. 2020). More recently, an increasing number of studies have focused on sector-specific technologies used by manufacturing and services firms. Some of these studies

FIGURE 1.1 **While Countries Are Converging in Their Adoption of Technology, They Are Diverging in the Intensity of Use**

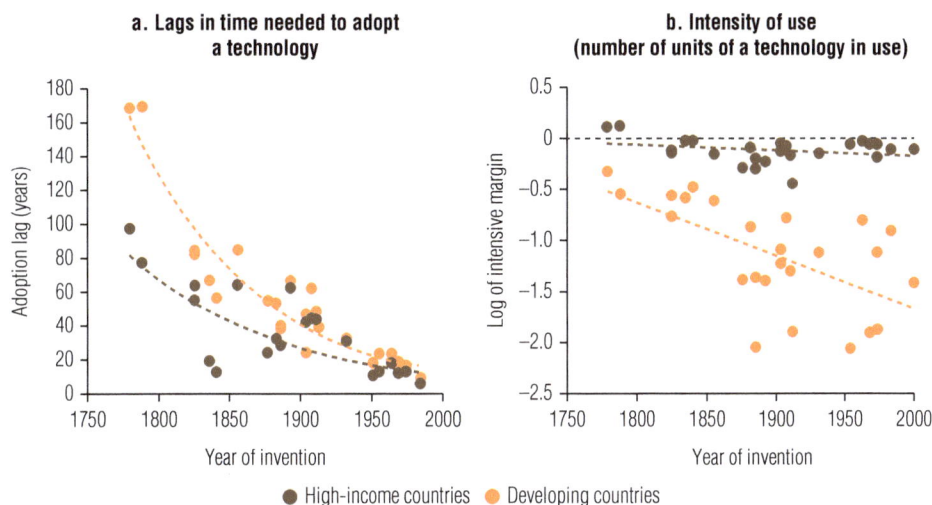

a. Lags in time needed to adopt a technology

y-axis: Adoption lag (years)
x-axis: Year of invention

b. Intensity of use (number of units of a technology in use)

y-axis: Log of intensive margin
x-axis: Year of invention

● High-income countries   ● Developing countries

Source: Adapted from Comin and Mestieri 2018.

Note: Each dot shows the average margin of adoption for high-income countries and developing countries, based on the World Bank income classification. The technologies are presented in the following chronological order: 1. spindles; 2. ships; 3 and 4. railway, passenger and freight; 5. telegraph; 6. mail; 7. steel; 8. telephone; 9. electricity; 10. cars; 11. trucks; 12. tractors; 13 and 14. aviation, passenger and freight; 15. electric arc furnaces; 16. fertilizer; 17. harvesters; 18. synthetic fiber; 19. blast oxygen furnaces; 20. kidney transplant; 21. liver transplant; 22. heart surgery; 23. personal computers; 24. mobile phones; 25. internet. Adoption lag refers to the number of years that it took on average for the technology to arrive in the country, from the time of its invention. The intensive margin refers to the number of units of technology (such as number of tractors per firm) in the country.

have linked the adoption of technologies—particularly information and communication technology (ICT)—to the variation in productivity growth across sectors over time.[4] As firm-level data are becoming more widely available, researchers are posing more relevant questions about technology applied to manufacturing and services on a variety of issues.[5] Finally, many firm-level studies aim to understand technology adoption with a focus on a few GPTs. For example, Hjort and Poulsen (2019) show that the access to fast internet connection increases firm entry, productivity, and exports in African countries.[6]

Although these different approaches tend to converge in identifying and highlighting the economic importance of technology adoption, it is difficult to integrate them in terms of measurement. A key gap is associated with the lack of appropriate comparable measures that provide representative information of technologies used by firms to perform specific tasks and that can be aggregated at different levels (such as firm size, sector, country, and region).

Moving from Measuring Adoption of GPTs to Measuring the Actual Use of Technologies for Particular Business Functions within the Firm

From the standpoint of technology adoption and use, firms remain black boxes (Demsetz 1997). The applied microeconomics literature has used granular measures of technology adoption by firms, but most of these measures apply to very specific sectors, and therefore face constraints for purposes of comparability. Many attempts have been made to understand the dynamics of technology through innovation surveys and patent data, but they do not capture some essential features of technology adoption, particularly for developing countries.[7]

The relevance and emergence of digital technologies have motivated researchers to measure the use of advanced technologies by firms in numerous sectors. As a result, statistical offices from advanced economies have developed ICT surveys for that purpose, including the US Census Bureau (Information Communication Technology Survey [ICTS] and Annual Business Survey [ABS]); the European Union's Eurostat (Community Survey of ICT Usage); and Statistics Canada (Survey of Advanced Technology [SAT]). Recently, the Canadian SAT has extended the scope of these measurement efforts to measure whether firms use a significant number of advanced technologies (between 41 and 50, depending on the round), with a focus on manufacturing.

Despite significant progress, existing measures of technology still fall short of providing a comprehensive characterization of technologies used by firms. First, the number of technologies covered is rather limited when compared to how many technologies are involved in production and management processes. Second, their focus on the presence of advanced technologies makes it impossible to understand how production takes place in companies without such technologies. This concern is most relevant in developing countries where advanced technologies have diffused more slowly. Third, because their unit of analysis is the firm, existing surveys are not designed to examine technology at the level of business functions undertaken by the firm, and cannot measure which business functions benefit from each particular technology. This drawback is particularly problematic for GPTs that can be relevant for multiple business functions. Finally, existing surveys largely omit questions about how intensively a technology is employed in the firm. Therefore, they do not reveal whether a technology that is present is widely utilized or used only marginally.[8]

To overcome these limitations, this volume proposes a new approach to measure technology that shifts the unit of analysis from the firm to the business function level. This approach, described by Cirera et al. (2020), led to the development of a new survey instrument by the World Bank Group in collaboration with several sector and technology experts. The survey, described in the next section, has been designed to collect detailed information for a representative sample of firms about the technologies that each firm uses to perform key business functions necessary to operate in its respective sector of economic activity.

Opening the Black Box: The Firm-level Adoption of Technology (FAT) Survey

The World Bank Group's new approach to measuring technology at the firm level, the FAT survey, has been piloted to a representative sample of firms in 11 countries. Much of the analysis in this volume draws on the survey results and comparisons with other surveys and studies.

The 11 countries included are: Bangladesh; Brazil (only the state of Ceará); Burkina Faso; Ghana; India (only the states of Tamil Nadu and Uttar Pradesh); Kenya; the Republic of Korea; Malawi; Poland; Senegal; and Vietnam. For those countries, subnational data were collected for 51 regions. Data collection is ongoing or planned for 2022 in Brazil (the state of Paraná); Cambodia; Chile; Croatia; Ethiopia; Georgia; Indonesia; Mauritania; and Peru. Preliminary results from Georgia are used in chapter 5 to discuss the relationship between technology and resilience focusing on green technology.

The FAT survey has five modules. Module A collects information about general characteristics of the firm.[9] Module B covers technologies used to perform general business functions that are common across all firms, while module C focuses on sector-specific technologies. Module D focuses on barriers and drivers of technology adoption, while module E gathers information about the firm's balance sheet and employment. To attain a wide coverage that allows a meaningful study of sector-specific technologies, sector-specific modules were developed for 12 significant sectors in the economy: agriculture and livestock; manufacturing (food processing, wearing apparel, leather and footwear, motor vehicles, and pharmaceuticals); and services (wholesale and retail, financial services, land transport services, accommodation, and health services). These sectors have been selected to cover all three major types of industry (agriculture, manufacturing, and services) and are based on their share in a country's aggregate value added, employment, and number of establishments. The discussion that follows describes in more detail the approach developed to measure technology as part of modules B and C of the survey.

Linking Technologies to Business Functions

The approach to measure technology at the firm level starts by differentiating firm-level business functions in two groups: general business functions (GBFs) and sector-specific business functions (SBFs). The unit of analysis of this approach is the business function, rather than the firm. GBFs are tasks that all firms conduct regardless of the sector in which they operate (such as businesses' administration-related tasks, production planning, sourcing and procurement, sales, and payment methods). SBFs are tasks relevant only for companies in a given sector (such as harvesting in agriculture, cooking in food processing, or sewing in apparel). Figure 1.2 summarizes the way technologies are measured through business functions.

A key step for this approach is to determine what business functions and technologies associated with them best represent the overall technology level of the firm. To this end, the methodology follows three steps. First, the team conducted desk research revisiting the specialized literature. Second, experts across the World Bank Group in each of the sectors covered provided inputs and feedback. Third, the team reached out to external consultants with significant experience in the field (at least 15 years).[10] This process allowed the team to

FIGURE 1.2 Conceptual Framework for the Firm-level Adoption of Technology (FAT) Survey

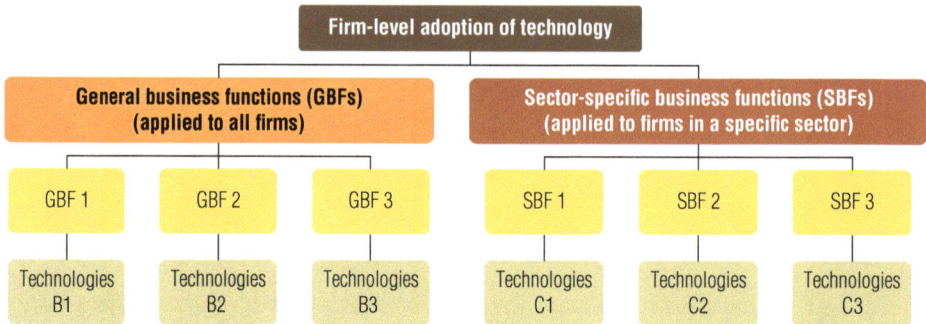

```
                    ┌──────────────────────────────────┐
                    │  Firm-level adoption of technology │
                    └──────────────────────────────────┘
              ┌──────────────────────┴──────────────────────┐
┌─────────────────────────────────────┐  ┌─────────────────────────────────────────┐
│ General business functions (GBFs)    │  │ Sector-specific business functions (SBFs) │
│ (applied to all firms)               │  │ (applied to firms in a specific sector)   │
└─────────────────────────────────────┘  └─────────────────────────────────────────┘
   ┌──────┬──────────┬──────┐              ┌──────┬──────────┬──────┐
┌───────┐ ┌───────┐ ┌───────┐           ┌───────┐ ┌───────┐ ┌───────┐
│ GBF 1 │ │ GBF 2 │ │ GBF 3 │           │ SBF 1 │ │ SBF 2 │ │ SBF 3 │
└───────┘ └───────┘ └───────┘           └───────┘ └───────┘ └───────┘
┌────────┐┌────────┐┌────────┐          ┌────────┐┌────────┐┌────────┐
│Technol.││Technol.││Technol.│          │Technol.││Technol.││Technol.│
│  B1    ││  B2    ││  B3    │          │  C1    ││  C2    ││  C3    │
└────────┘└────────┘└────────┘          └────────┘└────────┘└────────┘
```

Source: Original figure for this volume.

identify the main business functions, both general and specific to the sector, conducted in firms and the technologies that can be used to perform the key tasks in each of the identified functions (corresponding to "why" firms use a given technology).

The proposed approach normalizes the technology measures by the *technology frontier* in each business function. Previous measures of technology sophistication focused on sectors—such as Lall (2000), which is widely used in the area of international trade—do not capture the fact that regardless of the sector they are in, some firms are closer to the technology frontier for a particular business function than others. For example, a firm in agriculture in a given country might be much closer to the technology frontier than another firm in manufacturing when considering their respective relevant business functions. By normalizing the technology measures based on the frontier of each business function in each country, this approach allows for the possibility of comparing firms in sectors with different levels of intensity of technology use (*technology intensity*).

Technology Use across General Business Functions

What are the key business functions and technologies used across GBFs? The exercise conducted with the support of private sector experts has identified seven key general business functions that are common across all firms: business administration (such as accounting, finance, and human resources); production or service operations planning; sourcing and procurement (supply chain management); marketing and product development; sales; payment methods; and quality control. These GBFs have in common the fact that all firms tend to perform them, irrespective of their sector or activity. Figure 1.3 presents the GBFs and the possible technologies that can be used to conduct each of them, identified through the discussions with sector experts.

Evidence from the FAT data suggests that most of the sampled firms tend to rely on manual processes or basic digital technologies to perform these GBFs. Figure 1.4 provides some descriptive statistics from the FAT data to better illustrate the GBF measures.

FIGURE 1.3   General Business Functions and Their Associated Technologies

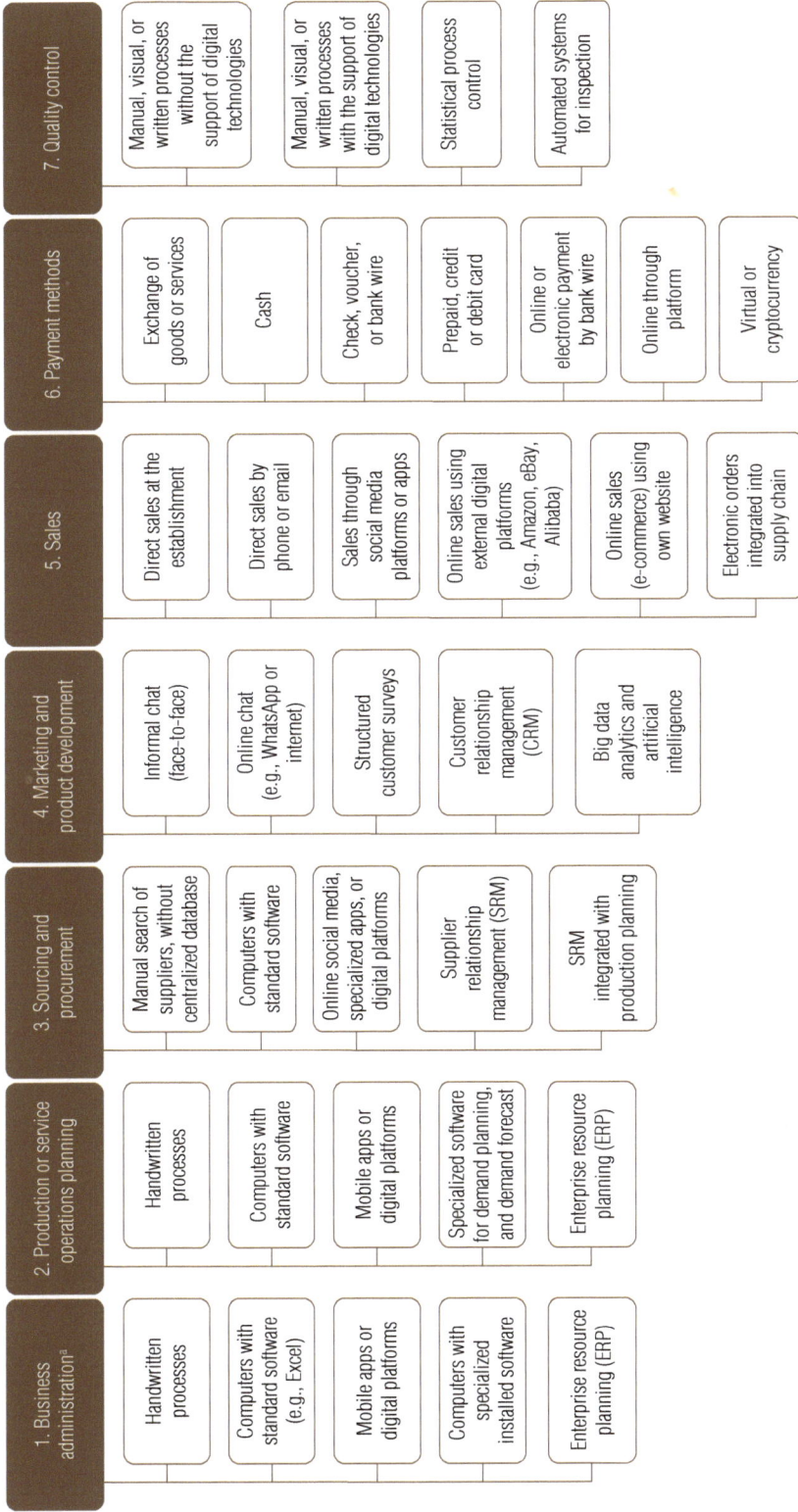

1. Business administration[a]	2. Production or service operations planning	3. Sourcing and procurement	4. Marketing and product development	5. Sales	6. Payment methods	7. Quality control
Handwritten processes	Handwritten processes	Manual search of suppliers, without centralized database	Informal chat (face-to-face)	Direct sales at the establishment	Exchange of goods or services	Manual, visual, or written processes without the support of digital technologies
Computers with standard software (e.g., Excel)	Computers with standard software	Computers with standard software	Online chat (e.g., WhatsApp or internet)	Direct sales by phone or email	Cash	Manual, visual, or written processes with the support of digital technologies
Mobile apps or digital platforms	Mobile apps or digital platforms	Online social media, specialized apps, or digital platforms	Structured customer surveys	Sales through social media platforms or apps	Check, voucher, or bank wire	Statistical process control
Computers with specialized installed software	Specialized software for demand planning, and demand forecast	Supplier relationship management (SRM)	Customer relationship management (CRM)	Online sales using external digital platforms (e.g., Amazon, eBay, Alibaba)	Prepaid, credit or debit card	Automated systems for inspection
Enterprise resource planning (ERP)	Enterprise resource planning (ERP)	SRM integrated with production planning	Big data analytics and artificial intelligence	Online sales (e-commerce) using own website	Online or electronic payment by bank wire	
				Electronic orders integrated into supply chain	Online through platform	
					Virtual or cryptocurrency	

Source: Original figure based on the Firm-level Adoption of Technology (FAT) survey.
a. Business administration includes accounting, finance, and human resources.

A New Approach to Measure Technology Adoption by Firms

FIGURE 1.4 Share of Firms Using Technologies Applied to Various General Business Functions, All Countries

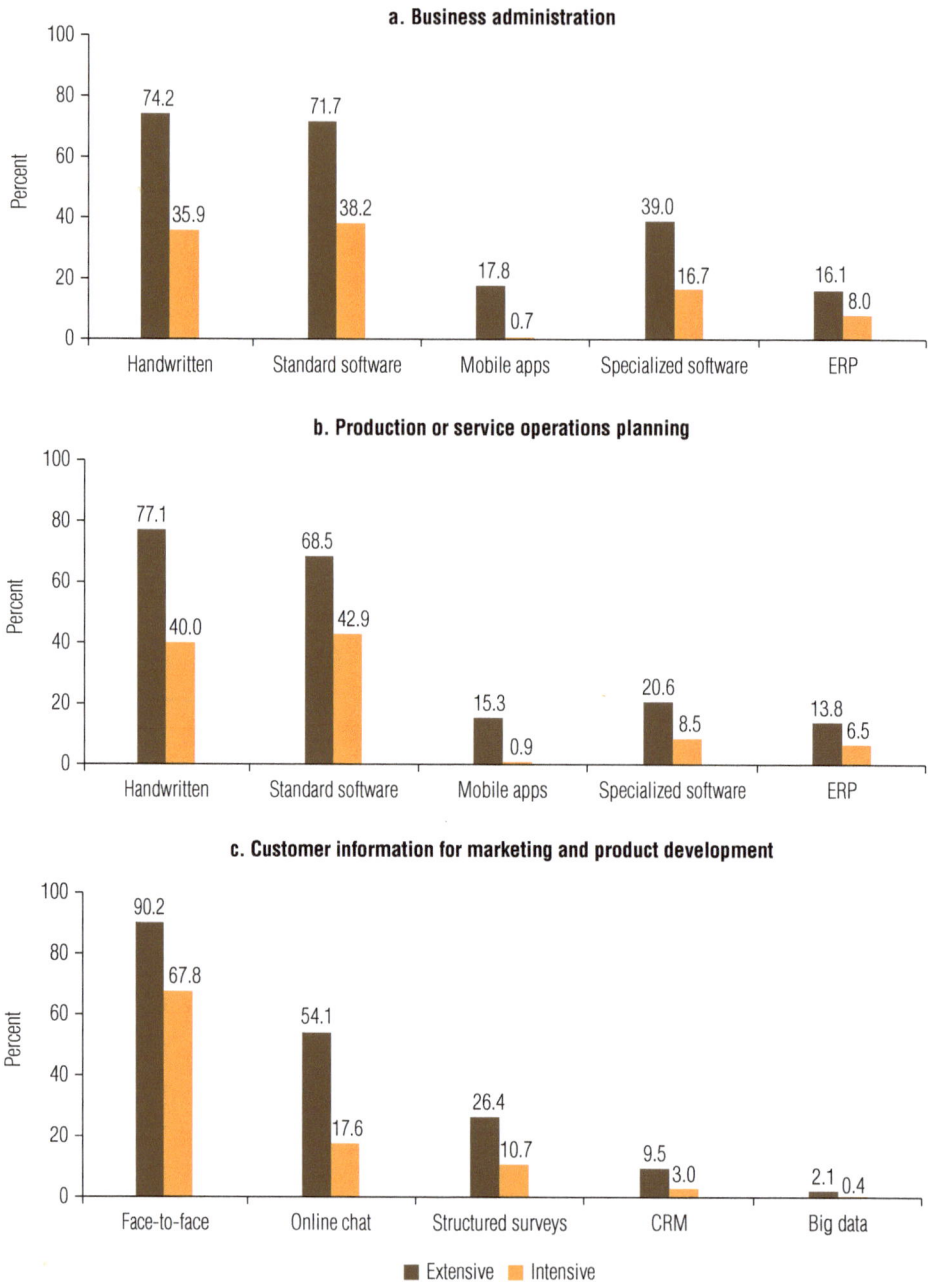

a. Business administration

Handwritten: Extensive 74.2, Intensive 35.9
Standard software: Extensive 71.7, Intensive 38.2
Mobile apps: Extensive 17.8, Intensive 0.7
Specialized software: Extensive 39.0, Intensive 16.7
ERP: Extensive 16.1, Intensive 8.0

b. Production or service operations planning

Handwritten: Extensive 77.1, Intensive 40.0
Standard software: Extensive 68.5, Intensive 42.9
Mobile apps: Extensive 15.3, Intensive 0.9
Specialized software: Extensive 20.6, Intensive 8.5
ERP: Extensive 13.8, Intensive 6.5

c. Customer information for marketing and product development

Face-to-face: Extensive 90.2, Intensive 67.8
Online chat: Extensive 54.1, Intensive 17.6
Structured surveys: Extensive 26.4, Intensive 10.7
CRM: Extensive 9.5, Intensive 3.0
Big data: Extensive 2.1, Intensive 0.4

■ Extensive ■ Intensive

(Figure continues on the following page.)

FIGURE 1.4 **Share of Firms Using Technologies Applied to Various General Business Functions, All Countries** *(continued)*

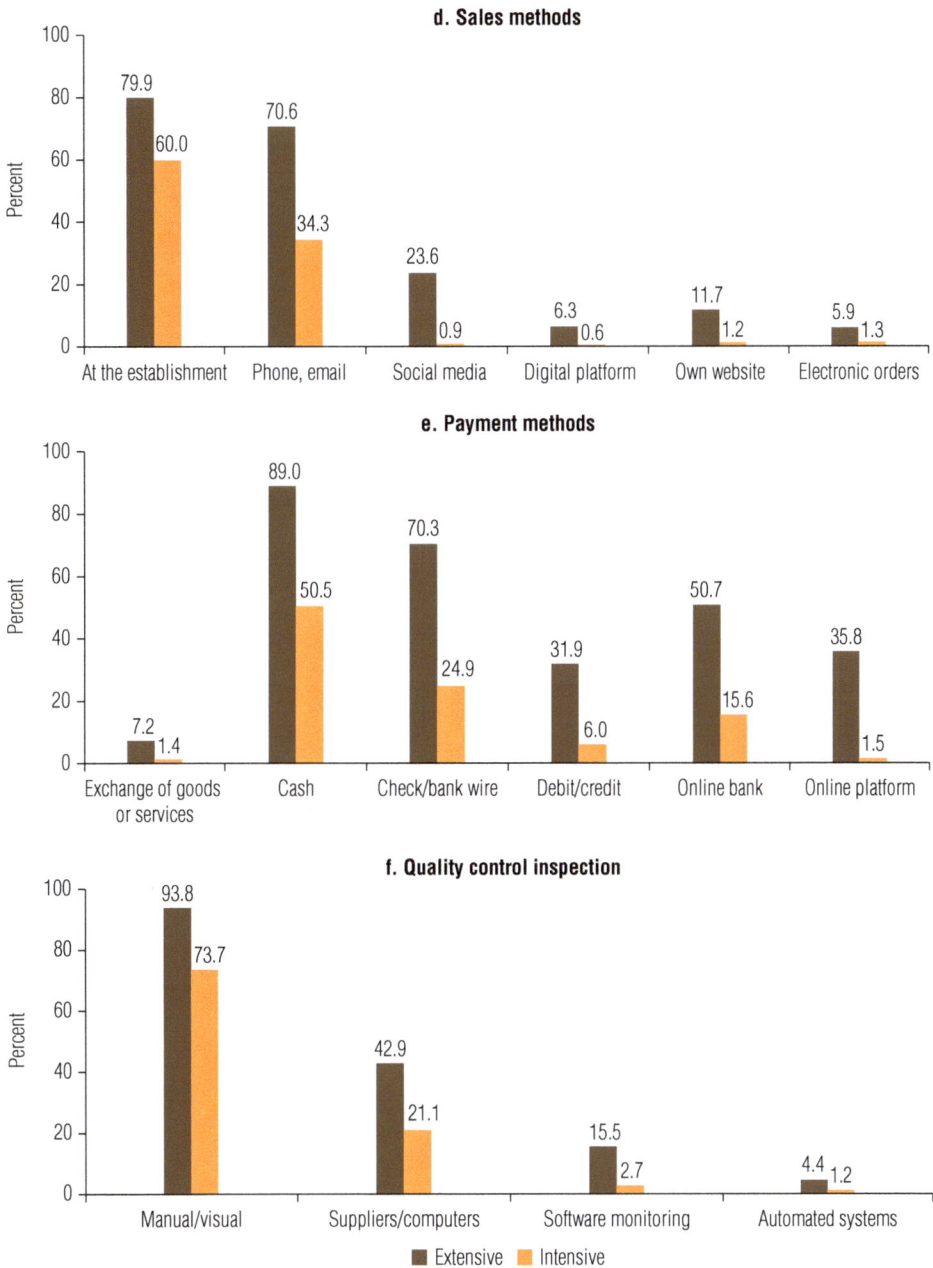

d. Sales methods

	At the establishment	Phone, email	Social media	Digital platform	Own website	Electronic orders
Extensive	79.9	70.6	23.6	6.3	11.7	5.9
Intensive	60.0	34.3	0.9	0.6	1.2	1.3

e. Payment methods

	Exchange of goods or services	Cash	Check/bank wire	Debit/credit	Online bank	Online platform
Extensive	7.2	89.0	70.3	31.9	50.7	35.8
Intensive	1.4	50.5	24.9	6.0	15.6	1.5

f. Quality control inspection

	Manual/visual	Suppliers/computers	Software monitoring	Automated systems
Extensive	93.8	42.9	15.5	4.4
Intensive	73.7	21.1	2.7	1.2

■ Extensive ■ Intensive

Source: Original figure based on Firm-level Adoption of Technology (FAT) survey data.

Note: Estimates based on cross-country average weighted by sampling weights. The 11 countries covered are Bangladesh; Brazil (only the state of Ceará); Burkina Faso; Ghana; India (only the states of Tamil Nadu and Uttar Pradesh); Kenya; Korea, Rep.; Malawi; Poland; Senegal; and Vietnam. The extensive measure captures the array of technologies used by the firm. The intensive measure captures the nature of the most used technology in the business function. Business administration includes accounting, finance, and human resources. CRM = customer relationship management; ERP = enterprise resource planning.

These are tasks for which digital technologies are prevalent, including the frontier technology. Therefore, firms from any sector could potentially benefit from a digital upgrade in these functions. Starting with business administration and production or service operations planning, about 70 percent of firms use standard software, such as Excel, but more than one-third of firms still rely mostly on handwritten methods. Panels a and b of figure 1.4 present the average share of firms across countries using different methods to perform tasks related to business administration processes and production or service operations planning, at both the *extensive margin* (whether they use the technology at all) and *intensive margin* (whether the technology is the most frequently used one to perform that particular task/business function). The results also show that less than 1 percent of businesses rely mostly on mobile apps to perform these tasks, and less than 9 percent rely mostly on ERP.

In the areas of marketing, sales, and payment, the adoption of more sophisticated technologies is more prevalent for payment, but with a large gap between the extensive and the intensive margins. These three business functions have in common the fact that they involve interactions with actors (customers or suppliers) outside the firm, with high potential for *network economies* in which products and services are created and value is added through social networks operating on large or global scales. Figure 1.4 shows that digital payments (e.g., online bank, online platform) are widely diffused technologies among firms, but half of firms still rely mostly on cash and 25 percent rely mostly on checks. For marketing, big data and artificial intelligence (AI) are still very rare among firms. Only 2 percent use these technologies and 1 percent use them intensively. For quality control tasks, most firms still rely on manual procedures as the most frequently used method.

Technology Use across Sector-Specific Business Functions

For the sector-specific technologies, a similar approach was used to identify key business functions and associated technologies in 12 sectors of activity across agriculture, manufacturing, and services (agriculture, livestock, food processing, wearing apparel, leather and footwear, motor vehicles, pharmaceuticals, wholesale and retail, financial services, land transport services, accommodation, and health services). An additional business function, fabrication, was also included for all manufacturing sectors. The identification of key business functions and the frontier in each sector required a significant interaction with several sector specialists. These functions tend to be associated with sector-specific production processes. Figure 1.5 exemplifies for agriculture, food-processing (manufacturing), and retail (services) how the FAT survey unpacks sector-specific production or service provision activities into the main business functions and the technologies that can be used to accomplish them.[11] For more information on the business functions and associated technologies for other sectors, see appendix A.

FIGURE 1.5 Sector-Specific Business Functions and Technologies

a. Agriculture: crops

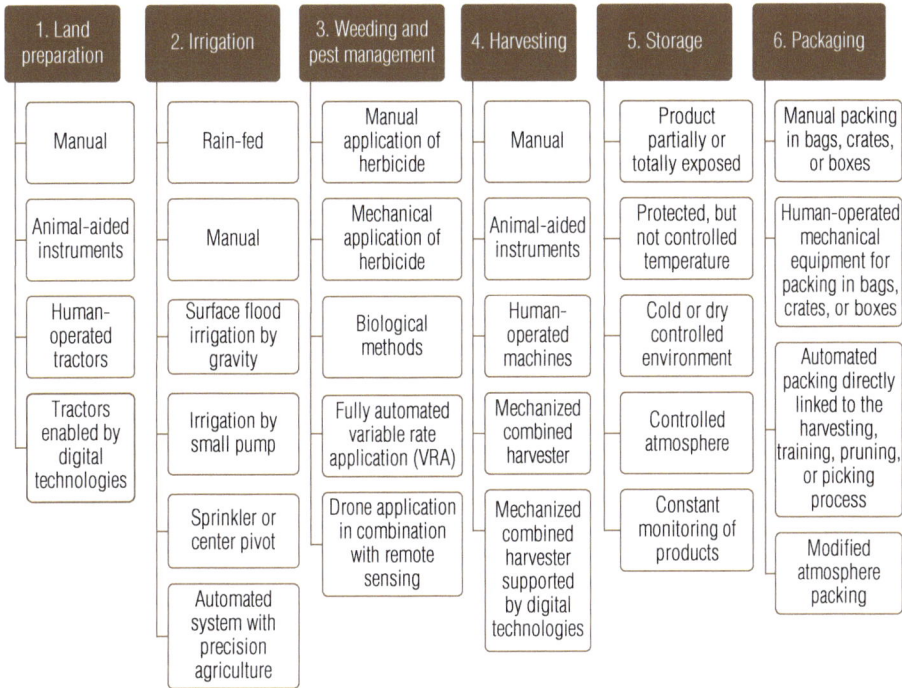

1. Land preparation	2. Irrigation	3. Weeding and pest management	4. Harvesting	5. Storage	6. Packaging
Manual	Rain-fed	Manual application of herbicide	Manual	Product partially or totally exposed	Manual packing in bags, crates, or boxes
Animal-aided instruments	Manual	Mechanical application of herbicide	Animal-aided instruments	Protected, but not controlled temperature	Human-operated mechanical equipment for packing in bags, crates, or boxes
Human-operated tractors	Surface flood irrigation by gravity	Biological methods	Human-operated machines	Cold or dry controlled environment	Automated packing directly linked to the harvesting, training, pruning, or picking process
Tractors enabled by digital technologies	Irrigation by small pump	Fully automated variable rate application (VRA)	Mechanized combined harvester	Controlled atmosphere	Modified atmosphere packing
	Sprinkler or center pivot	Drone application in combination with remote sensing	Mechanized combined harvester supported by digital technologies	Constant monitoring of products	
	Automated system with precision agriculture				

b. Manufacturing: food processing

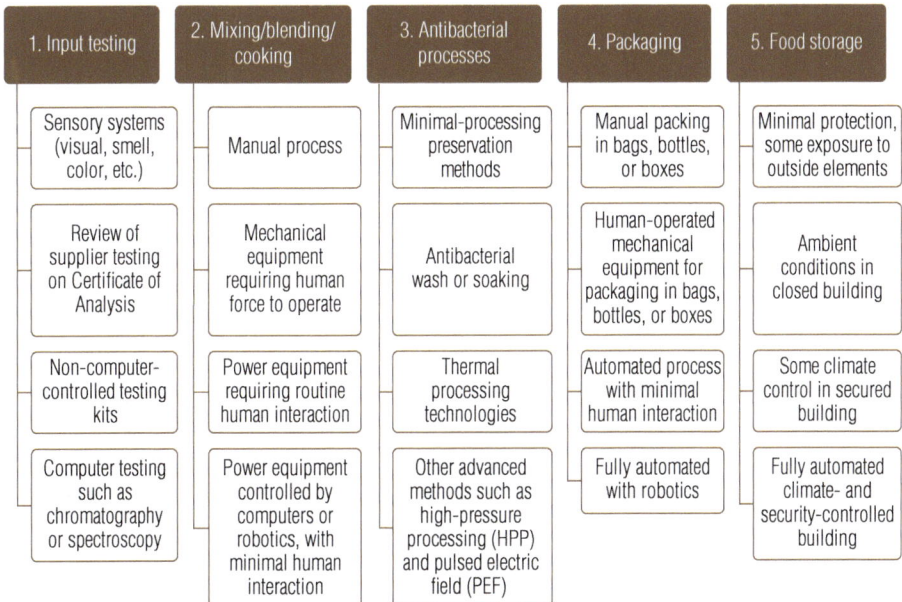

1. Input testing	2. Mixing/blending/ cooking	3. Antibacterial processes	4. Packaging	5. Food storage
Sensory systems (visual, smell, color, etc.)	Manual process	Minimal-processing preservation methods	Manual packing in bags, bottles, or boxes	Minimal protection, some exposure to outside elements
Review of supplier testing on Certificate of Analysis	Mechanical equipment requiring human force to operate	Antibacterial wash or soaking	Human-operated mechanical equipment for packaging in bags, bottles, or boxes	Ambient conditions in closed building
Non-computer-controlled testing kits	Power equipment requiring routine human interaction	Thermal processing technologies	Automated process with minimal human interaction	Some climate control in secured building
Computer testing such as chromatography or spectroscopy	Power equipment controlled by computers or robotics, with minimal human interaction	Other advanced methods such as high-pressure processing (HPP) and pulsed electric field (PEF)	Fully automated with robotics	Fully automated climate- and security-controlled building

(Figure continues on the following page.)

A New Approach to Measure Technology Adoption by Firms

31

FIGURE 1.5 Sector-Specific Business Functions and Technologies *(continued)*

c. Services: wholesale and retail

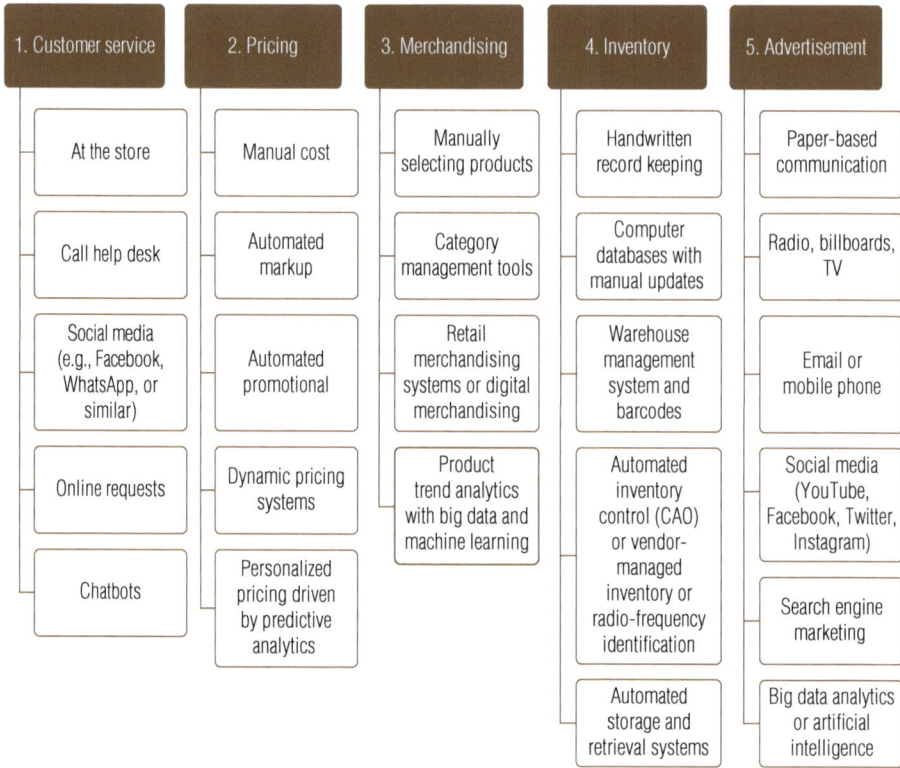

1. Customer service	2. Pricing	3. Merchandising	4. Inventory	5. Advertisement
At the store	Manual cost	Manually selecting products	Handwritten record keeping	Paper-based communication
Call help desk	Automated markup	Category management tools	Computer databases with manual updates	Radio, billboards, TV
Social media (e.g., Facebook, WhatsApp, or similar)	Automated promotional	Retail merchandising systems or digital merchandising	Warehouse management system and barcodes	Email or mobile phone
Online requests	Dynamic pricing systems	Product trend analytics with big data and machine learning	Automated inventory control (CAO) or vendor-managed inventory or radio-frequency identification	Social media (YouTube, Facebook, Twitter, Instagram)
Chatbots	Personalized pricing driven by predictive analytics		Automated storage and retrieval systems	Search engine marketing
				Big data analytics or artificial intelligence

Source: Original figure based on the Firm-level Adoption of Technology (FAT) survey.

For sector-specific business functions, digital technologies tend to be embedded in other technologies that are usually at the frontier. This is a common feature, particularly in agriculture and manufacturing, and has important implications in terms of the costs of adoption and the importance of network effects. For example, among methods commonly used by agricultural firms to perform harvesting (figure 1.5, panel a), the most basic option is to harvest manually, followed by animal-aided instruments; human-operated machines or a single tractor with one specific function (such as a single-axle tractor); a combined harvester (machines or tractors that combine multiple functions fully operated by the worker); and a combined harvester supported by digital technologies (such as a global positioning system [GPS] or computing systems integrated with the tractor). Unlike for GBFs, the application of digital technologies for the sector-specific business function of harvesting requires other sophisticated equipment or machines.

The different measures of technology used by firms are converted into *indexes of technology sophistication* for comparability and analytical purposes. One important element of the data is the fact that most firms use more than one technology to perform similar tasks (such as handwritten processes, Excel, and specialized software for business administration) with different levels of intensity. The next section describes how this information is converted into an index that is informative about the firm's level of technology sophistication to perform each business function. The sections that follow provide a short summary of the technology indexes widely used in this volume.

The Technology Index

The FAT survey asks two types of questions about the technologies used to perform a business function. The first type inquires about the use of each of the technologies listed by the experts as relevant in a given business function (corresponding to whether or not firms adopt technology). The answer to these questions characterizes the full array of technologies that the firm uses. The second type of question gathers information about which of the technologies used is employed more intensively (corresponding to "what" and "how" firms use technology).[12] The answer to this question is used to construct technology measures that reflect the nature of the main technology used in the business function (the intensive measure) as opposed to the most sophisticated technology from the array of technologies used in the business function (extensive measure).[13] This distinction is relevant because firms do not use all the technologies available to perform a business function with the same intensity, and the impact of a technology on the firm's productivity may depend on the importance of the technology used most intensively.

To measure the technology gap of the most intensively used technology, the technologies are combined into an index capturing the technology sophistication for each business function. The index varies between 1 and 5, where 1 stands for the most basic level of technology and 5 reflects the most sophisticated.[14] With the help of experts for each industry, a rank was assigned to the technologies in each business function according to their sophistication. The sophistication of a technology measures its complexity, which corresponds to its capacity to conduct more tasks and/or tasks of greater difficulty, or to perform them with greater accuracy or precision. Naturally, technology sophistication tends to be correlated with the novelty of the technology.[15] Figure 1.6 provides a simple example of the technology index for two functions: business administration (GBF); and storage for agriculture (SBF).[16] Box 1.1 presents an example of applying the technology index to different sizes of firms (small and large) in a particular sector (food processing) in a particular country (Senegal).

These measures of technology provide a very rich description of the overall level of sophistication of a firm, as well as the variation of technology sophistication across functions. They can be aggregated at different levels for which the FAT data are representative, such as country, subnational regions, sector of activity, firm size, and firm formality status.[17]

FIGURE 1.6   An Example of the Technology Index

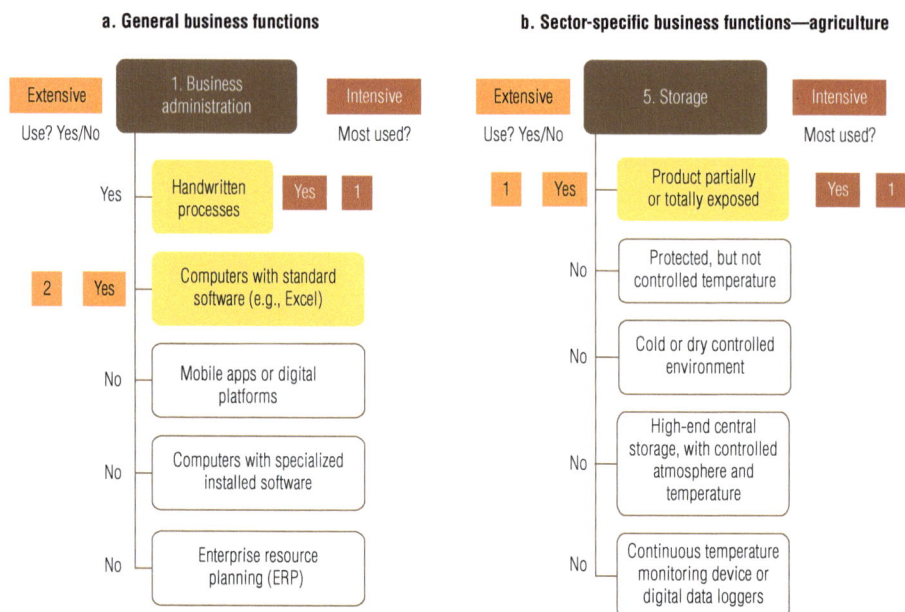

a. General business functions

Extensive		Intensive
Use? Yes/No	1. Business administration	Most used?

Yes — Handwritten processes — [Yes] [1]

[2] Yes — Computers with standard software (e.g., Excel)

No — Mobile apps or digital platforms

No — Computers with specialized installed software

No — Enterprise resource planning (ERP)

b. Sector-specific business functions—agriculture

Extensive		Intensive
Use? Yes/No	5. Storage	Most used?

[1] Yes — Product partially or totally exposed — [Yes] [1]

No — Protected, but not controlled temperature

No — Cold or dry controlled environment

No — High-end central storage, with controlled atmosphere and temperature

No — Continuous temperature monitoring device or digital data loggers

Source: Original figure based on the Firm-level Adoption of Technology (FAT) survey.
Note: Business administration includes accounting, finance, and human resources.

The Technology Index at the Firm Level: An Example from the Food-Processing Sector in Senegal

The measure of technology sophistication developed for this volume can characterize the technology landscape of firms with a high level of granularity. Figure B1.1.1 presents two spider charts that display the measures for each of the general business functions (GBFs) (panel a) and sector-specific business functions (SBFs) (panel b) for the two firms in the food-processing sector in Senegal: a small firm (Firm A), shown with the solid brown line; and a large firm (Firm B), shown with the dashed orange line. In general, the large firm uses more sophisticated technologies than the small one, but there is significant variation in the gap across different functions (Cirera et al. 2020). However, the gap between the sophistication of technologies used in both companies varies considerably depending on the technology measure, the type of business function, and the specific business function considered.

With the exception of cooking, for all other business functions Firm B has a level of technology sophistication greater than or equal to Firm A. The average sophistication for Firm B across business functions is 2.3 versus 1.4 for Firm A. Firm B has greater sophistication in both GBFs and SBFs, though the gap in sophistication is slightly larger in SBFs (2.6 minus 1.7 = 0.9) than in GBFs (2.0 minus 1.2 = 0.8). Beyond differences in average sophistication, there is significant variation in sophistication across business functions within a firm. For example, the sophistication for both firms is the same in business administration, planning, sourcing, and marketing, but Firm B has greater sophistication in sales, payment, and quality control. For SBFs, the two firms have the

(Box continues on the following page.)

BOX 1.1

The Technology Index at the Firm Level: An Example from the Food-Processing Sector in Senegal *(continued)*

same sophistication in only one function: packaging. Firm B has greater sophistication in three of the remaining functions and Firm A has greater sophistication in cooking. This suggests that there is greater variation in sophistication within firms across SBFs than across GBFs. Similarly, figure B1.1.1 also suggests that there is more variation within Firm B than within Firm A (1.8 versus 0.36).

FIGURE B1.1.1 Comparing Technology Sophistication of a Large and a Small Firm in the Food-Processing Sector

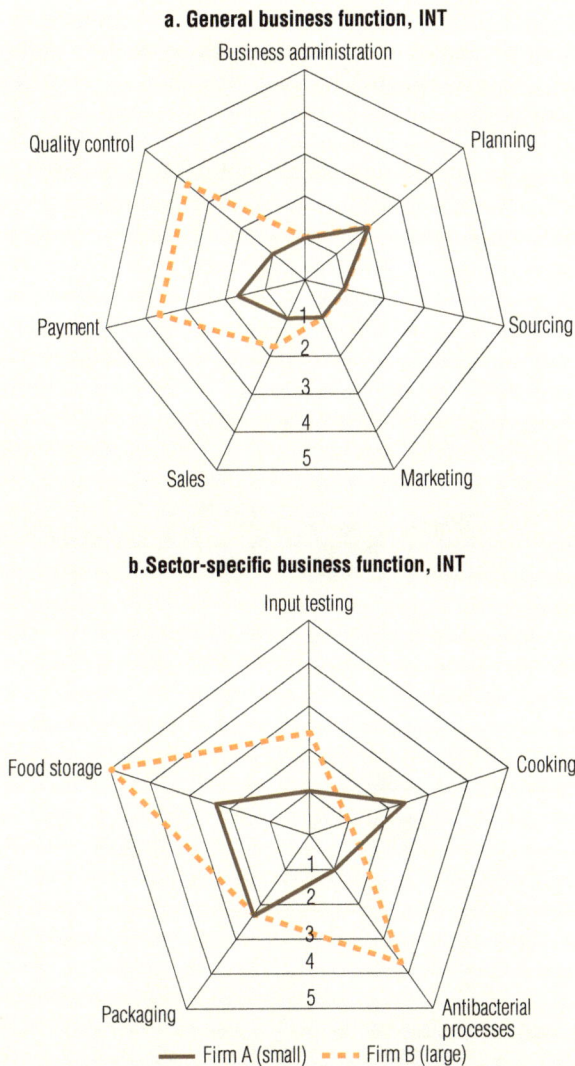

a. General business function, INT

b. Sector-specific business function, INT

Source: Cirera et al. 2020.

Note: Firm A (the small firm) has 16 workers. Firm B (the large firm) has 300 workers. INT = an index reflecting the sophistication of the most widely used technology in a business function. The higher the index, the greater the sophistication.

The Data Used in This Volume

This volume relies mostly on primary firm-level data from representative samples from 11 countries. The data were collected from 2019, before the COVID-19 pandemic, to 2021, in the midst of the pandemic. Table 1.1 shows the number of establishments interviewed, which totaled more than 13,000 and represent around 1.3 million establishments.[18] The Bangladesh data only include manufacturing, and the India and Malawi data exclude agriculture. The survey was stratified by firm size (small, medium, and large), sectors, and regions within countries. Because of stratification, the shares of firms in agriculture and manufacturing are proportionately large relative to services, compared to the distribution in the universe of firms. Particularly in the case of manufacturing, this improves the statistical power of the analysis. In the case of Senegal, informal firms are also included given that they are available in the sampling frame of Senegal's national statistical office. In this case, the survey was also stratified by formal and informal firms, which allows the team to measure the technology gap between formal and informal firms in the country. For the remaining countries, the data are representative of the formal sector only. Thus, in the case of countries where the share of informality is high among firms with 5 or more workers, especially in African countries, the analysis may overestimate the technology sophistication of the average firm, by excluding informal ones.[19]

TABLE 1.1 Number of Establishments Surveyed, by Sector and Firm Size

Country	Total	Sector			Firm size		
		Agriculture	Manufacturing	Services	Small	Medium	Large
Bangladesh	903	—	903	—	361	232	310
Brazil[a]	711	72	387	252	205	322	184
Burkina Faso	600	80	140	380	335	187	78
Ghana	1,262	85	275	902	774	382	106
India[b]	1,519	—	791	728	629	598	292
Kenya	1,305	155	335	815	499	421	385
Korea, Rep.	1,551	129	652	770	656	569	326
Malawi	482	—	137	345	284	122	76
Poland	1,500	90	607	803	779	394	327
Senegal	1,786	204	679	903	1,219	395	172
Vietnam	1,499	110	806	583	774	426	299
Total	**13,118**	**925**	**5,712**	**6,481**	**6,515**	**4,048**	**2,555**

Source: Original table based on Firm-level Adoption of Technology (FAT) survey data.

Note: Firm size refers to the number of workers: small (5–19), medium (20–99), and large (100 or more). — = not available.

a. The Brazil sample covers only the state of Ceará.

b. The India sample covers only the states of Tamil Nadu and Uttar Pradesh.

To ensure comparability, the team implemented a standardized data collection protocol across all countries. Data collectors included national statistical agencies in Malawi, Poland, and Vietnam; public-private institutions such as the State Industry Association (FIEC) in Ceará, Brazil; and specialized data collection firms in the remaining countries, with the sampling frame provided by national statistical offices. The same protocols were followed, as specified in a standard terms of reference for implementation. For each country, each survey item was professionally translated from English to the local language and back again, with interactions and revisions from World Bank team members who are fluent or native speakers in the local language.[20] The FAT data were collected through both face-to-face interviews and by telephone. The analyses presented in this book are performed using sampling weights. When computing cross-country analysis, the weights were rescaled so that all countries are equally weighted. See appendix A for more details about the FAT data and the weights used.

The richness of these data sets, over the period of 2019–21, offers a unique perspective to explore new questions and provide new evidence on the adoption and use of technology by firms. The next section uses the FAT data to illustrate the importance of granular measures of technologies used by firms to explain why some of the standard measures of technology provide a limited perspective.

Using the FAT Data to Understand Some of the Limitations of Standard Measures of Technology

In addition to measuring technologies at the business function level, the FAT survey also provides standard measures of GPTs. These measures include access to and quality of electricity, and use of ICT (such as mobile phones, computers, and the internet), as well as advanced digital technologies (such as cloud computing, robots, big data, and AI). These measures also provide an overall perspective on access to infrastructure and the conditions that enable technology use. Thus, before going into the specifics of technologies linked with business functions, the next section provides a general perspective on where firms in developing countries stand with respect to the adoption of technologies that are usually associated with different stages of industrial revolution. The section also explains the reason why these measures provide a limited perspective of the level of technology sophistication of firms, and the importance of linking the use of technologies to specific functions within a firm, as proposed by the FAT survey.

The Incomplete Transition from Industry 2.0 to Industry 4.0 in Developing Countries

Different stages of technological transitions, popularly defined as Industry 2.0, 3.0, and 4.0, are associated with the diffusion of disruptive GPTs. Industry 2.0 encompasses the diffusion of technologies powered by electricity, which are technologies from the 1880s. Industry 3.0 refers to the ICT revolution, including the use of mobile phones, computers, and the internet. These technologies became available over the 1970–80 period.[21] Industry 4.0 refers to technologies that in most cases have some digital component, but a higher level of autonomy, connection, and integration of information across different devices and machines to perform tasks. Among the GPTs usually associated with Industry 4.0 are the Internet of Things, big data analytics, AI, 3D printing, advanced robotics, and cloud computing.[22]

Standard measures of GPTs can only partially identify and explain where firms stand in the use of technologies associated with each technological transition. The adoption of Industry 2.0 technologies is incomplete in some firms in developing countries, which in some cases use manual processes. Access to the internet is wider, but adoption of Industry 3.0 technologies is partial. Most firms are very far from using Industry 4.0 technologies (figure 1.7). In addition to serving as technologies themselves, GPTs act as infrastructure for the development of applied technologies.

Access to GPTs is not the only factor that matters for adoption of these applied technologies: quality is also very important. For example, although most firms in developing countries have access to electricity, quality, measured by the small share of firms that do not experience outages, is often poor (panel a). These shortages occur for all types of firms. Also, there is a clear gap in how firms respond to this low quality of infrastructure access. Large firms are much more likely to have a generator to minimize electricity shortages (panel a). This difference in the response to low-quality electricity creates differences in technology use that limit, for example, the possibility of *leapfrogging*—skipping over a less sophisticated level of technology to use a more sophisticated one. Leapfrogging will be discussed in chapter 3.

Similarly, for Industry 3.0 technologies, even if access is widespread, adoption and use of particular technologies differ (panel b). There are not large gaps in access to mobile phones by large, medium, or small firms in developing countries. The pattern is different for computers and the internet, which almost all large firms use, while less than 75 percent of small firms do. Despite widespread access, quality differs across firms, but as shown in the next section, even with the same quality of access, firms differ greatly in their use and adoption of applied technologies. In the case of Industry 4.0 technologies (panel c), a very small share of firms uses these technologies. The exception is cloud computing, for which there is also a clear gap across firm size.

The incomplete technological transitions across countries are not fully captured by standard measures of technology adopted by firms. The simultaneous rapid spread of ICT general-purpose technologies alongside the persistence of a large share of firms still struggling to gain basic access to reliable electricity is one of the many paradoxes of technology in developing countries. First, it shows the power and the limits of technology disruptions associated with the digital revolution.[23] Second, there is large variation in

FIGURE 1.7 Firms Vary Widely in the Status of Their Adoption of General-Purpose Technologies

a. Industry 2.0

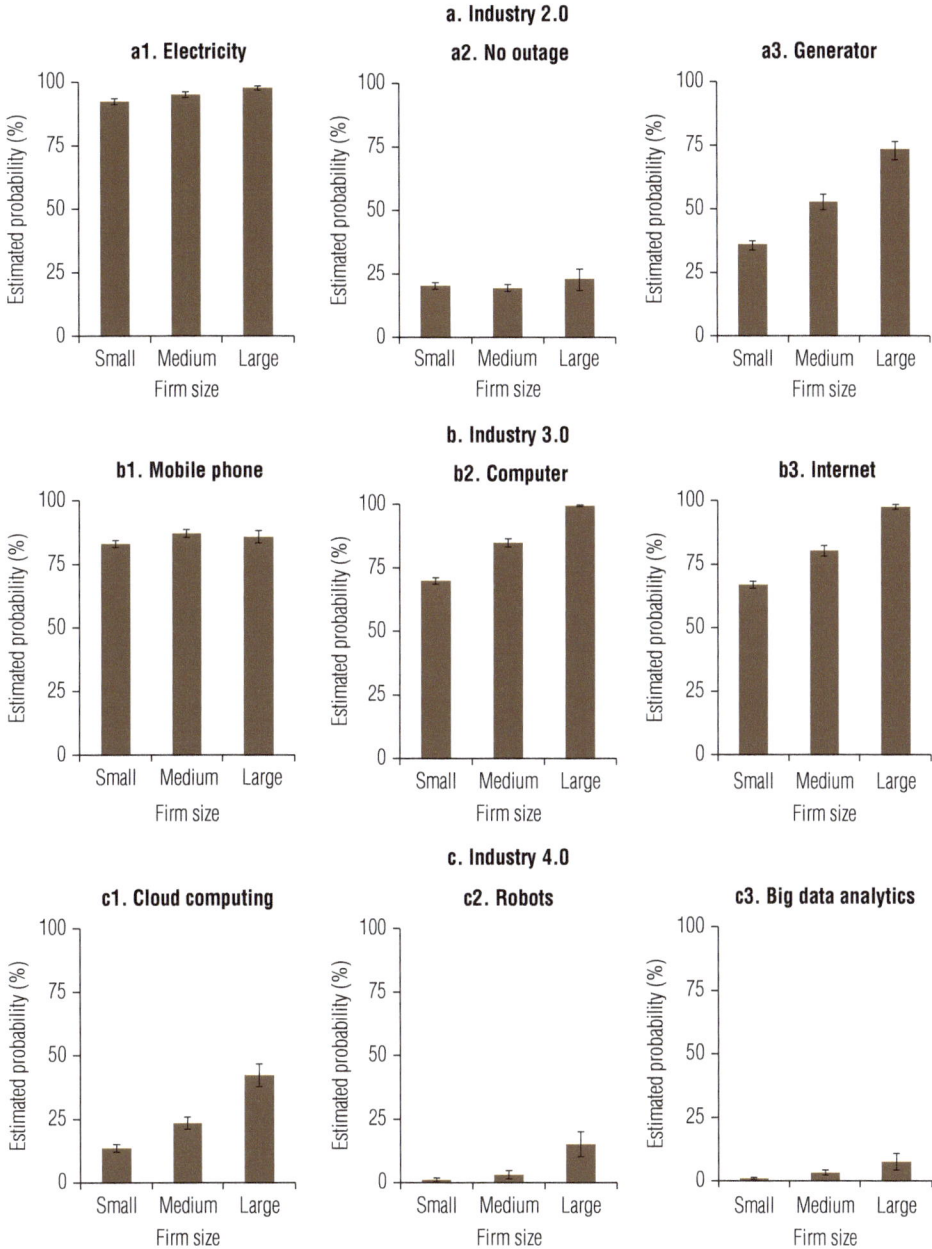

Source: Original figure based on Firm-level Adoption of Technology (FAT) survey data.

Note: The data cover 11 countries: Bangladesh; Brazil (only the state of Ceará); Burkina Faso; Ghana; India (only the states of Tamil Nadu and Uttar Pradesh); Kenya; Korea, Rep.; Malawi; Poland; Senegal; and Vietnam. Firm size refers to the number of workers: small (5–19), medium (20–99), and large (100 or more). Estimates are weighted by sampling weights.

terms of the quality of supply and potential for network economies across different uses of digital technologies. Thus, while the focus of the media and policy makers is on the latest technological transition (or industrial revolution), many firms, particularly in developing countries, have yet to complete previous transitions. This is partly due to the quality of the infrastructure underlying these technologies, but also partly due to other factors to be discussed next. But one clear lesson is that these technology differences are not visible using standard measures of access to GPTs.

How Are Firms Actually Using Computers and the Internet and for What Purposes?

Measuring the adoption of GPTs to characterize the degree of technology sophistication of a firm can be misleading without identifying the purpose for and intensity of a firm's use of those technologies. Beyond the problems with accessing reliable infrastructure—which could facilitate the adoption of applied technologies—for a given level of adoption of a given digital technology, the sophistication of use varies widely among firms.

A simple example is provided by comparing the technologies used by firms to perform business administration tasks, conditional on having computers and the internet. Figure 1.8 shows the share of firms using different levels of technology on both the extensive margin (whether they use it or not) and the intensive margin (which technology they use most intensively) to perform business administration tasks related to accounting, finance, and human resources, conditional on having computers and/or the internet. Most of those firms use standard software (such as Excel) to perform this task (extensive margin). This is also the technology used most frequently by those firms (intensive margin). But about 21 percent of firms rely on specialized software, while 11 percent use enterprise resource planning (ERP). There are significant differences in terms of technology sophistication between processing data manually, using standard Excel software, and utilizing ERP in terms of the capabilities to perform tasks, the efficiency gains of the processes, and the outputs produced. But there are also important differences in terms of just using a technology (the extensive margin) or using it intensively as the most used technology (intensive margin).

The results presented by the first two sets of bars (use of handwritten methods or standard software) in figure 1.8 describe another anomaly of adoption when looking merely at adoption of GPTs. Why do approximately one-fifth of firms (with 5 or more workers) still rely mostly on handwritten methods despite the fact that those firms have access to computers or the internet? Although the indicators, such as access to computers and the internet, used in traditional surveys provide a general picture on the adoption of a few GPTs, they fail to provide information on what technologies firms are effectively using to perform different tasks and functions, as shown in figure 1.8. This is a critical

FIGURE 1.8 **Among Firms with Access to Computers and the Internet, a Large Share Relies Mostly on Less Sophisticated Methods to Conduct Business Functions**

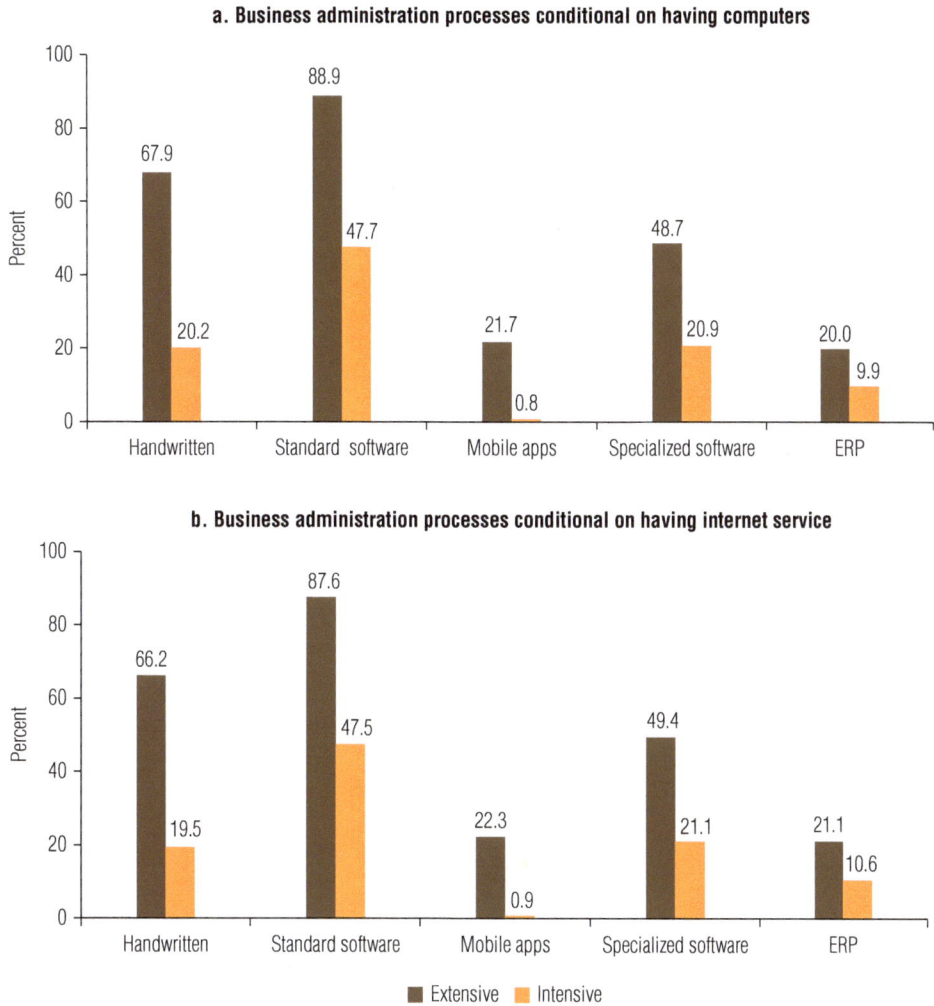

a. Business administration processes conditional on having computers

b. Business administration processes conditional on having internet service

■ Extensive ■ Intensive

Source: Original figure based on Firm-level Adoption of Technology (FAT) survey data.

Note: This figure presents firm-level data from eight countries (Bangladesh; Brazil [only the state of Ceará]; Ghana; India [only the states of Tamil Nadu and Uttar Pradesh]; Kenya; Korea, Rep.; Senegal; and Vietnam) on general business functions conditional on having computers and the internet. Business administration processes are those related to accounting, finance, and human resources. The extensive measure captures the array of technologies used by the firm. The intensive measure captures the nature of the most used technology in the business function. ERP = enterprise resource planning.

element because firms can use the internet in many different ways, ranging from using email for a few marketing activities to having fully digitalized and integrated management processes. Understanding this range of applications is essential to learn about firm performance, given that different uses result in very differentiated effects on productivity and profits. But traditional measures of ICT are not well suited to measure the granularity needed to explain firms' adoption and use of specific technologies.

Summing Up

This chapter puts forward a new framework to measure technology adoption. The framework has four core principles. First, the firm is at the center of the analysis. Second, it is grounded at the business function and task level. Third, it includes all technologies that can be used for a given business function. Fourth, it measures what kinds of technologies firms use and which technology they use more intensively. This new approach is necessary to measure the multiple dimensions of technology from the perspective of the firm. The scope and granularity of the framework can help researchers and policy makers thoroughly understand the process of technology adoption and use, including existing heterogeneity in patterns of adoption; differences between sectors; the impact on firm performance; and the main barriers to and drivers of technology adoption and use.

To illustrate the benefits of this framework and the data collected for this volume compared to standard GPT measures, this chapter provides an example in a context of industrial revolutions. The FAT data show that many firms in developing countries are still struggling with an incomplete transition from Industry 2.0 to Industry 3.0. Moreover, despite having computers and the internet, many firms still rely on handwritten methods to conduct business functions that could benefit from digital technologies. The granular information obtained through the FAT survey approach is critical to describe the reality of firms in both developed and developing countries. More important, the granularity of the data yielded by the survey and analysis is needed to design more targeted and effective policies that aim to increase technology adoption and use by firms. The chapters that follow use the data collected from the FAT survey to shed some light on all these issues.

Notes

1. See Mansfield (1961); Krueger (1993); Foster and Rosenzweig (1995); DiNardo and Pischke (1997); Bartel, Ichniowski, and Shaw (2007); Duflo, Kremer, and Robinson (2011); Atkin, Khandelwal, and Osman (2017); and Juhász, Squicciarini, and Voigtländer (2020).

2. The Cross-country Historical Adoption of Technology (CHAT) data set provides aggregated measures of adoption of more than 100 GPTs across more than 150 countries since 1800 (Comin and Mestieri 2018). The data set defines technologies as a group of production methods that are used to produce an intermediate good or service. It covers major technologies related to transportation, telecommunications, information technology (IT), health care, steel production, and electricity.

3. See, for example, Ryan and Gross (1943); Griliches (1957); Foster and Rosenzweig (1996); Suri (2011); Bustos, Caprettini, and Ponticelli (2016); and Gupta, Ponticelli, and Tesei (2020).

4. See, for example, Comin (2000); Jorgenson, Ho, and Stiroh (2005, 2008); Oliner, Sichel, and Stiroh (2007); and Van Ark, O'Mahoney, and Timmer (2008).

5. Examples of these studies vary from identifying the positive effects of adopting computer numerically controlled (CNC) machines and computer-aided design (CAD) software in the productivity of valve manufacturing (Bartel, Ichniowski, and Shaw 2007) to measuring the presence of CT scanners in hospitals (Trajtenberg 1990) to the impact of adopting onboard computers in trucks (Hubbard 2003).

6. Other examples of studies measuring the presence of some ICTs such as computers or access to the internet include Brynjolfsson and Hitt (2000); Stiroh (2002); Bresnahan, Brynjolfsson, and Hitt (2002); and Akerman, Gaarder, and Mogstad (2015).

7. Innovation surveys are widely available in many countries, but they usually do not provide information about how far a given firm is from the technology frontier. The questions are usually relative (for example, innovation in terms of process or product with respect to the local, national, or international market). Patent data identify some relevant aspects of the dynamics on the technology frontier, but most of them do not apply to an average firm in developing countries or advanced economies.

8. One exception is Mansfield (1963), and the papers that have followed this study, which examine the diffusion of a technology within a company, providing a proxy for the intensity with which the technology is used.

9. The survey is designed, implemented, and weighted at the establishment level. For multi-establishment firms, the survey targets the establishment randomly selected in the sample.

10. The external experts in agriculture and livestock were agricultural engineers and researchers from Brazil's Embrapa (Empresa Brasileira de Pesquisa Agropecuária, Brazilian Agricultural Research Corporation). For food processing, wearing apparel, motor vehicles, pharmaceuticals, transport, finance, and retail, as well as for the GBFs, the team relied on senior external consultants selected by a large management consulting organization. For health services, the team relied on consultants and physicians with practical experience in developing countries and advanced economies.

11. Appendix A provides more details on business functions and technologies covered by the other sector-specific variables.

12. In the pre-pilot stage, the team experimented with an alternative survey design that asked about the fraction of time/output/processes that were conducted with each of the technologies in the business function. However, this approach was harder to implement and contained larger errors because respondents found it difficult to answer precisely, and the more subjective interpretation made it harder to compare answers across business functions and companies.

13. The technology indexes are defined as:

$$EXT_{f,j} = 1 + 4 \times \hat{r}_{f,j}^{EXT}$$
$$INT_{f,j} = 1 + 4 \times \hat{r}_{f,j}^{INT}$$

$EXT_{f,j}$ is the most advanced technology (extensive margin) used in a business function f within a firm j. $INT_{f,j}$ is the index for most widely used technology (intensive margin). $\hat{r}_f$ is a relative rank of technology defined as $\dfrac{r_{f-1}}{R_{f-1}}$, where r_f is a rank of technology and R_f is the maximum rank in a business function.

14. Cirera et al. (2020) provide a detailed discussion and several robustness checks on the rationale and consistency of using a cardinal measure of technology based on an ordinal ranking.

15. The construction of technology sophistication rankings predated the administration of the survey and was not influenced by attributes (such as productivity) of firms that use a given technology.

16. Cirera et al. (2020) also develop a technology sophistication index to measure adoption at the extensive margin. Appendix A provides more details about this alternative index (EXT). This index is used in chapter 6 to provide more heterogeneity when discussing key barriers of adoption.

17. For example, in Senegal the sample is also representative for formal and informal firms.

18. The survey covers a universe of 1.3 million establishments with the following distribution across countries: Bangladesh (15,358); Brazil's state of Ceará (23,364); Burkina Faso (57,328); Ghana (42,165); India's states of Tamil Nadu and Uttar Pradesh (92,061); Kenya (74,255); Korea (545,515); Malawi (2,123); Poland (244,983); Senegal (9,583); and Vietnam (179,713).

19. To control for some of the differences in samples, stratification, and economic structure when comparing countries in the sample, dummies for sector, firm size, and formality are used to calculate correlations and different cross-country estimates.

20. Cirera et al. (2020) describe the design features implemented to minimize measurement bias and errors.

21. Comin and Mestieri (2018) present the reference year of invention for these technologies: electricity (1882); personal computers (PCs) (1973); cell phones (1973); and the internet (1983).

22. Hallward-Driemeier and Nayyar (2017) provide further discussions on the emergence of Industry 4.0. Although some of these technologies, such as AI, have been available since the 1960s, they have been increasingly available in recent years.

23. While almost all firms use mobile phones, clearly benefiting from an extraordinary process of leapfrogging, only a small share has reported no outages in electricity. There is a large gap in access to generators, particularly for small firms.

References

Akerman, A., I. Gaarder, and M. Mogstad. 2015. "The Skill Complementarity of Broadband Internet." *Quarterly Journal of Economics* 130 (4): 1781–824.

Atkin, D., A. K. Khandelwal, and A. Osman. 2017. "Exporting and Firm Performance: Evidence from a Randomized Experiment." *Quarterly Journal of Economics* 132 (2): 551–615.

Bartel, A., C. Ichniowski, and K. Shaw. 2007. "How Does Information Technology Affect Productivity? Plant-Level Comparisons of Product Innovation, Process Improvement, and Worker Skills." *Quarterly Journal of Economics* 122 (4): 1721–58.

Bresnahan, T. F., E. Brynjolfsson, and L. M. Hitt. 2002. "Information Technology, Workplace Organization, and the Demand for Skilled Labor: Firm-Level Evidence." *Quarterly Journal of Economics* 117 (1): 339–76.

Brynjolfsson, E., and L. M. Hitt. 2000. "Beyond Computation: Information Technology, Organizational Transformation and Business Performance." *Journal of Economic Perspectives* 14 (4): 23–48.

Bustos, P., B. Caprettini, and J. Ponticelli. 2016. "Agricultural Productivity and Structural Transformation: Evidence from Brazil." *American Economic Review* 106 (6): 1320–65.

Cirera, X., C. Comin, M. Cruz, and K. M. Lee. 2020. "Anatomy of Technology in the Firm." NBER Working Paper 28080, National Bureau of Economic Research, Cambridge, MA.

Comin, D. 2000. "An Uncertainty-Driven Theory of the Productivity Slowdown in Manufacturing." PhD thesis, Harvard University, Cambridge, MA.

Comin, D., and M. Mestieri. 2018. "If Technology Has Arrived Everywhere, Why Has Income Diverged?" *American Economic Journal: Macroeconomics* 10 (3):137–78.

Demsetz, H. 1997. "The Firm in Economic Theory: A Quiet Revolution." *American Economic Review* 87 (2): 426–29.

DiNardo, J. E., and J.-S. Pischke. 1997. "The Returns to Computer Use Revisited: Have Pencils Changed the Wage Structure Too?" *Quarterly Journal of Economics* 112 (1): 291–303.

Duflo, E., M. Kremer, and J. Robinson. 2011. "Nudging Farmers to Use Fertilizer: Theory and Experimental Evidence from Kenya." *American Economic Review* 101 (6): 2350–90.

Foster, A. D., and M. R. Rosenzweig. 1995. "Learning by Doing and Learning from Others: Human Capital and Technical Change in Agriculture." *Journal of Political Economy* 103 (6): 1176–1209.

Foster, A. D., and M. R. Rosenzweig. 1996. "Technical Change and Human-Capital Returns and Investments: Evidence from the Green Revolution." *American Economic Review* 86 (4): 931–53.

Foster, A. D., and M. R. Rosenzweig. 2010. "Microeconomics of Technology Adoption." *Annual Review of Economics* 2 (1): 395–424.

Fuglie, K., M. Gautam, A. Goyal, and W. F. Maloney. 2020. *Harvesting Prosperity: Technology and Productivity Growth in Agriculture.* World Bank Productivity Project series. Washington, DC: World Bank.

Griliches, Z. 1957. "Hybrid Corn: An Exploration in the Economics of Technological Change." *Econometrica* 25 (4): 501–22.

Gupta, A., J. Ponticelli, and A. Tesei. 2020. "Information, Technology Adoption and Productivity: The Role of Mobile Phones in Agriculture." NBER Working Paper 27192, National Bureau of Economic Research, Cambridge, MA.

Hallward-Driemeier, M., and G. Nayyar. 2017. *Trouble in the Making? The Future of Manufacturing-Led Development.* Washington, DC: World Bank.

Hjort, J., and J. Poulsen. 2019. "The Arrival of Fast Internet and Employment in Africa." *American Economic Review* 109 (3):1032–79.

Hubbard, T. N. 2003. "Information, Decisions, and Productivity: Onboard Computers and Capacity Utilization in Trucking." *American Economic Review* 93 (4): 1328–53.

Jorgenson, D. W., M. S. Ho, and K. Stiroh. 2005. *Productivity, Volume 3: Information Technology and the American Growth Resurgence.* Cambridge, MA: MIT Press.

Jorgenson, D. W., M. S. Ho, and K. Stiroh. 2008. "A Retrospective Look at the US Productivity Growth Resurgence." *Journal of Economic Perspectives* 22 (1): 3–24.

Juhász, R., M. P. Squicciarini, and N. Voigtländer. 2020. "Technology Adoption and Productivity Growth: Evidence from Industrialization in France." NBER Working Paper 27503, National Bureau of Economic Research, Cambridge, MA.

Krueger, A. B. 1993. "How Computers Have Changed the Wage Structure: Evidence from Microdata, 1984–1989." *Quarterly Journal of Economics* 108 (1): 33–60.

Lall, S. 2000. "The Technological Structure and Performance of Developing Country Manufactured Exports, 1985–98." *Oxford Development Studies* 28 (3): 337–69.

Mansfield, E. 1961. "Technical Change and the Rate of Imitation." *Econometrica* 29 (4): 741–66.

Mansfield, E. 1963. "Intrafirm Rates of Diffusion of an Innovation." *Review of Economics and Statistics* 45 (4): 348–59.

Oliner, S. D., D. E. Sichel, and K. J. Stiroh. 2007. "Explaining a Productive Decade." *Brookings Papers on Economic Activity* 2007 (1): 81–137.

Ryan, B., and N. Gross. 1943. "The Diffusion of Hybrid Seed Corn in Two Iowa Communities." *Rural Sociology* 8 (1):15–24.

Stiroh, K. J. 2002. "Information Technology and the U.S. Productivity Revival: What Do the Industry Data Say?" *American Economic Review* 92 (5): 1559–76.

Suri, T. 2011. "Selection and Comparative Advantage in Technology Adoption." *Econometrica* 79 (1): 159–209.

Trajtenberg, M. 1990. *Economic Analysis of Product Innovation: The Case of CT Scanners.* Harvard Economic Studies, Vol. 160. Cambridge, MA: Harvard University Press.

Van Ark, B., M. O'Mahoney, and M. P. Timmer. 2008. "The Productivity Gap between Europe and the United States: Trends and Causes." *Journal of Economic Perspectives* 22 (1): 25–44.

2. Facts about Technology Adoption and Use in Developing Countries

Introduction

This chapter presents some stylized facts that have emerged from the Firm-level Adoption of Technology (FAT) survey data in relation to the adoption and use of technology by firms. The data provide granular information for developing and high-income countries to address some previously unexplored questions about the size of the technology gaps between business functions, firms, sectors, regions, and countries.[1] To this end, the technology index described in the previous chapter is used to characterize the level of technology sophistication across and within firms.

Specifically, this chapter addresses the following questions:

- How far from the technology frontier are the average firms in developing countries?
- What is the association between the average level of technology sophistication of firms and the productivity of the regions where they are located?
- How does the technology gap vary across countries, regions, sectors, firms, and business functions?
- Based on the patterns of adoption by firms, what do the data reveal about technology leapfrogging—jumping stages in the process of technology convergence, such as from manual to advanced digital technologies?
- Are firms aware about their technology gap?

To address these questions, this chapter presents 10 stylized facts related to comparisons across countries, regions, sectors, firms, and business functions within firms. Among the most novel findings are the large variations in the sophistication of technologies at all levels of aggregation (from countries to sectors to firms); the more micro the unit of analysis—from country to business function within the firm—the larger the variance in sophistication. Moreover, not only is the average technology sophistication positively correlated with productivity, but so is the dispersion of technology sophistication across countries, firms, and business functions within a firm.

In line with a rich firm-level literature (see Syverson 2014), the analysis reveals considerable heterogeneity across and within firms regarding the adoption and use of technology. It also demonstrates that this heterogeneity matters for performance. This implies that firms have different incentives to upgrade different technologies.

Accordingly, policy support should consider that upgrading different technologies may require different approaches and face different barriers.

Cross-Country Technology Facts

Fact 1. Most firms are far from the technology frontier.

Most firms, especially in developing countries, are far from the technology frontier. Figure 2.1 presents the estimated country average of technology sophistication in manufacturing firms. First, the figure shows that the average firm (orange dot) in each country is far from the frontier (starting in the shaded area).[2] Second, using the top (20 percent) manufacturing firms in the Republic of Korea and Poland as a benchmark to the frontier, most firms in developing countries, including their best firms (brown dot), are far from the frontier.[3] The country rankings based on average technology sophistication tend to coincide with country income levels. The results also show a gap between formal and informal firms in Senegal.

Agricultural and services firms are also far from the technology frontier (figure 2.2). There are important peculiarities about those sectors. In agriculture

FIGURE 2.1 **Estimated Technology Sophistication, by Country: Manufacturing**

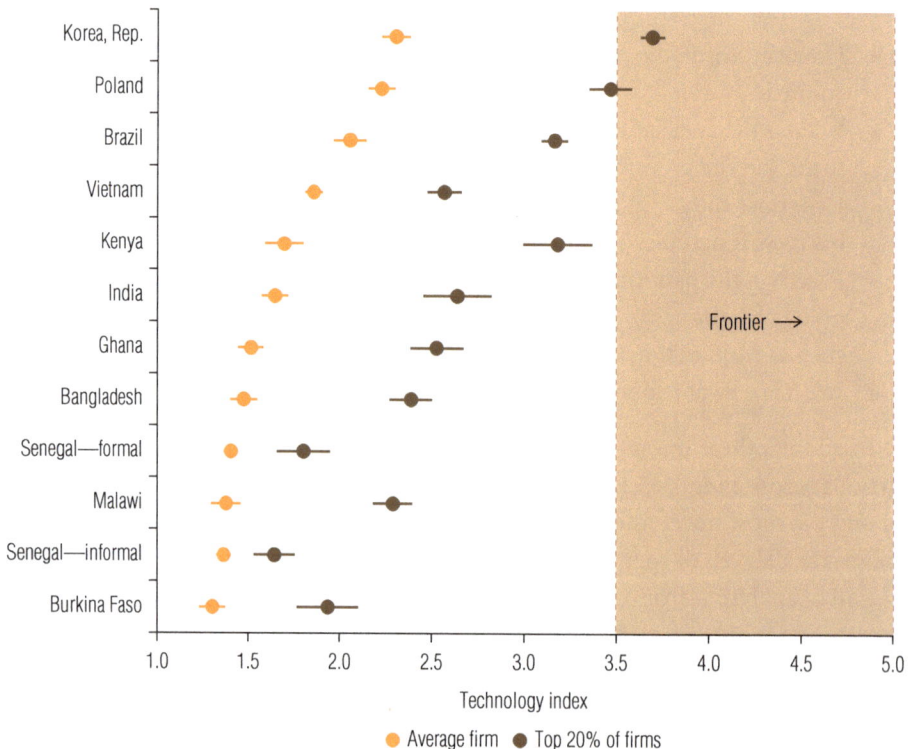

Source: Original figure based on Firm-level Adoption of Technology (FAT) survey data.

Note: The figure plots for each country the average level of technology sophistication of the firm across all business functions (ABF), including general business functions (GBFs) and sector-specific business functions (SBFs). Results are based on ordinary least squares (OLS) estimation using sampling weights and controlling for sector, country, formality, firm size group, and age group.

FIGURE 2.2 Estimated Technology Sophistication, by Country: Agriculture and Services

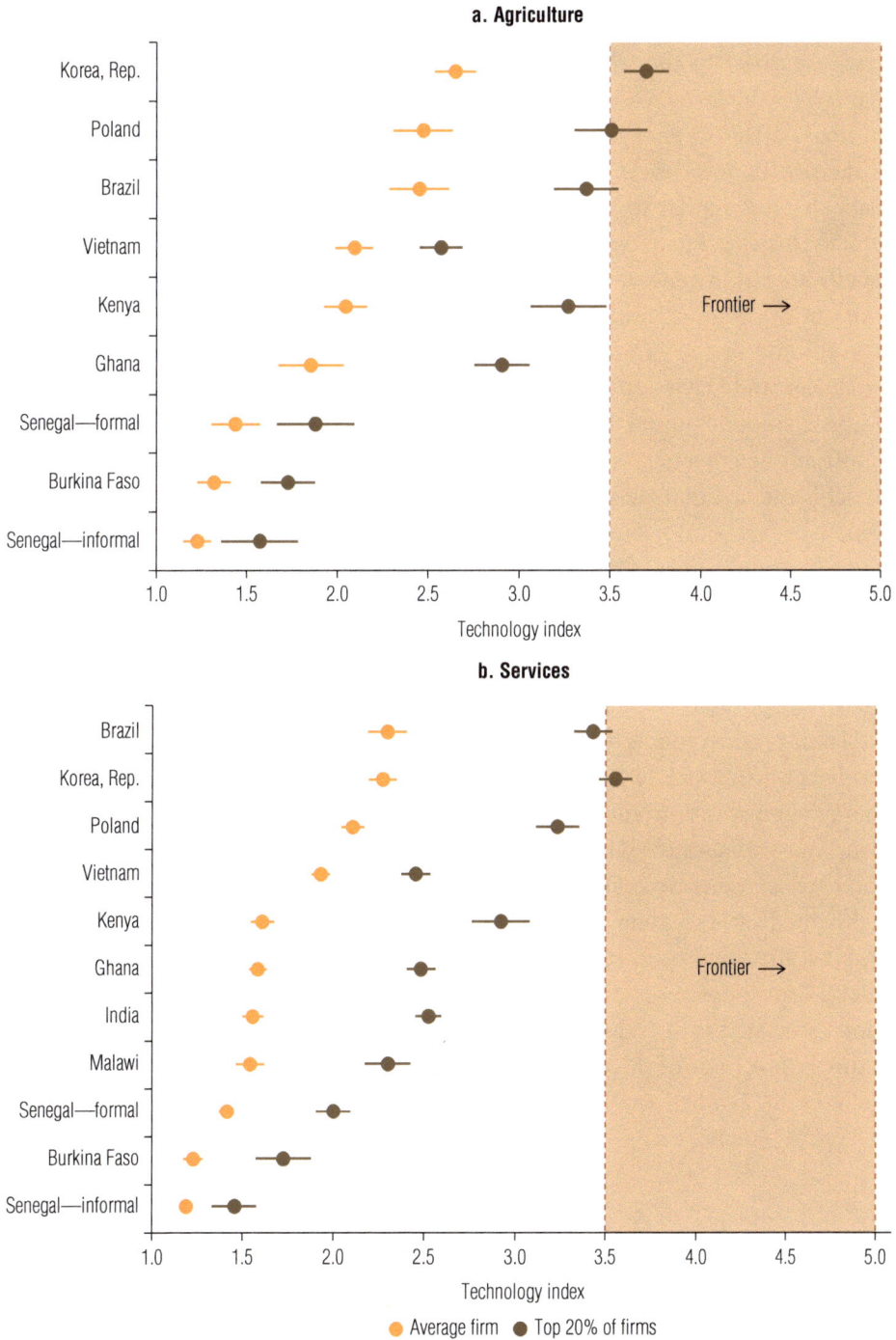

a. Agriculture

b. Services

● Average firm   ● Top 20% of firms

Source: Original figure based on Firm-level Adoption of Technology (FAT) survey data.

Note: The figure plots for each country the average business function, which reflects the average level of technology sophistication of the firm across all business functions, including general business functions (GBFs) and sector-specific business functions (SBFs). Results are based on ordinary least squares (OLS) estimation using sampling weights and controlling for sector, country, formality, firm size group, and age group.

(panel a), top firms in Brazil and Kenya tend to be relatively closer to top firms in Korea and Poland, compared to manufacturing. This suggests that in some developing countries where agricultural exports are important, agricultural firms are relatively closer to the frontier than in manufacturing. But as the discussion in chapter 4 will clarify, there is still a large gap in agricultural firms in developing countries driven by many informal and less capable firms, which still absorb many workers with low levels of productivity. The pattern for services is different (panel b): it is similar to agriculture and less correlated to a country's income per capita. This is partially explained by the rapid diffusion of certain technologies, usually related to general business functions (GBFs) (such as digital payment systems) in some countries. Yet, as discussed in chapter 3 and as highlighted in the fifth volume in the World Bank Productivity Project series (Nayyar, Hallward-Driemeier, and Davies 2021), despite the relevance of digital technologies for providing economic opportunities for services in developing countries, there is significant heterogeneity in adoption across services activities. Another important aspect is the fact that these measures do not capture differences in the number of firms (see fact 3), nor are they weighted by the number of workers they employ, which has implications for the per capita GDP ranking.

Fact 2. More productive regions are closer to the technology frontier.

The strong positive association between the variation of technology sophistication and labor productivity is observed not only across countries but also across regions within countries. Figure 2.3 presents a scatterplot of the regional measures of technology sophistication against regional productivity as the weighted average of firm-level variables for 44 subnational regions across 10 countries.[4] The correlation between these two variables is 0.87, confirming the cross-country association highlighted earlier.[5] There is also a strong positive correlation between technology sophistication and productivity at the firm level, unconditional or conditional on several firm characteristics (as will be discussed in chapter 4). The significant variation associated with technology and productivity across regions is also described in the sixth volume of the World Bank Productivity Project series (Grover, Lall, and Maloney 2022) when analyzing the several complementary factors driving the gap in laggard regions.

Fact 3. Advanced economies have many more sophisticated firms.

Why is the technology gap between the average firm in Korea and the other countries not as large as the gap in per capita income? The technology gap across countries (and regions) is driven not only by the sophistication of average firms, but also by the density (quantity of those firms per capita). There is a large difference

FIGURE 2.3 **There Is a Strong Correlation between the Technology Sophistication of a Region and Regional Productivity**

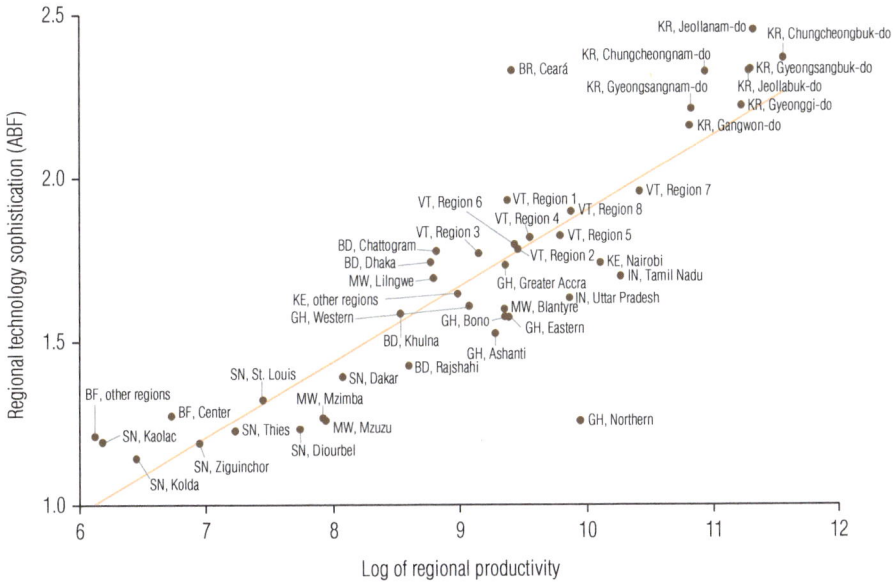

Source: Original figure based on Firm-level Adoption of Technology (FAT) survey data, following Cirera et al. 2020a.

Note: The regional average of technology sophistication by business function (ABF) is plotted on the y-axis. The regional productivity is plotted on the x-axis. The regional productivity is measured as the average value added per worker based on a representative sample of the FAT data for each region, using sampling weights. Countries are as follows: Bangladesh (BD); Brazil (BR); Burkina Faso (BF); Ghana (GH); India (IN); Kenya (KE); Korea, Rep. (KR); Malawi (MW); Senegal (SN); and Vietnam (VT). The eight regions sampled in Vietnam (VT) are: Region 1 (Bắc Ninh, Hải Phòng, Ninh Bình); Region 2 (Bắc Giang, Thái Nguyên); Region 3 (Bình Định, Hà Tĩnh, Thanh Hoá); Region 4 (Kon Tum, Lâm Đông); Region 5 (Bình Dương, Đông Nai); Region 6 (Long An, Vĩnh Long); Region 7 (Hà Nôi); and Region 8 (Hồ Chì Minh City).

between the number of formal firms across countries. Comparing Korea and Kenya, countries with similar populations (around 50 million), not only is the average firm in Korea closer to the technology frontier but there are also many more of those firms (with 5 or more workers) absorbing many more workers (see box 2.1). The number of firms in Korea in the top 20 percent in terms of technology sophistication is almost double the full number of formal firms with 5 or more workers in Kenya in the FAT sample. Figure 2.4 shows that the gap between Vietnam, Kenya, and Senegal with respect to Korea is explained not only by the average sophistication (vertical axis), but also by having many more firms with those technologies (circle size), and more workers absorbed by those firms (horizontal axis).[6] This highlights the importance of more capable entrepreneurs who are able to enter developing countries' markets, grow, and absorb the knowledge created elsewhere (see the third volume in the World Bank Productivity Project series, Grover Goswami, Medvedev, and Olafsen 2019).[7]

FIGURE 2.4 **Cross-Country Differences in Technology Are Also Explained by the Number of Firms Using Sophisticated Technology**

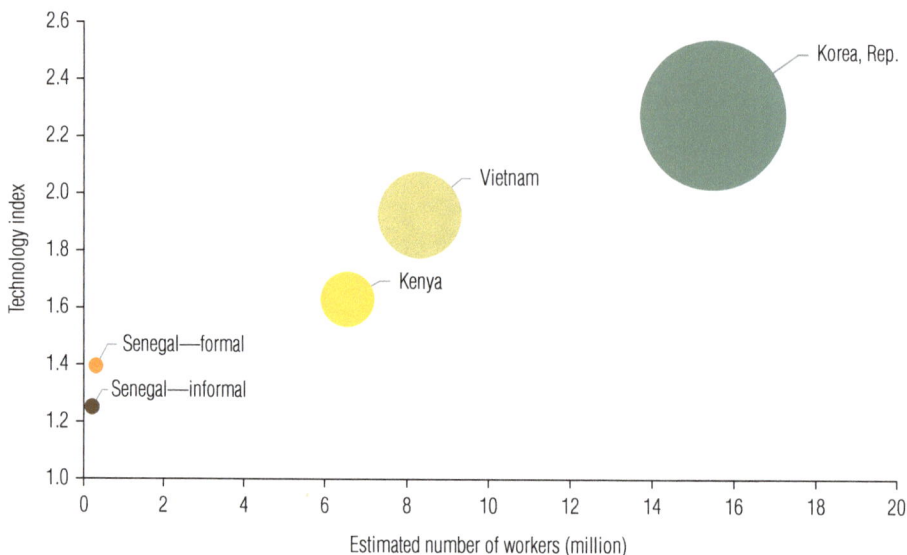

Source: Original figure based on Firm-level Adoption of Technology (FAT) survey data.

Note: Technology index estimates at the firm level across all business functions. Results are based on ordinary least squares (OLS) estimation controlling for sector, country, formality, firm size group, age group, and using sampling weights (vertical axis), number of workers (horizontal axis), and number of firms (size of the bubble). All estimations are based on sampling weights. For Senegal, the total number of workers is adjusted based on the latest establishment census to cover firms from all regions.

BOX 2.1

The Large Gap in Technology Sophistication between Formal and Informal Firms

Is the difference between the Republic of Korea and Kenya in the number of firms with 5 or more workers explained by the informal nature of firms (informality)? The literature has documented that the share of firms not reported as formal establishments in developing countries tends to be more prevalent among micro firms (those with less than 5 workers), but informal firms are still present among firms with 5 or more workers, as suggested by the Firm-level Adoption of Technology (FAT) survey results for Senegal (see figure 2.4). The implication for some other countries in the sample—especially in Africa, where informality is more prevalent—is that if the informal sector were taken into account, the average technology sophistication would be reduced, increasing the average distance to the frontier. Malawi, for example, has about half the number of formal firms observed in Senegal, despite having a larger population, and thus has a higher incidence of informality.

Estimates from Senegal help explain the implications of informality on the differences in the number of firms, the aggregated distance from the frontier, and workers' access to sophisticated technologies through firms. On a plot like that shown in figure 2.4, including informal firms increases the size of the circle (by adding more firms), but moves the circle down (farther away from the frontier) and to the right (adding more workers). Figure B2.1.1 shows that average

(Box continues on the following page.)

The Large Gap in Technology Sophistication between Formal and Informal Firms *(continued)*

FIGURE B2.1.1 **Technology Sophistication Is Significantly Greater among Formal Firms in Senegal**

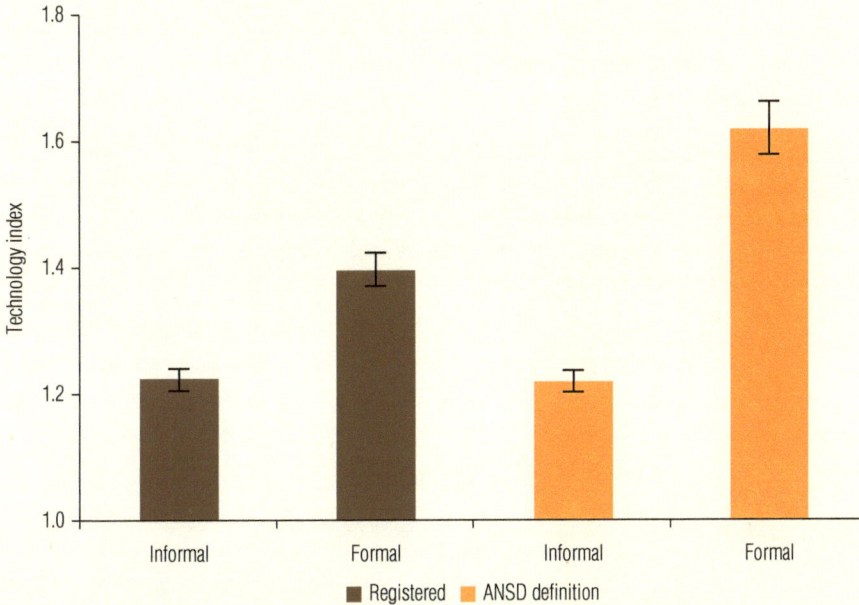

Source: Original figure based on Firm-level Adoption of Technology (FAT) survey data.

Note: Technology index estimates based on weighted sample controlling for sector, country, formality, firm size group, and age group. ANSD refers to the stricter definition of formality by Senegal's National Agency of Statistics and Demography (ANSD).

technology sophistication for formal firms—controlling for sector, firm size group, firm age group, and region—is significantly greater than for informal firms. Although the number of firms will increase, informal firms tend to be smaller (because informality tends to be unlikely among larger firms), limiting the shift to the right. Moreover, the definition of "formality" can also vary across countries. To be considered formal by Senegal's National Agency of Statistics and Demography (ANSD), for instance, a firm must not only be registered but also must have a standard accounting system. Results show that this stricter definition of formality would reduce the number of firms in this group, introducing more bias—with respect to the average firm—toward higher technology sophistication.

It is important to highlight that while informality contributes significantly to the large technology gap across countries, a gap would still persist if all informal firms were formalized and were able to achieve the level of sophistication of formal firms. This is illustrated by the technology gaps between frontier firms in Korea and Poland with the most sophisticated firms in Senegal.

Cross-Firm Technology Facts

Fact 4. Technology sophistication varies across business functions.

Firms are closer to the technology frontier in some business functions than in others. Figure 2.5 compares the average technology sophistication in seven general business functions (GBFs)—business administration (accounting, finance, and human resources); production or service operations planning; sourcing, procurement, and supply chain management; marketing and product development; sales; payment methods; and quality control—across top firms (those in the 90th percentile, p90) with the average across all firms (mean) and the median firms (50th percentile, p50), as well as with firms in the bottom 10th percentile (p10) of technology sophistication. While, on average, firms in the 90th percentile have higher scores than those in the 10th percentile, there is great variation in proximity to the frontier across functions. Top firms tend to score well on business administration, but poorly on quality control. The gap between firms in the 90th and 10th percentiles is also larger in business administration than in other GBFs. An important characteristic of some of these functions (such as sourcing, marketing, sales, and payment) is that the intensive use of some of these technologies often also requires their adoption by customers and suppliers through network effects, which may explain the distance from the frontier even among top

FIGURE 2.5 **The Level of Technology Sophistication for General Business Functions Varies Greatly**

Intensive margin

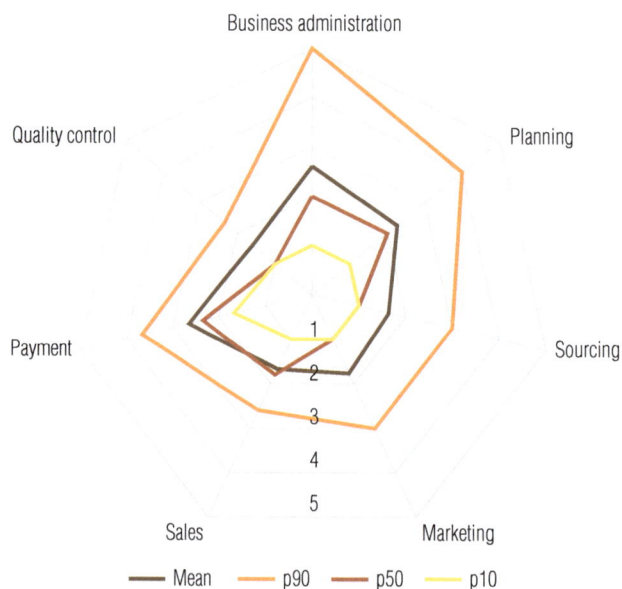

Source: Original figure based on Firm-level Adoption of Technology (FAT) survey data.

Note: The figure covers all 11 countries in the sample. The intensive margin refers to the most frequently used technology to perform that particular task/business function. p90, p50, and p10 refer to the 90th, 50th, and 10th percentiles of firms, respectively. The mean is the average across all firms using sampling weights.

firms. Many of these firms are using more sophisticated technologies in those functions, but not as the most intensively used technology.

These patterns of heterogeneity in sophistication at the business level are also replicated at the country level. First, the average sophistication level varies significantly across business functions within each country. Second, differences across countries in the use of technologies for particular business functions are not maintained. For example, while there is a large gap in the technologies used more intensively for business administration or planning across countries, the differences are very narrow for payment systems or quality control, where low adoption is common across countries regardless of income. Technology gaps across countries vary depending on the business function and level of aggregation.

Fact 5. Larger firms use more sophisticated technologies, but this scale effect varies across technologies.

The adoption and use of more sophisticated technologies are positively correlated with the size of the firm. Figure 2.6 shows the average level of technology sophistication for both general and sector-specific business functions (SBFs) by size groups for firms, defined as small (5 to 19 workers), medium (20 to 99 workers), and large (100 or more workers). Larger firms tend to use more sophisticated technologies, on average, for GBFs and SBFs, as well as ABF (all business functions), which takes a simple average of the index across all business functions.

There is, however, significant variation for different types of technologies and business functions. Figure 2.7 shows the estimated probability of adopting particular

FIGURE 2.6 Technology Sophistication Varies across Firm Size

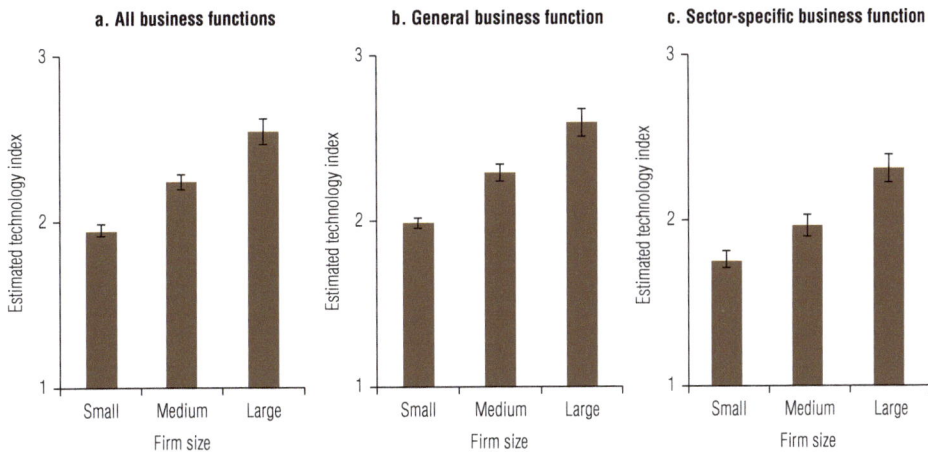

a. All business functions   b. General business function   c. Sector-specific business function

Source: Original figure based on Firm-level Adoption of Technology (FAT) survey data.

Note: The figure covers all 11 countries in the sample. Marginal effect estimates based on weighted sample controlling for sector, country, formality, firm size group, and firm age group. Firm size refers to the number of workers: small (5–19), medium (20–99), and large (100 or more).

FIGURE 2.7   **The Likelihood of Adopting Frontier Technologies for General Business Functions Varies across Firm Size**

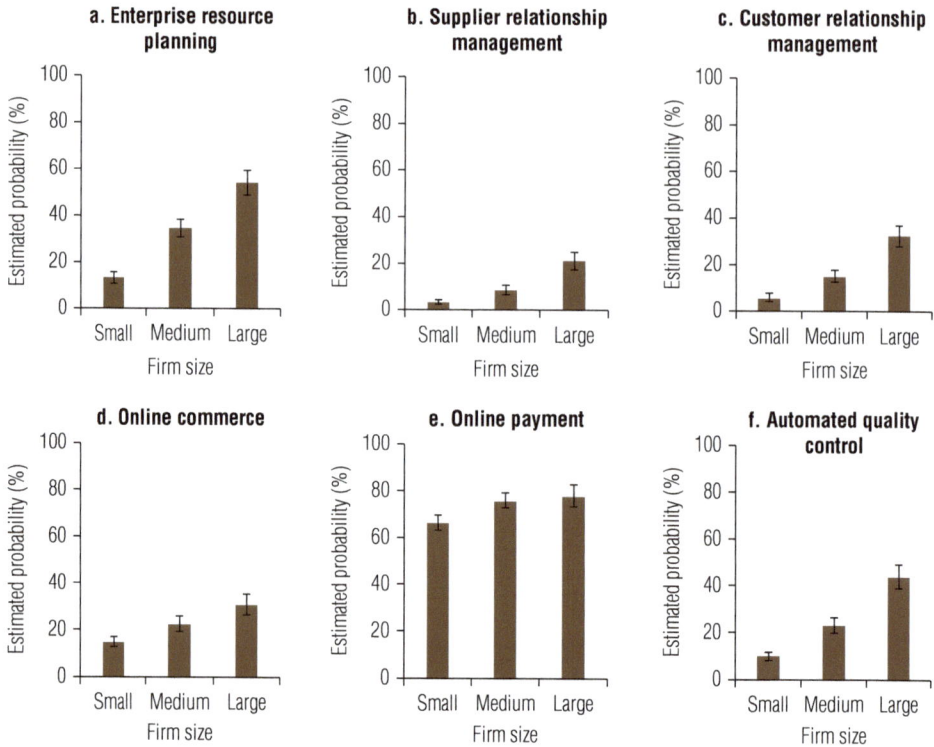

a. Enterprise resource planning

b. Supplier relationship management

c. Customer relationship management

d. Online commerce

e. Online payment

f. Automated quality control

Source: Original figure based on Firm-level Adoption of Technology (FAT) survey data.

Note: Estimated probability of technology adoption using sampling weights and controlling for country, firm size, and sector. Firm size refers to the number of workers: small (5–19), medium (20–99), and large (100 or more).

technologies that are in the frontier across different GBFs by firm size groups. Sophisticated digital technologies for GBFs include enterprise resource planning (ERP); sourcing, procurement, and supplier relationship management (SRM); customer relationship management (CRM); use of online sales through digital platforms or a firm's own website (online commerce); use of online payment through platform or commercial banks (online payment); and use of statistical software or automated systems for quality control (automated quality control). The comparison of the likelihood of using these advanced technologies—in the frontier of different GBFs—across size groups of firms shows that the gap between small and large firms regarding the adoption of these technologies varies significantly. For example, the gap between small and large firms is much wider for ERP than for e-payment.

This variation is also present, and even more pronounced, across sector-specific functions. Figure 2.8 shows the estimated probability of adoption by size groups for particular technologies that are in the frontier across sector-specific business functions in agriculture (irrigation, harvesting, storage); manufacturing/food processing (input

FIGURE 2.8 The Likelihood of Adopting Frontier Technologies for Sector-Specific Business Functions Varies across Firm Size

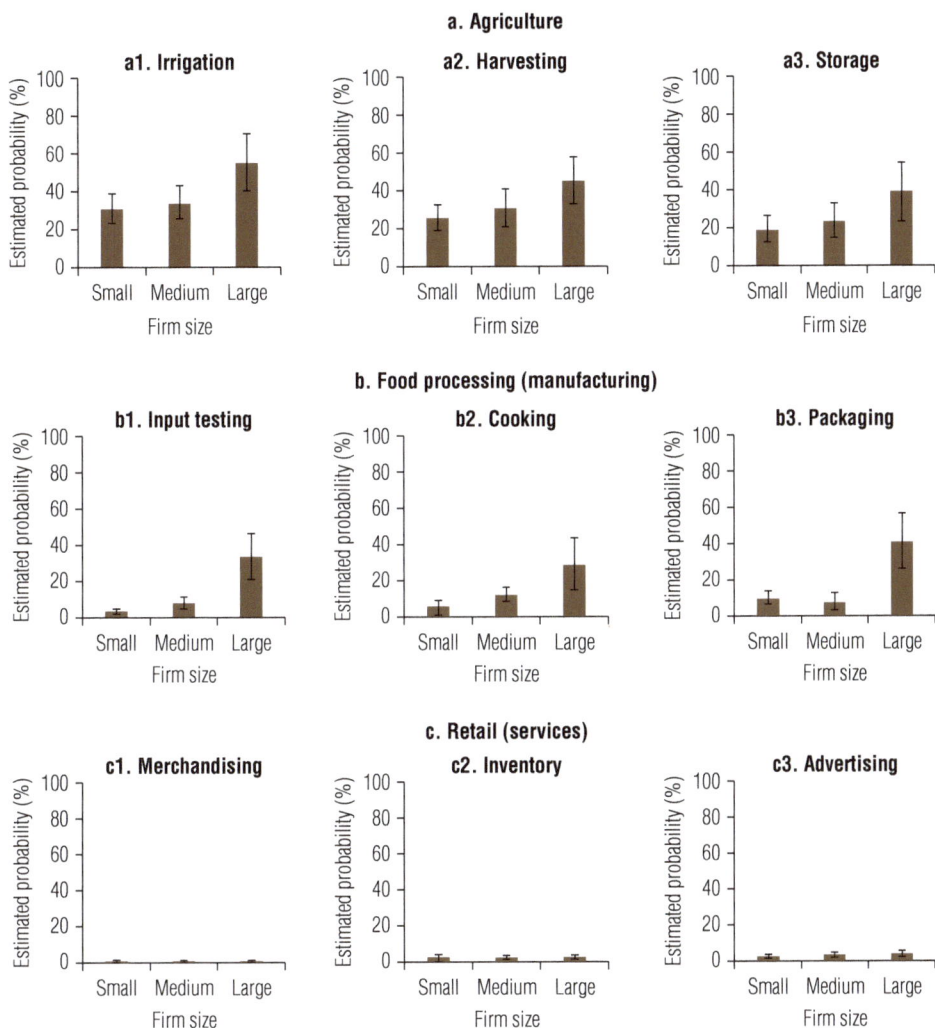

a. Agriculture

a1. Irrigation   a2. Harvesting   a3. Storage

b. Food processing (manufacturing)

b1. Input testing   b2. Cooking   b3. Packaging

c. Retail (services)

c1. Merchandising   c2. Inventory   c3. Advertising

Source: Original figure based on Firm-level Adoption of Technology (FAT) survey data.

Note: Estimated probability of technology adoption using sampling weights and controlling for country, firm size, and sector. Firm size refers to the number of workers: small (5–19), medium (20–99), and large (100 or more).

testing, cooking, packaging); and services/retail (merchandising, inventory, advertising). The gap between small and large firms in the likelihood of adopting frontier technologies in the functions related to food processing is larger than in agriculture and services.

Fact 6. The largest technology gaps occur within countries, not between countries.

Underlying the significant differences in the average technology sophistication across countries, regions, sectors, and firm size lies a large variation of sophistication across firms. A key advantage of a firm-level data set such as FAT is that it allows researchers and practitioners to go beyond country or regional comparisons of average technology sophistication by characterizing the entire distribution of technology sophistication across firms. Figure 2.9 plots the kernel density of the distribution of the firm-level technology sophistication for Burkina Faso, Korea, and Vietnam. Visual inspection of the densities suggests the possibility of consistent rank orderings (first-order stochastic dominance), which suggests that for any point of the cumulative distribution of technology across firms in each country, firms in Korea tend to be more or at least as sophisticated as firms in Vietnam, which tend to be more or at least as sophisticated as firms in Burkina Faso.[8]

In addition, the within-country variance in technology sophistication is larger than the between-country variation. Cirera et al. (2020b) conduct a variance-covariance decomposition to measure the magnitude of the dispersion of firm-level technology sophistication within and between countries. They find that there is significant dispersion in technology across firms within each country, which is consistent with large cross-firm dispersion in management practices, as highlighted by Bloom and Van Reenen (2007). The findings suggest that cross-firm differences in technology

FIGURE 2.9   **Rank Orderings of the Distribution of Technology Sophistication Are Consistent across Select Countries**

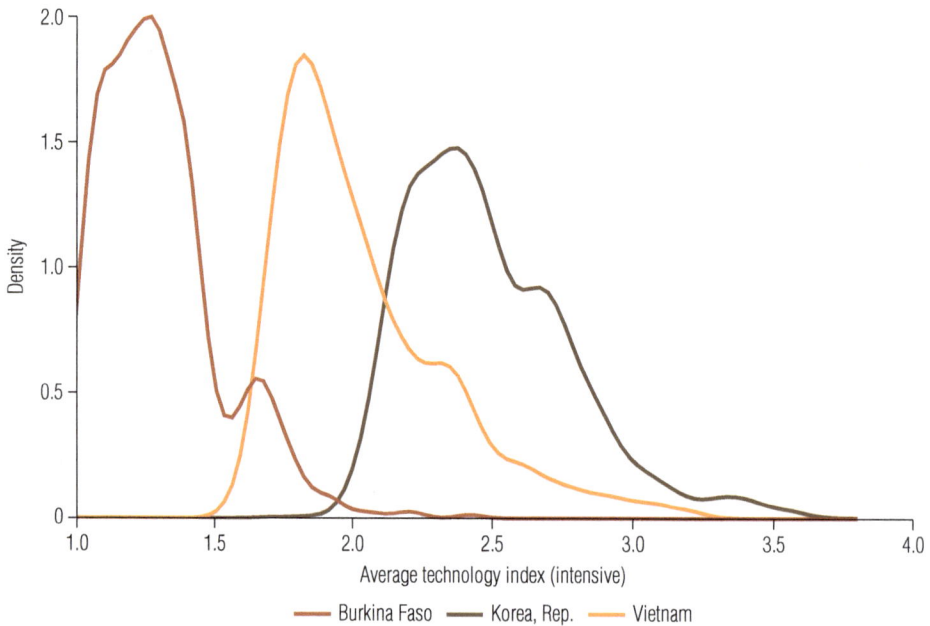

Source: Original figure based on Firm-level Adoption of Technology (FAT) survey data.
Note: Average technology index (intensive) reflects the average sophistication of the technology most frequently used to perform all business functions performed by the firm using sampling weights.

Bridging the Technological Divide

sophistication are larger than cross-country differences, regardless of the technology measures considered and whether the focus is on general, sector-specific, or all business functions. The implication of this finding is that contrary to some popular beliefs that tend to associate technology gaps with cross-country differences, the largest technology gaps occur within countries.

Fact 7. More productive regions have more dispersion in regional technology sophistication.

There is also a strong correlation between cross-firm variance and regional productivity levels. Figure 2.10 plots the cross-firm variance in technology sophistication in each subnational region against the regional productivity level. The figure confirms the positive association between the two variables (with a correlation of 0.68). More-developed

FIGURE 2.10   Most Productive Countries and Regions Have Firms That Use More Sophisticated Technologies on Average

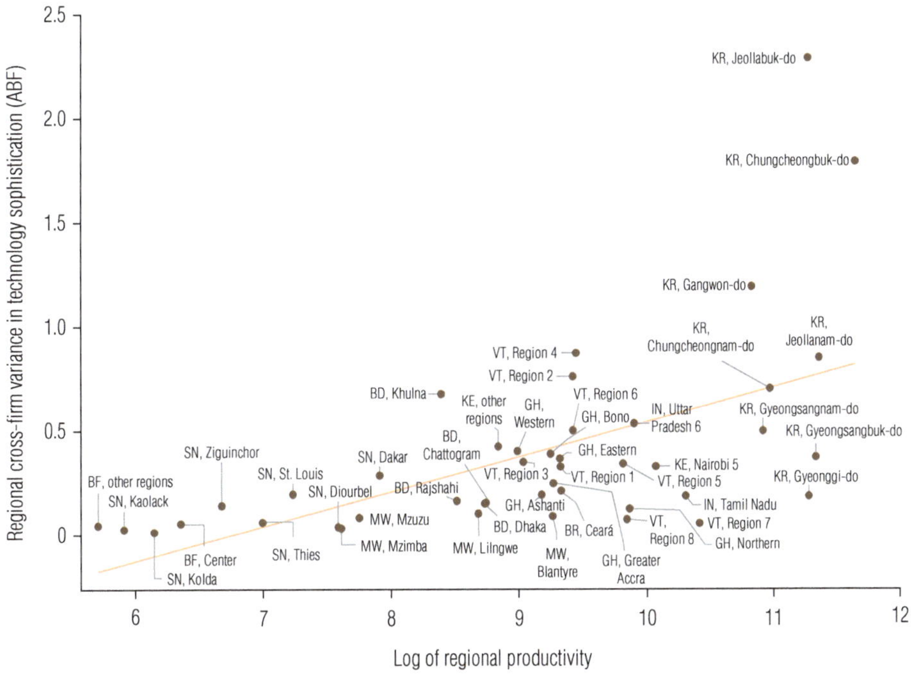

Source: Original figure based on Firm-level Adoption of Technology (FAT) survey data, following Cirera et al. 2020a.

Note: The regional-level cross-firm variance of technology sophistication for all business functions (ABF) is on the y-axis. The regional productivity is on the x-axis. The regional productivity is measured as the average value added per worker based on a representative sample of the FAT data for each region using sampling weights. Countries are as follows: Bangladesh (BD); Brazil (BR); Burkina Faso (BF); Ghana (GH); India (IN); Kenya (KE); Korea, Rep. (KR); Malawi (MW); Senegal (SN); and Vietnam (VT). The eight regions sampled in Vietnam (VT) are: Region 1 (Bắc Ninh, Hải Phòng, Ninh Bình); Region 2 (Bắc Giang, Thái Nguyên); Region 3 (Bình Định, Hà Tĩnh, Thanh Hoá); Region 4 (Kon Tum, Lâm Đồng); Region 5 (Bình Dương, Đồng Nai); Region 6 (Long An, Vĩnh Long); Region 7 (Hà Nội); and Region 8 (Hồ Chí Minh City).

regions tend to have more dispersion of technology, with some firms closer to the frontier and others lagging.[9] Intuitively, these results suggest that all countries and regions have firms with low levels of technology sophistication on average, but most productive countries and regions also have firms that adopt and intensively use more sophisticated technologies.

Other Technology Facts

Fact 8. There is a large variation in technology sophistication within firms, and it is positively associated with regional productivity.

There is a larger variation in technology sophistication within firms than across firms. The findings from Cirera et al. (2020a) suggest that firms that are relatively closer to the frontier on average use more sophisticated technologies for some functions but not for others. Cirera et al. (2020a) explore this topic in more detail with data from Brazil, Senegal, and Vietnam. The analysis shows that the paths of technology upgrading are different across business functions, reflecting the existence of heterogeneous costs and benefits of the different available technologies. Moreover, the study shows a positive relationship between within-firm variance and productivity across countries and regions. Figure 2.11 plots the average within-firm variance in each of the 44 regions against the log of regional productivity. The figure reveals a strong positive correlation between both variables (0.76).[10]

Fact 9. Leapfrogging a technology in a business function is rare.

Technology upgrading by firms is mostly a continuous process. The technology disruption caused by the diffusion of mobile phones is a prominent example frequently used to illustrate the process of leapfrogging.[11] The first mobile phone call was made in the early 1970s, but it was not until the 2000s that the technology started to diffuse rapidly across middle- and lower-middle-income countries, disrupting the diffusion of fixed-line telephones (figure 2.12). Low-income countries jumped directly to the new technology. The successful case of telecommunications shows the potential for developing countries to benefit from leapfrogging, especially with digital technologies.

Using large firms as a proxy for early adopters of technology,[12] panel a of figure 2.13 shows that the pattern observed in firms' use of mobile versus fixed-line phones is consistent with leapfrogging. However, this pattern is not maintained for other technologies.[13] In fact, leapfrogging is not commonly observed across technologies used by firms across different business functions. Indeed, the adoption and use of many specific technologies by firms tend to follow a mostly continuous process (with incremental improvements), rather than disruptive patterns.

FIGURE 2.11 Within-Firm Variance of Technology Sophistication Is Positively Associated with Regional Productivity

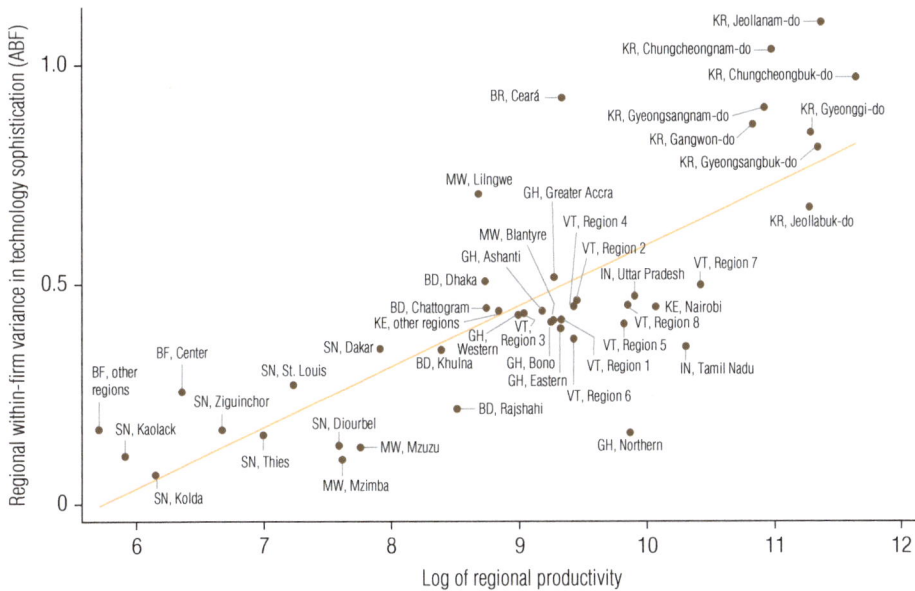

Source: Original figure based on Firm-level Adoption of Technology (FAT) survey data, following Cirera et al. 2020a.

Note: The regional-level within-firm variance of technology sophistication for all business functions (ABF) is on the y-axis. The regional productivity is on the x-axis. The regional productivity is measured as the average value added per worker based on a representative sample of the FAT data for each region using sampling weights and adjusted by purchasing power parity. Countries are as follows: Bangladesh (BD); Brazil (BR); Burkina Faso (BF); Ghana (GH); India (IN); Kenya (KE); Korea, Rep. (KR); Malawi (MW); Senegal (SN); and Vietnam (VT). The eight regions sampled in Vietnam (VT) are: Region 1 (Bắc Ninh, Hải Phòng, Ninh Bình); Region 2 (Bắc Giang, Thái Nguyên); Region 3 (Bình Định, Hà Tĩnh, Thanh Hoá); Region 4 (Kon Tum, Lâm Đồng); Region 5 (Bình Dương, Đồng Nai); Region 6 (Long An, Vĩnh Long); Region 7 (Hà Nội); and Region 8 (Hồ Chí Minh City).

To better illustrate this point, panel b of figure 2.13 presents the estimated probability of firms using digital and frontier technologies. It includes the use of the internet and computers, as general-purpose technologies (GPTs), Excel and ERP used for business administration, as GBFs, as well as four frontier sector-specific business function (SBF) technologies used by food-processing firms: computer testing such as chromatography or spectroscopy used for "input testing"; power equipment controlled by computers or robotics for "cooking, mixing, and blending"; advanced methods such as high-pressure processing used as an antibacterial process for "preserving"; and machines fully automated with robotics used for "packaging." The probability of using the internet, computers, and Excel follows a similar shape, suggesting that most firms, except small ones, are very likely to use these technologies. For the other advanced technologies, including ERP and other frontier technologies for SBFs—all of them with advanced digital components—there is a significant gap between small (late adopter) and large (early adopter)

FIGURE 2.12   Technology Disruption in Telecommunications

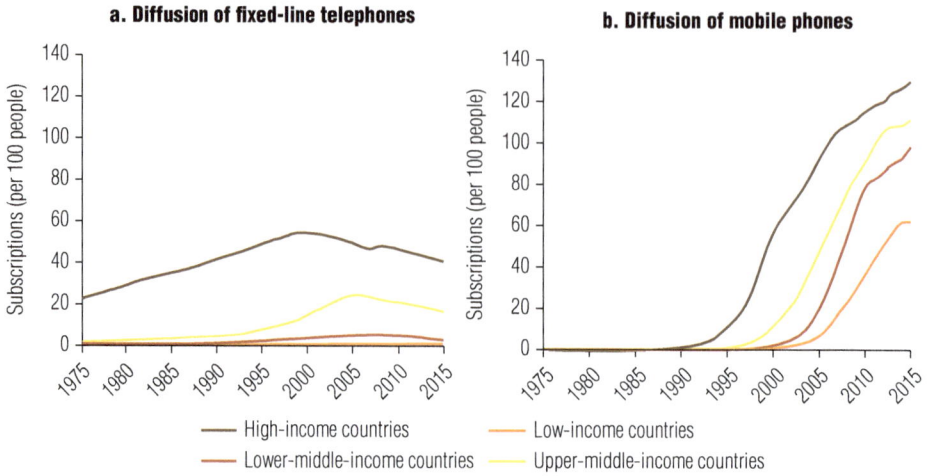

a. Diffusion of fixed-line telephones

b. Diffusion of mobile phones

- High-income countries
- Lower-middle-income countries
- Low-income countries
- Upper-middle-income countries

Source: Original figure based on World Bank World Development Indicators.

FIGURE 2.13   Diffusion Curves, by Firm Size (Early versus Late Adopters)

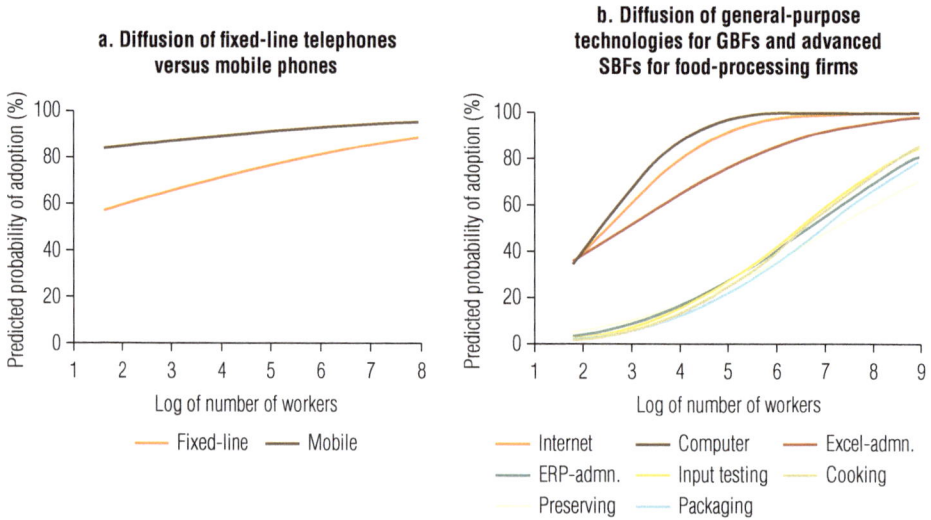

a. Diffusion of fixed-line telephones versus mobile phones

b. Diffusion of general-purpose technologies for GBFs and advanced SBFs for food-processing firms

- Fixed-line
- Mobile

- Internet
- Computer
- Excel-admn.
- ERP-admn.
- Input testing
- Cooking
- Preserving
- Packaging

Source: Original figure based on Firm-level Adoption of Technology (FAT) survey data.

Note: The diffusion curves analyze the probability of adopting a given technology across firm size. Assuming that larger firms adopt earlier than smaller firms, this is a representation of the diffusion over time of specific technologies. The figure presents estimates of the probability of adoption across all 11 countries in the FAT survey sample for the extensive margin (whether a technology is used or not) as a function of the log of the number of workers and controlling for age group and sector using sampling weights. Adm. = administration; ERP = enterprise resource planning; GBFs = general business functions; SBFs = sector-specific business functions.

firms. The curve has an S-shape—a pattern that is well established in the literature on technology diffusion (Gort and Klepper 1982; Skinner and Staiger 2007).

Technology upgrading within firms is mostly a continuous process. While using Excel—an old technology—for business administration closely follows the pattern of the adoption of computers and the internet, there is still a large gap with respect to ERP, which follows a pattern that is much closer to the sector-specific technologies. Low-cost digital technologies (such as standard software or social media) are easily available to perform some of the GBFs (such as standard software or apps for business administration tasks and online payments). By contrast, SBFs usually require more sophisticated and customized application of digital technologies, usually embedded in expensive machines—such as global positioning system (GPS) in tractors or equipment controlled by computers for mixing and cooking. Despite some differences across sectors and technologies, these patterns tend to be consistent across most functions, where earlier adopters (larger firms) tend to move much more quickly in adopting and using more sophisticated technologies. This topic is discussed further in chapters 3 and 5.

Fact 10. Firms with low levels of technology sophistication are overconfident about their technological capabilities.

An important element to explain delayed adoption of more sophisticated technologies is the willingness to adopt. Entrepreneurs can have important biases against adoption. For example, if entrepreneurs or managers believe that they are already adopting more sophisticated technologies in relative terms, it is unlikely that they will invest in adopting new technologies. Then the question is whether firms are aware of their actual technology gap.

To address this question, figure 2.14 compares the entrepreneurs' self-assessment of their technology level with the actual measurement index in the survey. The FAT survey asks for a self-assessment of technology from 1 to 10 (here rescaled to 1 to 5), comparing the respondent's firm with other firms within the country (here distributed by quintiles).[14, 15]

Along the 45-degree line, the predicted technology sophistication of the manager matches the actual level of sophistication. However, the results suggest that firms with lower levels of technological capabilities are more likely to overestimate their technology sophistication in relation to other firms.[16] These results capture a type of behavioral bias labeled *reference group neglect* (Camerer and Lovallo 1999) by which entrepreneurs tend to underestimate their competitors' abilities—in this case, technological capabilities. The importance of this type of bias, as described in chapter 6, is that firms may not upgrade their technologies if they do not perceive that they need them to compete. Thus, reference group neglect can act as a strong deterrent for technology upgrading and firms' take-up of policy support programs. Chapter 7 highlights the important role of public-private partnerships to address this bias by providing information and benchmarking to firms.

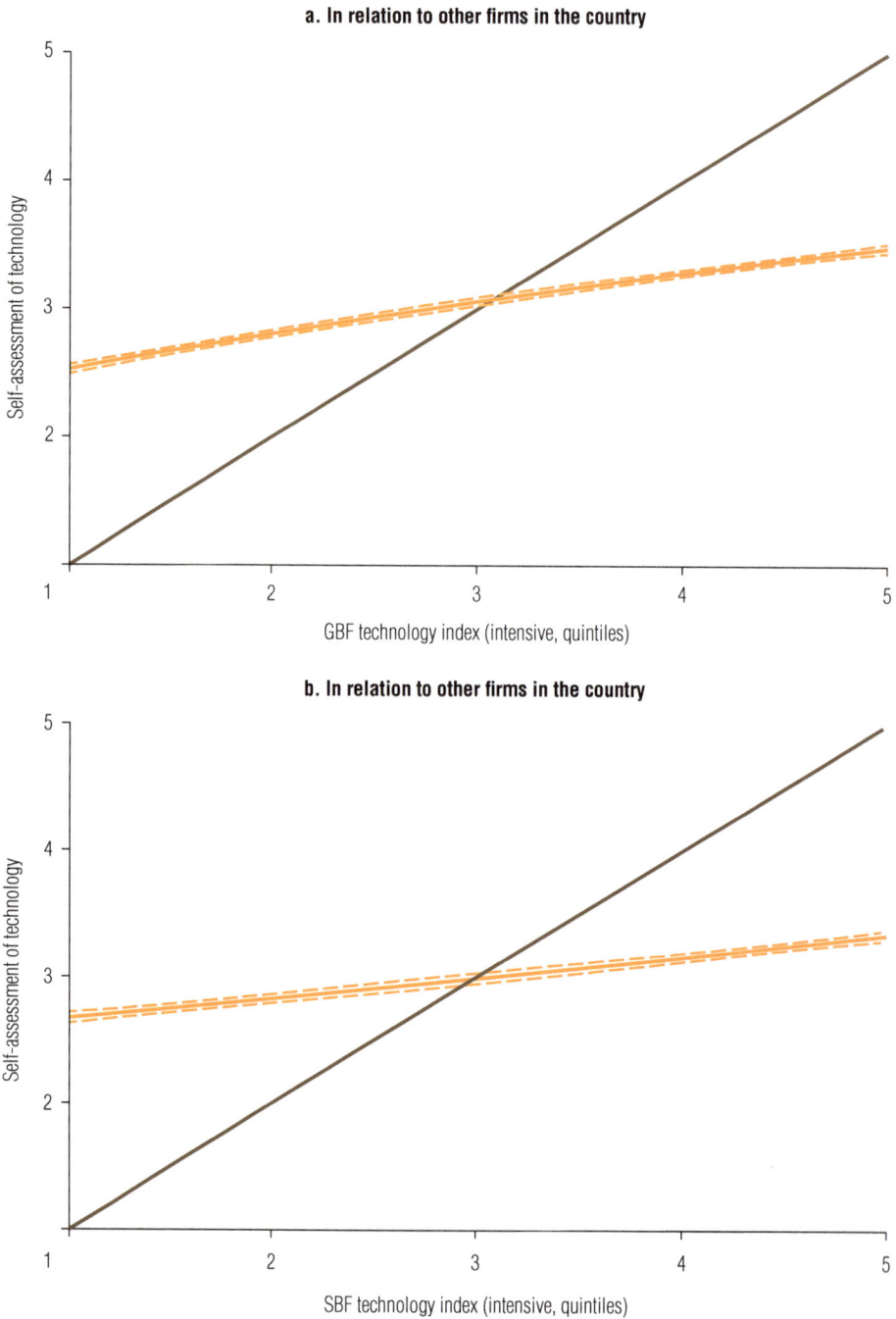

FIGURE 2.14 Firms with Lower Levels of Technological Capabilities Tend to Overestimate Their Technological Sophistication

a. In relation to other firms in the country

b. In relation to other firms in the country

Source: Original figure based on Firm-level Adoption of Technology (FAT) survey data.

Note: The orange line shows the quadratic fit with 95 percent confidence interval using sampling weights. GBF = general business function; SBF = sector-specific business function.

Summing Up

This chapter has presented results from implementing the novel methodology proposed by the FAT survey to measure technology adoption and use at the firm level in 11 countries over 51 regions and all income levels. The chapter provides a snapshot of old and new stylized facts that characterize the process of technology adoption and use in developing countries. The results open the black box of the firm (Demsetz 1997) and describe previously poorly understood elements of diffusion of technology within the firm. While previous work on the diffusion of technology within a firm focused on the increase in the intensity of use of a specific technology (Battisti and Stoneman 2005) or the diffusion across establishments, the data presented here also describe the process of diffusion within the firm across business functions and tasks.

Some of the stylized facts uncovered were already known and complement more macro facts presented in Comin and Hobijn (2004), especially around cross-country differences in technology sophistication. In this volume, however, the findings are presented from the point of view of the firm as the main decision-maker on whether to adopt a technology and for what purpose. Other findings are novel, adding nuance and rigor to the identification of existing technology gaps. Specifically, the chapter shows that:

1. Most firms in developing countries are far from the technology frontier.
2. More productive regions are closer to the technology frontier.
3. Advanced economies have many more sophisticated firms.
4. Technology sophistication varies significantly across business functions, and differences across countries are not maintained at the business function level.
5. Scale and size are important in explaining technology sophistication. Larger firms use more sophisticated technologies, but this scale effect varies across technologies.
6. The largest technology gaps occur within countries, not between countries.
7. More productive regions have more dispersion in regional technology sophistication.
8. There is a large variation in technology sophistication within firms, and it is positively correlated with productivity.
9. Technology upgrading by firms is a continuous process. Leapfrogging technologies is rare.
10. Firms with low levels of technological capabilities are overconfident about their capabilities to adopt and use technology.

The granularity that this methodology provides by focusing on the business function or task opens a promising new research and policy agenda regarding what technologies matter most for performance and whether policies should focus equally on all technologies. The data can also provide important insights about the differences in technology adoption across sectors and their role in structural transformation.

These are all elements that have been largely explored with aggregated data, but lacking strong micro foundations.

While this chapter has provided a general characterization of firm-level technology adoption and use, the next few chapters focus on specific elements that merit further analysis, such as sector differences, the impact of technology on performance, and the role of technologies for firms' resilience to shocks.

Notes

1. The chapter presents and analyzes data collected in 11 representative countries varying across income levels, world regions, and differences in technology adoption and use: Bangladesh, Brazil, Burkina Faso, Ghana, India, Kenya, the Republic of Korea, Malawi, Poland, Senegal, and Vietnam. The sample for each country is nationally representative, except for Brazil (covering only the state of Ceará) and India (covering only the states of Tamil Nadu and Uttar Pradesh). This chapter reports some original findings from Cirera et al. (2020a, 2020b).

2. The analysis considers the frontier to be above an average of 3.5, which loosely corresponds to firms utilizing digital technologies for most business functions and using some frontier technologies in sector-specific business functions, and using those intensively. A score of 5.0 corresponds to the use of frontier technologies for all business functions, which in the FAT survey sample occurs for only two firms in Korea.

3. This finding is consistent with a literature that links further investments of frontier firms in technology in sectors close to the technology frontier (Aghion et al. 2009).

4. Poland is excluded in figure 2.3 because productivity estimates were not available for cross-country comparison.

5. This high and positive correlation also provides ex post validation of the team's measure of technology sophistication, originally based on experts' assessments.

6. The sampling frames providing the number of establishments for Kenya, Korea, Senegal, and Vietnam were provided by the respective national statistical offices, based on the latest establishment census available in the respective country.

7. Maloney and Zambrano (2021) develop a model of entrepreneurial capital and show the importance of migrants in explaining the industrialization process in Latin America.

8. Cirera et al. (2020b) test this hypothesis for Brazil (the state of Ceará), Senegal, and Vietnam, and find first-order stochastic dominance among these countries.

9. This contrasts with empirical results that show large productivity dispersion in developing economies (Hsieh and Klenow 2009) and suggests that what may be driving these differences are distortions that create the wedges in revenue total factor productivity (TFPR), which are larger in developing countries.

10. For more details about these results, see Cirera et al. (2020a).

11. Both fixed-line telephones and mobile phones have high sunk costs. Yet, the lower marginal cost of diffusion associated with mobile phones has disrupted the slow expansion of the previous existing market of fixed-line phones.

12. Large firms use more sophisticated technologies, as illustrated in figure 2.6. If one assumes that they were also faster to adopt—earlier adopters—the likelihood of leapfrogging can be represented by the likelihood that a small firm will use a new technology compared to a large firm. If the probability is similar and the technology is new and sophisticated, that implies that small firms adopt quickly and can leapfrog.

13. Is the leapfrog pattern observed at the country level (figure 2.12) also observed for firms? A constraint to address this question with FAT data is the lack of a time series that allows one to observe adoption of a given technology by firms over time. Yet, under the assumption that larger firms are earlier adopters, it is possible to observe the pattern of adoption across firm size as a continuum variable. Given that only one point in time in the data can be observed (around the latest year of figure 2.12), one would expect: (a) a gap between mobile and fixed-line telephone use, with firms being more likely to use mobile phones; and (b) a smaller gap between mobile and fixed-line phone use among earlier adopters (larger firms). Panel a of figure 2.13 suggests that both conditions hold. On average, a very large share of firms is using mobile phones for business purposes, and there is no significant difference across firm size, after controlling for other characteristics, such as country fixed effects.

14. The question also asks the firm to compare with firms that are global technology leaders in their sector of activity.

15. The self-assessment question is asked before any of the technology adoption questions to prevent any bias in the self-assessment from potential framing.

16. These results are similar when using the actual technology sophistication index instead of quintiles of the distribution of the index within countries.

References

Aghion, P., R. Blundell, R. Griffith, P. Howitt, and S. Prantl. 2009. "The Effects of Entry on Incumbent Innovation and Productivity." *Review of Economics and Statistics* 91 (1): 20–32.

Battisti, G., and P. Stoneman. 2005. "The Intra-Firm Diffusion of New Process Technologies." *International Journal of Industrial Organization* 23 (1): 1–22.

Bloom, N., and J. Van Reenen. 2007. "Measuring and Explaining Management Practices across Firms and Countries." *Quarterly Journal of Economics* 122 (4): 1351–408.

Camerer, C., and D. Lovallo. 1999. "Overconfidence and Excess Entry: An Experimental Approach." *American Economic Review* 89 (1): 306–18.

Cirera, X., D. Comin, M. Cruz, and K. M. Lee. 2020a. "Anatomy of Technology in the Firm." NBER Working Paper 28080, National Bureau of Economic Research, Cambridge, MA.

Cirera, X., D. Comin, M. Cruz, and K. M. Lee. 2020b. "Technology within and across Firms." CEPR Discussion Paper 15427, Center for Economic and Policy Research, Washington, DC.

Comin, D., and B. Hobijn. 2004. "Cross-Country Technology Adoption: Making the Theories Face the Facts." *Journal of Monetary Economics* 51 (1): 39–83.

Demsetz, H. 1997. "The Firm in Economic Theory: A Quiet Revolution." *American Economic Review* 87 (2): 426–29.

Gort, M., and S. Klepper. 1982. "Time Paths in the Diffusion of Product Innovations." *Economic Journal* 92 (367): 630–53.

Grover, A., S. V. Lall, and W. F. Maloney. 2022. *Place, Productivity, and Prosperity: Revisiting Spatially Targeted Policies for Regional Development*. World Bank Productivity Project series. Washington, DC: World Bank.

Grover Goswami, A., D. Medvedev, and E. Olafsen. 2019. *High-Growth Firms: Facts, Fiction, and Policy Options for Emerging Economies*. World Bank Productivity Project series. Washington, DC: World Bank.

Hsieh, C.-T., and P. J. Klenow. 2009. "Misallocation and Manufacturing TFP in China and India." *Quarterly Journal of Economics* 124 (4): 1403–48.

Maloney, W. F., and A. Zambrano. 2021. "Learning to Learn: Experimentation, Entrepreneurial Capital, and Development." Policy Research Working Paper 9890, World Bank, Washington, DC.

Nayyar, G., M. Hallward-Driemeier, and E. Davies. 2021. *At Your Service? The Promise of Services-Led Development.* World Bank Productivity Project series. Washington, DC: World Bank.

Skinner, J., and D. Staiger. 2007. "Technology Adoption from Hybrid Corn to Beta-Blockers." In *Hard-to-Measure Goods and Services: Essays in Honor of Zvi Griliches,* edited by E. R. Berndt and C. R. Hulten, 545–70. University of Chicago Press for the National Bureau of Economic Research.

Syverson, C. 2014. "The Importance of Measuring Dispersion in Firm-level Outcomes." *IZA World of Labor* 53: 1–53.

3. Adoption of Sector-Specific Technologies

Introduction

This chapter provides a deep dive into differences in production technologies adopted by firms in different sectors. Agriculture has been the focus of many studies of technology in the empirical microeconomic literature.[1] The effects of cutting-edge production technologies have also captured the public imagination. Images of robots carrying out large-scale manufacturing, drones engaged in agriculture, or automated delivery of goods and services appear in any discussion of Industry 4.0 and frontier technologies. But as described in chapters 1 and 2, this advanced state of technology is not the reality for most firms, particularly in developing countries. Connecting policy makers with the reality of technology used in production is important for identifying and defining key policy priorities that are feasible and relevant in a given context.[2]

A key challenge for measuring and comparing production technologies is that they are usually specific to particular sectors because they implement sector-specific business functions (SBFs). For example, while land preparation and irrigation are core functions for agriculture, weaving is for apparel, and cooking is for food processing. The Firm-level Adoption of Technology (FAT) survey takes these variations across sectors into account. It not only measures technologies adopted to perform tasks that are common across all firms (general business functions, GBFs) such as business administration and payment, but it also collects data for sector-specific business functions that reflect technology use in core production processes or provisions of services in selected sectors. To account for the fact that the range and sophistication of technologies available—the *technology domain*—is different in each sector and business function, these sector-specific measures are normalized to the technology frontier in each business function. This provides a comparable measure of sophistication that is relative to the relevant technologies available in each function.

Sector-specific technology measures can also inform the discussion about outsourcing, which is an important aspect of economic development.[3] A firm's decision to outsource a sector-specific task is related to the availability and cost of technologies and the overall capabilities of the firm to perform the task or outsource it. The FAT survey asks whether the business function is performed by the establishment, insourced to another establishment of the same firm, or outsourced. This level of detail allows for further investigation in this topic.

The survey covers firms and SBFs in agriculture, manufacturing, and services. Thus, it can analyze the relative technological gap in different sectors within those broad industries, and differences in the process of technology upgrading, including leapfrogging. Specifically, this chapter explores the following questions:

- Where do firms in specific sectors stand with respect to the technology frontier for technologies they apply to general business functions (GBF technologies) and sector-specific business functions (SBF technologies)?
- Is leapfrogging commonly observed for sector-specific technologies?
- What is the relationship between technology adoption and outsourcing in sector-specific business functions?

Technology Differences across and within Sectors

Are the differences in technology sophistication observed across sectors driven by GBF technologies or SBF technologies? As the previous chapter discussed, with respect to GBFs, manufacturing is not the sector with the most sophisticated use of technology in most countries in the sample, particularly upper-middle-income countries, such as Brazil and Vietnam, and those with high per capita income levels, such as the Republic of Korea. With respect to SBFs, agricultural firms in the FAT sample tend to be closer to the technology frontier than manufacturing and services firms. The technology gap between agriculture, manufacturing, and services tends to be larger for SBFs. These differences can be partly attributed to the fact that while the GBF measure captures the same functions and technologies for each firm, the SBF measure provides a comparison that is relative to specific frontiers, and the technology domains can be different.

For sector-specific technologies, figure 3.1 shows the cross-country differences for four sectors: agriculture (crops and livestock); food processing; wearing apparel; and wholesale and retail services. The patterns across countries are similar in terms of rankings of technology sophistication. The patterns for food processing and apparel are very similar (panels b and c), and there is less of a difference across countries for wholesale and retail services (panel d). In general, sophistication of technologies in services appears to be more equal across countries on average than for other sectors.

Another important dimension of sector-specific technology is the variance of technologies across business functions within sectors. As shown in chapter 2, there is large variation in the use of GBF technologies. The discussion that follows provides a deep dive into differences within sectors and SBF technologies in agriculture, manufacturing—including two manufacturing activities of particular interest for developing countries, food processing and wearing apparel—and retail activities in the services sector.

Agriculture

Agricultural firms face larger technology gaps with respect to the frontier in some general and sector-specific business functions than manufacturing or services firms face.

FIGURE 3.1 Firms in Agriculture Tend to Use More Sophisticated Technologies in Sector-Specific Business Functions

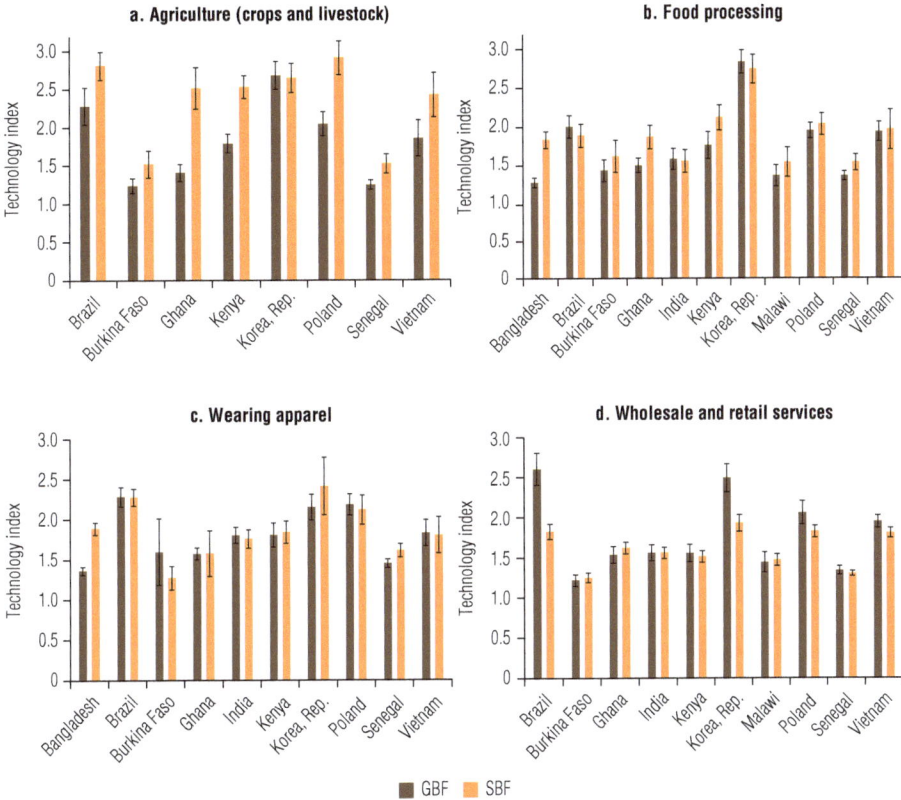

a. Agriculture (crops and livestock)

b. Food processing

c. Wearing apparel

d. Wholesale and retail services

■ GBF   ■ SBF

Source: Original figure based on Firm-level Adoption of Technology (FAT) survey data.
Note: Technology index estimates controlling for size of the firm and age groups using sampling weights. GBF = general business function; SBF = sector-specific business function.

Firms tend to apply more sophisticated technologies to perform sector-specific core functions and low levels of digitalization to perform GBFs. Figure 3.2 compares an average agricultural firm in Brazil (state of Ceará), Kenya, and Senegal. It shows a consistent pattern across countries, suggesting a smaller distance to the frontier for SBFs than for GBFs. For example, the relative technology sophistication in irrigation is closer to the frontier than in management and customer-related technologies (such as in marketing and sales).

Many agricultural firms use relatively advanced technologies in irrigation, while using very basic methods for storage or packaging. Photo 3.1 provides an example of a small agricultural establishment located near Dakar, Senegal. It uses a drip irrigation system (panel a), while relying on the most basic option for storage (defined by the FAT survey questionnaire as "precarious facilities, with products totally or partially exposed to sun, rain, and wind") (panel b). These photos capture the typical reality of an average agricultural establishment with 5 or more workers in Senegal—particularly among informal firms, and reflect the heterogeneity of technology across business functions within firms.[4]

FIGURE 3.2 The Technology Gaps Are Larger in General Business Functions in Agriculture Compared to Sector-Specific Business Functions

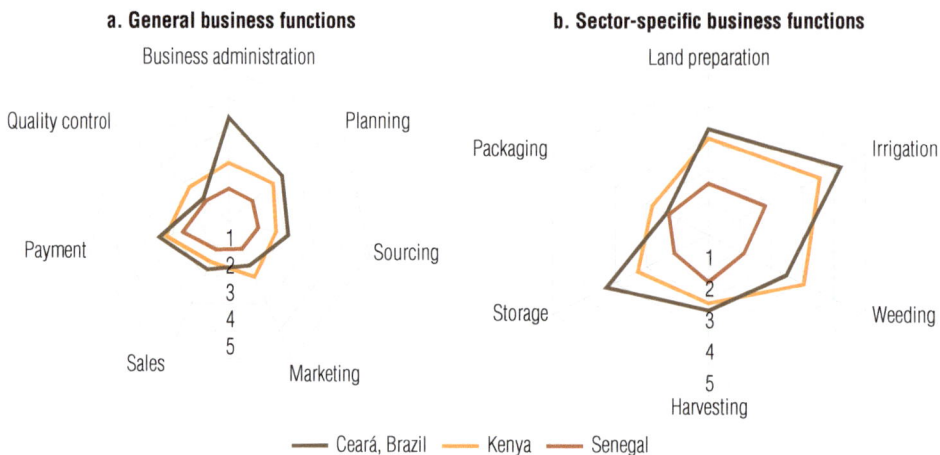

a. General business functions

b. Sector-specific business functions

—— Ceará, Brazil   —— Kenya   —— Senegal

Source: Original figure based on Firm-level Adoption of Technology (FAT) survey data.

Note: The figure covers three countries: Brazil (only the state of Ceará), Kenya, and Senegal. Technology index based on FAT survey using sampling weights.

PHOTO 3.1 Technologies Used for Irrigation and Storage in Senegal Vary Greatly in Sophistication

a. Irrigation

b. Storage

Source: World Bank.

Note: Photos taken during the pilot of the Firm-level Adoption of Technology (FAT) survey in Senegal of a one-acre farm with eight workers.

Manufacturing

Most manufacturing firms in developing countries are far from using advanced fabrication technologies, such as robots or 3D printers (figure 3.3). Yet the experiences of firms in advanced economies are often projected onto firms in developing countries, citing the extraordinary advances (leapfrogging) made with cell phones or anecdotes about exceptional firms. The reality of most manufacturing firms in developing countries is far from Industry 4.0. On average, 83 percent of businesses use manual

FIGURE 3.3 **Technology Sophistication for Fabrication in Manufacturing Is Low in Developing Countries**

Share of firms

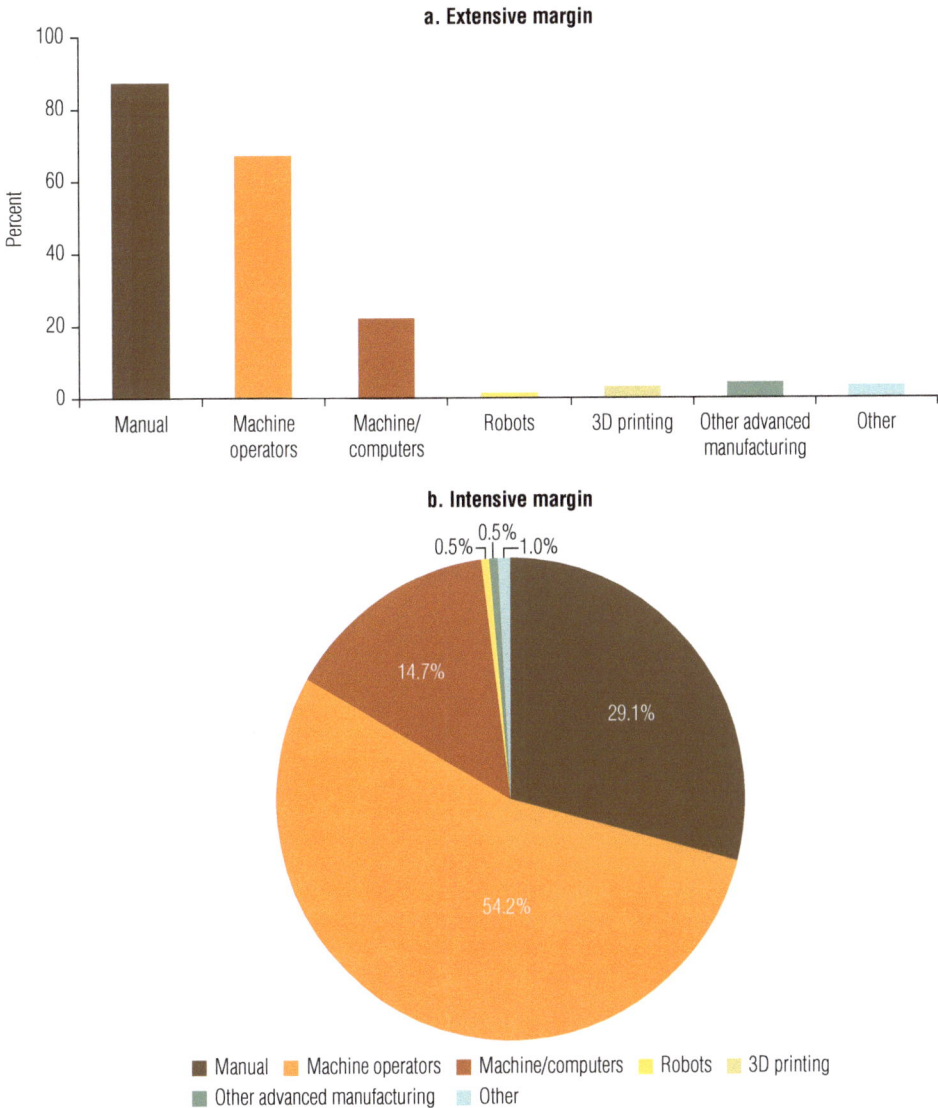

a. Extensive margin

b. Intensive margin

Legend: Manual, Machine operators, Machine/computers, Robots, 3D printing, Other advanced manufacturing, Other

Source: Original figure based on Firm-level Adoption of Technology (FAT) survey data.

Note: Average estimates across all 11 countries in the FAT survey sample using sampling weights. The extensive margin captures the share of firms using a technology. The intensive margin refers to the share of firms for which the technology is the most frequently used for fabrication.

processes or machines that are manually operated to fabricate their main product at the intensive margin, but there are important variations across sectors (see box 3.1). Photo 3.2 shows a manual procedure for filling the bottle used by a food-processing business in Bangladesh. Although this is not the stereotype of a manufacturing firm, the data suggest that similar methods are indeed the most frequently used by firms in Bangladesh and other developing countries performing similar tasks. The discussion that follows explores examples for some specific sectors.

Food Processing

In the case of food processing, the technology gap between GBFs and SBFs is less obvious. Generally, for most business functions, SBFs use more sophisticated technologies, but there are some exceptions where the gap is narrow (figure 3.4). The comparison across firms in Burkina Faso, Korea, and Vietnam suggests that the average firm uses mechanical equipment manually operated for mixing/cooking, but in all business functions they are at least one step above the most basic (usually manual) method to perform the task. Firms in Korea are relatively closer to the frontier for this function. The country ranking according to per capita income holds for average technology indexes for both GBFs and SBFs, with firms in Korea using more advanced technologies, followed by Vietnam and Burkina Faso, but with the differences between the last two countries much narrower for some functions.

Wearing Apparel

For wearing apparel, the differences in both GBFs and SBFs are narrower across countries, especially those that export significantly, although with low

PHOTO 3.2 Small Firms in Developing Countries Still Perform Many Functions Manually

Source: World Bank.

Note: Photo taken during the pilot of the Firm-level Adoption of Technology (FAT) survey in Bangladesh in a food-processing firm with 90 workers, showing the packaging process. The worker is checking the amount of liquid in each bottle, which was filled with a manually operated machine. If she decides that there is too much liquid, she pours the excess in the blue bucket. Then she adds the excess to another bottle if she decides that it is not full enough.

The Strong Sector Composition of the Use of Industry 4.0 Technologies

The world is undergoing a significant technological transformation. Some are calling it the fourth industrial revolution (Schabb 2016) or Industry 4.0, while others see this process as a continuation of the information and communication technology (ICT) revolution. The term "Industry 4.0" originated with a project led by the German government promoting the computerization of manufacturing. It is associated with a new industrial revolution, characterized by the adoption of cyber-physical systems such as robotics and drones, 3D printing, artificial intelligence (AI), and machine learning across all sectors of the economy, reshaping both the way in which and where manufacturing is done.

While Industry 4.0 is a concept that extends broadly across manufacturing activities, some of its technologies are very sector specific. In the case of robotics and despite the hype around it, most of the adoption of this technology has been concentrated in the motor vehicles and electronics sectors, although it is increasingly becoming more relevant to other manufacturing activities, data from the International Federation of Robotics suggest. Results from the Firm-level Adoption of Technology (FAT) survey also show this allocation of robots across sectors. Firms in the motor vehicles sector are significantly more likely to use robots than firms in other manufacturing sectors (see figure B3.1.1). Moreover, in sectors such as apparel and leather, 3D printing is a more relevant technology than robots.

FIGURE B3.1.1 The Likelihood of Adopting Advanced Manufacturing Technologies Varies Widely across Sectors

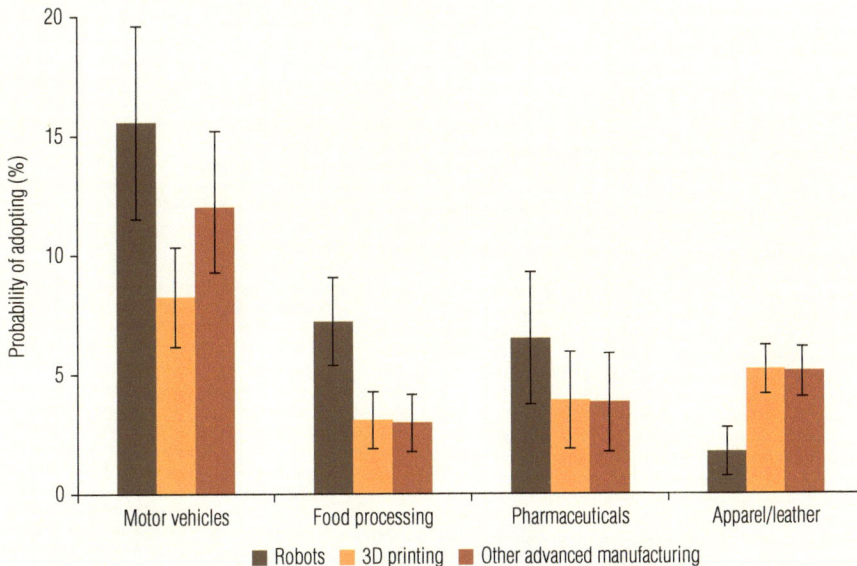

Source: Original figure based on Firm-level Adoption of Technology (FAT) survey data.

Note: Average estimates across all 11 countries in the FAT survey sample using sampling weights, except for motor vehicles (excluding data from Bangladesh and Senegal) and pharmaceuticals (excluding data from Brazil and Senegal).

(Box continues on the following page.)

The Strong Sector Composition of the Use of Industry 4.0 Technologies (continued)

In agriculture, these advanced technologies have been used to achieve greater efficiency through integration of information and production, which also requires investment in physical capital. Practitioners have been referring to "precision agriculture" as a broadly defined method of improving crop yields and assisting management decisions using high-technology sensors and analytic tools. The application of these techniques also requires significant investment in machinery and equipment, in which the digital component is usually embedded, such as tractors enabled by global positioning system (GPS) technologies. Such digitally enhanced machinery and equipment is known as the Internet of Things. Figure B3.1.2 shows that both precision agriculture and automated irrigation systems are significantly more likely among agricultural firms that are more capital intensive, measured by the number of tractors, split into three groups (more than 5 tractors, between 1 and 5 tractors, no tractors). Among firms that do not own a tractor, the likelihood of adopting precision agriculture is also very low.

The adoption and impact of some of these technologies will depend on the sector composition of a country's production structure. In most developing countries there is little production of cars and electronics, and thus the potential for robotics is limited. Moreover, even among more traditional manufacturing sectors, such as food-processing, which is common in developing countries, there is large variation across countries. Food-processing firms in the Republic of Korea, for example, are significantly more likely to use robots than similarly sized food-processing firms in developing countries.

FIGURE B3.1.2   More Capital-Intensive Agricultural Firms Are More Likely to Adopt Advanced Technologies

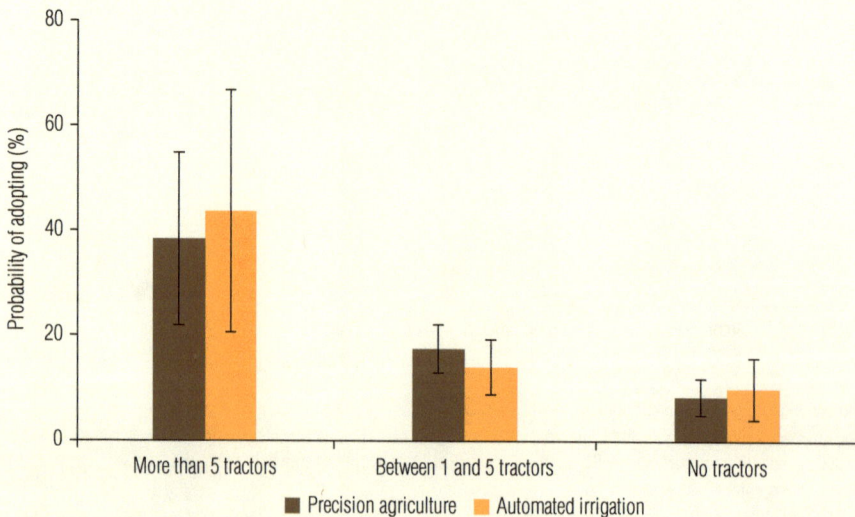

Source: Original figure based on Firm-level Adoption of Technology (FAT) survey data.

Note: The number of tractors a firm owns is a proxy for capital intensity. Average estimates across eight countries (Brazil, Burkina Faso, Ghana, Kenya, Republic of Korea, Poland, Senegal, and Vietnam) in the FAT survey sample using sampling weights.

FIGURE 3.4 Differences in Technology across Countries Roughly Follow Income Differences in the Food-Processing Sector

a. General business functions

b. Sector-specific business functions

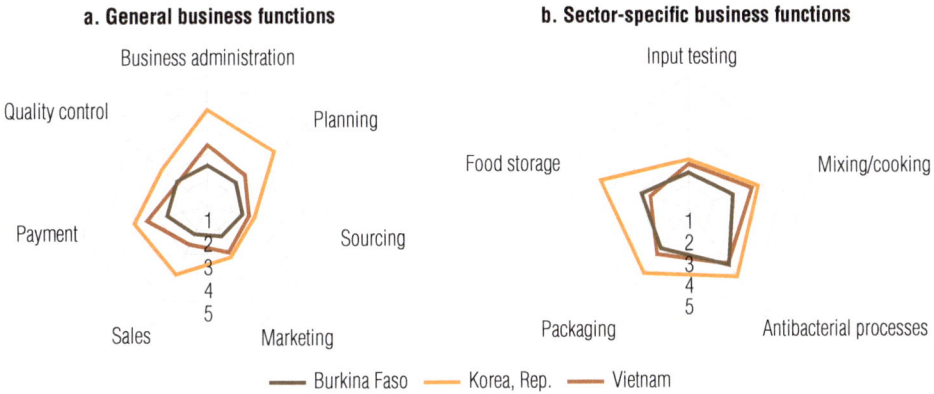

Source: Original figure based on Firm-level Adoption of Technology (FAT) survey data.
Note: Technology measures using sampling weights.

FIGURE 3.5 Cross-Country Comparisons in Wearing Apparel Are Not So Large among Exporter Countries

a. General business functions

b. Sector-specific business functions

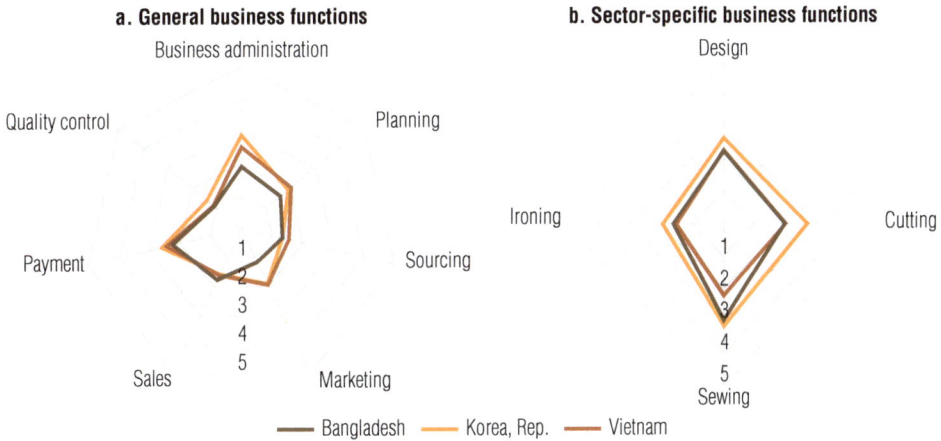

Source: Original figure based on Firm-level Adoption of Technology (FAT) survey data.
Note: Technology measures using sampling weights.

sophistication (figure 3.5). Design and ironing are the SBFs for which the most firms are using manual processes. Firms in Bangladesh are particularly advanced in the use of more sophisticated sewing machines, compared to firms in Vietnam, while firms in Vietnam use more advanced technologies for GBFs, particularly payment and sales, on average. The pattern observed in Bangladesh could be explained by a large insertion of their firms in global value chains for apparel, with more specialization in sewing tasks. This proximity of the technology across the average firm is not observed in other manufacturing sectors integrated into global value chains, such as pharmaceutical products (see box 3.2).

The Closeness of Pharmaceutical Firms to the Technology Frontier

Pharmaceutical manufacturing firms in high-income countries tend to be close to the frontier for sector-specific business function (SBF) technologies. This sector became particularly relevant in the context of the COVID-19 pandemic. Figure B3.2.1 shows that, on average, firms in Poland are closer to the technology frontier in general business functions (GBFs) and most SBFs compared to India (based on the states of Tamil Nadu and Uttar Pradesh). India plays an important role as a global exporter in pharmaceutical products. Exports from India for pharmaceutical products represented 3 percent of global value exported in 2020—considerably larger than the share from Poland (0.7 percent) or Vietnam (0.4 percent), data compiled by the Observatory of Economic Complexity suggest. Yet, results from the Firm-level Adoption of Technology (FAT) survey show that there is still significant room for an average pharmaceutical firm in India to upgrade its technology.

FIGURE B3.2.1 **Pharmaceutical Firms Are Relatively Close to the Technology Frontier, but There Is Significant Room for Improvement in Developing Countries**

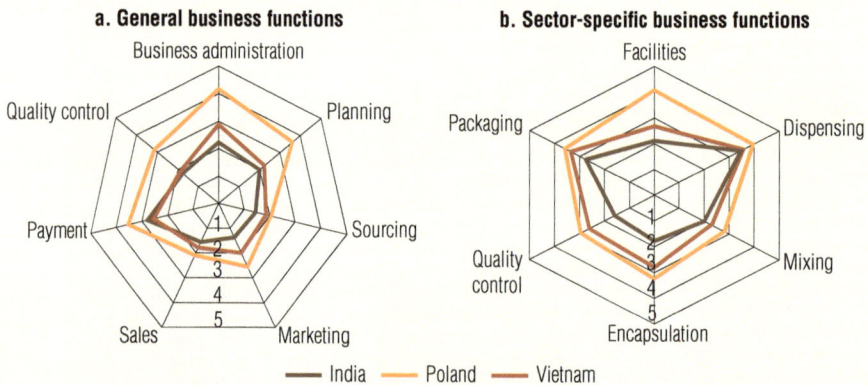

a. General business functions

b. Sector-specific business functions

— India   — Poland   — Vietnam

Source: Original figure based on Firm-level Adoption of Technology (FAT) survey data.

Note: Data for India are for two states only: Tamil Nadu and Uttar Pradesh. Technology measures using sampling weights.

Services–Retail

Most firms in retail are still at an early stage of digitalization applied to sector-specific tasks (figure 3.6). The gap between average firms across countries, comparing Kenya, Korea, and Vietnam, is wider among GBFs than SBFs in retail. Even if they adopt digital technologies, they do not use them intensively. Retail is an important activity of the services sector for developing countries because it usually represents a large share of formal establishments and employment. Most firms in retail still rely on manual technologies as the most frequently used method to perform tasks related to customer service, pricing, merchandising, inventory, and advertisement. Yet, the use of low-cost digital technologies is increasing in the extensive margin.

FIGURE 3.6 **Digitalization of Sector-Specific Business Functions Is at an Early Stage in Retail Services**

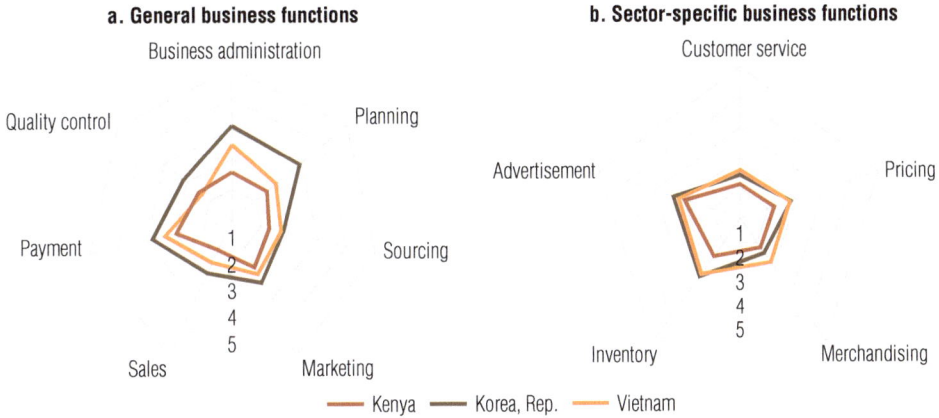

a. General business functions

b. Sector-specific business functions

— Kenya — Korea, Rep. — Vietnam

Source: Original figure based on Firm-level Adoption of Technology (FAT) survey data.
Note: Technology measures using sampling weights.

Technology Upgrading and the Limits to Leapfrogging

Sector-Specific Technology Upgrading as a Continuous Process

Do certain technologies allow firms to skip some stages of technology upgrading and jump from the most basic to the most sophisticated technologies? This question is often asked by policy makers and is often part of the policy discussions related to the potential of digital technologies.

Firms face many challenges to leapfrog in sector-specific technologies. As described in chapter 2, given the lack of information over time in the FAT survey, the analysis assumes that larger firms are earlier adopters. Based on this assumption and the fact that more sophisticated technologies covered in the FAT survey tend to be relatively newer than more basic technologies, two conditions for leapfrogging might be expected. First, the predicted likelihood for leapfrogging with more sophisticated technologies would occur on top of the diffusion of more basic technologies for smaller firms (late adopters). Second, the gap between earlier adopters (large firms) and later adopters (small firms) would be relatively small, with a high likelihood of adoption for all firms. In addition, the probability of using technologies that are obsolete or are being phased out would decrease over firm size.

There is no clear evidence of leapfrogging in sector-specific technologies. Figure 3.7 shows the predicted probability of adoption of technologies by firm size—the diffusion curves—with different levels of sophistication for sector-specific business functions in agriculture (weeding and harvesting, panels a and b), wearing apparel (design and sewing, panels c and d), and retail (pricing and merchandising, panels e and f).

FIGURE 3.7 The Diffusion Curves of Newer Sector-Specific Technologies Do Not Suggest Leapfrogging

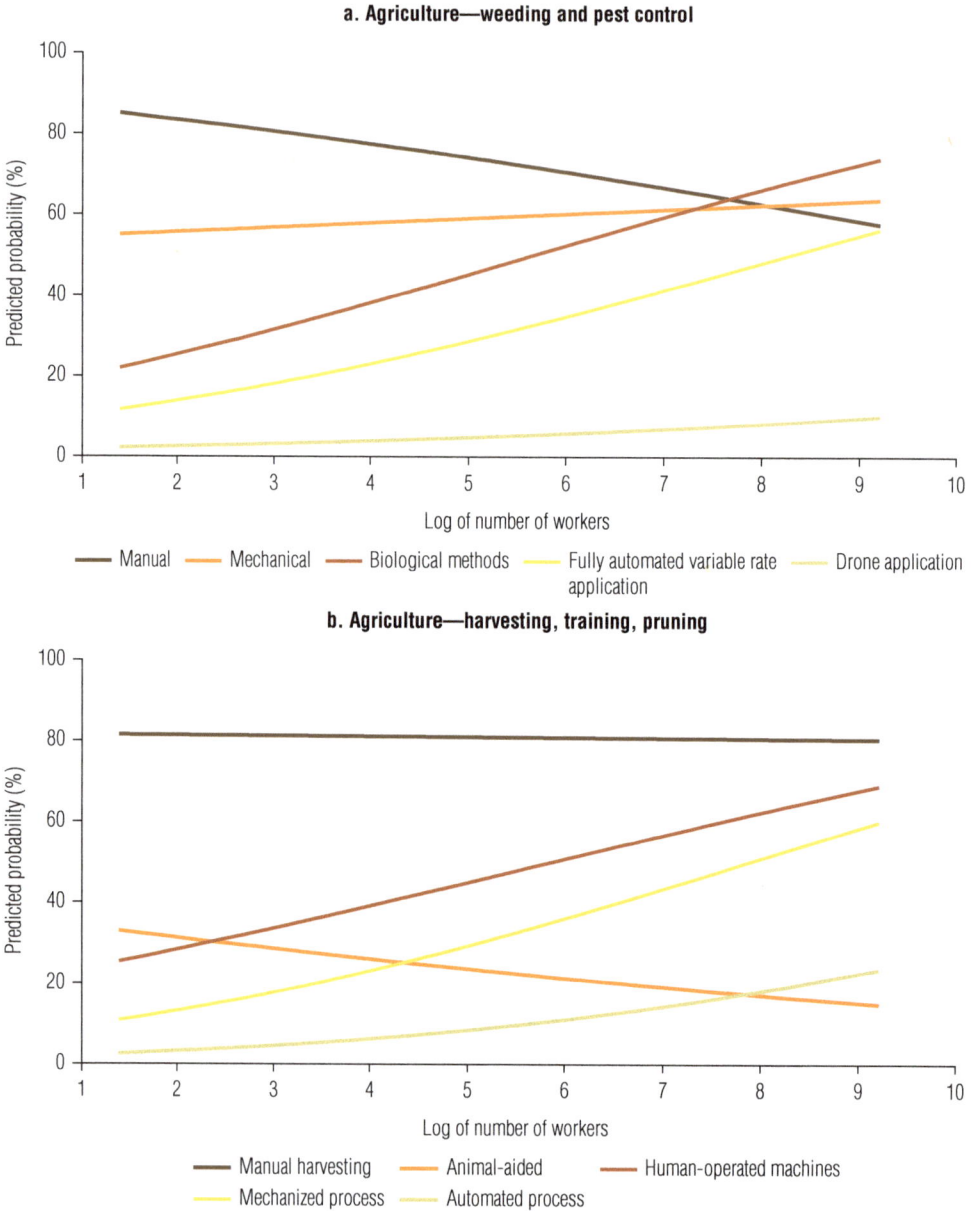

a. Agriculture—weeding and pest control

Legend: Manual — Mechanical — Biological methods — Fully automated variable rate application — Drone application

b. Agriculture—harvesting, training, pruning

Legend: Manual harvesting — Animal-aided — Human-operated machines — Mechanized process — Automated process

(Figure continues on the following page.)

FIGURE 3.7 The Diffusion Curves of Newer Sector-Specific Technologies Do Not Suggest Leapfrogging *(continued)*

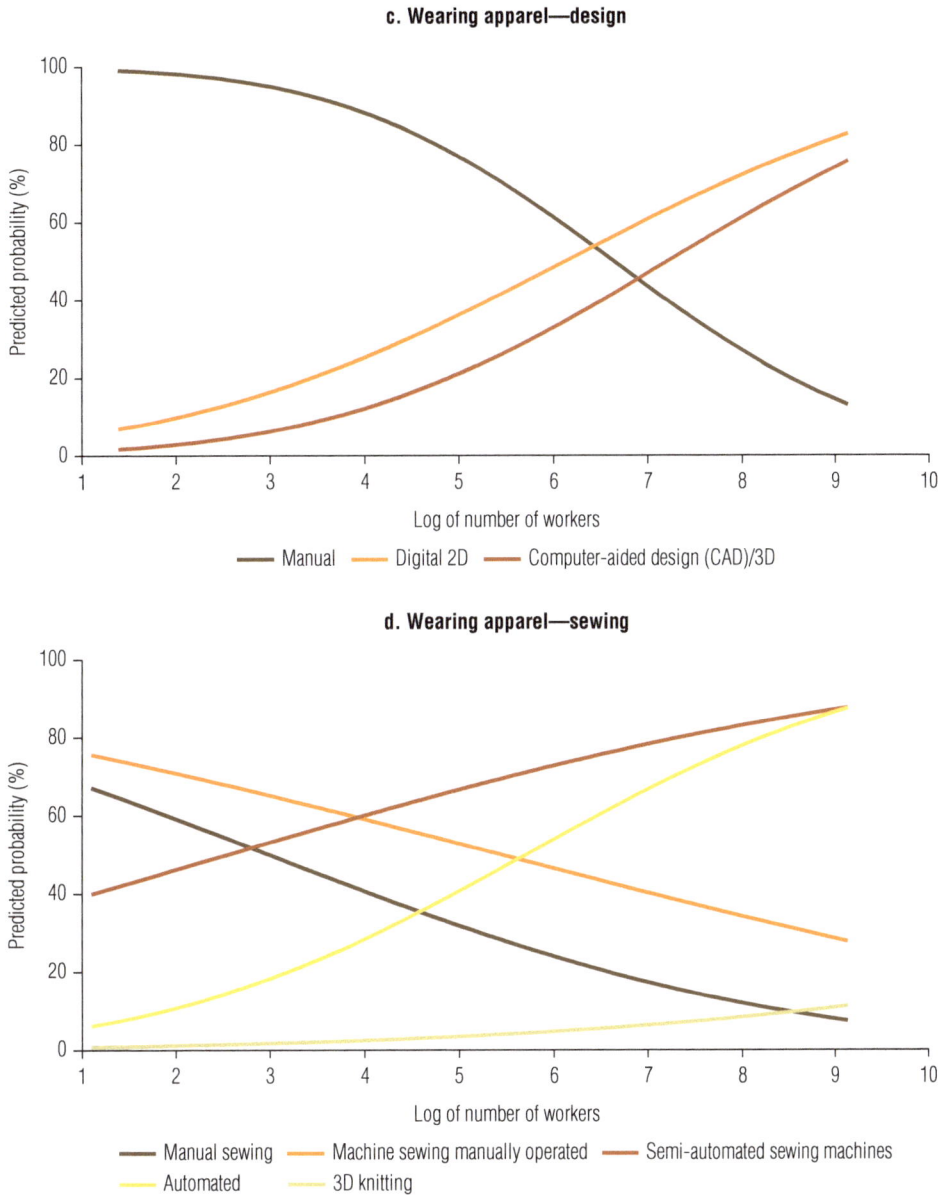

c. Wearing apparel—design

Manual — Digital 2D — Computer-aided design (CAD)/3D

d. Wearing apparel—sewing

Manual sewing — Machine sewing manually operated — Semi-automated sewing machines
Automated — 3D knitting

(Figure continues on the following page.)

e. Retail—pricing

Legend: Manual cost — Automated markup — Automated promotional — Dynamic pricing — Personalized pricing

f. Retail—merchandising

Legend: Manual selection — Category management tools — Digital merchandising — Product trend analytics

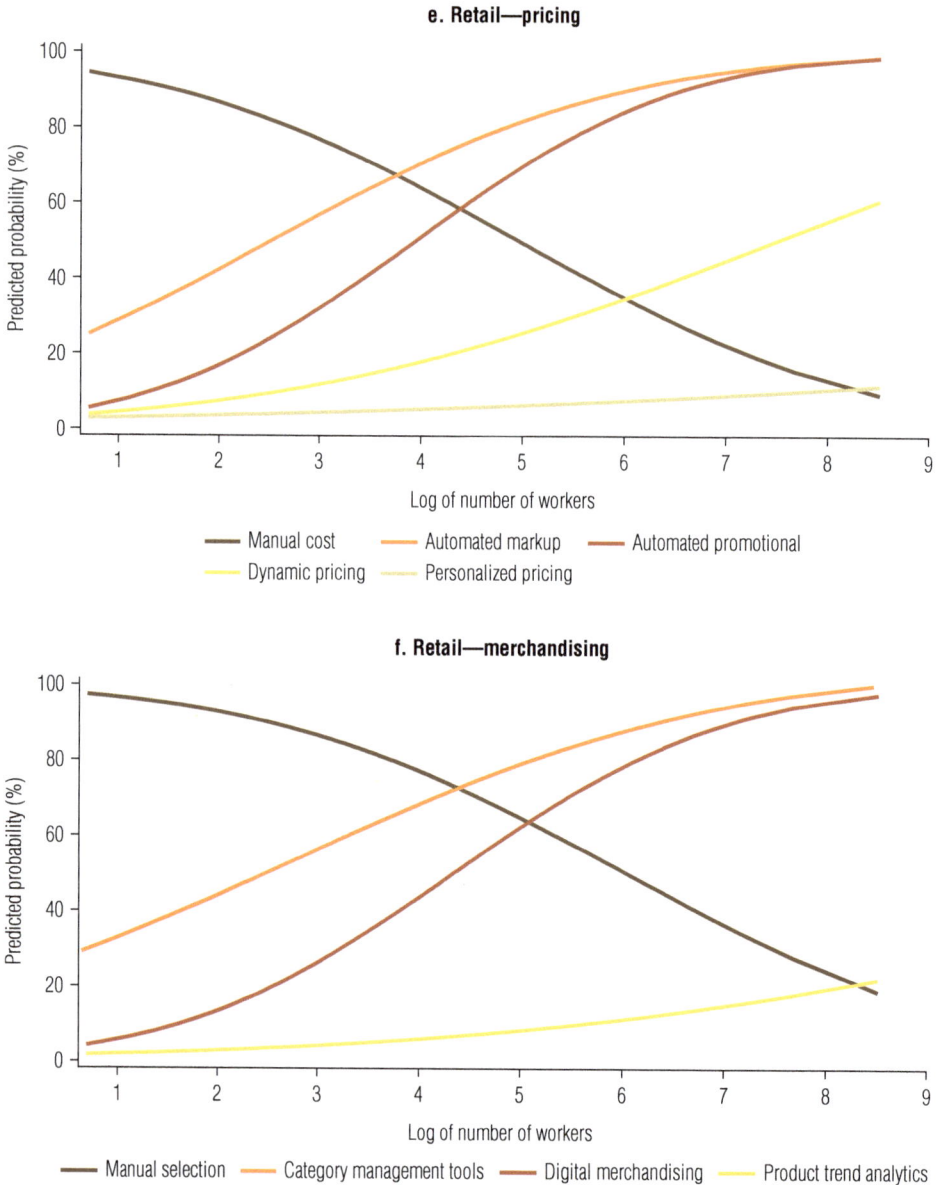

Source: Original figure based on Firm-level Adoption of Technology (FAT) survey data.

Note: The diffusion curves analyze the probability of adopting a given technology across firm size. Assuming that larger firms adopt earlier, this is a representation of the diffusion over time of specific technologies. The figure presents estimates of the probability of adoption across all 11 countries in the FAT survey sample for the extensive margin (whether a technology is used or not) as a function of the log of the number of workers based on a probit using sampling weights. Panels a and b: Agriculture data are from eight countries (Brazil, Burkina Faso, Ghana, Kenya, Republic of Korea, Poland, Senegal, and Vietnam); panels e and f do not include Bangladesh, for which data on retail are not available.

These functions have in common the fact that they can be performed manually (the most basic option), but the most sophisticated technology is digital. As figure 3.7 shows, manual technologies are becoming obsolete at different speeds: obsolescence is occurring more slowly in agriculture than in retail and in manufacturing.

The results are consistent across most business functions in the FAT data. They support the hypothesis that technology upgrading is mostly a continuous process, and the speed of upgrading for newer and more sophisticated technologies is slow. The likelihood of adopting more sophisticated technologies increases with firm size, following the order of sophistication of the technologies available. There are two exceptions. The use of manual methods for harvesting (agriculture) is not associated with firm size. The use of manually operated machines for sewing (wearing apparel) follows a pattern similar to manual processes in general.[5] In agriculture, most of the frontier technologies are linked to the Internet of Things (IoT) and the use of the global positioning system (GPS), which is embedded in frontier technologies for weeding or harvesting, for example. Upgrading to these technologies has been very slow. For some frontier technologies, although the cost of adoption might be low for replication of the necessary software, they still require expensive equipment, good infrastructure, and/or high levels of capabilities. Thus, there might be opportunities for leapfrogging in a few technologies, but they tend to be rare.

Can Digital Platforms Support Leapfrogging in Sector-Specific Technologies?

Most peer-to-peer platforms focus on providing solutions that are more applicable to general business functions (such as sales and payment). But there are some interesting experiences built on the concept of the "sharing economy" that are trying to reduce transaction costs and improve access to more sophisticated and efficient equipment and machines applied to SBFs in agriculture. A well-known example is "Hello Tractor," an innovative digital platform based in Kenya that aims to connect tractor owners to smallholder farmers searching for tractor service, resembling breakthrough platforms like Uber. Such platforms, if successful, can help small firms use more sophisticated technologies without bearing the full cost of upgrading. The question is, therefore, when available, how often is this type of digital solution being used?

Consider an illustration. Renting tractors was a common practice among farmers before such digital platforms became available. This market has three important characteristics: (1) the equipment is easily mobile; (2) there is seasonality in agricultural activities that imply time peaks in use; and (3) the equipment is needed for a limited period of time. This leads to allocation and coordination problems (for example, the owner of a tractor could benefit from renting it in a period the machine is not being used; or the acquisition of the machine is justified only if used by a group of farmers). This is a sort of problem that can be efficiently addressed through better (and cheaper) access to information through digital platforms if it is widely used by actors interested in this market exchange.

Cross-country data for Brazil, Kenya, Senegal, and Vietnam suggest that on average 37 percent of establishments in agriculture (with 5 or more workers) rent tractors. Kenya has the largest share of tractors rented (55 percent) as well as the largest share of tractors rented through a digital platform. Among the establishments that report that they rent a tractor, 37 percent use digital platforms, compared to 8 percent in Senegal, and none in Brazil or Vietnam. Panel a of figure 3.8 shows a positive relationship between owning a tractor and the level of a firm's technology sophistication, controlling for the size of the firm. This correlation is also positive and significant for renting, with a smaller coefficient, and positive but not significant if the rental is through a digital platform. Panel b shows the estimated probability of owning or renting a tractor by firm size. Small firms are significantly more likely to rent a tractor than own it, and this is potentially an important segment that could benefit from digital platforms. Yet, results based on FAT data suggest that large firms are significantly more likely to rent tractors through digital platforms.[6]

These results do not imply a causal relationship and do not exclude the hypothesis that under some conditions, digital platforms could improve the efficiency in the allocation of existing resources to facilitate technology adoption—and potentially help with leapfrogging. But as noted, there are several characteristics that are very specific to this market and are unlikely to apply to other technologies.

FIGURE 3.8 Tractor Ownership, Renting, and Digital Renting Do Not Suggest Leapfrogging through Digital Platforms

a. Type of access to tractor and harvesting

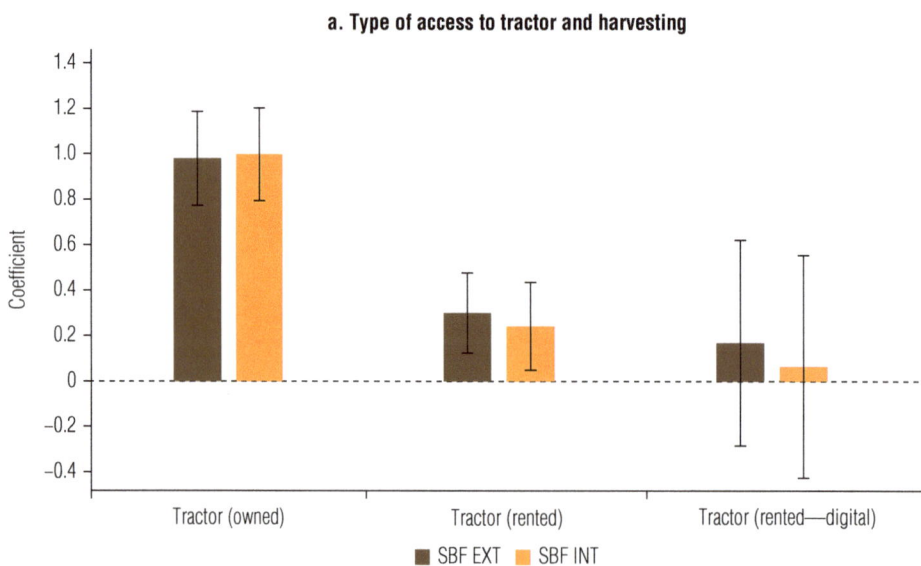

(Figure continues on the following page.)

FIGURE 3.8 **Tractor Ownership, Renting, and Digital Renting Do Not Suggest Leapfrogging through Digital Platforms** *(continued)*

b. Probability of using tractor, by firm size

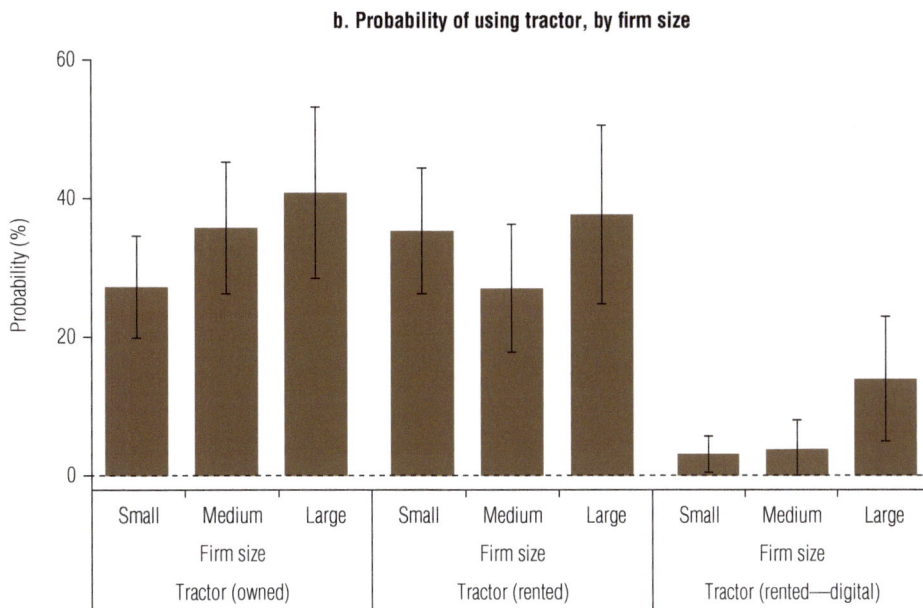

Source: Original figure based on Firm-level Adoption of Technology (FAT) survey data.

Note: Estimation using sampling weights for Brazil, Burkina Faso, Ghana, Kenya, Republic of Korea, Poland, Senegal, and Vietnam. In panel a, SBF EXT refers to the extensive margin of the sector-specific business function; SBF INT refers to the intensive margin. In panel b, firm size refers to the number of workers: small (5–19), medium (20–99), and large (100 or more).

Specialization, Technology, and Outsourcing

For some tasks, firms face a choice between outsourcing or performing it internally (in house), and if done in house, investing in a specific technology or delaying adoption.[7] These decisions are affected by the technologies available,[8] but the boundaries of the firm, which define what tasks are conducted within or outside the firm (Coase 1937; Williamson 1981), are also critically important in the process of technology adoption: how specialized the firm is; what its core functions are; the scale of its operations; what markets it serves; and so on. A first-order question is what are the particular tasks and functions that a firm needs to implement as it transforms resources in its production process—what Demsetz (1997) called the "black box" of the firm.

As the world becomes more globalized, firms are becoming more integrated in global value chains (GVCs) and specializing in particular tasks (Taglioni and Winkler 2016; World Bank 2020). GVCs are not only present in manufacturing; they have also expanded rapidly in services and are important in agriculture. But manufacturing activities, particularly those that are capital intensive (such as in basic metals and chemicals), are driving participation in GVCs. Among manufacturing activities, three low-end manufacturing sectors are of particular interest for developing countries: food processing; wearing apparel; and leather and footwear. These are sectors for which the entry costs are relatively lower and labor cost advantages are more important. They have been often the entry point for a country's industrialization process. The FAT survey data allow us to identify what sector-specific functions firms in these sectors have outsourced, and investigate whether this has any association with levels of technology adopted, insertion in GVCs, and economies of scale.

To start, there is a large variation in outsourcing decisions across sectors. Figure 3.9 shows that outsourcing in sector-specific business functions is not uncommon in various sectors, even in developing countries. On average, 11 percent of firms outsource some core functions. In some sectors, such as livestock, this figure reaches almost 40 percent of firms. In other sectors, such as health care, it is hard for firms to outsource core functions given the way the service is delivered.

A deep dive in two important manufacturing sectors—wearing apparel and food processing—reveals interesting differences across business functions in the sectors.

FIGURE 3.9 Across Sectors, There Is Large Heterogeneity in Outsourcing Sector-Specific Business Functions

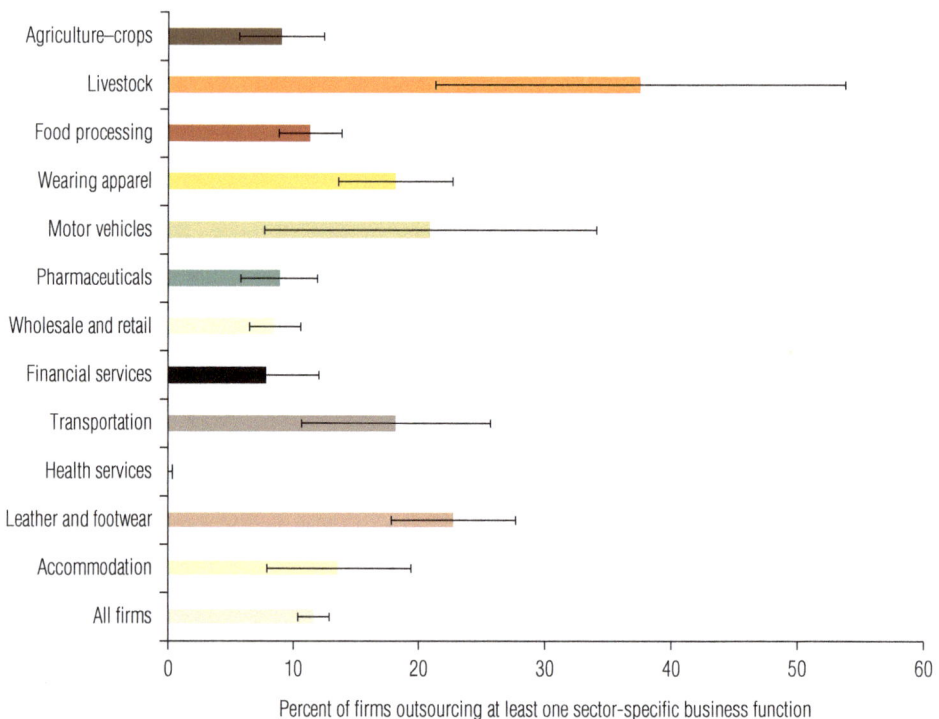

Percent of firms outsourcing at least one sector-specific business function

Source: Original figure based on Firm-level Adoption of Technology (FAT) survey data.

Note: The figure covers all 11 countries in the FAT survey sample. Estimates of outsourcing using sampling weights, except for the following categories: accommodation (excluding Bangladesh, Brazil, Malawi, Senegal, and Vietnam); agriculture–crops (excluding Bangladesh, India, and Malawi); motor vehicles (excluding Bangladesh and Senegal); financial services (excluding Bangladesh, Brazil, and Burkina Faso); leather and footwear (excluding Brazil, Malawi, and Senegal); livestock (excluding Bangladesh, India, and Malawi); pharmaceuticals (excluding Brazil and Senegal); transportation (excluding Bangladesh); and wholesale and retail (excluding Bangladesh).

About 18 percent of firms in wearing apparel outsource at least one sector-specific function, while only 12 percent of firms do in food processing. This ranking, whereby firms in apparel are more likely to outsource activities than firms in food processing, is consistent with the larger share of GVC participation in the respective sectors (World Bank 2020). Figure 3.10 shows that the most common function outsourced

FIGURE 3.10 Within Sectors, There Is Heterogeneity in the Degree of Outsourcing within Sector-Specific Business Functions

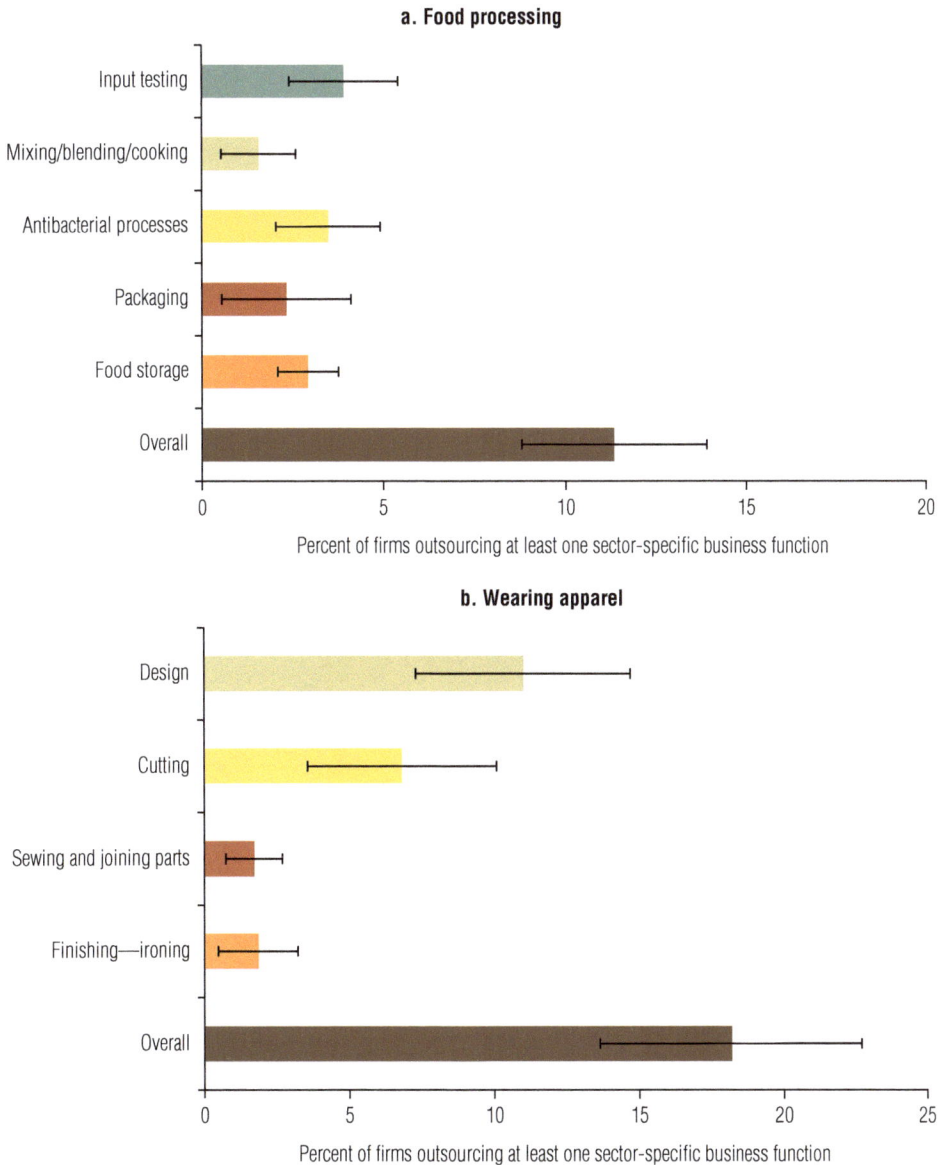

a. Food processing

Percent of firms outsourcing at least one sector-specific business function

b. Wearing apparel

Percent of firms outsourcing at least one sector-specific business function

Source: Original figure based on Firm-level Adoption of Technology (FAT) survey data.
Note: The panels cover all 11 countries in the FAT survey sample. Estimates of outsourcing using sampling weights.

by firms in wearing apparel is design (11 percent), while in food processing it is antibacterial processes and input testing (4 percent).

One potential explanation for the decision to outsource is that less sophisticated firms outsource those business functions that need more complex technologies. This would imply a negative correlation between outsourcing and technology sophistication. The FAT survey data reveal that outsourcing in design in apparel, controlling for country fixed effects, is negatively associated with average levels of technology sophistication in other functions (figure 3.11). Design is a knowledge-driven task that may require a higher level of firm capabilities, which may not be economically viable for the average small firm. However, as figure 3.11 shows, storage in food processing also exhibits a negative correlation, which is likely to be more related to issues of scale and the fact that smaller firms have lower levels of technology sophistication. The pattern for other business functions is not pronounced, which suggests that other factors are at play.

Finally, to test the hypothesis of whether the decision of outsourcing these tasks is associated with integration in GVCs, an empirical analysis was conducted to

FIGURE 3.11 The Significant Correlation between Outsourcing Tasks and Technology Sophistication (All Business Functions) Is Restricted to Some Business Functions

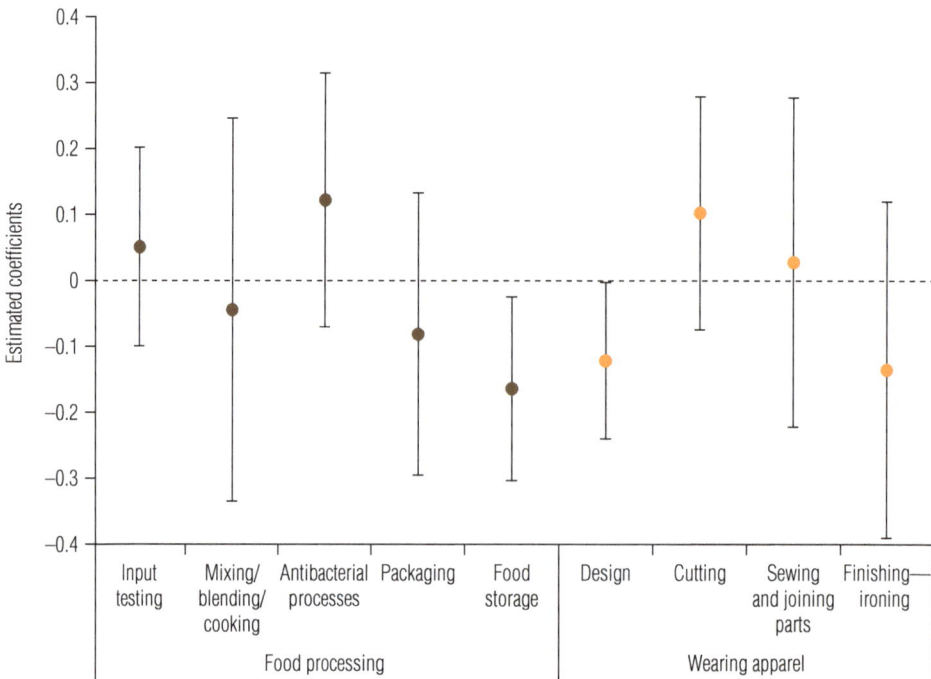

Source: Original figure based on Firm-level Adoption of Technology (FAT) survey data.

Note: The y-axis shows the coefficient estimates for the relationship between outsourcing business functions and all business functions—including general business functions and sector-specific business functions—controlling by country for all 11 countries in the FAT survey sample. Estimates are weighted by sampling weights. The x-axis refers to specific business functions in each sector.

investigate what business functions are more likely to be outsourced by firms based on traders (exporters or importers) versus nontraders that do not participate in international trade. Overall, the analysis does not find that the decision to outsource is associated with trading status. For apparel, only one activity—cutting—is more likely to be outsourced if a firm trades in international markets. For food processing, only packaging seems to be more likely to be outsourced if the firms are nontraders (figure 3.12). A potential explanation is that traders are not more likely to outsource business functions because although participation in GVCs is likely to

FIGURE 3.12 **There Are No Significant Differences between Traders and Nontraders in Outsourcing Business Functions**

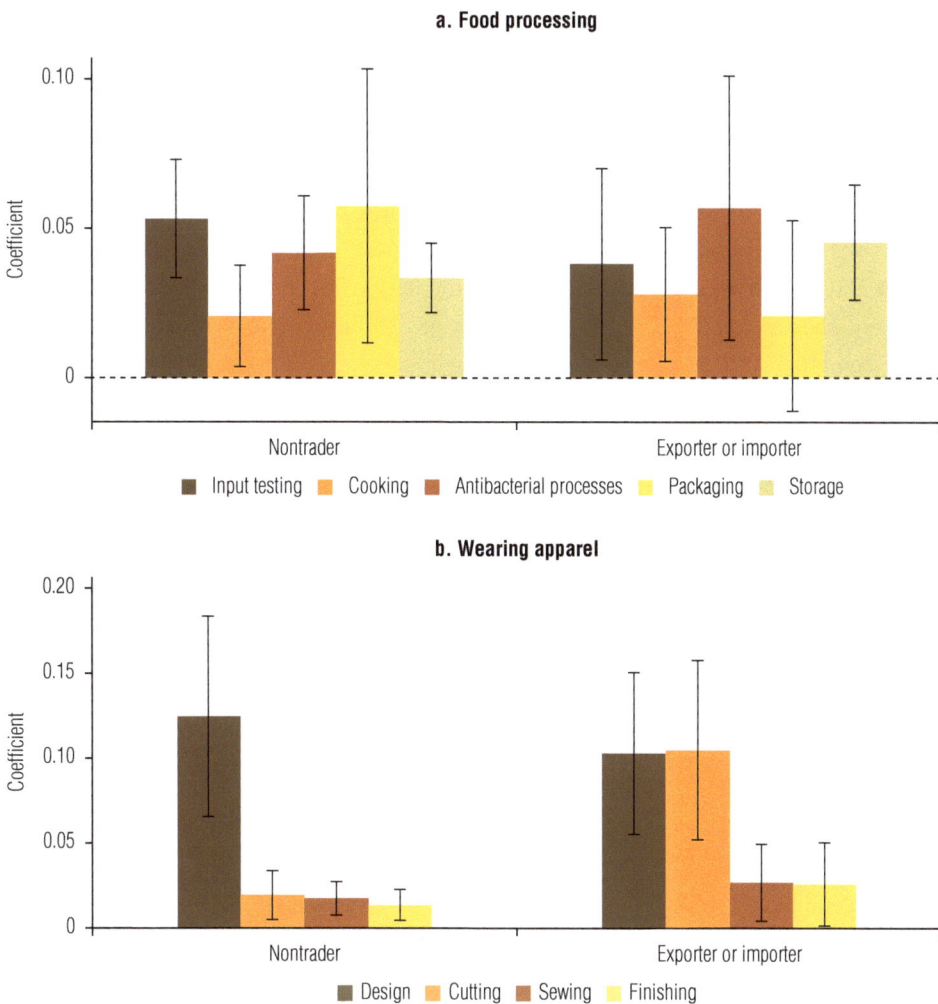

a. Food processing

b. Wearing apparel

Source: Original figure based on Firm-level Adoption of Technology (FAT) survey data.

Note: For each business function, this figure includes firms' technologies from the 11 countries in the FAT survey sample, except for panel a that excludes Ghana and Malawi and panel b that excludes Ghana. Technology measures are weighted by sampling weights. Results are conditioned on not being a foreign firm.

lead to more sophisticated technologies, it does not necessarily lead to more domestic specialization in terms of what business functions to perform in-house.

Summing Up

The chapter started by providing a basic comparison of technology adoption in specific sectors. Having a more comprehensive and nuanced picture of what the key business functions and technologies associated with them are in specific sectors, as well as where firms stand on technology adoption, is critical to inform the policy debate and avoid a biased view of production technologies used by firms. For example, a more detailed analysis of technologies shows that despite the rapid diffusion of general-purpose digital technologies used by businesses, such as access to the internet and mobile phones, there are still large gaps in technologies used to perform production tasks in agriculture or light manufacturing (such as tractors for harvesting or electric sewing machines in apparel).

The chapter also shows that the reality for most firms is that leapfrogging in SBF technologies is rare and the diffusion of newer and more sophisticated technologies is mostly gradual. Finally, the chapter shows that firms can outsource some business functions or use platforms when they do not have sufficient capabilities to implement them. But overall, most functions are implemented within the boundaries of the firm, and the reasons for outsourcing go beyond production complexity and can include scale and other factors.

Notes

1. Studies have focused on the types of production technologies (such as fertilizer, seeds, and tractors) that more directly affect the productivity of farms. Examples range from the seminal work of Griliches (1957) and Mansfield (1963) to more recent work by Conley and Udry (2010); Duflo, Kremer, and Robinson (2011); and Suri (2011). For an overview of the literature, see the fourth volume in the World Bank Productivity Project series (Fuglie et al. 2020).

2. Policy makers update their beliefs when informed of the findings of research, Hjort et al. (2021) show in an experiment in Brazil.

3. It also informs an even more important topic for economic development, structural change, which is discussed in the next chapter.

4. The owner reported that he did not have access to capital to build a more appropriate storage unit and conducts most GBFs manually—despite having access to a computer and the internet, and eventually using them with the support of his children.

5. The manual sewing machine is an old technology. It has been available since the 1930s and is relatively affordable.

6. If the subsample is restricted to small firms, renting a tractor through a digital platform becomes statistically significantly associated with more sophisticated technology at the intensive margin, but not for harvesting.

7. Acemoglu, Antràs, and Helpman (2007) develop a model based on the Grossman and Hart (1986) framework to explain adoption decisions, where a firm chooses its technology and investment

levels in activities that can be contracted to suppliers of intermediate inputs, depending on the quality of the contracting institutions in the country.

8. Bakos and Brynjolfsson (1993) developed a model that explains the decisions to outsource based on new opportunities brought about by information and communication technologies. ICT lowers coordination costs, which in turn facilitates outsourcing of tasks domestically or abroad (offshoring). Using data for US manufacturing firms, Fort (2017) finds that the adoption of ICT technologies between 2002 and 2007 is associated with a 3.1 percentage point increase in its probability of outsourcing. This effect is 20 percent higher in industries with production specifications that are easier to codify in an electronic format.

References

Acemoglu, D., P. Antràs, and E. Helpman. 2007. "Contracts and Technology Adoption." *American Economic Review* 97 (3): 916–43.

Bakos, J. Y., and E. Brynjolfsson. 1993. "From Vendors to Partners: Information Technology and Incomplete Contracts in Buyer-Supplier Relationships." *Journal of Organizational Computing* 3 (3): 301–28.

Coase, R. H. 1937. "The Nature of the Firm." *Economica* 4 (16): 386–405.

Conley, T. G., and C. R. Udry. 2010. "Learning about a New Technology: Pineapple in Ghana." *American Economic Review* 100 (1): 35–69.

Demsetz, H. 1997. "The Firm in Economic Theory: A Quiet Revolution." *American Economic Review* 87 (2): 426–29.

Duflo, E., M. Kremer, and J. Robinson. 2011. "Nudging Farmers to Use Fertilizer: Theory and Experimental Evidence from Kenya." *American Economic Review* 101 (6): 2350–90.

Fort, T. C. 2017. "Technology and Production Fragmentation: Domestic versus Foreign Sourcing." *Review of Economic Studies* 84 (2): 650–87.

Fuglie, K., M. Gautam, A. Goyal, and W. F. Maloney. 2020. *Harvesting Prosperity: Technology and Productivity Growth in Agriculture.* World Bank Productivity Project series. Washington, DC: World Bank.

Griliches, Z. 1957. "Hybrid Corn: An Exploration in the Economics of Technological Change." *Econometrica* 25 (4): 501–22.

Grossman, S. J., and O. D. Hart. 1986. "The Costs and Benefits of Ownership: A Theory of Vertical and Lateral Integration." *Journal of Political Economy* 94 (4): 691–719.

Hjort, J., D. Moreira, G. Rao, and J. F. Santini. 2021. "How Research Affects Policy: Experimental Evidence from 2,150 Brazilian Municipalities." *American Economic Review* 111 (5): 1442–80.

Mansfield, E. 1963. "Intrafirm Rates of Diffusion of an Innovation." *Review of Economics and Statistics* 45 (4): 348–59.

Schwab, Klaus. 2016. *The Fourth Industrial Revolution.* New York: Crown Business.

Suri, T. 2011. "Selection and Comparative Advantage in Technology Adoption." *Econometrica* 79 (1): 159–209.

Taglioni, D., and D. Winkler. 2016. *Making Global Value Chains Work for Development.* Washington, DC: World Bank Group.

Williamson, O. E. 1981. "The Economics of Organization: The Transaction Cost Approach." *American Journal of Sociology* 87 (3): 548–77.

World Bank. 2020. *World Development Report 2020: Trading for Development in the Age of Global Value Chains.* Washington, DC: World Bank.

PART 2

The Implications of the Technological Divide for Long-Term Economic Growth

4. Technology Sophistication, Productivity, and Employment

Introduction

The centrality of technology in economic development rests on the relationship between technology adoption and firm performance. At the macro level, economists widely agree that variation in technology accounts for a large share of the differences in GDP per capita across countries.[1] This positive view of the aggregate impact of technology is supported by Joseph Schumpeter's concept of "creative destruction," and more generally by the positive impact that technology-based firms have on disrupting markets and enhancing business dynamism.

At the firm level, technology is a key driver of productivity growth. If firms use better technologies, they are able to produce more and better-quality products and services with the same inputs. This can allow for higher remuneration of all factors involved in production, including higher wages for labor—given that the marginal product of labor is likely to increase, and workers may also capture part of the economic rents generated by the innovations brought to the market.

Yet every new wave of industrial revolution tends to raise concerns about job displacement. Since the Luddites railed against modern technology in nineteenth-century Europe, the potential negative effects of the diffusion of new technologies for the quality and quantity of jobs have been highlighted in the policy debate. This concern is especially relevant for policy makers in developing countries that are facing an increasing diffusion of advanced digital technologies and automation that could undermine labor cost advantages. The question is whether the adoption of the latest round of technologies is characterized by the same or different dynamics on employment than past ones.

While many studies and a considerable body of evidence focus on the country level and high-income economies, this chapter looks at these issues from the perspective of the firm and developing countries. Specifically, the chapter addresses the following questions:

- What is the relationship between adopting more sophisticated technologies and productivity at the firm level?

- How are the technology and productivity gaps across sectors associated with structural change?
- What is the association between technology adoption and employment growth at the firm level?
- Is the adoption of more sophisticated technologies associated with better jobs, proxied by higher wages?

Technology and Firm-Level Productivity

There are three main channels through which better technology can boost productivity over time: (1) labor reallocation from less productive firms to more productive firms; (2) technology upgrading within the firm across business functions; or (3) entry and exit of firms. In the first case, workers are moving from firms that are far from the technology frontier to firms that are closer to the frontier. In the second case, firms upgrade their technologies to become more efficient. In the third case, firms that are far from the frontier exit the market and are replaced by new firms that are closer to the frontier. Figure 4.1 provides a conceptual framework developed in the second volume in the World Bank Productivity Project series (Cusolito and Maloney 2018) describing the drivers of productivity growth through a decomposition exercise. Technology upgrading is central in explaining productivity gains within the firm and through the entry margins, but it also likely affects reallocation across sectors. Estimates for Ethiopia, India, Malaysia, and Slovenia suggest that within-firm performance upgrading may account for a large share of productivity gains over the 2000s. Estimates range from about one-third in Chile over 1996 to 2006 to more than half in China over 2000 to 2007 (Melitz and Polanec 2015; Cusolito and Maloney 2018).

FIGURE 4.1 Several Drivers Affect the Margins of Productivity Growth

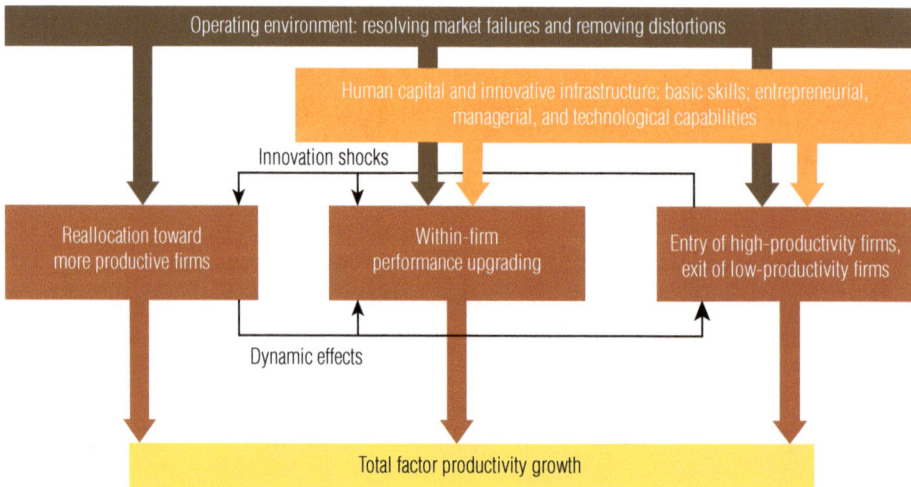

Source: Cusolito and Maloney 2018.

The Strong and Positive Association between Technology Sophistication and Labor Productivity

Evidence from the Firm-level Adoption of Technology (FAT) survey data show a positive and robust relationship between technology and labor productivity. Given the limitations of estimating total factor productivity (TFP) robustly without longitudinal data,[2] rather than estimating the contribution of these channels for productivity growth, this section focuses on aggregate effects on labor productivity. Specifically, the correlation between labor productivity (value added per worker)[3] and technology is estimated.[4] Figure 4.2 plots a representation of the relationship between labor productivity and the measure of the average sophistication of the technology index for all business functions (ABF) at the intensive margin (that is, the average sophistication of the technologies most intensively used for all business functions). While causal interpretations cannot be drawn, the results reinforce the finding that the various measures of technology used in this analysis are positively and significantly associated with labor productivity.

FIGURE 4.2 Technology Sophistication Is Correlated with Labor Productivity

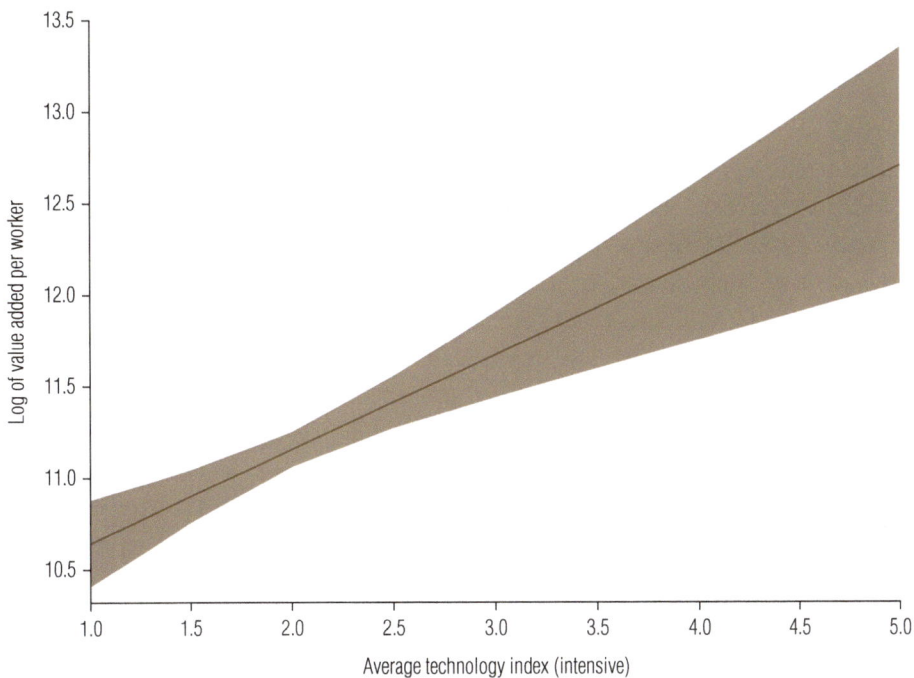

Source: Original figure based on Firm-level Adoption of Technology (FAT) survey data.

Note: The figure plots the predicted productivity as a function of technology sophistication using sampling weights and controlling for country, sector, formality, and employment. Estimates based on 10 countries in the FAT survey sample (productivity data for Poland were not available). The x-axis plots the average technology sophistication across all business functions (ABF) at the intensive margin. ABF includes general business functions (GBFs) and sector-specific business functions (SBFs).

Sector Technology, the Productivity Gap, and Structural Change

As labor is reallocated toward activities with higher levels of productivity and technology content, it can lead to large-scale sector reallocation of employment and capital—a process commonly known as structural change or structural transformation (Kaldor 1961; Kuznets 1973; Maddison 1980). In most developed countries, this process is characterized by increases in the share of manufacturing in the economy, both in terms of jobs and value added. It is followed by a reduction in the share of employment in agriculture and a continued increasing share of employment in services, as workers migrate to urban areas to find job opportunities in other sectors. Some recent literature has emphasized the predominant role of manufacturing in the growth process (Rodrik 2011), the risks of premature deindustrialization (Rodrik 2016), and the prospects of services-led development (Nayyar, Cruz, and Zhu 2021; Nayyar, Hallward-Driemeier, and Davies 2021).

A granular picture of FAT data yields a more nuanced view of manufacturing as a technological leader. Figure 4.3 shows that in some cases, technology use is relatively closer to the frontier in agriculture and some services sectors (such as financial and health services). While technologies still may yield larger productivity gains in manufacturing than in agriculture and services, there is significant dynamism in these other sectors too. Diao et al. (2021) suggest that one key problem in the process of structural transformation in Africa may be related to the types of technologies that are available, especially in manufacturing, which are more capital intensive than those that would correspond to the region's income per capita or factor endowments (Africa's abundance of land and unskilled labor)—which would favor more labor-intensive and less skill-intensive use of technologies. While it is true that the technologies that are available for firms in Africa are similar to those in developed economies, the FAT data reveal less adoption in African countries of more capital-intensive and sophisticated technologies. For example, large firms in Kenya use sector-specific technologies that are similar to those used by small firms in Brazil and Vietnam, and that are much less sophisticated than those used by large firms in the Republic of Korea. The extent to which these technologies are more labor saving depends on the sector, but overall, actual adoption appears aligned with their income levels and less capital-intensive endowments. What remains to be validated is whether the reason not to upgrade to more sophisticated technologies and accelerate the process of structural transformation is related to the mismatch in endowments or how appropriate these technologies are—as Diao et al. (2021) suggest—or to some of the factors described in chapter 6.

Cross-Country Productivity and Technology Gaps in Agriculture

Despite the controversies concerning the relative roles that manufacturing versus services play in the relationship between structural change and economic

FIGURE 4.3 **The Level of Technology Sophistication Varies Considerably across Agriculture, Manufacturing, and Services Sectors**

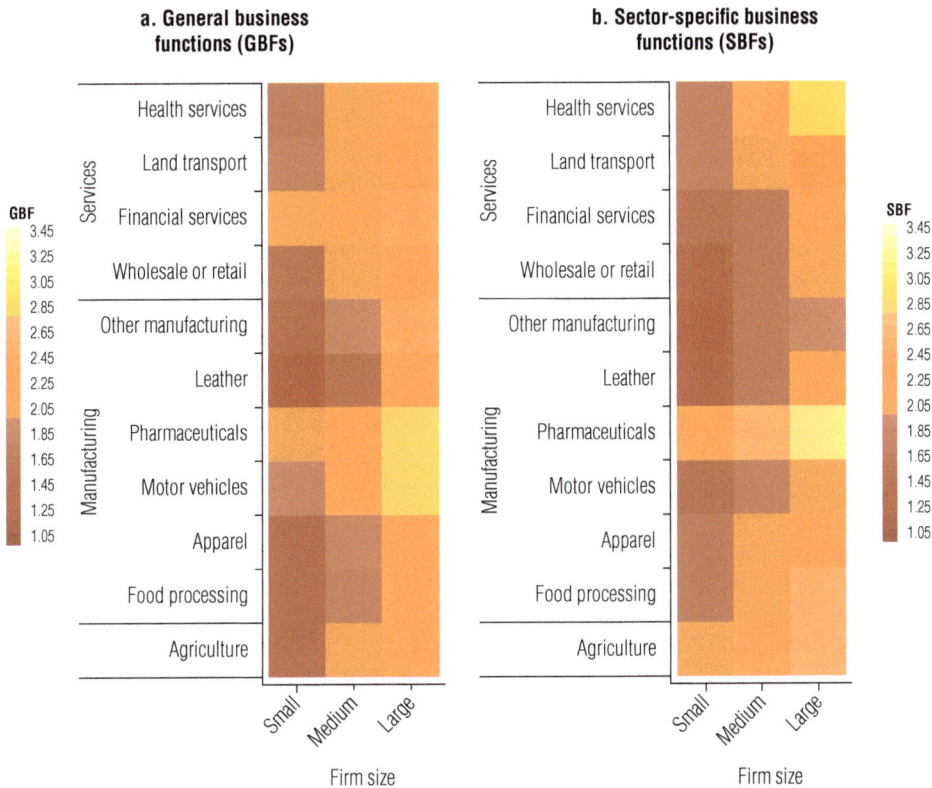

a. General business functions (GBFs)

b. Sector-specific business functions (SBFs)

Source: Original figure based on Firm-level Adoption of Technology (FAT) survey data.

Note: Average technology index across all 11 countries in the FAT survey sample using sampling weights and controlling for country, firm size, and sector. The higher the index measure (moving from brown to orange to yellow), the greater the level of technology sophistication. Firm size refers to the number of workers: small (5–19), medium (20–99), and large (100 or more).

development, there is more consensus among economists around the view that increasing productivity in agriculture is key (see the fourth volume in the World Bank Productivity Project series, Fuglie et al. 2020). As productivity increases in agriculture due to mechanization and use of more advanced technologies, and the population's income grows in a way that the resulting increases in demand shift from basic food products to manufacturing products and services, less employment is needed in agriculture and more is required in manufacturing and services. This reduction of the labor share in agriculture is observed across countries that have moved into higher-income status (Comin, Lashkari, and Mestieri 2021).

In this context, one of the big puzzles in the productivity literature is the large variation across agriculture, manufacturing, and services sectors observed in productivity differences across countries. In particular, Caselli (2005) shows that cross-country differences in productivity are 10 times larger in agriculture than in nonagricultural sectors.[5] Panel a of figure 4.4 focuses on Korea and Senegal and compares the technology

FIGURE 4.4 Differences in Technology Sophistication between the Republic of Korea and Senegal Are Larger in the Agricultural Sector than in Nonagricultural Sectors and Are Driven Mainly by the Low Sophistication of Informal Firms

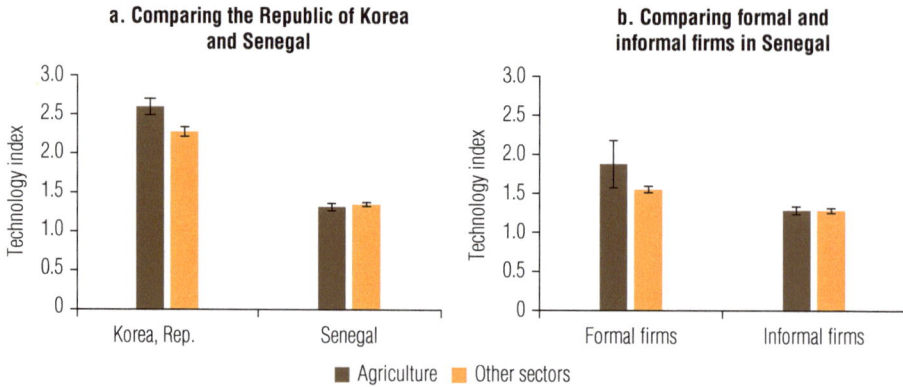

a. Comparing the Republic of Korea and Senegal

b. Comparing formal and informal firms in Senegal

Y-axis (both panels): Technology index, scale 0 to 3.0

Panel a categories: Korea, Rep.; Senegal
Panel b categories: Formal firms; Informal firms

Legend: ■ Agriculture ■ Other sectors

Source: Original figure based on Firm-level Adoption of Technology (FAT) survey data.

Note: Estimated levels of technology index using sampling weights and controlling for sector, firm size, and country.

gap between agriculture and nonagricultural sectors, based on FAT survey data. It shows that the gap between agriculture is larger than the gap between nonagricultural sectors, on average. Moreover, agricultural firms in Senegal are not relatively closer to the technology frontier, unlike in Korea and other countries as observed in the FAT survey data. Panel b shows that this pattern of a larger agriculture gap in Senegal is driven mainly by informal firms, which are more prevalent among agricultural firms in the country, even among those with 5 or more workers.

Part of the sectoral differences in productivity also reflect the larger cross-country differences in firm size in agriculture compared to nonagricultural sectors. As smaller production units tend to be less productive, the greater difference in average firm size between higher-income and lower-income countries in agriculture versus nonagriculture explains some of the cross-sector difference in the relative productivity gap.

Technology Adoption and Employment

For centuries, technology has been associated by some groups and commentators with fear of mass unemployment. In the past decade, this negative view of the effects of technology adoption on employment has gained significant traction with the emergence of advanced labor-saving technologies and evidence in more advanced economies of job polarization (Acemoglu and Autor 2011; Autor 2015), with significant decreases in the demand for routine and often medium-skilled occupations, and resulting increases in income inequality. This evidence focuses mainly on advanced economies. The few studies that focus on developing countries find different dynamics of polarization (Maloney and Molina 2016).

FIGURE 4.5 Firms Generally Keep the Same Number of Jobs When They Adopt New Technologies

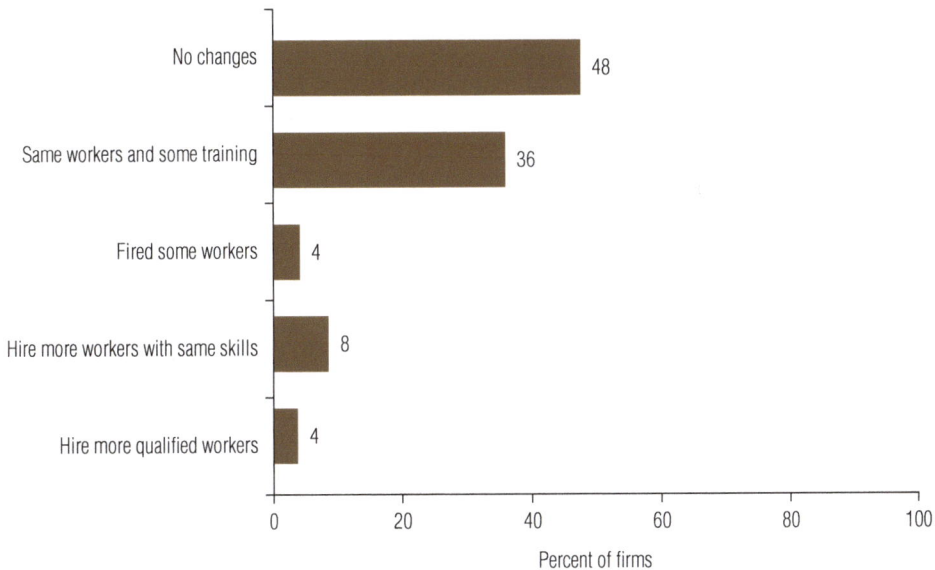

Source: Original figure based on Firm-level Adoption of Technology (FAT) survey data.

Note: The figure covers six countries (Bangladesh, Brazil [only the state of Ceará], India [only the states of Tamil Nadu and Uttar Pradesh], Malawi, Senegal, and Vietnam) in the FAT survey sample using sampling weights.

This discussion of the impact of technology on employment, including the literature on polarization, refers to economywide effects over the medium and long term—which cannot be analyzed with FAT survey data. Yet an important question is whether a direct association between adopting more sophisticated technologies and changes in employment can be observed. The survey directly asks firms how they adjust their employment levels after they adopt new technologies: specifically, after they acquire a new machine, equipment, or software. The survey results are summarized in figure 4.5. The vast majority (84 percent) of firms report that they do not change the number of workers (48 percent reported no changes at all; 36 percent reported they offer some training to current workers). Only a small share of firms (4 percent) report a reduction in the number of workers as a mechanism of adjustment for the acquisition of new technologies. This share is much smaller than the number of firms that report an increase in the number of workers with the same skills (8 percent) or hire more workers with higher skills (4 percent). At face value, there is little evidence that technology upgrading in these firms has led to job losses.

Technology Sophistication and Job Growth

Firms that use more sophisticated technology also have higher employment growth. Figure 4.6 shows the association between technology sophistication and employment changes in the firm in the interval between the last fiscal year before the

FIGURE 4.6 Firms That Have Adopted Better Technology Have Increased Employment

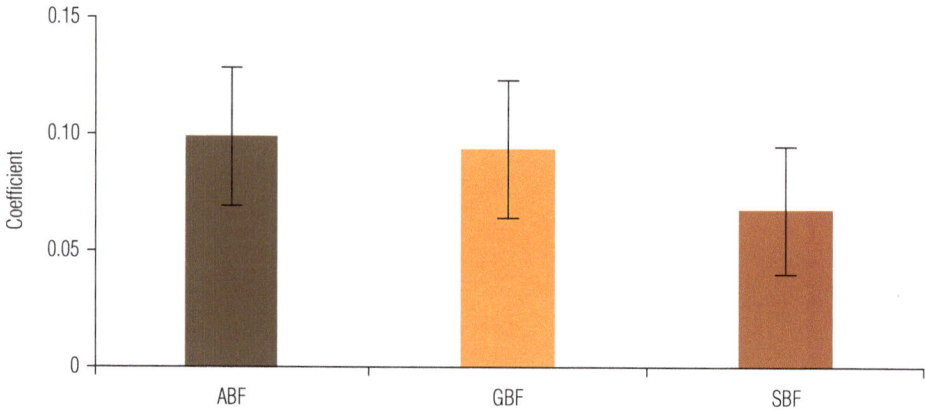

Source: Original figure based on Firm-level Adoption of Technology (FAT) survey data.

Note: The figure provides the coefficients and 95 percent confidence intervals from regressions. Job growth is regressed on all business functions (ABF), general business function (GBF), and sector-specific business function (SBF) at the intensive margin using sampling weights, while controlling for sector, firm size, and regions. It includes 10 countries in the FAT survey sample (data for Poland not included).

interview and two years earlier. The results suggest a positive and statistically significant association between employment growth and technology sophistication for all the technology indexes—for general business functions (GBFs), sector-specific business functions (SBFs), and the aggregate index for all business functions (ABF)—after controlling for firm characteristics such as the initial size of the firm, their age, sector, region, foreign ownership, and exporting status. Although these results do not infer a causal relationship, they are in line with other findings in the literature suggesting that firms with better technologies tend to be more productive and benefit from opportunities to expand. For example, evidence on the impact of innovation on employment also suggests an expansion effect (see summary in Dosi and Mohnen [2019] and other articles on the impact of innovation on employment in the same volume).

The correlation between firms' employment growth and the level of technology is also robust for individual general business functions at the intensive margin. This suggests that some of these general business functions have a stronger association with employment growth. Indeed, figure 4.7 shows that the association of most GBFs with employment growth is positive and statistically significant.

Technology and Skill Composition

Does adoption of more sophisticated technologies tilt the skill composition toward skilled workers? The hypothesis of skill-biased technological change suggests that a shift in the production technology may favor skilled over unskilled workers by

FIGURE 4.7 **More Sophisticated Technologies in Some Business Functions Are More Associated with Employment Growth**

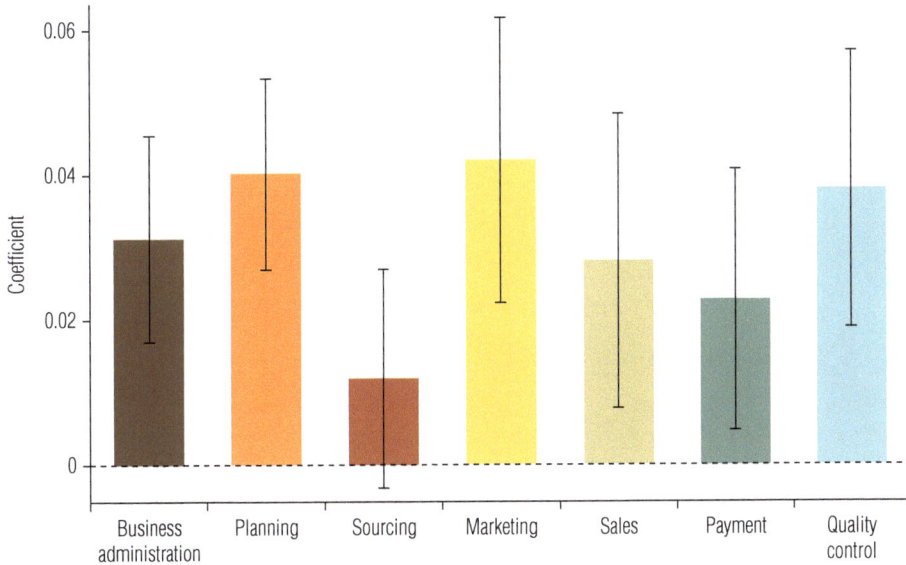

Source: Original figure based on Firm-level Adoption of Technology (FAT) survey data.

Note: The figure provides the coefficients and 95 percent confidence intervals from regressions. Job growth is regressed on each specific general business function at the intensive margin using sampling weights, while controlling for sector, firm size, and regions. It includes data for 10 countries in the FAT survey sample (data for Poland not available).

increasing skilled workers' relative productivity and, therefore, their relative demand. To investigate this relationship, the authors analyzed the correlation between the technology index and changes in the skill composition of the firm based on existing occupations. To measure the intensity of high-skilled workers, the analysis uses the share of chief executive officers and managers, professionals, and technicians to total workers. The low-skilled category includes clerks, production workers, and services workers. The analysis then takes the difference of this share in the interval between the last fiscal year before the interview and two years earlier, and uses it as a dependent variable. Figure 4.8 shows a negative correlation between changes in the skill intensity and the level of technology, controlling for the initial size of the firm, their age, sector, and region. Results are not statistically significant for the average index (ABF) and GBFs, for which no significant skills changes are observed in the short term associated with increased technology sophistication. The correlation is significant for sector-specific technology sophistication. The results suggest that firms with higher level of technologies are generating more jobs and not necessarily reducing the share of unskilled workers in their payroll. If anything, the negative significant correlation with SBF suggests that for some technologies the share of unskilled workers increases.[6, 7]

FIGURE 4.8 **Firms with a Higher Level of Technology Are Creating More Jobs but Not Changing Their Share of Low-Skilled Workers**

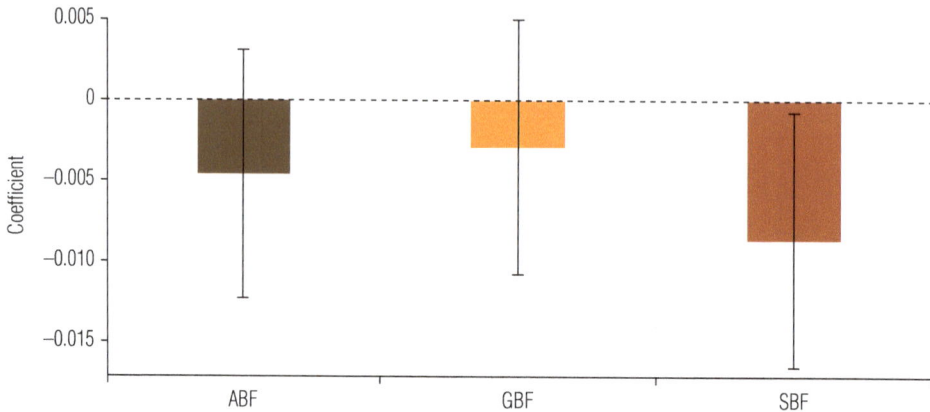

Source: Original figure based on Firm-level Adoption of Technology (FAT) survey data.

Note: The figure provides the coefficients and 95 percent confidence intervals from regressions. Change in the share of high-skilled occupations is regressed on all business functions (ABF), general business function (GBF), and sector-specific business function (SBF) at the intensive margin using sampling weights, while controlling for sector, firm size, and regions. It includes data for 10 countries in the FAT survey sample (data for Poland not included).

These results are consistent with related work on knowledge hierarchies. Garicano and Rossi-Hansberg (2015) suggest that managing firm expansion requires increasing employment in low-skilled workers as well. More recently, Aghion et al. (2019) show the complementarity between high- and low-skilled workers in innovative firms; the increase in the demand for high-skilled workers from introducing an innovation in the firm also demands additional tasks of low-skilled workers to complement and support high-skilled workers, so the net effect can be zero or small.

Technology Adoption and the Wage Premium

Another important aspect of the impact of technology adoption on the labor market is how the adoption of technology increases or decreases wages. In other words, is there a wage premium associated with using more advanced technologies? An extensive literature has examined how firms' characteristics affect wages. For instance, many findings have indicated the existence of a wage premium associated with firms that are large (Bloom et al. 2018), are foreign-owned (Hijzen et al. 2013), are exporters (Schank, Schnabel, and Wagner 2008), or are more innovative (Cirera and Martins-Neto 2020; Aghion et al. 2018). However, although technology adoption relates to some of these characteristics, the literature has not explicitly examined the existence of a technology wage premium. The FAT survey allows this hypothesis to be tested. In doing so, the analysis focuses on data from the state of Ceará in Brazil. The analysis first matches FAT survey data with 2018 data from a matched employer-employee database compiled by the Brazilian Ministry of Economy considered to be a high-quality census of the Brazilian formal labor market (Relação Anual de Informações Sociais, RAIS). A Mincer-type wage equation is then estimated controlling for firm and individual observable characteristics.

Figure 4.9 shows the coefficients of regressions of the logarithm of workers' monthly wages on the logarithm of the four different technology indexes. Regressions control for individuals' age, gender, length of employment, education, and occupation. At the establishment level, the regressions control for firm characteristics such as sector, size, exporting status, and foreign ownership, as well as a dummy indicating whether the establishment has employees dedicated to research and development (R&D). Vertical markers show estimated 95 percent confidence intervals based on robust standard errors.

FIGURE 4.9 **Firms Using More Sophisticated Technologies Pay Higher Wages**

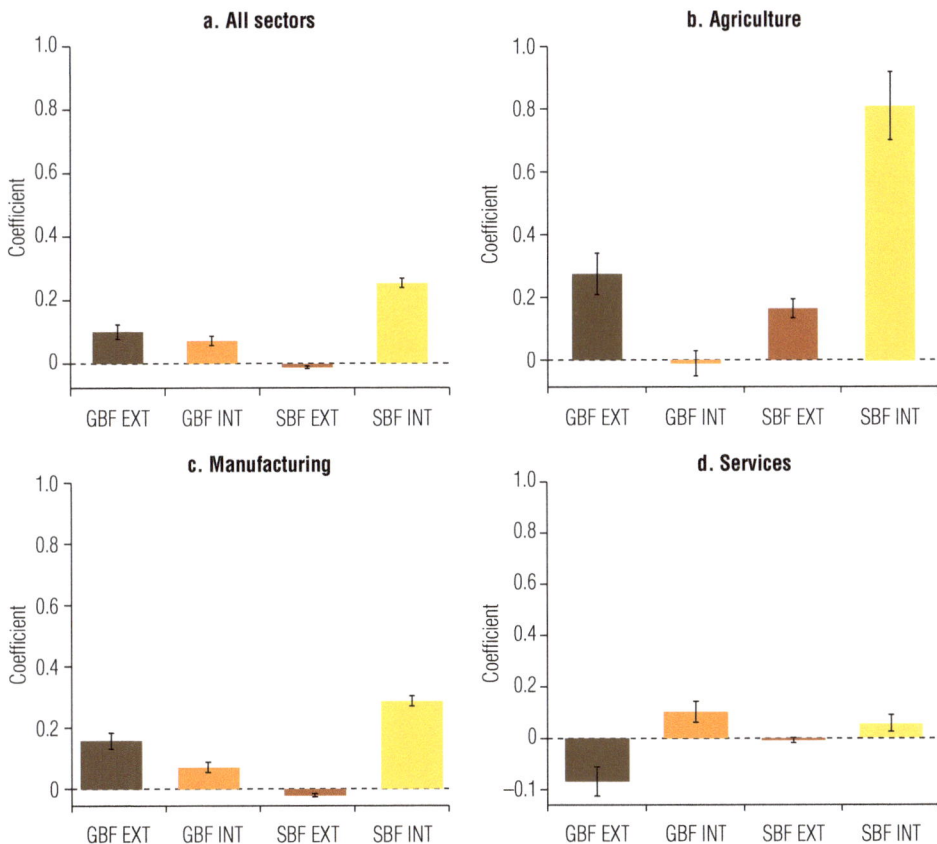

Source: Original figure based on Firm-level Adoption of Technology (FAT) survey data and RAIS data.

Note: The figure uses data from the state of Ceará in Brazil. EXT = extensive margin; GBF = general business function; INT= intensive margin; SBF = sector-specific business function. RAIS is a matched employer-employee database covering formal firms and formal workers in Brazil.

There is a positive and significant wage premium associated with technology adoption, especially for sector-specific business functions (figure 4.9).[8] For instance, an SBF index that is 1 percent higher at the intensive margin is associated with 0.27 percent higher monthly wages. The results are significant even when controlling for other important firms characteristics. Panels b, c, and d show the coefficients of a similar exercise, now disaggregated by broad sectors. Panel b shows that the premium is larger for firms in agriculture, but not significant for GBFs at the intensive margin. In contrast, the premium is smaller for services and not significant at the extensive margin for both GBFs and SBFs. Firms with more sophisticated technologies pay higher wages.

Given the existence of a premium linked to the adoption of more sophisticated technologies, another important question is whether higher-paid individuals capture most of the premium with respect to those at the bottom of the distribution: that is, whether technology is associated with within-firm wage inequality. Recent literature has underlined the importance of within-firm variation in explaining earnings variance (see Song et al. 2018). For instance, Alvarez et al. (2018) document a significant decrease in earnings inequality in Brazil from 1992 to 2012 and find that within-firm variance accounts for 40 percent of the total decline in inequality.

To test for the relationship between technology adoption and wage inequality, the authors used the matched database in the state of Ceará in Brazil and constructed, for each establishment, a measure of wage inequality based on the ratio of the 90th to 10th percentiles log wage differential. Figure 4.10 reports the coefficients of regressions of the logarithm of wage inequality (90/10 log wage differential) on the logarithm of the

FIGURE 4.10 Technology Sophistication Contributes to Wage Inequality within Firms

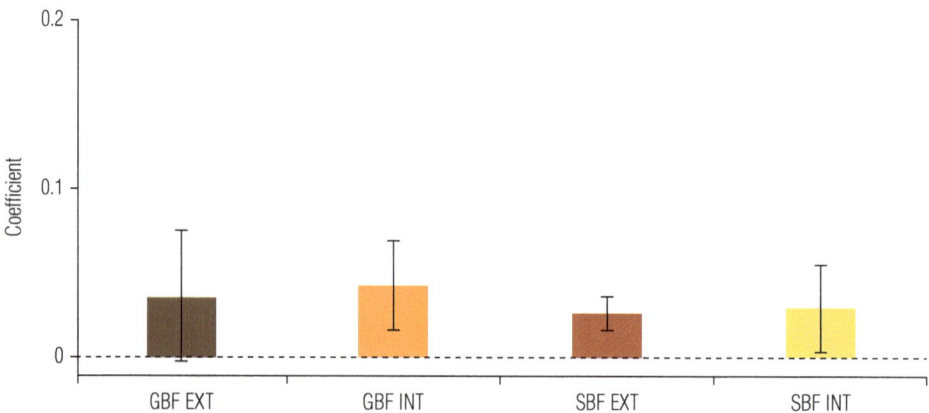

Source: Original figure based on Firm-level Adoption of Technology (FAT) survey data and RAIS data.

Note: The figure uses data from the state of Ceará in Brazil. EXT = extensive margin; GBF = general business function; INT= intensive margin; SBF = sector-specific business function. RAIS is a matched employer-employee database covering formal firms and formal workers in Brazil.

Bridging the Technological Divide

four different technology indexes. Regressions control for firm characteristics (the establishment's sector, size, exporting status, foreign ownership, share of high-skilled occupations, and share of workers who are college graduates), as well as a dummy indicating whether the establishment has employees dedicated to R&D. Vertical markers show the estimated 95 percent confidence intervals based on robust standard errors. The figure shows a small but significant association between technology sophistication and wage inequality for all the intensive measures, indicating that technology sophistication is also associated with larger within-firm wage inequality.

Summing Up

This chapter has illustrated the links between technology sophistication, productivity, and employment. For productivity, a large literature has shown the importance of technology sophistication at the macro, meso, and micro levels. The evidence presented in this chapter confirms the positive relationship between technology and labor productivity. This chapter has also emphasized the need to put technology adoption at the center of the discussions on the agriculture productivity gap and on structural transformation from one broad sector to another (see also the fourth and fifth volumes in the World Bank Productivity Project series, Fuglie et al. 2020 and Nayyar, Hallward-Driemeier, and Davies 2021), but to have a more nuanced view of technology and productivity differences in particular sectors.

Regarding employment, the chapter shows that with respect to direct impacts on firms, there is no evidence that technology sophistication is associated with job losses in the firm and across skills groups. More sophisticated technologies are associated with greater employment growth, including the growth of low-skilled jobs. This suggests that the expansion effect of these technologies can be larger than any job losses (labor savings). The many dimensions of technology included in the technology index suggest that some of the labor-saving effects can be related more to automated processes in production but less to adoption of other technologies in management and general business functions. Finally, workers in firms utilizing more sophisticated technology tend to receive higher wages, likely as a result of capturing some of the productivity rents associated with working in more productive firms. Overall, these results call for a more nuanced view of the impact of technology on employment by business function and technology, but also highlight a positive impact of technology sophistication on employment growth at the level of the firm.

Notes

1. Comin and Hobijn (2010) estimate that the cross-country variation in the adoption of technologies accounts for at least one-quarter of per capita income differences.
2. For a review of methods to estimate TFP, see Van Biesebroeck (2007).
3. Specifically, labor productivity is measured as nominal value added in US dollars divided by the number of workers.

4. The following regression was estimated:

$$\ln(VAPW)f,c = \alpha c + \beta s + \gamma * Tf,c + \rho * Xf,c + vf,c,$$

where αc and βs are country and sector fixed effects, Tf,c is a vector of firm-level technology measures, and Xf,c is a vector of controls that includes the observable variables discussed plus 12 dummies for the sectors for which the sample includes data on sector-specific technologies and other services.

5. Caselli (2005) uses purchasing power parity (PPP) adjustments to compute sectoral productivity. This may induce additional discrepancies in cross-country productivity gaps across sectors if the PPP price index differs more across countries in agriculture than in nonagricultural sectors.

6. This does not necessarily mean that these technologies are biased toward unskilled workers, given that the results could be driven by the growth effect. Yet, evidence in the literature suggests that technologies such as online platforms used for export sales can lead to reduction in the wage skill premium (Cruz, Milet, and Olarreaga 2020).

7. There is, however, significant heterogeneity across countries. In Senegal, for example, there is a positive and strong correlation between technology sophistication and changes in the share of low-skilled workers.

8. The results do not claim any causal relationship, given that the analysis is unable to control for unobservable characteristics for workers and firms and the fact that more productive or higher-ability workers self-select into firms that use more advanced technologies.

References

Acemoglu, D., and D. Autor. 2011. "Skills, Tasks and Technologies: Implications for Employment and Earnings." Chapter 12 in *Handbook of Labor Economics*, Vol. 4, edited by David Card and Orley Ashenfelter, 1043–171. Elsevier.

Aghion, P., U. Akcigit, A. Hyytinen, and O. Toivanen. 2018. "On the Returns to Invention within Firms: Evidence from Finland." *AEA Papers and Proceedings* 108: 208–12.

Aghion, P., A. Bergeaud, R. Blundell, and R. Griffith. 2019. "The Innovation Premium to Soft Skills in Low-Skilled Occupations." CEPR Discussion Paper 14102, Center for Economic and Policy Research, Washington, DC.

Alvarez, J., F. Benguria, N. Engbom, and C. Moser. 2018. "Firms and the Decline in Earnings Inequality in Brazil." *American Economic Journal: Macroeconomics* 10 (1): 149–89.

Autor, D. A. 2015. "Why Are There Still So Many Jobs? The History and Future of Workplace Automation." *Journal of Economic Perspectives* 29 (3): 3–30.

Bloom, N., F. Guvenen, B. S. Smith, J. Song, and T. von Wachter. 2018. "The Disappearing Large-Firm Wage Premium." *AEA Papers and Proceedings* 108: 317–22.

Caselli, F. 2005. "Accounting for Cross-Country Income Differences." Chapter 9 in *Handbook of Economic Growth*, Vol. 1, Part A, 679–741. Elsevier.

Cirera, X., and A. S. Martins-Neto. 2020. "Do Innovative Firms Pay Higher Wages? Micro-Level Evidence from Brazil." Policy Research Working Paper 9442, World Bank, Washington, DC.

Comin, D., and B. Hobijn. 2010. "An Exploration of Technology Diffusion." *American Economic Review* 100 (5): 2031–59.

Comin, D., D. Lashkari, and M. Mestieri. 2021. "Structural Change with Long-Run Income and Price Effects." *Econometrica* 89 (1): 311–74.

Cruz, M., E. Milet, and M. Olarreaga. 2020. "Online Exports and the Skilled-Unskilled Wage Gap." *PLOS one* 15 (5): e0232396.

Cusolito, A. P., and W. F. Maloney. 2018. *Productivity Revisited: Shifting Paradigms in Analysis and Policy*. World Bank Productivity Project series. Washington, DC: World Bank.

Diao, X., M. Ellis, M. S. McMillan, and D. Rodrik. 2021. "Africa's Manufacturing Puzzle: Evidence from Tanzanian and Ethiopian Firms." NBER Working Paper 28344, National Bureau of Economic Research, Cambridge, MA.

Dosi, G., and P. Mohnen. 2019. "Innovation and Employment: An Introduction." *Industrial and Corporate Change* 28 (1): 45–49.

Fuglie, K., M. Gautam, A. Goyal, and W. F. Maloney. 2020. *Harvesting Prosperity: Technology and Productivity Growth in Agriculture.* World Bank Productivity Project series. Washington, DC: World Bank.

Garicano, L., and E. Rossi-Hansberg. 2015. "Knowledge-Based Hierarchies: Using Organizations to Understand the Economy." *Annual Review of Economics* 7 (1): 1–30.

Hijzen, A., P. Martins, T. Schank, and R. Upward. 2013. "Foreign-Owned Firms around the World: A Comparative Analysis of Wages and Employment at the Micro-Level." *European Economic Review* 60 (C): 170–88.

Kaldor, N. 1961. "Capital Accumulation and Economic Growth." *The Theory of Capital: Proceedings of a Conference Held by the International Economic Association*, edited by D. C. Hague, 177–222. London: Palgrave Macmillan UK.

Kuznets, S. 1973. "Modern Economic Growth: Findings and Reflections." *American Economic Review* 63 (3): 247–58.

Maddison, A. 1980. "Economic Growth and Structural Change in the Advanced Countries." In *Western Economies in Transition: Structural Change and Adjustment Policies in Industrial Countries*, edited by I. Leveson and J. Wheeler, 41–60. Boulder, CO: Westview Press.

Maloney, W. F., and C. A. Molina. 2016. "Are Automation and Trade Polarizing Developing Country Labor Markets, Too?" Policy Research Working Paper 7922, World Bank, Washington, DC.

Melitz, M. J., and S. Polanec. 2015. "Dynamic Olley-Pakes Productivity Decomposition with Entry and Exit." *Rand Journal of Economics* 46 (2): 362–75.

Nayyar, G., M. Cruz, and L. Zhu. 2021. "Does Premature Deindustrialization Matter? The Role of Manufacturing versus Services in Development." *Journal of Globalization and Development* 12 (1): 63–102.

Nayyar, G., M. Hallward-Driemeier, and E. Davies. 2021. *At Your Service? The Promise of Services-Led Development.* World Bank Productivity Project series. Washington, DC: World Bank.

Rodrik, D. 2011. "Unconditional Convergence." NBER Working Paper 17546, National Bureau of Economic Research, Cambridge, MA.

Rodrik, D. 2016. "Premature Deindustrialization." *Journal of Economic Growth* 21 (1): 1–33.

Schank, T., C. Schnabel, and J. Wagner. 2008. "Higher Wages in Exporting Firms: Self-Selection, Export Effect, or Both? First Evidence from German Linked Employer-Employee Data." Friedrich-Alexander University Erlangen-Nuremberg, Labour and Regional Economics Discussion Paper 55.

Song, J., D. J. Price, F. Guvenen, N. Bloom, and T. von Wachter. 2018. "Firming Up Inequality." *Quarterly Journal of Economics* 134 (1): 1–50.

Van Biesebroeck, J. 2007. "Robustness of Productivity Estimates." *Journal of Industrial Economics* 55: 529–69.

5. Digital Technologies and Resilience to Shocks

Introduction

The widespread diffusion of computers, smartphones, and the internet has enabled a wide variety of information and communication technologies (ICT) used for business purposes. Indeed, the technology options firms use to perform general business functions (GBFs) (such as business administration, business planning, sales, and payment) are predominantly digital, and they are applied by firms with different levels of sophistication.[1] In this regard, digitalization and technology sophistication are almost synonymous. Policy and academic discussions for at least a decade—and well before the COVID-19 pandemic—have focused on promoting digitalization to improve productivity and promote growth (for an extended discussion in the context of Europe, see Hallward-Driemeier et al. 2020). This focus has resulted in the proliferation of policy strategies that prioritize the digitalization of businesses and that include other areas such as government services or finance.

As a response to the pandemic, businesses worldwide have significantly increased their use of digital technologies. Despite this overall increase, the intensity in the use of digital tools has varied considerably. For example, larger firms and firms that that had already gone digital before the pandemic have intensified their digitalization more than other types of firms. This trend is raising concerns that the digital divide between countries and firms is widening. Thus, while the quick response from businesses to adopt digital technologies represents an important opportunity for technology upgrading, additional efforts are needed to facilitate this process for laggard firms to avoid leaving some firms and workers behind, but also closing the productivity gap and increasing aggregate productivity. The next part of this chapter explores the patterns of digitalization across firms and their implications.

The rest of the chapter explores the role of digital technologies in increasing firms' resilience to shocks. Digital technologies allow firms to integrate information systems into their operations, significantly reducing transaction costs. This has proven essential to respond to the large and widespread shock caused by the COVID-19 pandemic and highlights the role of technology as an engine for resilience to shocks, which is not confined only to health shocks and future pandemics, but also to climate shocks. Both climate change mitigation and adaptation require the adoption of technologies to reduce emissions and adapt to increasing climate shocks and rising temperatures.

This chapter addresses the following questions:

- What are the patterns of digital adoption across firms?
- How does the supply side of digital business solutions affect technology adoption by firms? To what extent do market concentration and anticompetitive practices by suppliers of digital solutions raise prices, restrict access, or lower quality and innovation in solutions?
- How much has the COVID-19 shock accelerated digitalization, and what are the risks of an increasing digital gap across firms?
- What role has the "technology readiness" of firms before the pandemic played in explaining their digital response and firm performance during the COVID-19 shock? Did firms that have been using more digital technologies perform better in terms of curtailing the loss of sales and building sales—that is, were they more resilient?
- How are firms mitigating climate change and adapting to climate shocks, and how is this related to the overall technological capabilities of the firm?

Digital Technologies

As shown in previous chapters, a large share of firms in developing countries have access to computers, smartphones, and the internet. These general-purpose technologies (GPTs) play an important role as enablers to access digital technologies, but as discussed in chapter 1, many questions remain about the purposes for which firms are using digital technologies and with what intensity. This section focuses on disentangling those purposes and describes the patterns of digitalization within firms. Understanding this process is critical for policy makers when considering digital upgrading programs and more specifically about how to prioritize technologies for support.

Patterns of Digitalization across Firms

The data from the Firm-level Adoption of Technology (FAT) survey show that there are significant gaps across firms in the use of digital technologies, but this gap varies across digital enablers. For example, there is a relatively small gap between large and small firms in their access to the internet or the use of digital platforms that cost little to access (such as social media) (figure 5.1, panels a and b), compared to the likelihood of having their own website (figure 5.1, panel c). Reducing the gap between small and large firms with respect to digital enablers may be a necessary condition for providing better opportunities for businesses in developing countries, but as discussed, it will not be sufficient to guarantee adoption of digital technologies. Therefore, it is important to understand how and for what purposes these businesses are using digital technologies.

FIGURE 5.1 Use of Internet and Adoption of Applications of Digital Technologies Vary by Sophistication and Firm Size

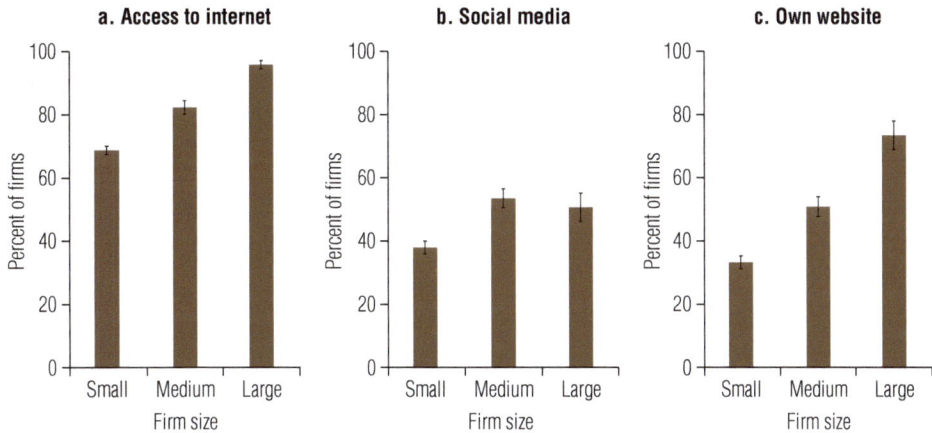

a. Access to internet   **b. Social media**   **c. Own website**

Source: Original figure based on Firm-level Adoption of Technology (FAT) survey data.

Note: Average estimates using sampling weights. Firm size refers to the number of workers: small (5–19), medium (20–99), and large (100 or more).

Digital technologies significantly reduce costs associated with searching, replication, transportation, tracking, and verification of information (Goldfarb and Tucker 2019). From this perspective, business functions comprising tasks that are intensive in processing information (such as business administration, marketing, and sales) can be expected to benefit more from digital technologies.

Indeed, the prevalence of digital technologies, defined by how many of the technologies mapped by the FAT survey are digital, varies across business functions. Figure 5.2 displays the range of digital intensity in each business function, comparing GBFs with a selected group of sector-specific business functions (SBFs). The heat map shows that GBFs are more digitally intensive than SBFs. On average, 80 percent of the technologies identified to perform GBFs are predominantly digital. Among SBFs, there are important differences between agriculture and manufacturing firms, which tend to have sophisticated digital technologies embedded in frontier technologies (such as new machines and equipment), and services, which tend to have a wider variety of digital technologies to perform each function. The important takeaway from figure 5.2 is the fact that digital technologies cannot be equated with frontier technologies for all functions of the firm, especially SBFs.

The Main Purposes for which Firms Are Using Digital Technologies

Because digital technologies tend to be embedded in/applied to more sophisticated machines and equipment in SBFs, firms' use of digital technologies tends to start through their application on GBFs (such as digital payment, online sales, and the use of

FIGURE 5.2 Digital Technology Intensity Varies across Sectors and Business Functions

Business function	GBFs	SBFs						
		Agriculture	Food processing	Apparel	Pharmacy	Retail	Finance	Transport
BF1	0.8	0.3	0.3	0.7	0.1	0.6	0.6	0.5
BF2	0.8	0.2	0.3	0.4	0.2	0.6	0.7	0.8
BF3	0.8	0.3	0.3	0.4	0.3	0.5	0.3	0.4
BF4	0.8	0.2	0.3	0.2	0.2	0.6	0.8	0.4
BF5	0.8	0.2	0.3	n.a.	0.5	0.7	0.7	0.5
BF6	0.7	0.5	n.a.	n.a.	0.6	n.a.	n.a.	n.a.
BF7	0.8	n.a.	n.a.	n.a.	n.a.	n.a.	n.a.	n.a.
Average	0.8	0.3	0.3	0.4	0.3	0.6	0.6	0.5

Source: Original figure based on Firm-level Adoption of Technology (FAT) survey questionnaire.

Note: Colors range from light green (least prevalent among technology options in the business function) to dark green (most prevalent). The values refer to the share of technologies identified as digital in that business function. In most cases, each business function has about five technologies, ranging from most basic to most sophisticated. Thus, a value of 0.8 suggests that four in five technologies identified to perform that task have a digital component, which is based on the technologies identified for the FAT questionnaire. Business functions (BFs) 1–7 refer to individual business functions associated with the general business function (GBF) or each sector-specific business function (SBF) described in the table. For example, for GBFs: business administration (BF1); planning (BF2); supply chain management (BF3); marketing (BF4); sales (BF5); payment (BF6); and quality control (BF7). For SBFs, for agriculture: land preparation (BF1); irrigation (BF2); weeding (BF3); harvesting (BF4); storage (BF5); and packaging (BF6). For food processing: input testing (BF1); cooking (BF2); antibacterial processes (BF3); packaging (BF4); and food storage (BF5). For other SBFs, see figure 1.5 in chapter 1 for agriculture, food processing, and retail, and the figures in appendix A for apparel, pharmacy, finance, and transport. n.a. = not applicable.

Excel for administrative functions).[2] As a result, digital adoption applied to GBFs constitute most technology projects supported in government-backed policies and programs aiming to promote digitalization of small and medium enterprises (SMEs). These have been the functions (such as digital administrative tools, online marketing, sales, and payment) for which rapid digital response became critical during the pandemic and for which demand for support has been greatest.

In addition to differences in the extent of digitalization between GBFs and SBFs, there is also important variation across GBFs. In part, these differences may be explained by the fact that for some of these functions (such as sales, payment, and marketing) there are significant network effects associated with the larger benefits of adopting when customers and other firms also adopt (see chapter 1). Figure 5.3 plots patterns of the likelihood of diffusion of different technologies to perform similar GBFs across firm size. These functions were more likely to be used in adjusting to the COVID-19 pandemic. The plots are similar to the diffusion curves presented in chapter 3.[3] While the use of most basic technologies, usually involving manual methods (such as hand-written methods for business administration), is in decline, the diffusion curves of digital technologies increase with firm size, and tend to have an S-shape for more sophisticated technologies. More important, some digital technologies such as enterprise resource planning (ERP) (panels a and b) seem to diffuse more rapidly than customer relationship management (CRM) (panel c) or electronic orders (panel d).

FIGURE 5.3   Some Technologies Diffuse More Rapidly than Others

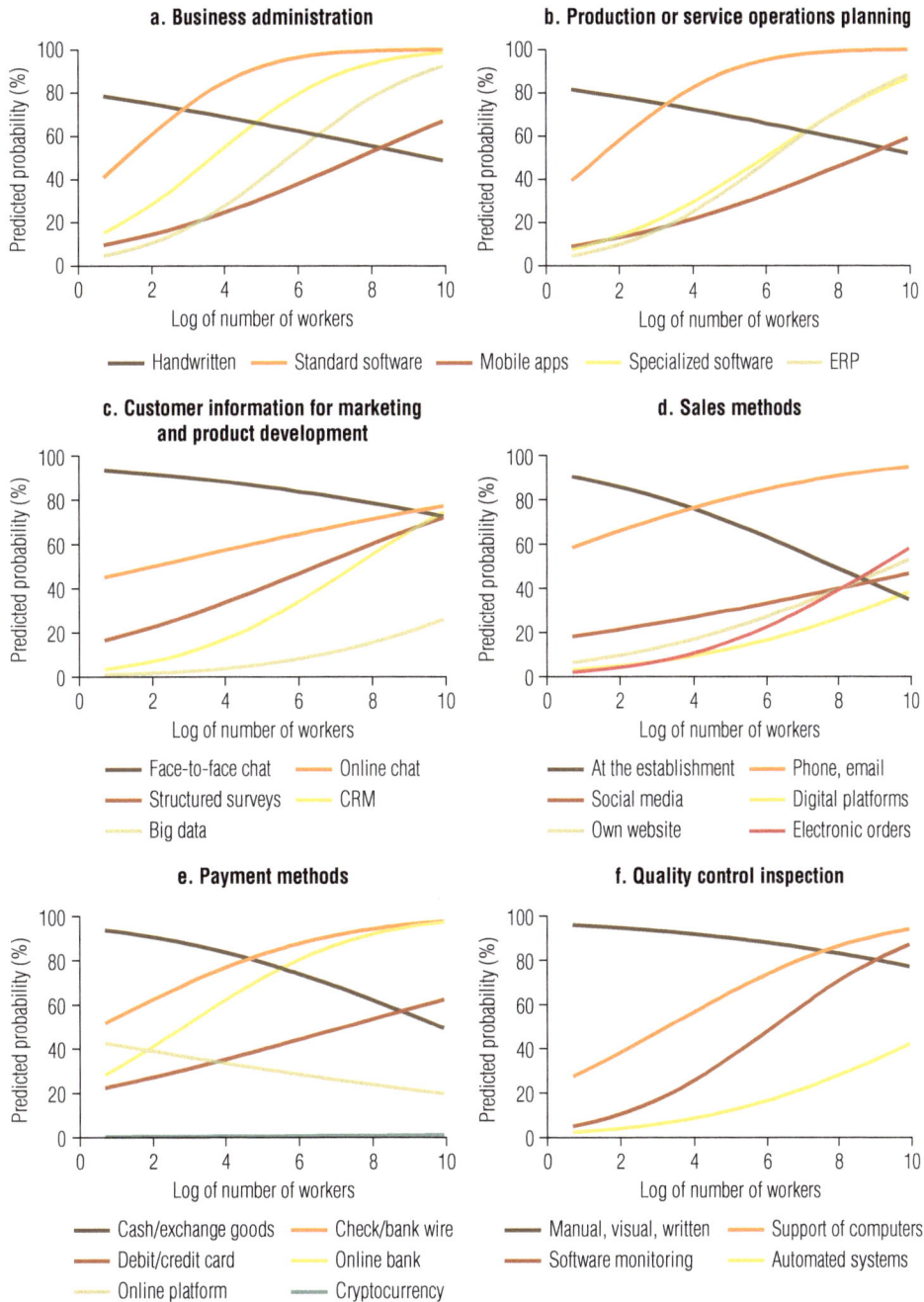

a. Business administration

b. Production or service operations planning

Legend (panels a and b): Handwritten · Standard software · Mobile apps · Specialized software · ERP

c. Customer information for marketing and product development

d. Sales methods

Legend (panel c): Face-to-face chat · Online chat · Structured surveys · CRM · Big data

Legend (panel d): At the establishment · Phone, email · Social media · Digital platforms · Own website · Electronic orders

e. Payment methods

f. Quality control inspection

Legend (panel e): Cash/exchange goods · Check/bank wire · Debit/credit card · Online bank · Online platform · Cryptocurrency

Legend (panel f): Manual, visual, written · Support of computers · Software monitoring · Automated systems

Source: Original figure based on Firm-level Adoption of Technology (FAT) survey data.

Note: The diffusion curves analyze the probability of adopting a given technology across firm size. Assuming that larger firms adopt earlier, this is a representation of the diffusion over time of specific technologies. The figures present estimates of the probability of adoption for each technology for the extensive margin (whether a technology is used or not) as a function of the log of the number of workers and age group based on a probit. For panel a, business administration includes processes related to accounting, finance, and human resources. CRM = customer relationship management; ERP = enterprise resource planning.

This can be the result of higher costs of implementation, more demanding capabilities required for implementing them, or, for the latter, the presence of network effects; integrating orders may require suppliers or buyers to also have digital systems.

An important exception is for payment methods. In this case, the diffusion patterns along firm size suggest potential leapfrogging. Panel e shows that the likelihood of small businesses adopting online platforms is higher than their likelihood of using credit or debit cards or online banking as a payment method. The likelihood of using online platforms also decreases with firm size, suggesting wide opportunity for financial technology (fintech) to enhance the diffusion to financial instruments.

Digital Platforms and the Supply of Digital Business Solutions

An important factor to understand the adoption of digital technologies is to understand the role of digital platforms and the supply of digital technologies. Digital platforms can allow access to technologies and increasing firm performance, via the sharing economy as well as access to markets and suppliers. Also, the role of the supply of digital solutions in the diffusion of digital technologies is often ignored in developing countries.[4]

The Many Roles of Platforms

Digital technologies have made firm boundaries more flexible, facilitating outsourcing of tasks in a timely and cost-effective manner (Cusolito 2021). One example is the emergence of peer-to-peer technologies, commonly known as digital platforms. These digital platforms create peer-to-peer markets (Einav, Farronato, and Levin 2016), reducing matching, search, and transaction costs between supply and demand and buyers and sellers, and allowing firms to expand their customer base and access talent globally.

More important, this significant reduction in frictions and matching costs has resulted in a reconfiguration of the boundaries of the firm. The use of digital platforms allows firms to externalize the use of some technologies, in some cases reducing the need to invest in technologies by using platform services. For example, sales and payments are often done through the platform marketplace, reducing the tasks done internally. At the same time, new tasks are adopted, increased, or outsourced. For instance, for a firm to maintain its reputation in these platforms, it may need to significantly increase its customer services. This can be accomplished by insourcing—increasing tasks and personnel in the marketing department and customer services—or by outsourcing certain services to service providers that can perform those tasks for the firm.

These double-sided platforms extend beyond the goods marketplace (such as Amazon, eBay, MercadoLibre, or Alibaba) to sharing platforms for equipment (Hello Tractor, Grab) (see chapter 3); workers and hiring (Workable, WUZZUFF); and payments (M-Pesa, Mercado Pago). More important, these platforms are not confined to advanced economies. Developing countries are also experiencing a boom in the proliferation of these platforms, which often allow the creation of new markets that either were very imperfect or simply did not exist. Consider the role of M-Pesa in Kenya in occupying and developing a financial market that was absent for the poorest segments of the population.

Platforms such as Uber facilitate work arrangements between workers and consumers through a shadow employer (Friedman 2014; Gandini 2019), while e-commerce platforms such as MercadoLibre and eBay reduce transaction costs and facilitate digitalization and market access (UNCTAD 2019), especially for small and medium-size enterprises (Jin and Hurd 2018). The results are apparent in many industries. Anderson and Magruder (2012) show that positive restaurant ratings on Yelp.com increase demand. Rivares et al. (2019) develop a proxy for platform use across four industries—hotels, restaurants, taxis, and retail trade—and find evidence of productivity gains and labor reallocation toward more productive firms in these industries. The authors also find that "aggregator" platforms are associated with higher productivity, profits, and employment of existing services firms. In contrast, more disruptive platforms that enable new entrants are associated with a decline in markups, employment, and wages of existing providers.

While much of the literature has focused on the employment effects of digital platforms in high-income countries, the COVID-19 pandemic has reinforced the critical role those digital platforms can play in the economy (see discussion later in the chapter). As an example, the pandemic has increased the number of average daily tasks/jobs posted and filled on digital platforms (Umar, Xu, and Mirza 2020).

Adopting or integrating into these platforms often requires firms to make adjustments that are different from those needed for more traditional nonplatform technologies and also present risks. Some of the obstacles to connect to these platforms are often more related to regulatory issues. Moreover, the nature of digital technologies can favor incumbents and lead to concentration of market power in the hands of a few major platforms. In addition, platforms have used their intermediary role to take over firms in "adjacent" subsectors and extend their activities into nondigital industries as they become increasingly digitalized. These expansions are driven by economies of scope from owning large amounts of data.

Digital Solutions

Accelerating businesses' digital transformation requires strengthening the links of the nondigital sector with the growth of the digital sector, and the opening of new market opportunities.[5] This includes ensuring that, on the supply side, digital entrepreneurs, platforms, and sectors can grow, providing digital solutions to nondigital business.

Thus, understanding the supply side of digital technologies is important to foster digitalization. In an effort to evaluate how the two forces are playing out, the World Bank has built a global database of 200,000 investment-ready technology solution firms in 190 countries (the digital business database), drawing from three different data sources (CB Insights, PitchBook, Briter Bridges) and cross-checked with national economic censuses when possible (Zhu et al., forthcoming). This data set allows examination of whether there is evidence regarding: (1) the existence of a digital growth pathway in developing countries; (2) the digital divide between developed and developing countries; and (3) the digital market structure in both developed and developing countries and the tendency toward conglomeration.

A first glance at the data confirms that building economies of scope and network effects constitute key digital development pathways. This finding has implications for how to incentivize traditional firms to enter digital platforms—or incorporate data-intensive solutions if no network effects exist yet. This means that to identify market and government failures, the unit of analysis relevant for policy interventions for technology adoption will likely have to include market-level analysis that yields a better understanding of the dynamics of competition between firms and the vertical integration of digital services. For example, if a seller's incentive to adopt a digital platform depends on how many other sellers and buyers are already using the platform, or whether a digital payment and fulfillment/logistics services exist, there is a need to evaluate digital market policies that enable the trusted use and scaling of online commerce so more users and firms are crowded in. These policies could include e-transaction laws, online consumer and supplier protection, and industry data policies that allow data-driven market intelligence to be shared with sellers and customers.

Another key opportunity to drive technology adoption by leveraging supply-side interventions is to incentivize local digital solution firms to design tailored business-to-business (B2B) solutions that match local user needs, skills level, language(s), and infrastructure endowments. A breakdown in the digital business database by subsector in the number of digital solution firms and investment flows to these firms shows that developing countries are generally catching up with consumer-facing digital solutions such as e-commerce and fintech, but less so on B2B solutions. Incentivizing local firms to develop B2B products tailored for local needs can not only increase supply but also provide more technology options for traditional businesses that fit their specific needs, lowering barriers to adoption.

New analysis based on the Enlyft database of digital technologies used by firms in developing countries shows that the supply of digital technologies is moderately to highly concentrated across all segments in all regions.[6] Each digital technology market segment typically has two providers that make up more than half the segment, with one major company typically serving 30 percent to 40 percent of the market. The most concentrated product segment is "intelligence and analytics." Google is the major provider in all regions through its web analytics services. Concentrations are also high across all regions in other market segments that are key for job growth as shown by the FAT survey—such CRM and ERP. Google holds the largest share of marketing/CRM, and SAP holds the largest share of ERP across all regions (figure 5.4).

Market concentration and winner-takes-most dynamics in supply-side markets may have implications for the exercise of market power, and therefore for market outcomes such as access and affordability. They also raise the risk of anticompetitive

FIGURE 5.4 Market Concentration Poses a Challenge for the Supply of Digital Business Solutions

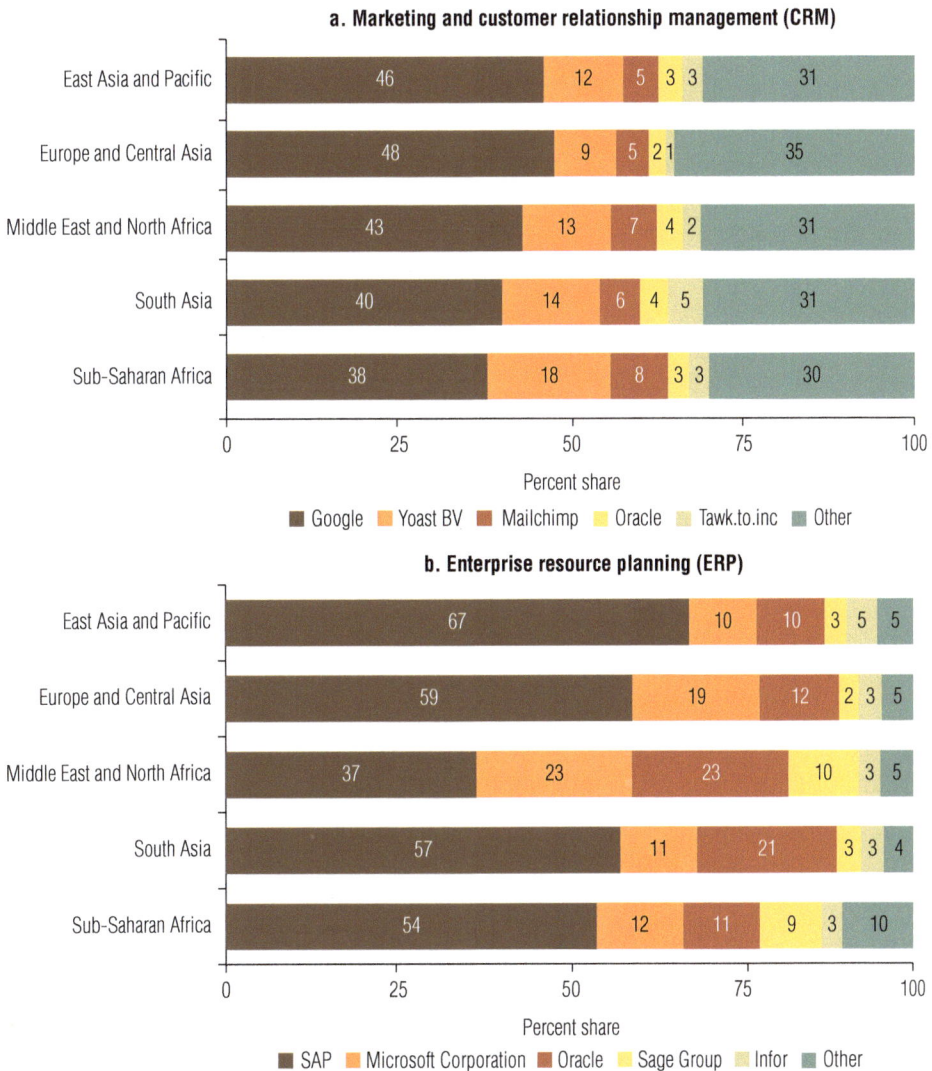

a. Marketing and customer relationship management (CRM)

Region	Google	Yoast BV	Mailchimp	Oracle	Tawk.to.inc	Other
East Asia and Pacific	46	12	5	3	3	31
Europe and Central Asia	48	9	5	2	1	35
Middle East and North Africa	43	13	7	4	2	31
South Asia	40	14	6	4	5	31
Sub-Saharan Africa	38	18	8	3	3	30

Percent share

■ Google ■ Yoast BV ■ Mailchimp ■ Oracle ■ Tawk.to.inc ■ Other

b. Enterprise resource planning (ERP)

Region	SAP	Microsoft Corporation	Oracle	Sage Group	Infor	Other
East Asia and Pacific	67	10	10	3	5	5
Europe and Central Asia	59	19	12	2	3	5
Middle East and North Africa	37	23	23	10	3	5
South Asia	57	11	21	3	3	4
Sub-Saharan Africa	54	12	11	9	3	10

Percent share

■ SAP ■ Microsoft Corporation ■ Oracle ■ Sage Group ■ Infor ■ Other

Source: Nyman and Ukhaneva, forthcoming.

Note: Data are not available for Latin America and the Caribbean.

practices by suppliers of digital solutions (such as collusion and abuse of dominance) that can raise prices, restrict access, or lower quality and innovation in solutions. Exclusionary abuse of dominance can also restrict potential competitors in supply-side markets from entering or expanding and thus limit innovation in products provided. A database compiled recently by the World Bank found more than 100 finalized antitrust cases involving digital platforms. Nearly 40 percent of those are in developing countries. Meanwhile, antitrust scrutiny in other digital markets is steadily increasing. For instance, the European Commission is currently investigating SAP over allegedly abusing its dominance in the ERP market by preventing users from switching to other vendors or connecting to competitors' applications.

Further research is needed on the question of how these supply-side market dynamics affect technology adoption by firms. In some cases, pricing of digital technologies may play a lesser role in firms' adoption compared to other types of inputs because a number of digital solutions are provided at no cost or at a low price to the user, and free open-source solutions are readily available. After digital technologies provided by Google and Microsoft, the next most popular choice for digital technologies overall are open-source systems (such as WordPress, PHP, and Apache). Together they provide 14 percent of all technologies in Sub-Saharan Africa, and 11 percent to 12 percent in other regions. Smaller firms are more likely than their larger counterparts to use these open-source technologies. The share of Apache and PHP (Hypertext Preprocessor) used by small firms is twice the share used by large firms. At the same time, it is possible that even if market power does not result in higher prices it may manifest in a lack of incentives to develop products targeted to smaller firms, developing countries, or niche markets.

Technology and Resilience

Technology is central to resilience to different shocks. Previous findings suggest that firms with more diversified technologies are less subject to the impact of shocks such as natural disasters (Hsu et al. 2018) or overall external shocks (Koren and Tenreyro 2013). The COVID-19 pandemic put those findings to the test. The discussion that follows uses granular data from both the FAT survey and the World Bank Business Pulse Survey (BPS) to investigate the role that digital technologies, in particular, can play in helping firms weather shocks.[7]

The discussion examines the role of digital readiness—whether firms that used more sophisticated digital tools before a shock fare better during and after a shock. In the case of the COVID-19 pandemic, firms with a high level of digital readiness performed better, regardless of the extent and type of their digital response during the pandemic. This finding also has implications for firms' adjustment to climate change. Firms' adoption of green technologies to adapt to and mitigate climate change is examined at the end of this section.

Digital Responses to Adjust to the COVID-19 Pandemic

The COVID-19 pandemic was unique in imposing both supply shocks (associated with measures to stop the pandemic, including restrictions that limited worker mobility, curtailed or shut down operations on premises, and created supply chain bottlenecks) and simultaneous demand shocks (stemming from restrictions on consumer mobility and job losses), while being both sudden and worldwide. Businesses were plunged into stress around the world.

The negative impact of the COVID-19 pandemic on sales has been large and widespread across firms. Results from the BPS show that about 84 percent of firms on average, across more than 60 countries, reported a reduction in sales, compared to the same period in the previous year, at the early stage of the pandemic (Apedo-Amah et al. 2020). While the biggest impact of the COVID-19 crisis occurred during the initial shock in March and April 2020, the drop in sales was persistently large even 10 weeks later. The drop in sales was particularly significant for microenterprises and small firms, compared to medium and larger businesses. By the end of 2020, firms started to recover (Cirera et al. 2021), but for a large share of firms the negative change in sales persisted (figure 5.5).[8]

FIGURE 5.5 The Large Drop in Sales at the Beginning of the COVID-19 Pandemic Persisted for Many Firms, and the Loss Was Greater for Microenterprises and Small Firms

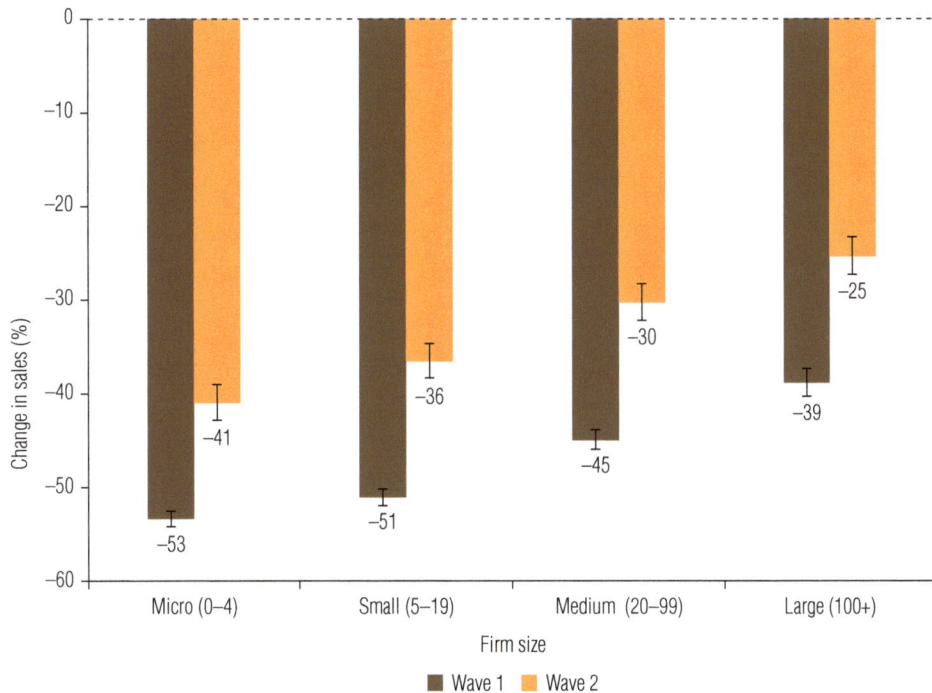

Source: Business Pulse Survey (BPS) data based on Avalos et al., forthcoming.
Note: Wave 1 and Wave 2 refer to different rounds of the BPS. Firm size is defined in terms of number of workers.

COVID-19 as an Unprecedented Driver of Digital Adoption

A significant amount of anecdotal evidence suggests that the COVID-19 shock led to an unprecedented increase in the demand for digital technologies. Despite the lack of historical data to address this question, data on online shopping trends and the BPS data provide some evidence that reinforces the large increase in digitalization during the pandemic. First, there was a sharp spike in the interest for digital solutions. Google trend indexes in different languages for measuring "online shopping" suggest that interest in the use of digital technologies for this purpose reached an historical peak around the time that further restrictions on mobility were adopted in response to the pandemic (figure 5.6, panel a). Second, there was a significant increase in the share of firms that started using digital technologies in response to COVID-19, as well as firms that increased their use of technologies, in both developing and high-income countries (panel b). While a larger share of firms in high-income countries use digital technologies, almost 40 percent were already using and did not increase during the pandemic, while in developing countries 20 percent started using digital tools during the pandemic.

A more detailed examination of the type of digital investments shows that firms are going digital across different dimensions. Cross-country data for more than 60 countries suggest that around 45 percent of firms started or increased the use of digital platforms in response to the pandemic; 44 percent used online sales; 28 percent invested in digital solutions; and 23 percent increased telecommuting, allowing employees to work remotely (figure 5.7).[9] Comparing the BPS data for firms in which a panel is available with two rounds of the BPS suggests that the probability of starting or increasing the use of digital technologies in response to the COVID-19 shock continuously increased over time across different firm size groups. Although the gap between large and small firms in the digital response has shrunk, it has persisted as the shock has continued.

Among firms that started or increased the use of digital technologies in response to the pandemic, there is also large variation in the business functions they digitalized. Digital responses by firms were largely concentrated among functions related to customer relations. Specifically, 64 percent of firms increased digitalization in marketing, 55 percent in sales, 52 percent used it for internal tasks (such as business administration), and 37 percent in payment (figure 5.8). Overall, among firms that have adopted digital technologies in response to the pandemic, external functions (sales, marketing, payment) have become more digitalized. This is consistent with the severity of the demand shock. Another 34 percent used it only for external purposes, while around 10 percent used it only for internal tasks.

A Widening Digital Divide

Despite the opportunities generated by an increasing demand for digitalization, there is also the risk of widening the digital divide. The push for digitalization associated with the pandemic and the intensification of digitalization have not been equal across firms, sectors, and countries.

FIGURE 5.6 **Demand for Digital Solutions Increased Greatly in Response to the COVID-19 Pandemic**

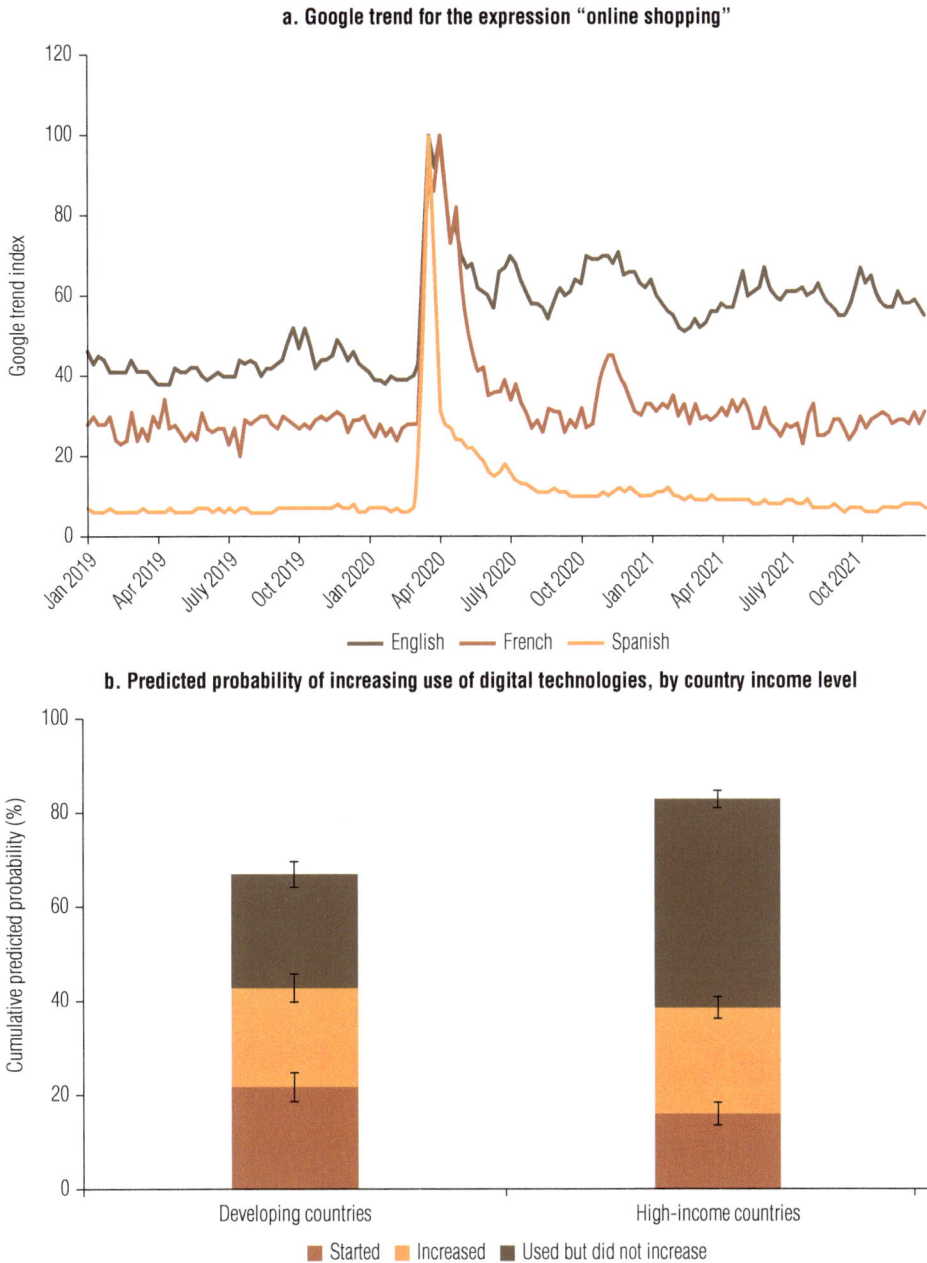

a. Google trend for the expression "online shopping"

b. Predicted probability of increasing use of digital technologies, by country income level

Sources: Google trend data and World Bank Business Pulse Survey (BPS) data.

Note: Panel a shows the trend for the expression "online shopping" in English, French, and Spanish. Panel b shows the estimated share of firms that started or increased the use of digital technologies in response to the COVID-19 pandemic, as well as the share of firms that used digital technology before COVID-19 but did not increase the use in response to the shock, by income group.

FIGURE 5.7   A Large Share of Businesses Digitalized during the COVID-19 Pandemic

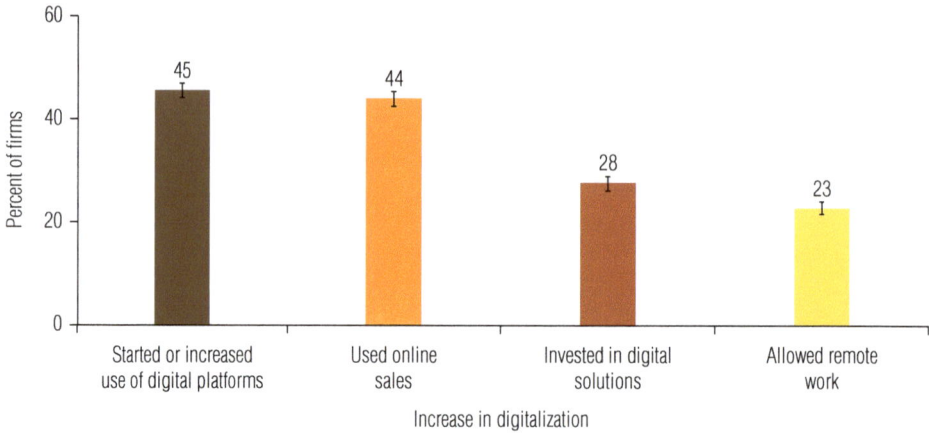

Source: Business Pulse Survey (BPS) data based on Avalos et al., forthcoming.

FIGURE 5.8   Among Firms That Used and Invested in Digital Technologies, Investments in Digitalizing External, Customer-Related Functions Dominated

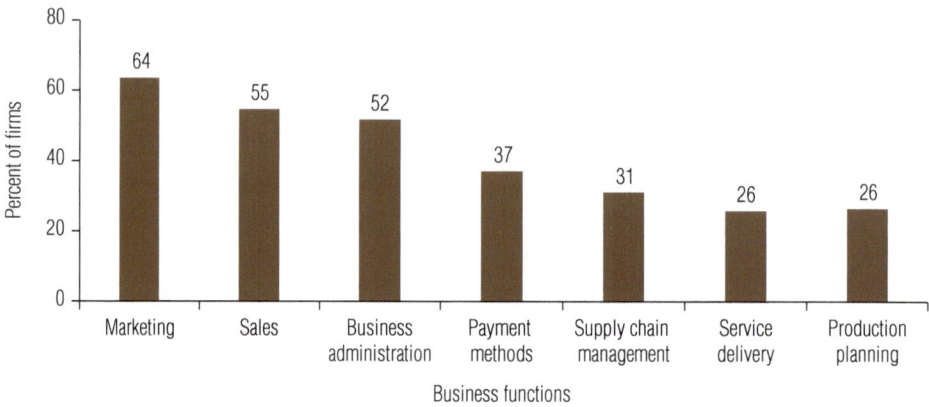

Source: Business Pulse Survey (BPS) data based on Avalos et al., forthcoming.
Note: Percentages are conditional on firms using digital platforms.

There are significant differences in the use and increase of digital tools across countries (figure 5.9), and this variation is not explained by country income. Firms in some countries in Africa and Latin America have responded with widespread digital investments, while some other countries in Europe and Central Asia have shown a lower digital response. Part of this regional composition may be related to the fact that firms in some European countries were already using digital technologies and did not need to start or increase the use of digital technologies. Nevertheless, figure 5.9 shows that differences across countries and regions in firms responding to the pandemic are quite heterogenous.

At the firm level, the gap between small and large firms has persisted during the pandemic in the use of digital solutions and investment (figure 5.10), as well as in

FIGURE 5.9 There Is Large Variation across Countries in the Use of Digital Technologies to Respond to the COVID-19 Pandemic

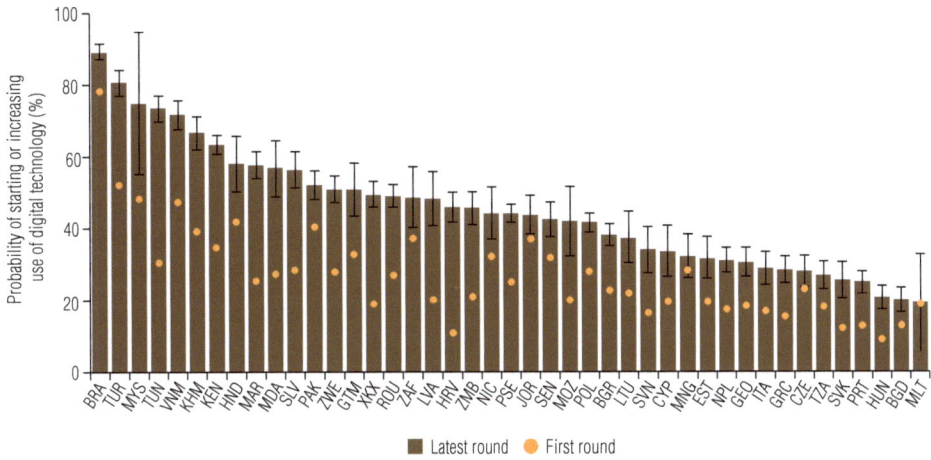

Source: Business Pulse Survey (BPS) data based on Avalos et al., forthcoming.

Note: Results from probit estimates controlling for country, firm size, sector, severity of the shock from mobility restrictions, and their interactions with the wave. Results are weighted by the inverse of the number of observations by country-wave. Results are at means of the sample (bar chart) in the latest round and depicted by orange dots in the first round of data collection in the country. Country labels use International Organization of Standardization (ISO) country codes. Results for Brazil are based on one state—São Paulo—which likely overestimates the results.

FIGURE 5.10 Smaller Firms Have Used and Invested Less in Digital Solutions

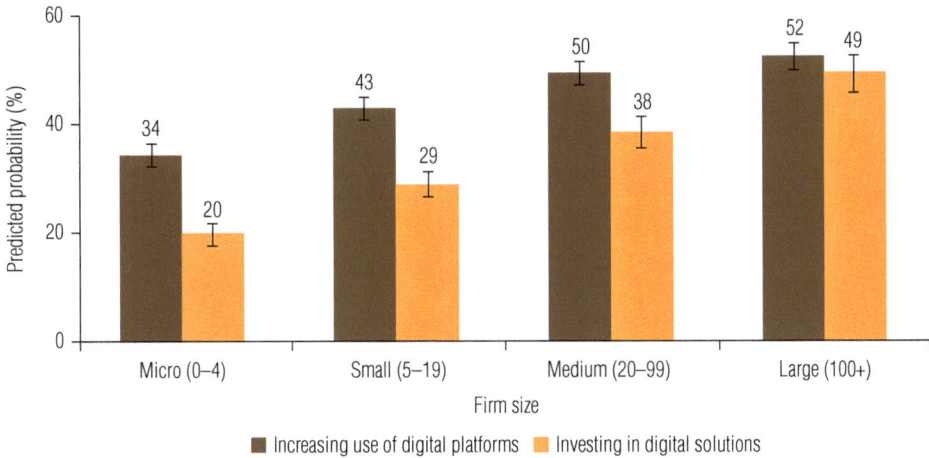

Source: Business Pulse Survey (BPS) data based on Avalos et al., forthcoming.

Note: Results from probit controlling for country, firm size, sector, severity of the shock from mobility restrictions, and their interactions with the wave. Results are weighted by the inverse of the number of observations by country-wave. Firm size is defined in terms of number of workers.

online sales and home-based work. Even if COVID-19 led to a significant response from micro and small firms by starting and increasing the use of digital technologies, because there was a large digital divide before the pandemic, the digital gap by firm size might be increasing, particularly in the intensive margin. Therefore, to better understand this process it is important to analyze this gap by taking into consideration the level of digital technology sophistication used by firms (digital readiness) before the pandemic.

This gap in the digital responses to COVID-19 between small and large firms observed using the BPS data is also consistent with the digital gap observed using the FAT data (before the pandemic). This persistence in the gap should not come as a surprise, and it reinforces the hypothesis that "digital readiness" before the pandemic was a key factor driving the capacity of firms to respond to the COVID-19 shock through the use of more digital technologies. Figure 5.11, based on BPS data across several countries, shows that digital readiness is strongly associated with the likelihood that firms increased the use of digital technologies or invested in digital solutions.

FIGURE 5.11   The Probability of a Digital Response to the COVID-19 Pandemic Is Larger for Firms That Were Digitally Ready before the Pandemic

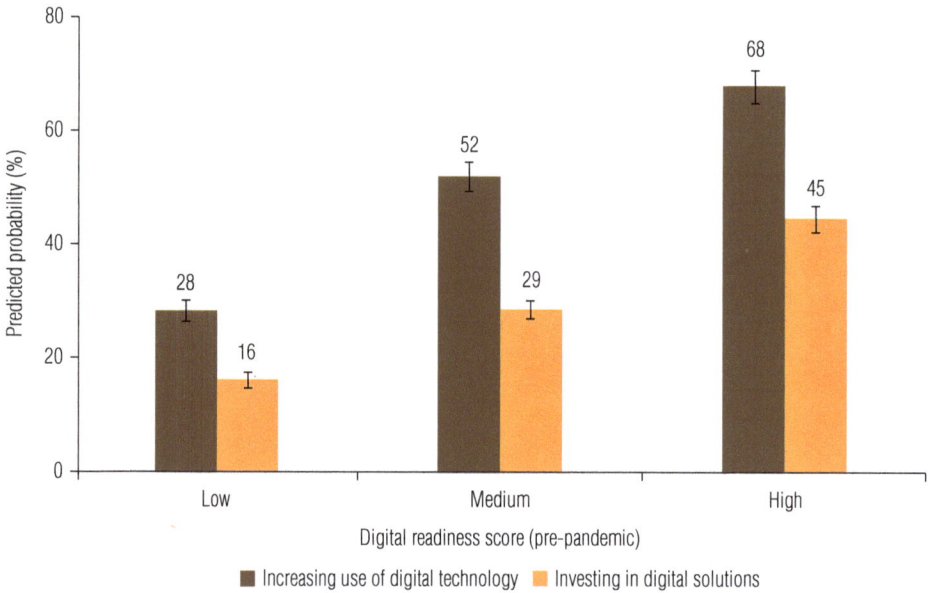

Source: Business Pulse Survey (BPS) data based on Avalos et al., forthcoming.

Note: Results from probit estimates controlling for country, firm size, sector, severity of the shock from mobility restrictions, and their interactions with the wave. Results are weighted by the inverse of the number of observations by country-wave. Firm size is defined in terms of number of workers. The digital readiness score is based on four questions included in the BPS to measure digital readiness before COVID-19: (1) use of online sales and/or digital payment; (2) use of online tools for marketing and product development; (3) use of customer or supplier relationship management (CRM or SRM); (4) use of enterprise resource planning (ERP) for business administration. The digital readiness groups sort firms by the number of digital technologies used: either low (0 technologies); medium (1 or 2 technologies); or high (3 or 4 technologies). This is a simplified version of the questions extracted from the Firm-level Adoption of Technology (FAT) survey and incorporated into the BPS.

Technology Readiness and Resilience to the COVID-19 Shock

These results lead to the key question of how the use of digital technologies affected firm performance during the pandemic. Many factors might explain differences across firms.[10] As discussed, digital technologies played an important role, allowing firms to reach out to consumers during closures and to reduce the impacts of restrictions to mobility in the management of the business. Recent evidence on the increased use of digital technologies in response to the pandemic suggests that the pandemic increased the returns to digitalization (Apedo-Amah et al. 2020; Van Reenen and Valero 2021; Bellmann et al. 2021).

Firms that increased their use of digital technologies (or invested) did have better sales performance, regardless of their level of digital readiness before the pandemic (figure 5.12). Yet, the results also show that firms with a high level of digital readiness—that is, firms that used more sophisticated digital tools before the pandemic—performed better, regardless of the extent and type of their digital response during the pandemic. Because digital readiness also triggered a greater likelihood of increasing the digital response during the pandemic, it is important to disentangle the direct effects (from digital technologies in place before the pandemic) and indirect effects (via increasing adoption) of technology readiness.

FIGURE 5.12   Sales Fell Less during the COVID-19 Pandemic for Firms That Increased the Use of and/or Investment in Digital Technologies during the Pandemic

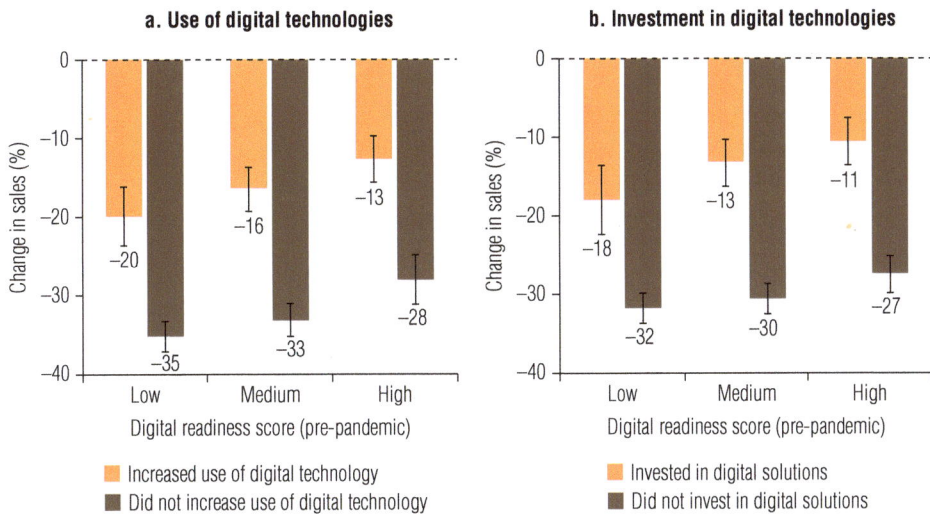

Source: Business Pulse Survey (BPS) data based on Avalos et al., forthcoming.

Note: Results from ordinary least squares regression controlling for country, firm size, sector, severity of the shock from mobility restrictions, and their interactions with the survey wave. Results are weighted by the inverse of the number of observations by country-wave. The digital readiness score is based on four questions included in the BPS to measure digital readiness before COVID-19: (1) use of online sales and/or digital payment; (2) use of online tools for marketing and product development; (3) use of customer or supplier relationship management (CRM or SRM); (4) use of enterprise resource planning (ERP) for business administration. The digital readiness groups sort firms by number of digital technologies used: either low (0 technologies); medium (1 or 2 technologies); or high (3 or 4 technologies). This is a simplified version of the questions extracted from the Firm-level Adoption of Technology (FAT) survey and incorporated into the BPS.

The Indirect and Direct Effects of Technology Sophistication before the Pandemic
To investigate the impact of technology on the performance during the pandemic, Comin et al. (2022) combine information on digital adoption by firms before and after the COVID-19 shock. They use data from Brazil, Senegal, and Vietnam for which granular measures of technology readiness before the pandemic are available from the FAT survey, and information on digital response and firm performance during the pandemic available from the BPS. The analysis quantifies the direct and indirect effects of technology sophistication before the pandemic using the treatment effect mediation framework first developed by Baron and Kenny (1986) and more recently detailed in Imai, Keele, and Yamamoto (2010) and Celli (2022).

More sophisticated businesses, for example, could better plan production adequately to reduce potential supply chain bottlenecks, or more quickly switch to home-based work (direct effect). Similarly, more sophisticated firms could more easily adopt additional technology and transition into digital platforms to sell their products online and reduce the impact of lower consumer mobility (indirect effect).

Firms with higher levels of technology before the pandemic were significantly more likely to start using or increase their use of digital technologies during the COVID-19 crisis. In line with the previous results, the analysis—using much more granular measures of technology sophistication from the FAT survey—shows that, on average, a change in one unit of increase in the GBF technology index (intensive margin) amounts to a 17 percentage point increase in the likelihood of starting or increasing the use of digital technologies in response to COVID-19, yielding a statistically significant coefficient (see figure 5.13).[11] Moreover, the likelihood of adopting additional digital solutions to respond to the crisis increases with technology sophistication. While businesses in the second quintile of technology sophistication were 25 percentage points more likely to start or increase the use of digital solutions than the bottom 20 percent, the additional likelihood for businesses in the third, fourth, and fifth quintiles is at least 35 percentage points.

Digital readiness helped firms become more resilient during the pandemic. The direct impact of technology sophistication before the pandemic on sales is significantly larger than the indirect effect through the adoption of digital solutions (figure 5.14). Both direct and indirect effects on sales are positive and their magnitude increases with pre-pandemic technology sophistication. The resulting total effect averages 6.5 percentage points (3.8 percentage points for an increase of one standard deviation in technology sophistication), and ranges from 5 percentage points when comparing businesses in the second quintile to those in the bottom 20 percent, to almost 14 percentage points for businesses in the fifth quintile. The direct effect accounts for most of the impact of technology sophistication before the pandemic, as shown in figure 5.14, because the impact of additional technology adoption on sales (6.6 percentage points, on average) is mediated by an estimated probability of additional adoption that

FIGURE 5.13 **Firms' Likelihood of Adopting Additional Digital Solutions to Respond to the COVID-19 Crisis Increased with Technology Sophistication**

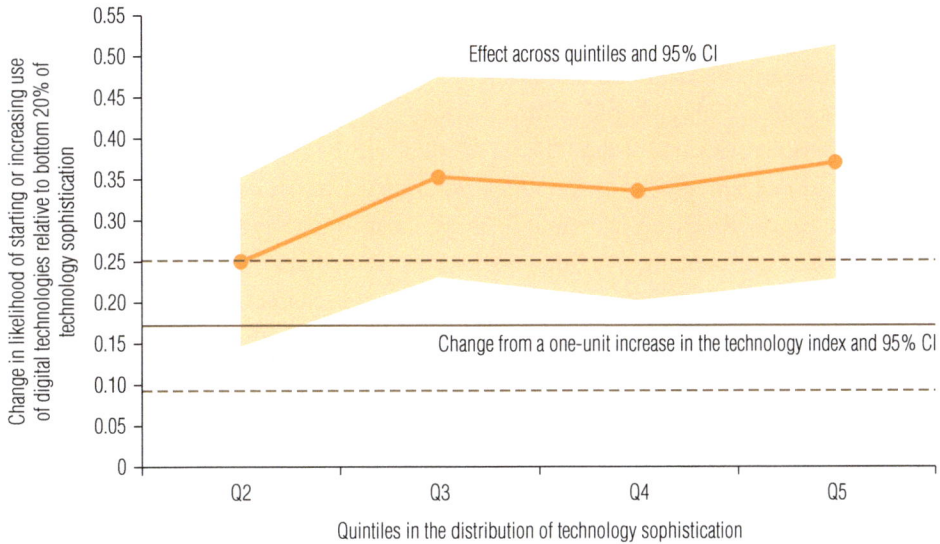

Source: Comin et al. 2022.

Note: The dots show the estimated average effect of the probability of increasing use of technology as a response to the pandemic across quintiles of the distribution from low (Q2) to most advanced (Q5) technology sophistication, relative to the most basic (Q1) technology sophistication. CI = confidence interval.

FIGURE 5.14 **The Direct Effect of Technology Readiness before the COVID-19 Pandemic Is Much Larger than the Indirect Effect on the Change in Sales during the Pandemic**

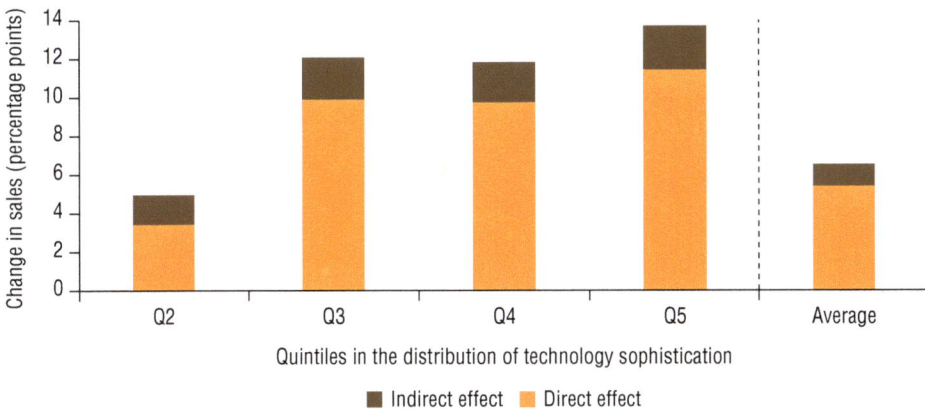

Source: Comin et al. 2022.

Note: The figure shows the estimates of the direct and indirect effects of technology before the pandemic on the percentage change in sales following the treatment effect mediator framework, as described in Comin et al. (2022). The columns show the estimations across quintiles of the distribution from low (Q2) to the most advanced (Q5) technology sophistication, in relation to the most basic (Q1). The last column shows the total effect for the full sample.

increases with technology sophistication but averages only 37 percent among the most sophisticated firms.

The Types of Digital Solutions that Helped during the Pandemic

These results are consistent across different types of digital solutions. In calculating the effects of technology sophistication before the pandemic, Comin et al. (2022) combine several measures of digital adoption during the crisis into a single indicator. The indicator comprises any of the following: starting to use or increasing the use of digital solutions; investing in new digital solutions; reporting a higher fraction of sales online; and reporting a higher fraction of workers working from home. Figure 5.15 shows the effects for the direct and indirect effects using each potential type of digital response as an indirect channel for realizing the effect of technology sophistication. The total effect remains close to 6.5 percentage points when the response is the additional use of digital platforms or the new investment in equipment, software, or digital solutions. When the response is more home-based work, the effect increases by 1 percentage point, and by nearly 2 percentage points when the response is a higher share of online sales.

FIGURE 5.15 The Direct and Indirect Effects of Digital Readiness Are Consistent across Different Types of Digital Solutions

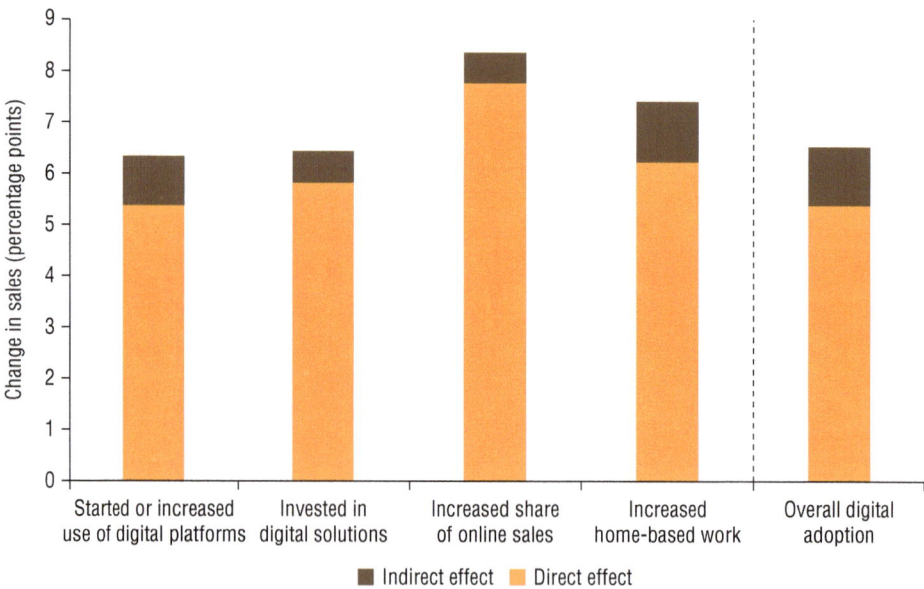

Source: Comin et al. 2022.

Note: The figure shows the estimates of the direct and indirect effects of technology before the pandemic on the percentage change in sales following the treatment effect mediator framework, as described in Comin et al. (2022), across different types of digital responses.

Technology as an Engine of Resilience to Adapt to and Mitigate Climate Shocks

Looking forward, some of the greatest and potentially most damaging global shocks may arise from climate change. Estimates of the impact of climate shocks suggest a significant negative and tangible impact already occurring in the past few decades. In low-income countries, a one-degree Celsius increase in temperature is associated with a reduction in economic growth by 1.3 percentage points (Dell, Jones, and Olken 2012). Rising temperatures have large negative impacts on agriculture and industrial value added, not only on output levels but also on growth. Plant-level estimates for China suggest that industrial output could decrease between 3 percent to 36 percent under the slowest scenario of temperature increases (Chen and Yang 2019). The effects are also important in other sectors beyond agriculture such as retail and tourism. Hsiang (2010) estimates that a one-degree Celsius increase in the Caribbean and Central America could result in a loss of output of 6.1 percent in retail, restaurants, and hotels and 4.2 percent in mining. These effects are similar in magnitude to the adverse effects of rising temperatures on labor productivity. Excessive heat causes physical discomfort and fatigue; affects cognitive functioning (Hancock, Ross, and Szalma 2007); increases workplace injuries (Park, Pankratz, and Behrer 2021); and reduces productivity (Seppanen, Fisk, and Lei 2006).

Minimizing the impact of these climate shocks requires adopting new technologies. On the one hand, adaptation to climate shocks—such as rising temperatures, drought, fire, cyclones, and flooding—requires technologies that account in real time to adjust to weather changes in agriculture, reduce excess temperature in premises, and minimize sourcing risks in supply chains for manufacturing and services. On the other hand, mitigation efforts require greener and more energy-efficient production, especially in the context of increasing energy prices and other geopolitical shocks.

Regarding adaptation to climate change, the FAT data show that most firms do not use supplier relationship management (SRM) software that can allow more flexibility in managing the supply chain in the event of climate or other shocks (see figure 2.7 in chapter 2). In fact, only 20 percent of firms in the sample, and less than 10 percent of medium and small firms, used SRM systems. Similarly, for agriculture, precision agriculture that can support higher yields during climate shocks by improving land preparation, irrigation, or weeding is only used in more advanced firms in Brazil, Kenya, and the Republic of Korea (see figure 2.8 in chapter 2). Most firms lag in the adoption of certain technologies that can help adapt to the impact of climate shocks and rising temperatures.

Recently collected data for 1,800 firms in Georgia expand the FAT survey questionnaire to include some information on green management practices and green technologies. Panel a of figure 5.16 shows the percentage of firms that use a set of energy-efficient practices and technologies. On average, most firms do not use any of these practices. Energy-efficient lighting and having VAC/HVAC (variable air volume/ heating, ventilation, and air conditioning) systems are the most used technologies, and have been adopted by almost 40 percent of firms, but very few firms use energy-efficient equipment, programmable thermostats, or sensors connected to the Internet of Things (IoT). Panel b presents another example: the use of sustainable practices in retail. The picture is similar, and adoption of retail sustainability practices is still incipient, with the exception of use of recyclable materials for packaging and considering sustainability when sourcing products. Overall, figure 5.16 shows a picture of very limited adoption of green technologies and practices for climate mitigation.

A critical question for climate mitigation is related to how adoption of general and sector-specific technologies is associated with adoption of green technologies. In other words, are firms using more sophisticated technologies for SBFs or GBFs also using more efficient energy and green practices and technologies? Energy efficiency can have significant effects on productivity. For instance, energy-efficient LED lighting increased productivity on hot days in Indian manufacturing plants, in addition to reducing energy costs (Adhvaryu, Kala, and Nyshadham 2020). Figure 5.17 shows the correlation between the FAT technology index and the adoption of energy-efficiency practices, based on the recently collected FAT data in Georgia. More technologically sophisticated firms, for both general and sector-specific business functions, tend to use more energy-efficient technologies. There may be some complementarities in adoption via the knowledge accumulated in the firm and a potential reduction in costs to adopt these

FIGURE 5.16   Adoption of Green Practices Is at a Very Early Stage in Georgia

a. Energy-efficiency practices and technologies | b. Retail sustainability practices

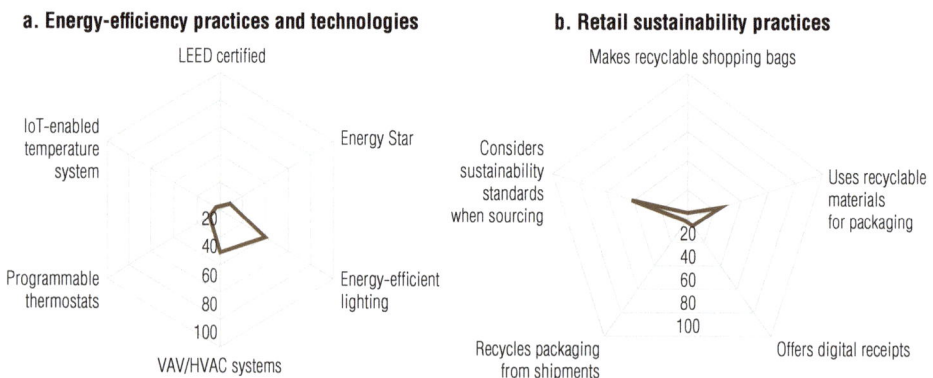

Source: Original figure based on the Firm-level Adoption of Technology (FAT) survey for Georgia.

Note: Panel a: Percentage of firms that use: LEED (Leadership in Energy and Environmental Design) certified; Energy Star/efficiency rated equipment; energy-efficient lighting (LED light-emitting diode/CFL compact fluorescent lamps); VAV (variable air volume)/HVAC (heating, ventilation, and air conditioning) systems; programmable thermostats, timers, robots, and motion sensors; Internet of Things (IoT)-enabled systems to control premises temperature, lighting system, and/or refrigeration units. Panel b: Percentage of firms in retail using the following sustainability retail practices: makes recyclable shopping bags; uses recyclable materials for packaging; offers digital receipts; recycles packaging from shipments; considers sustainability standards when sourcing products.

Bridging the Technological Divide

FIGURE 5.17 There Is a Positive Correlation between Technology Sophistication and Use of Energy-Efficient Technologies in Georgia

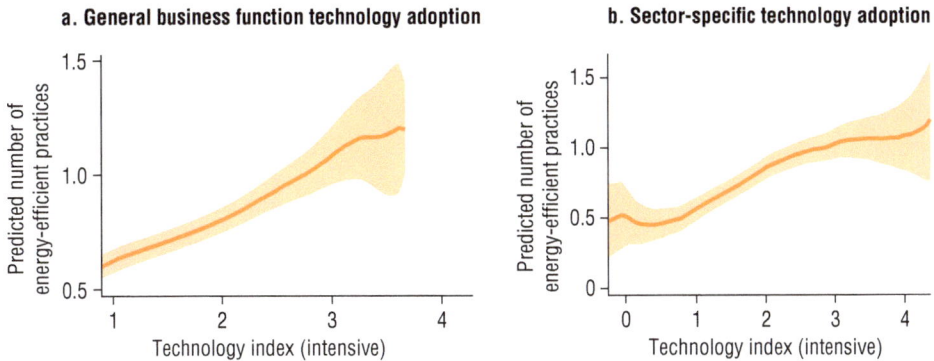

a. General business function technology adoption

b. Sector-specific technology adoption

Source: Original figure based on the Firm-level Adoption of Technology (FAT) survey for Georgia.

Note: The technology indexes used in panels a and b refer to the intensive margin, which captures the most widely used technology across business functions. The y-axis measures the number of energy-efficient technologies and practices used by the firm.

additional technologies. It also suggests that some of the barriers and drivers of technology adoption between "green" and "nongreen" technologies may be similar. More and better data are needed to measure and identify these complementarities, but there is a clear need to understand green technologies from the perspective of the firm and how the dynamics of adoption relate to the drivers and obstacles that other technologies face (see the next chapter) and what obstacles and drivers are specific to green technologies.

Summing Up

This chapter has described some key features of how digital technologies are used by firms and has illustrated the important role they can play by helping firms be more resilient to economic, health, and environmental shocks. It has also highlighted the importance of having an adequate supply of digital solutions, and the potential benefits of platforms to outsource certain tasks and the use of technologies. The potential benefits, however, come at the expense of some risk of market dominance of platforms and suppliers of digital solutions. Demand-side digital policies need to consider ways to ensure the quality and affordability of supply of these digital solutions and the role played by platforms.

Digital technologies provided firms with much-needed flexibility during the restrictions implemented to stop the COVID-19 pandemic, and those firms that were digitally "ready" before the pandemic experienced a lower drop in sales and were more likely to invest in more digital solutions. But the chapter also highlights the risks of an increasing digital divide across firms. Mitigating the risks of this growing technology gap requires removing existing barriers to adoption. The fact that firms in Brazil, Senegal, and Vietnam that were already more prepared with higher levels of technologies, particularly digital technologies, before the pandemic were significantly more likely to accelerate adoption during the pandemic suggests that existing barriers may be persistent. These barriers are explored in detail in the next chapter, but include issues related to the lack of managerial capabilities, uncertainty, and limited access to markets. Many of these conditions have deteriorated disproportionally for small and female-led businesses during the pandemic, which is further widening the digital divide.

The pandemic has increased the awareness about digital technologies and the incentives to digitalize. As a result, governments and business-support organizations are intensifying the use of policy instruments to promote digital adoption and upgrading (see chapter 7). A recent survey conducted by the World Bank of public programs supporting businesses in Kenya shows that many of these programs have adjusted the services they provide by increasing support to digital solutions (Cruz and Hernandez 2022). About 48 percent of the programs that existed before the pandemic reported that they have started to offer or have expanded their offer of training and technical support related to digital solutions. Similarly, management extension services in countries such as Brazil are experiencing a shift of demand toward digital upgrading programs, and new programs are being created to tailor to the needs of SMEs in this area. These programs combine the provision of information with technical assistance, and are taking advantage of greater interest among SMEs for technology upgrading. Policy makers should seize the opportunity to accelerate and complete the digital transformation of SMEs. To do so, they need to understand the main barriers and obstacles to technology adoption. That is the objective of the next chapter.

Finally, the chapter has emphasized the central role of technology adoption to support adaptation to and mitigation of climate shocks, and the need to understand the adoption of green technologies from the perspective of the firm and the drivers of and barriers to their adoption, and their complementarities with other technologies.

Notes

1. The digital presence in sector-specific business technologies is usually different, especially for agriculture and manufacturing, where digital technologies are usually embedded in more sophisticated machinery and equipment that are, in most cases, frontier technologies.
2. The data show that small firms, which are on average later adopters of new technologies than large firms, are significantly more likely to adopt digital technologies applied to GBFs than SBFs, on average.
3. The assumption behind building the curves is the fact that larger firms are earlier adopters. See chapter 3.
4. This section draws heavily on Cusolito (2021), Nyman and Ukhaneva (forthcoming), World Bank (2021), and Zhu et al. (forthcoming).

5. The spread of digital platforms has raised concerns about the changing nature of employment status, ushering in a more flexible workforce and eroding traditional employer-employee relationships. Blurring lines between formal and casual employment, characterized by independent or temporary work arrangements (such as on-call workers, contract workers, or freelancers) could be problematic. Workers face the risk of insecure working environments. Beyond occupations in transportation such as drivers or delivery, these platforms are affecting other occupations ranging from arts and design, media, and communication to other services. The growth of digital platforms has expanded the share of workers performing on-demand tasks—the so-called gig economy. With its allure of flexibility and compensation (Hall and Krueger 2018), the gig economy has grown exponentially and helped workers buffer against income and expense shocks (Farrell and Greig 2016). The incidence of alternative work arrangements has been rising in the United States, with the share of all workers growing from 10.7 percent in 2005 to as high as 15.8 percent in late 2015 (Katz and Krueger 2019).

6. Enlyft is a private digital platform providing a database on B2B technology based on machine learning.

7. The BPS is an initiative led by the World Bank Group to collect and harmonize firm-level data to understand the impact of COVID-19 on the private sector in developing countries. Apedo-Amah et al. (2020) summarize the first round of data collection. The severity of the effect of the COVID-19 shock on businesses has been well documented across countries and data sources. See Adams-Prassl et al. (2020); Bartik et al. (2020); Dai, Hu, and Zhang (2020); Fairlie (2020a, 2020b); and Humphries, Neilson, and Ulyssea (2020).

8. The average drop in sales in the first four weeks following the peak of the shock is between 60 percent and 75 percent. In the next four months, the drop in sales narrowed to 47 percent in week 8, 47 percent in week 12, and 43 percent after week 16. Although nearly 90 percent of businesses were open 10 weeks after the peak of the outbreak, the negative impact on sales still loomed large.

9. This section is based on Avalos et al. (forthcoming), a background paper for this volume.

10. This section is based on Comin et al. (2022), a background paper for this volume.

11. One standard deviation in pre-pandemic technology sophistication is associated with an increase of 10 percentage points in the likelihood of starting or increasing the use of digital technologies. Firms whose technology sophistication index is one standard deviation (0.62 percentage points) higher than the average (1.78) tend to rely on specialized software to perform business administration or production planning and sourcing; online chat or internet to interact with customers; debit/credit card and online payment; and computers for quality control. Firms whose technology index of 2.78 is 1 percentage point higher than the average tend to be very close to the frontier in performing tasks such as business administration and planning (for example, use ERP systems) and use basic to more sophisticated digital technologies in all other GBFs.

References

Adams-Prassl, A., T. Boneva, M. Golin, and C. Rauh. 2020. "Inequality in the Impact of the Coronavirus Shock: Evidence from Real Time Surveys." *Journal of Public Economics* 189 (September): 104245.

Adhvaryu, A., N. Kala, and A. Nyshadham. 2020. "The Light and the Heat: Productivity Co-benefits of Energy-Saving Technology." *Review of Economics and Statistics* 102 (4): 779–92.

Anderson, M., and J. Magruder. 2012. "Learning from the Crowd: Regression Discontinuity Estimates of the Effects of an Online Review Database." *Economic Journal* 122 (563): 957–89.

Apedo-Amah, M. C., B. Avdiu, M. Cruz, X. Cirera, E. Davies, A. Grover, L. Iacovone, U. Kilinc, D. Medvedev, F. O. Maduko, S. Poupakis, J. Torres, and T. T. Tran. 2020. "Unmasking the Impact of COVID-19 on Business: Firm-Level Evidence from around the World." Policy Research Working Paper 9434, World Bank, Washington, DC.

Avalos, E., X. Cirera, M. Cruz, I. Leonardo, D. Medvedev, G. Nayyar, and S. Reyes. Forthcoming. "Digital Divide across Firms through COVID-19: A Tale of Two Stories." World Bank, Washington, DC.

Baron, R. M., and D. A. Kenny. 1986. "The Moderator-Mediator Variable Distinction in Social Psychological Research: Conceptual, Strategic, and Statistical Considerations." *Journal of Personality and Social Psychology* 51 (6): 1173.

Bartik, A. W., M. Bertrand, Z. Cullen, E. L. Glaeser, M. Luca, and C. Stanton. 2020. "The Impact of COVID-19 on Small Business Outcomes and Expectations." *Proceedings of the National Academy of Sciences* 117 (30): 17656–66.

Bellmann, L., P. Bourgeon, C. Gathmann, C. Kagerl, D. Marguerit, L. Martin, L. Pohlan, and D. Roth. 2021. "Digitalisierungsschub in Firmen während der Corona-Pandemie." Working paper, Luxembourg Institute for Socio-Economic Research (LISER).

Celli, V. 2022. "Causal Mediation Analysis in Economics: Objectives, Assumptions, Models." *Journal of Economic Surveys* 36 (1): 214–34.

Chen, X., and L. Yang. 2019. "Temperature and Industrial Output: Firm-Level Evidence from China." *Journal of Environmental Economics and Management* 95 (C): 257–74.

Cirera, X., M. Cruz, A. Grover, L. Iacovone, D. Medvedev, M. Pereira-Lopez, and S. Reyes. 2021. "Firm Recovery during COVID-19: Six Stylized Facts." Policy Research Working Paper 9810, World Bank, Washington, DC.

Comin, D. A., M. Cruz, X. Cirera, K. M. Lee, and J. Torres. 2022. "Technology and Resilience." NBER Working Paper 29644, National Bureau of Economic Research, Cambridge, MA.

Cruz, M., and Z. Hernandez. 2022 "Entrepreneurship Ecosystems and MSMEs in Kenya: Strengthening Businesses in the Aftermath of the Pandemic." World Bank, Washington, DC. Unpublished.

Cusolito, A. P. 2021. "The Economics of Technology Adoption." World Bank, Washington, DC. Unpublished.

Dai, R., J. Hu, and X. Zhang. 2020. "The Impact of Coronavirus on China's SMEs: Findings from the Enterprise Survey for Innovation and Entrepreneurship in China." CGD Note, Center for Global Development, Washington, DC, and London.

Dell, M., B. F. Jones, and B. A. Olken. 2012. "Temperature Shocks and Economic Growth: Evidence from the Last Half Century." *American Economic Journal: Macroeconomics* 4 (3): 66–95.

Einav, L., C. Farronato, and J. Levin. 2016. "Peer-to-Peer Markets." *Annual Review of Economics* 8 (1): 615–35.

Fairlie, R. W. 2020a. "The Impact of Covid-19 on Small Business Owners: Evidence of Early-Stage Losses from the April 2020 Current Population Survey." NBER Working Paper 27309, National Bureau of Economic Research, Cambridge, MA.

Fairlie, R. W. 2020b. "The Impact of COVID-19 on Small Business Owners: The First Three Months after Social-Distancing Restrictions." NBER Working Paper 27462, National Bureau of Economic Research, Cambridge, MA.

Farrell, D., and F. Greig. 2016. "Paychecks, Paydays, and the Online Platform Economy: Big Data on Income Volatility." *Proceedings. Annual Conference on Taxation and Minutes of the Annual Meeting of the National Tax Association* 109: 1–40.

Friedman, G. 2014. "Workers without Employers: Shadow Corporations and the Rise of the Gig Economy." *Review of Keynesian Economics* 2 (2): 171–88.

Gandini, A. 2019. "Labour Process Theory and the Gig Economy." *Human Relations* 72 (6): 1039–56.

Goldfarb, A., and C. Tucker. 2019. "Digital Economics." *Journal of Economic Literature* 57 (1): 3–43.

Hall, J. V., and A. B. Krueger. 2018. "An Analysis of the Labor Market for Uber's Driver-Partners in the United States." *ILR Review* 71 (3): 705–32.

Hallward-Driemeier, Mary, Gaurav Nayyar, Wolfgang Fengler, Anwar Aridi, Indermit Gill. 2020. *Europe 4.0: Addressing the Digital Dilemma.* Washington, DC: World Bank.

Hancock, P. A., J. M. Ross, and J. L. Szalma. 2007. "A Meta-Analysis of Performance Response under Thermal Stressors." *Human Factors* 49: 851–77.

Hsiang, S. 2010. "Temperatures and Cyclones Strongly Associated with Economic Production in the Caribbean and Central America." *Proceedings of the National Academy of Sciences* 107: 15367–72. https://doi.org/10.1073/pnas.1009510107.

Hsu, P. H., H. H. Lee, S. C. Peng, and L. Yi. 2018. "Natural Disasters, Technology Diversity, and Operating Performance." *Review of Economics and Statistics* 100 (4): 619–30.

Humphries, J. E., C. Neilson, and G. Ulyssea. 2020. "The Evolving Impacts of COVID-19 on Small Businesses since the CARES Act." Cowles Foundation Discussion Paper 2230, Cowles Foundation for Research in Economics, Yale University, New Haven, CT.

Imai, K., L. Keele, and T. Yamamoto. 2010. "Identification, Inference and Sensitivity Analysis for Causal Mediation Effects." *Statistical Science* 25 (1): 51–71.

Jin, H., and F. Hurd. 2018. "Exploring the Impact of Digital Platforms on SME Internationalization: New Zealand SMEs Use of the Alibaba Platform for Chinese Market Entry." *Journal of Asia-Pacific Business* 19 (2): 72–95.

Katz, L. F., and A. B. Krueger. 2019. "The Rise and Nature of Alternative Work Arrangements in the United States, 1995–2015." *ILR Review* 72 (2): 382–416.

Koren, M., and S. Tenreyro. 2013. "Technological Diversification." *American Economic Review* 103 (1): 378–414.

Nyman, Sara, and Yana Ukhaneva. Forthcoming. "The Supply and Use of Digital Technologies by Businesses in Developing Countries: An Analysis Using Enlyft Data." World Bank, Washington, DC.

Park, J., N. Pankratz, and A. Behrer. 2021. "Temperature, Workplace Safety, and Labor Market Inequality." IZA Discussion Paper 14560, IZA Institute of Labor Economics, Bonn.

Rivares, A. B., P. Gal, V. Millot, and S. Sorbe. 2019. "Like It or Not? The Impact of Online Platforms on the Productivity of Incumbent Service Providers." OECD Economics Department Working Paper 1548, Organisation for Economic Co-operation and Development, Paris.

Seppanen, O., W. Fisk, and Q. Lei. 2006. "Effect of Temperature on Task Performance in Office Environment." Lawrence Berkeley National Laboratory, Berkeley, CA.

Umar, M., Y. Xu, and S. S. Mirza. 2020. "The Impact of Covid-19 on Gig Economy." *Economic Research-Ekonomska Istraživanja* 34 (1): 2284–96.

UNCTAD (United Nations Conference on Trade and Development). 2019. *Digital Economy Report 2019. Value Creation and Capture: Implications for Developing Countries.* Geneva: UNCTAD.

Van Reenen, J., and A. Valero. 2021. "How Is Covid-19 Affecting Firms' Adoption of New Technologies?" Economics Observatory, Science, Technology & Innovation, January 8.

World Bank. 2021. *Antitrust and Digital Platforms: An Analysis of Global Patterns and Approaches by Competition Authorities.* Equitable Growth, Finance and Institutions Insight. Washington, DC: World Bank.

Zhu, T. J., P. Grinsted, H. Song, and M. Velamuri. Forthcoming. "Digital Businesses in Developing Countries: New Insights for a Digital Development Pathway." World Bank, Washington, DC.

PART 3

What Countries Can Do to Bridge the
Technological Divide

6. What Constrains Firms from Adopting Better Technologies?

Introduction

If more sophisticated technologies lead to productivity gains, why don't firms adopt and use them more intensively? Understanding what drives firms to adopt a specific technology is essential to improve the effectiveness of policies aiming to support technology upgrading. This chapter analyzes the key obstacles firms face in adopting sophisticated technologies. Specifically, it addresses the following questions:

- What are the key determinants of technology adoption by firms highlighted by the literature?
- What are the main drivers and obstacles for adoption that entrepreneurs and managers themselves perceive?
- What is the association between the key determinants highlighted by the literature and the level of sophistication of the technology actually adopted by firms?

To respond to these questions, the first part of this chapter provides a brief summary of the literature on the main drivers of and barriers to adoption. The discussion looks at technology adoption from the perspective of the firm.[1] It then describes what entrepreneurs themselves perceive as the main obstacles and motivations to adopt new technologies. Finally, it analyzes the association between the key drivers and obstacles highlighted by the literature and the level of technology sophistication based on factual evidence from the Firm-level Adoption of Technology (FAT) data.[2]

Firm-Level Determinants of Adoption

What factors impede or prevent a firm from deciding to adopt a more sophisticated technology?[3] A good place to start answering this question is to consider the possibility of positive returns and profits for a firm. A general framework to empirically study firms' decisions to invest in a specific technology is described in Besley and Case (1993). The framework is based on optimizing a dynamic profit function where the present value of implementing a technology in time t depends on current profits and the discounted expected value of the technology.[4]

In practice, estimating the returns to technology upgrading is challenging, given the relevance of interacting factors inside and outside the firm.[5] In an influential experiment on the use of fertilizer in Kenya, Duflo, Kremer, and Robinson (2008) found that even when returns to fertilizer use were high, and even when farmers were offered free delivery in the period during the planting season that the fertilizer needed to be applied, adoption was low. They surmised that behavioral biases were important. Suri (2011) reexamined this empirical puzzle by using a methodology to estimate returns to specific farmers in the adoption of hybrid maize in Kenya and found that farmers with low net returns did not adopt the technology. These studies suggest that when looking at spatial differences in returns—and assuming that the technology is known and there is sufficient information about it—individual decision-makers will vary in their assessments of the benefits and costs of technologies, and that will drive variations in adoption.

In a developing country context, technology upgrading might be more challenging than in advanced economies because market failures and missing complementarities are likely to be more acute. This lack of complementary factors also affects the returns to technology upgrading for individual firms. This issue is documented in the first volume of the World Bank's Productivity Project series. Cirera and Maloney (2017) identify "the innovation paradox," noting that despite the vast potential returns to innovation, developing countries invest far less in technology and innovation than advanced economies, measured along a variety of dimensions. The main factor explaining this paradox is the lack of complementary factors. Some of these factors are internal investments in knowledge and management by the firm. Others are external to the firm, such as skills available in the labor market, access to finance, the cost of doing business, or the supply of knowledge and technologies.

More recently, Verhoogen (forthcoming) provides a comprehensive review of the literature on firm-level upgrading in developing countries, including technology adoption.[6] Verhoogen presents a conceptual framework focusing on the drivers of upgrading regarding the output side (such as exports and competition), the input side (such as imported and domestic inputs), and know-how factors (such as entrepreneurial ability and learning). The evidence reviewed suggests that international trade provides powerful channels to promote upgrading, but there is also an important role for learning.

In general, the literature has highlighted several factors that drive firm technology adoption. Some of these factors are outside the control of the firm and can affect the profits and returns of adopting a technology, but several factors relate to entrepreneurs and capabilities of the firm. Figure 6.1 summarizes some of the key factors emphasized by the literature, organized in two complementary sets of drivers: one internal to the firm and one external. Organizing the discussion around these two broad topics can help policy makers identify instruments that are available to support technology upgrading.

FIGURE 6.1 Technology Adoption Depends on a Set of Complementary Factors That Are External and Internal to the Firm

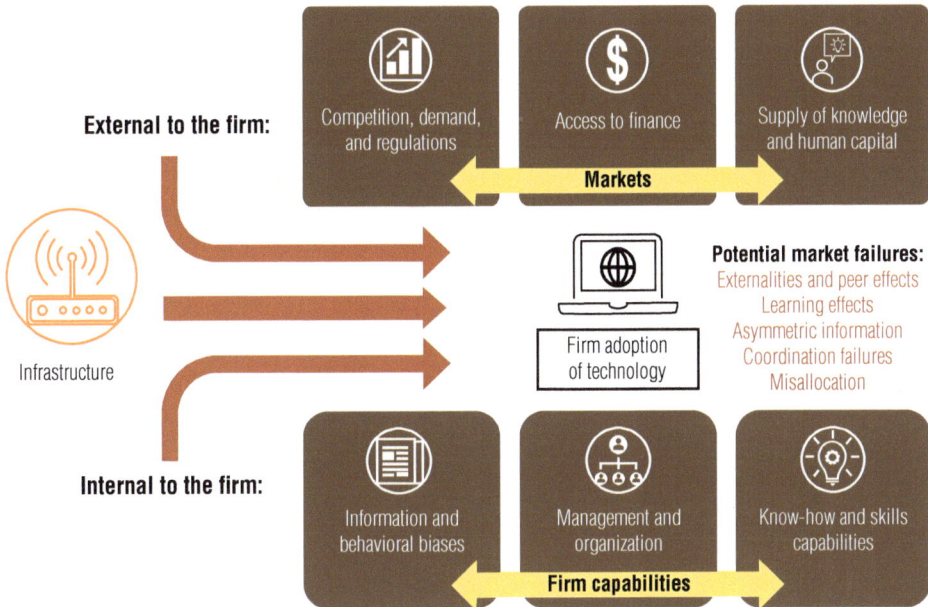

Source: Original figure for this volume.

In addition to having access to an enabling infrastructure, such as electricity, internet service, or a mobile network, other factors are important to explain firm-level adoption. Internal factors are related to building firm capabilities. This includes the knowledge and know-how accumulated and implemented through management and organizational practices, as well as the information available and biases of the entrepreneurs in the decision to adopt a technology. External factors include market dynamics and the regulatory environment, as well as access to funding to finance technology projects. The supply of knowledge and technology solutions from other firms or from public institutions is also very important. All these factors affect the decision to adopt and the diffusion of existing technologies. Different market failures affect these elements, from information frictions that result in the underprovision of finance to externalities and spillovers that are not appropriated and reduce investment in technology, or distortions that affect factor prices favoring more energy-intensive or labor-intensive technologies, for example.[7]

The rest of this chapter provides some evidence about the importance of these barriers as observed in the FAT data. First, entrepreneurs' perceptions of the main barriers they face are discussed. This analysis is complemented with factual data from the FAT survey about some of the key barriers and drivers to adoption.

Perceived Drivers of and Obstacles to Technology Adoption

Drivers

The FAT survey asks firms about their main motivations for upgrading technologies. Figure 6.2 shows the top motivations for adopting new technologies by firm size group. The pressure of competition, an external factor, is the main motivation for most firms. In particular, more than 40 percent of small and medium enterprises (SMEs) report this as their main reason. This finding is consistent with some of the literature reviewed in the first part of the chapter.

Interestingly, a second motivation is simply replacement from obsolescence or malfunction of existing equipment. The third and fourth most reported motivations are reducing costs to become more competitive and adjusting to new regulations. These factors are more relevant for large firms than for SMEs. The pattern is similar for the importance of other firms adopting. Product innovation and access to new markets is the main reason for about 20 percent of firms. This is consistent with the fact that a relatively small share of firms innovate and export.

FIGURE 6.2   **Competition Is a Top Driver for Technology Adoption**

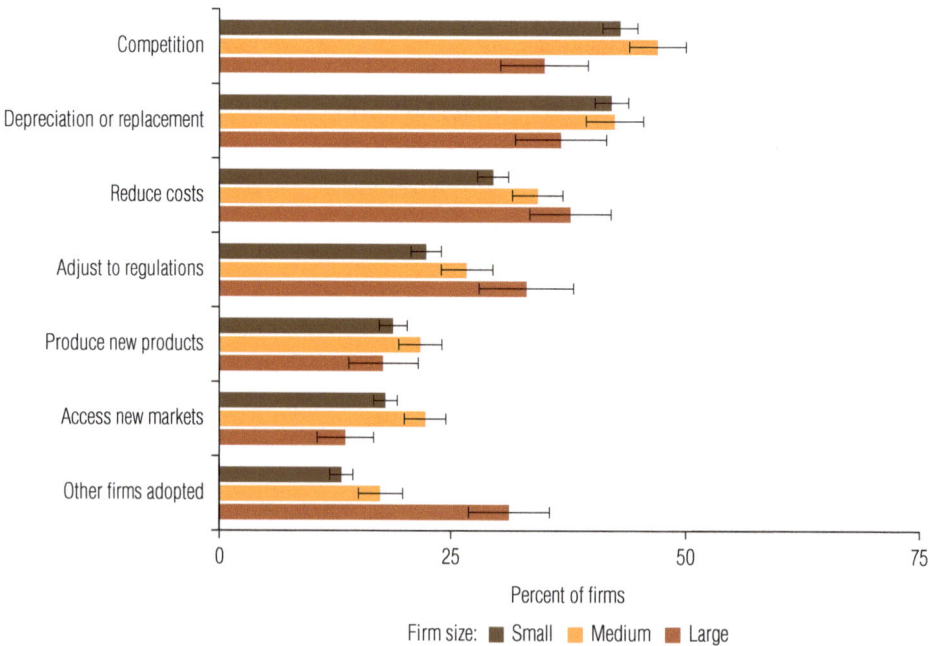

Source: Original figure based on Firm-level Adoption of Technology (FAT) survey data.

Note: Results are based on cross-country average using sampling weights. Firm size relates to the number of workers: small (5–19), medium (20–99), large (100 or more).

Obstacles

Figure 6.3 shows the share of firms reporting the top three obstacles to adoption by firm size group. The most common obstacle for all types of firms across countries is concern about sufficient demand or uncertainty about demand to justify investment in new technologies. More than 60 percent of firms cite this concern, which is an external factor. The high percentage is homogeneous across firm size, from large to small firms. The second most common factor reported is related to lack of capabilities, which includes the overall technical skills and know-how to implement new technologies. This is the main internal factor cited.

Around 20 percent to 25 percent of firms cite lack of finance and poor infrastructure, depending on the obstacle and firm size. Government regulations pose a critical barrier for less than 25 percent of firms, although the share is much higher in certain countries, such as Brazil. Compared with the review of the evidence, finance and infrastructure play a more important role in the mind of entrepreneurs and managers than the emphasis in the literature would suggest. In the case of infrastructure, this is likely because entrepreneurs and managers in the FAT survey sample are more diverse in sector and firm size and have a different focus than various studies looking more

FIGURE 6.3   **Lack of Demand and Firm Capabilities Are Key Obstacles for Technology Adoption**

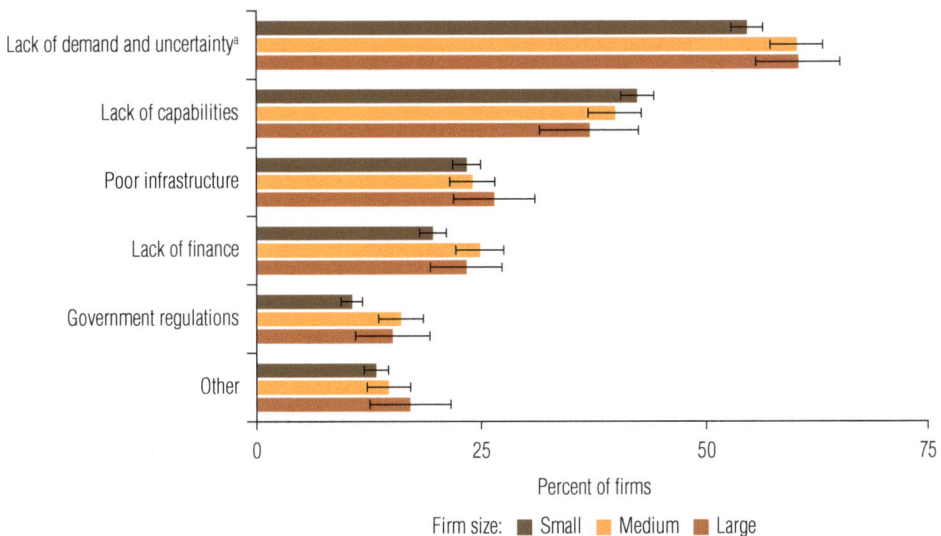

Source: Original figure based on Firm-level Adoption of Technology (FAT) survey data.

Note: The figure shows the share of firms reporting each obstacle as among its top three obstacles. Results based on cross-country average using sampling weights. Firm size refers to the number of workers: small (5–19), medium (20–99), large (100 or more).

a. Uncertainty refers to uncertainty about future demand.

narrowly at some sectors in developing countries. There is also some heterogeneity across countries regarding the identified main obstacle. Firms in Senegal cite lack of capabilities, while firms in Vietnam mention lack of demand.

Learning about perceived obstacles is important for policy makers. Addressing those issues that entrepreneurs already identify as main obstacles may facilitate political support to implement reforms. Yet, perceived obstacles and drivers do not necessarily imply that these are the most relevant issues faced by the firms. Firms do not know what they do not know. Having more factual evidence, including impact evaluations, about the elements that determine lack of adoption is critical to designing policy well.

Factual Evidence on Drivers of and Obstacles to Technology Adoption

This section reviews the factual evidence reported in the FAT survey about key drivers and obstacles for firm technology adoption. Following the framework in figure 6.1, these factors are divided into two groups: those external to the firm and in the enabling environment; and those internal to the firm. External factors that are part of the enabling environment include infrastructure, markets and competition, financial constraints, and access to external knowledge. Internal factors to the firms that affect firms' capabilities and knowledge include information and behavioral biases, management quality and organization, and know-how and skills.

Factors External to the Firm: An Enabling Environment

Infrastructure
Infrastructure in general, from electricity to roads and telecommunications, plays an important role as an enabler of technology adoption by firms. Evidence across African countries, for instance, suggests that the spread of fast internet connection has increased firm entry, productivity, and exports in African countries (Hjort and Poulsen 2019). The rapid spread of the internet, as described in chapter 1, and recent increase in the demand for digital technologies due to the COVID-19 pandemic have heightened the role of digital infrastructure.

To assess the effect of digital infrastructure on adoption, we use a unique data set for Senegal that allows the impact of geographic proximity to internet infrastructure to be measured.[8] In the spirit of Hjort and Poulsen (2019), the analysis, described in Berkes et al. (forthcoming), combines information on the GPS location of the firms that participated in the FAT survey in Senegal with the location of the node of the Senegalese internet backbone. It then explores the contribution of digital infrastructure to the adoption of technologies through the effects of the proximity to the nodes, which translate into having access to better quality internet service, which was improved through the arrival of submarine internet cables in 2011.

Map 6.1 shows the distribution of firms (blue dots) and the location of the nodes of the Senegalese internet backbone (red dots). Panel a describes the distribution of firms in the data, selected from a random sample drawn from the latest establishment census. Panel b replicates this information for firms with internet access.

The results show that the distance to a node of the Senegalese internet backbone is a strong predictor of having an internet connection. Specifically, doubling the distance from a node reduces the likelihood of having an internet connection by 5 percentage points (figure 6.4).[9] Interestingly, the effect is even stronger (7 percentage points) when considering only the subset of firms established more than 10 years ago, suggesting that these firms already existed before the arrival of submarine internet cables. As expected, proximity to a node increases the likelihood of having a high-speed DSL connection.[10]

More important, the analysis can be extended to explore the impact of having internet on the sophistication of technology use, using instrumental variables to better identify the causal effect.[11] Figure 6.5 shows that the quality of internet service can explain only adoption of more sophisticated technologies for general business functions at the extensive margin, but not for sector-specific business functions, on average, where digital may be less prevalent and internet service less of an enabler. Results are robust when restricting the sample for firms with 10 or more years of age.

Overall, the results confirm the importance of digital infrastructure as an enabler of technology for firms, but they also show that facilitating access to the internet due to improvement of infrastructure does not explain a large variation of technology sophistication across firms. In the case of sector-specific business functions (SBFs), the results can be explained by the fact that many SBFs—particularly in agriculture and manufacturing—are not fully digital or are embedded in sophisticated machines that many firms cannot afford or that pose other types of barriers in terms of firms' access to information or know-how.

Markets, Competition, and Regulation

Market structure and competition are critical external drivers for technology adoption. Competition provides incentives to adopt new technologies. For instance, competition from China has driven increases in innovation and the adoption of information and communication technologies (ICTs) in the United Kingdom (Bloom, Draca, and Van Reenen 2016). However, since work by Aghion et al. (2005) found an inverted-U relationship between innovation and competition, the literature has been more nuanced about this relationship depending on the type of market in which the firms operate. Generally, greater market competition can help enable innovation and technology adoption, especially in cases where competition is low to start with, but this pattern varies greatly by sector, and the regulatory environment can shape firms' decisions (Hannan and McDowell 1984). Regulatory issues are also critical when it comes to adoption of certain data-intensive technologies and access to digital platforms (see box 6.1).

MAP 6.1 **Firms in Senegal Are More Likely to Access the Internet in Clusters Surrounded by Digital Infrastructure**

a. Distribution of firms and internet nodes

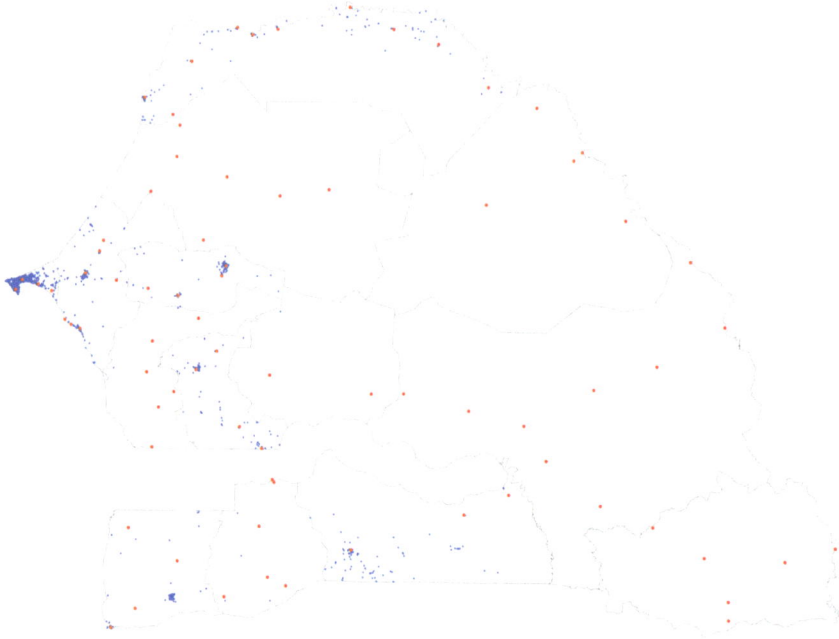

b. Firms with access to internet

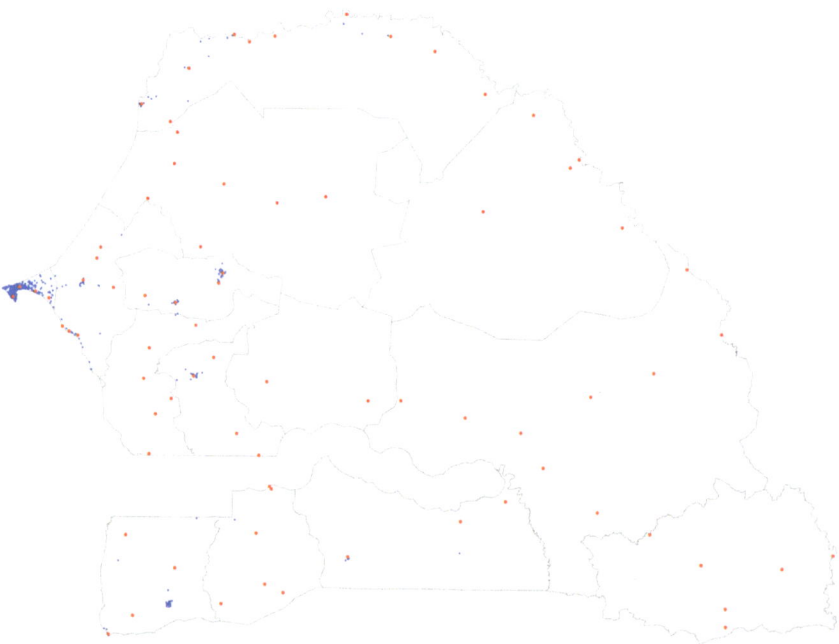

Source: Berkes et al., forthcoming.

Note: The sample targets seven regions in Senegal with internet access (Dakar, St. Louis, Thies, Diourbel, Ziguinchor, Kaolack, and Kolda). The red dots denote the location of the access nodes of the Senegalese internet backbone. The blue dots show the location of the firms in the Firm-level Adoption of Technology (FAT) survey (panel a) and firms with internet access (panel b).

Bridging the Technological Divide

FIGURE 6.4 **Longer Distances from Internet Nodes Significantly Reduce the Likelihood that Firms Will Adopt Internet Service**

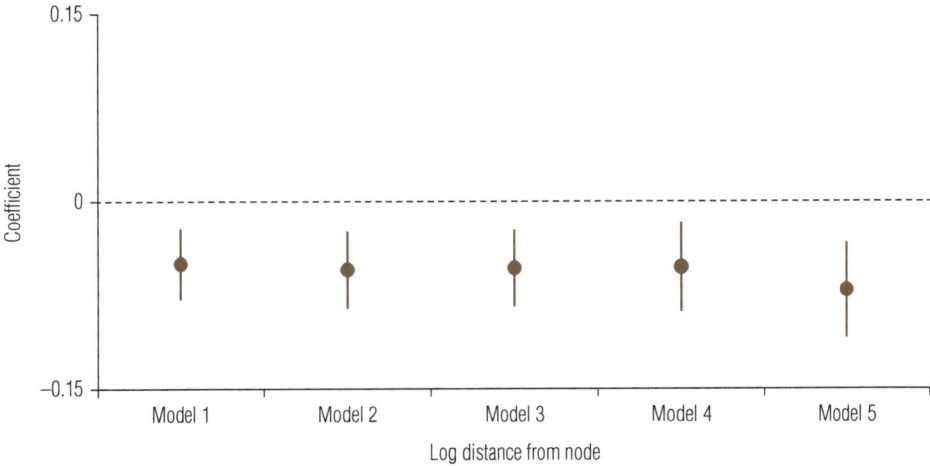

Source: Berkes et al., forthcoming.

Note: Model 1 reports the marginal effect from a probit specification controlling for region fixed effects, industry fixed effects, and basic firm characteristics. The results imply that doubling the distance from an access node reduces the likelihood of having an internet connection by 5 percentage points. This effect is about 10 percent of the sample mean (0.47) and hence economically significant. Model 2 introduces several variables that control for firm-level characteristics, such as age and size. Model 3 reports the estimates obtained when also controlling for managerial characteristics (such as experience), whereas Model 4 introduces region times industry fixed effects. Finally, Model 5 considers only those firms that were established more than 10 years before the survey was conducted. The idea is that these firms chose their location before the arrival of submarine internet cables in 2011.

FIGURE 6.5 **The Impact of Access to the Internet Is More Restricted to General Business Functions than to Sector-Specific Business Functions**

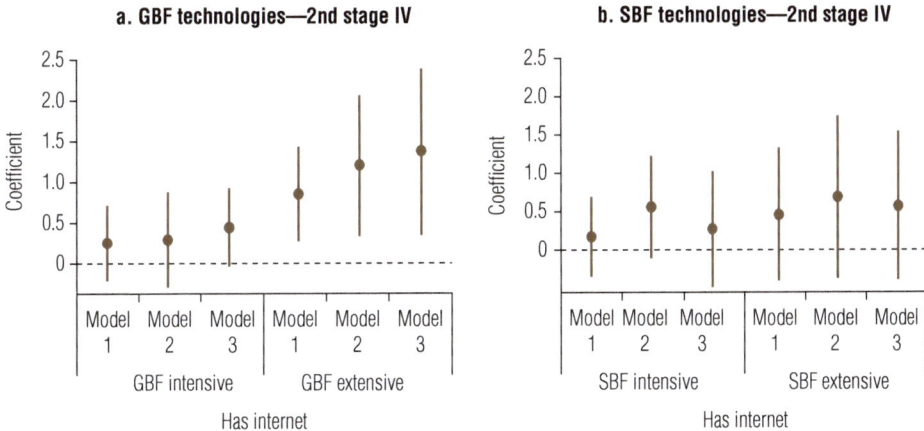

Source: Berkes et al, forthcoming.

Note: IV (instrumental variables) estimates for Senegal. The dependent variable is an index of technology adoption for GBFs (panel a) and SBFs (panel b). Extensive and intensive indexes refer to most advanced and most frequently used technology, following the methodology described in Cirera et al. (2020). The instrument used is the log distance from an access node of the Senegalese internet backbone. Model 1 includes the full sample for Senegal. Model 2 includes all firms with 10 years of age or more. Model 3 includes only formal firms with 10 years of age or more. All specifications (Models 1, 2, and 3) control for region fixed effects, sector fixed effects, and firm characteristics (age; log of number of workers; importer; exporter; multinational; manager experience in the same sector, large firms, studying abroad). Standard errors clustered at the industry-region level. GBF = general business function; SBF = sector-specific business function.

*** $p < 0.01$; ** $p < 0.05$; * $p < 0.1$.

Specific Barriers to the Use of Digital Platforms

Despite the benefits that digital platforms can bring to the economy in developing countries, there are also important adoption challenges. Cusolito (2021) summarizes these technology adoption challenges in five categories: (1) coordination problems; (2) lack of trust; (3) weak standard compliance and enforcement; (4) self-deregulation; and (5) regulatory loopholes. Coordination problems and regulatory issues are very common in developing countries. Coordination problems happen in the presence of network effects, given that the benefits that adoption of a digital platform brings to a potential user depend primarily on the size of the network effects, which are a function of the adoption decisions of other firms. To address coordination problems, many digital platforms try to subsidize or help firms (or service providers) with the initial investments they need to boost connection. This has significant implications for public policy given that the platform, rather than government, could solve the coordination problem. Indeed, several e-commerce platforms provide business support services to vendors. For example, the e-commerce platform Jumia has created Jumia University to train vendors to help them deliver the best shopping experience to their customers.[a]

Regulatory barriers can play an important role in delaying adoption. Platforms often face outdated regulations applied to activities that have been primarily provided offline in the past (such as ride-sharing or accommodation). Regulatory bottlenecks are especially present in the area of e-commerce. Enabling regulations are needed regarding electronic documentation and signatures, financial law related to e-payments, consumer protection, intellectual property, cybersecurity, personal privacy, and data protection, Daza Jaller, Gaillard, and Molinuevo (2020) emphasize. But many countries lack a well-designed regulatory framework that can enable online intermediation while protecting consumers. These regulatory bottlenecks apply not only to digital platforms but also to technologies more generally. For example, in Brazil, taxes on microchips and SIM cards, which were taxed individually, were impeding the diffusion of agricultural technologies connected to the Internet of Things.

Source: Cusolito 2021.
a. Jin and Sun (2020) evaluate training provided by a platform operator and find that it increases new sellers' likelihood of being found by consumers, improving the matching quality between consumers and sellers.

Access to international markets and competition in the domestic market are important drivers of adoption. About 40 percent of firms report "competition" as a key driver (see figure 6.2). Access to international markets has large effects on productivity via competition and learning, and these channels can also result in the use of more sophisticated technologies.[12] Panel a of figure 6.6 shows the relationship between exporting status and the technology index, while panel c shows the results of a similar exercise with importing status. Both exporting and importing activities have a significant correlation with technology use. Panels b and d also show that larger firms are significantly more likely to export and import, which is consistent with the behavior observed by the trade literature (Wagner 1995).

FIGURE 6.6   Globally Engaged Firms Are More Sophisticated Technologically

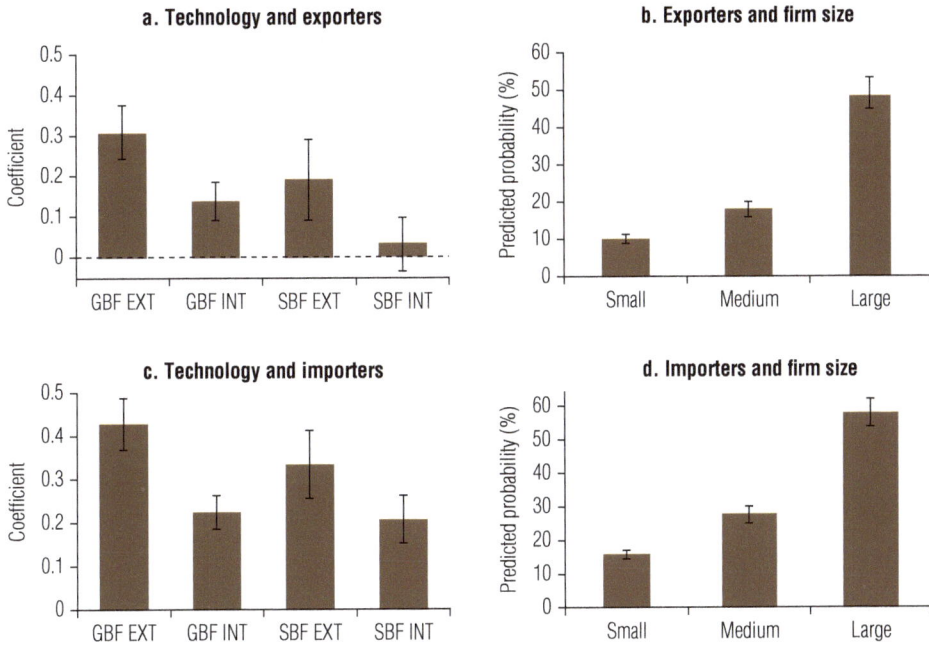

a. Technology and exporters

b. Exporters and firm size

c. Technology and importers

d. Importers and firm size

Source: Original figure based on Firm-level Adoption of Technology (FAT) survey data.

Note: Panels a and c provide the coefficients and 95 percent confidence intervals from regressions. Each technology measure is regressed on exporter/importer dummies, respectively, while controlling for country, sector, and firm size. Panels b and d show the predicted probability of exporter/importer status on firm size from the probit regressions with controlling for other baseline characteristics. All estimates are weighted by sampling and country weights. EXT = extensive margin; GBF = general business function; INT = intensive margin; SBF = sector-specific business function.

Scale and learning mechanisms through demand are important drivers of technology adoption. Bustos (2011) and Lileeva and Trefler (2010) show that following trade policy reforms for Argentina and Canada, scale effects through exports increased technology adoption by firms in both countries.

Firms integrated to international markets as exporters, importers, foreign-owned entities, or multinationals tend to use more sophisticated technologies across different business functions. Aside from payment methods, exporting companies use more advanced technologies for general business functions. In the intensive margin, the gap is particularly large for business administration tasks. The exercise of decomposing the technology index between domestic and foreign-owned companies is repeated in figure 6.7. Firms were considered to be foreign owned if they had more than 10 percent foreign ownership. Interestingly and despite the previous results, the differences between domestic and foreign-owned companies were found to be small on the intensive margin (that is, on the technology used more intensively). Yet, foreign firms use more sophisticated technologies, especially for business administration, planning, and sourcing.

Foreign-Owned Companies Tend to Have More Sophisticated Technologies across General Business Functions

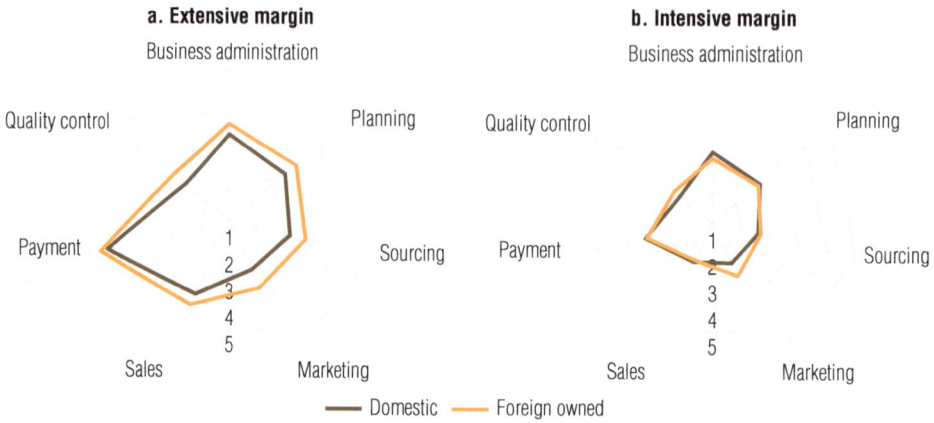

a. Extensive margin

b. Intensive margin

— Domestic   — Foreign owned

Source: Original figure based on Firm-level Adoption of Technology (FAT) survey data.

Financial Constraints

An inefficient financial system may make it harder for firms to access finance to invest in technology, and thus may deter technology adoption. A significant number of entrepreneurs and managers cited financial constraints as an important barrier to technology adoption. Thus, an important question is how correlated adoption of sophisticated technologies is to access to finance.

Panel a of figure 6.8 shows a positive and statistically significant relationship between the technology adoption measures for both GBFs and SBFs at both the extensive (EXT) and intensive (INT) margins and access to loans. The coefficient is larger for GBF-EXT, suggesting that firms that have access to loans for purchasing machines or software tend to use more sophisticated technologies in GBFs than in SBFs. Panel b shows the predicted probability of having access to financial loans for the acquisition of machines or software by firm size. Small firms have about a 22 percent probability of having a loan to acquire machines or software, compared to large firms, which have around a 38 percent probability. Given the correlation between access to finance and technology sophistication, the financial channel is likely to be a constraint to technology upgrading for smaller firms, which often need to use their own resources to finance technology.

This result is supported by some evidence in the literature. Previous studies suggest that an inefficient financial system, with large information asymmetries or distortions to finance, may reduce and underfinance firm-level technology adoption within a country even if the use of a technology would be more profitable. For example, Midrigan and Xu (2014) find that financial frictions distort firm entry and technology adoption decisions, which results in lower levels of aggregate productivity. Cole, Greenwood, and Sanchez (2016) show that the efficiency of the financial system determines which technologies are adopted by firms across countries. Other studies

FIGURE 6.8 **Constraints to Financial Credit Are a Larger Barrier to Technology Upgrading for Smaller Firms**

a. Technology adoption on loans for purchasing machines/software

b. Probability of having a loan to purchase machines/software, by firm size

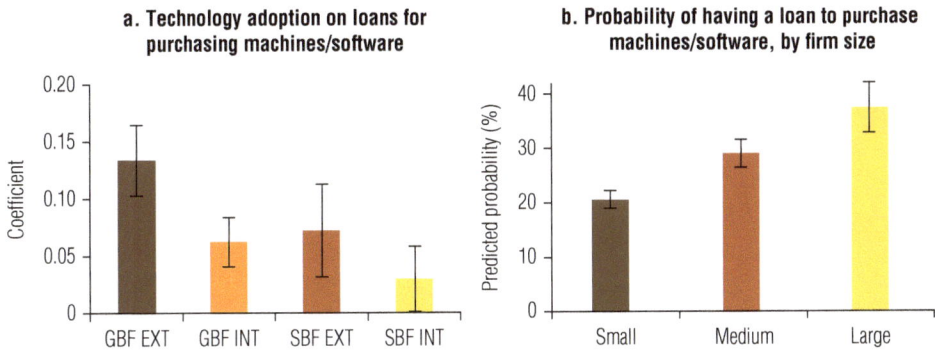

Source: Original figure based on Firm-level Adoption of Technology (FAT) survey data.

Note: Panel a provides the coefficients and 95 percent confidence intervals from regressions. Each technology measure is regressed on a dummy for taking loans to purchase machines/software and interest rates, respectively, while controlling for formality, sector, size, and regions. Panel b shows the predicted probability of getting loans by firm size groups and confidence intervals from the probit regression while controlling for other baseline characteristics. All estimates are weighted by sampling and country weights. Firm size refers to the number of workers: small (5–19), medium (20–99), and large (100 or more). EXT = extensive margin; GBF = general business function; INT = intensive margin; SBF = sector-specific business function.

have also found suggestive evidence that the improvement of local financial systems increases firm-level technology adoption in the Russian Federation (Bircan and De Haas 2019) and in agriculture in Ethiopia (Abate et al. 2016).

Access to External Knowledge and Human Capital

Firms can learn and improve their know-how through different sources, including knowledge transfer through other firms, within the firm, and from consultant services. Learning by exporting is another route. For instance, Atkin, Khandelwal, and Osman (2017) focus on carpet producers in the Arab Republic of Egypt and show evidence of learning by exporting that was induced by demand for high-quality products from knowledgeable buyers in high-income countries. A large body of evidence has explored the importance of learning and having access to better information for technology adoption, mostly focusing on agricultural firms (Foster and Rosenzweig 1995; Gupta, Ponticelli, and Tesei 2020; Beaman et al. 2021).

An important source of knowledge transfer to the firm may come from external consultants. Panel a of figure 6.9 shows that using an external consultant is significantly associated with a higher score in the technology index, by between 0.2 and 0.4 points. The likelihood of using external consultant services varies between 14 percent for small firms and 48 percent for large firms (panel b), suggesting that while half of large firms use these external consultants, only around one in six small firms uses this form of external knowledge.

Panel c shows that the most common type of consultant is from local firms, followed by business associations and foreign firms. Only a small share of firms benefit

FIGURE 6.9 Firms That Use External Business Consultants Have Higher Levels of Technology Sophistication

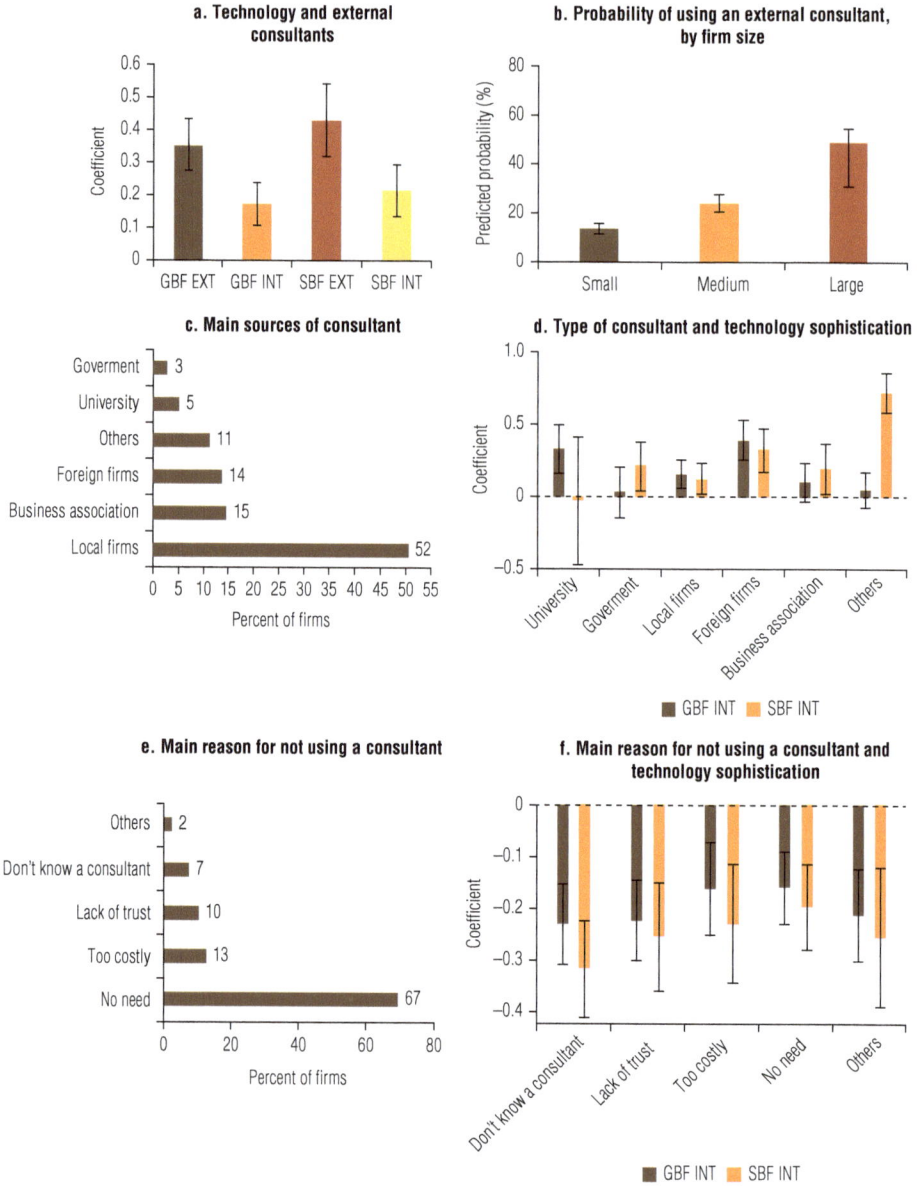

a. Technology and external consultants

b. Probability of using an external consultant, by firm size

c. Main sources of consultant

d. Type of consultant and technology sophistication

e. Main reason for not using a consultant

f. Main reason for not using a consultant and technology sophistication

Source: Original figure based on Firm-level Adoption of Technology (FAT) survey data.

Note: Panel a provides the coefficients and 95 percent confidence intervals from regressions. Each technology measure is regressed on a dummy for the use of external consultant by the firm, while controlling for country, sector, firm size, and regions. Panel b presents the likelihood that firms have used consultants by firm size group. Panel c shows the share of firms by type of consultant services received. Panel e shows the share of firms by main reason for not using a consultant. Panels d and f provide the coefficients and 95 percent confidence intervals from regressions analyzing the correlation between technology measures and the type of consultants or reason to not use consultants, controlling for country, sector, firm size, regions, and the use of consultants. All estimates are weighted by sampling and country weights. EXT = extensive margin; GBF = general business function; INT = intensive margin; SBF = sector-specific business function.

from consultants coming from a university or government. Panel d shows a positive relationship between technology sophistication and different types of consultants relative to not using consultants. Consulting services provided by local and foreign firms are both significantly correlated with technology sophistication, but the coefficient for foreign firms is larger. Panel e examines the main reason firms do not use consultants. The most common reason reported is the belief that firms do not need it. The negative coefficients in panel f for the different reasons for not using a consultant and technology sophistication, relative to using a consultant, reinforce the importance of accessing external knowledge.

In a recent systematic review looking at interventions to promote technology adoption, Alfaro-Serrano et al. (2021) find mixed evidence on the impact of various interventions to support technology adoption which are primarily based on the use of external consultants (see next chapter). While the context of the intervention differs from the normal use of external knowledge for technology adoption, the authors find a positive impact on technology adoption in 19 out of 33 studies for manufacturing and services firms. Providing access to external knowledge is a common type of support in developed economies via extension services.

Another important source of knowledge is associated with the availability of engineers, as a specialized type of human capital that plays a critical role on technology absorption. Maloney and Valencia Caicedo (2022) build an indicator of engineer intensity for US counties around 1880 and show that a one standard deviation increase in engineers in 1880 accounts for a 16 percent increase in US county income today. Maloney (2002) shows that one of the main reasons that explain the failure to take advantage of growth opportunities in the early twentieth century in some countries in Latin America, with similar factor endowments to Australia, Canada, and Scandinavia, was low investment in human capital and scientific infrastructure, which led to poor innovation and technology adoption.

Factors Internal to the Firm: Firm Capabilities

Information and Behavioral Biases

An important element to explain a firm's decision to adopt a more sophisticated technology is its willingness to do so. A behavioral bias that may influence this decision, as discussed in chapter 2, is *reference group neglect*: that is, entrepreneurs believe themselves to have a particular skill but neglect to realize that they are competing with others who also possess that skill (Camerer and Lovallo 1999). For example, if a firm believes that it is already adopting more sophisticated technologies relative to its competitors, it is unlikely that business will invest in additional technologies. Then the question is whether firms are aware of their actual technology gap.

To address this question, the FAT survey includes a question to managers to self-assess their technological level. The results of their self-assessment are compared with the actual measurement index in the survey. Specifically, the FAT survey asks for a self-assessment of technology from 1 to 10 (here rescaled to 1 to 5), comparing the respondent's firm with other firms within the country and with firms that are global technology leaders in their sector.[13]

Figure 6.10 replicates and expands figure 2.14 in chapter 2 and shows the predicted self-assessment of technology according to the technology adoption index and a 95 percent confidence interval. The 45-degree line shows the point where self-assessed and actual scores coincide. Panels a and b compare respondent firms with domestic firms, while panels c and d compare respondent firms to global leaders in the sector—the frontier. Interestingly, most firms are overconfident (shown by their location above the 45-degree line) since their perception of how sophisticated they are is greater than their

FIGURE 6.10 Firms with a Lower Level of Technology Are Especially Likely to Think They Are More Technologically Sophisticated than They Actually Are

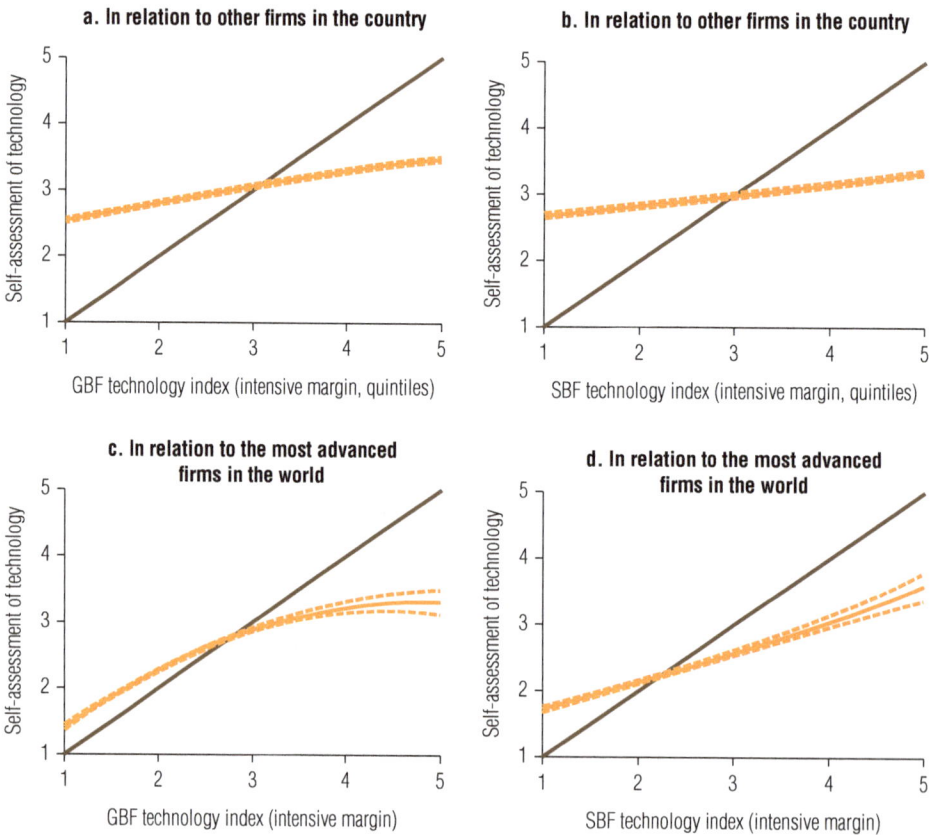

Source: Original figure based on Firm-level Adoption of Technology (FAT) survey data.

Note: The orange line shows the quadratic fit with 95 percent confidence interval using sampling weights. GBF = general business function; SBF = sector-specific business function.

actual level of technology. More important, this excess confidence or reference group neglect is larger for those firms that use less sophisticated technologies. This overconfidence constrains their willingness to adopt and use more sophisticated technologies. Firms' overconfidence is greater when they compare themselves with domestic firms, and it corrects itself when comparing with international firms. This pattern is common, on average, in firms whose technology index for GBFs and SBFs is relatively low (less than 3 on a 5-point scale). This overconfidence, especially among those competing in local markets, is an important deterrent of adoption. Similar overconfidence results are found for management quality (Bloom and Van Reenen 2007; Cirera and Maloney 2017), and suggest that some of these biases are not uncommon when it comes to firm upgrading in general, including upgrading management practices.

Flows of Information and Skills and Links to Large Firms and Multinational Enterprises

Even if potential returns are high, firms may not adopt a new technology if they lack information about these returns, have difficulty evaluating uncertainty, or lack knowledge about how to use the technology. In this context, learning is important. The dominant approach to explain technology adoption has been to frame adoption decisions in a learning environment where benefits and costs to the technologies are homogeneous but unknown and are learned over time. This leads to diffusion processes that resembles an S-shape, consistent with epidemic frameworks laid out by Griliches (1957) and Mansfield (1963). Although learning and externalities dominate adoption processes (Besley and Case 1993), uncertainty associated with market conditions and demand also plays an important role in investment decisions.

Among formal and larger firms, the flows of information and skills with multinational enterprises and other large firms can facilitate technology adoption. These flows tend to happen when firms are geographically closer to other large firms that produce similar products or provide similar services (Foster and Rosenzweig 1995; Bandiera and Rasul 2006; Conley and Udry 2010), and do business with those firms as well as with other multinational firms (Alipranti, Milliou, and Petrakis 2015). Figure 6.11, based on data from the FAT survey, shows a positive association between firms that do business with multinationals or have chief executive officers (CEOs) or top managers who have previous experience in large firms and technology adoption, especially for larger firms. Assuming that these CEOs/top managers are exposed to more firms with more advanced technologies, they become an important source of information on technology adoption. The shares of formal and large firms with CEOs or managers with previous experience in other large firms are more than twice the shares of informal and small firms. More important, as shown in panel a, the sources of information that are more correlated with higher scores on technology indexes are the links to multinational enterprises as suppliers and buyers and the experience of CEOs/top managers with larger firms.

FIGURE 6.11 Engagement with Multinational Enterprises or More Seasoned CEOs Is Positively Associated with Technology Sophistication

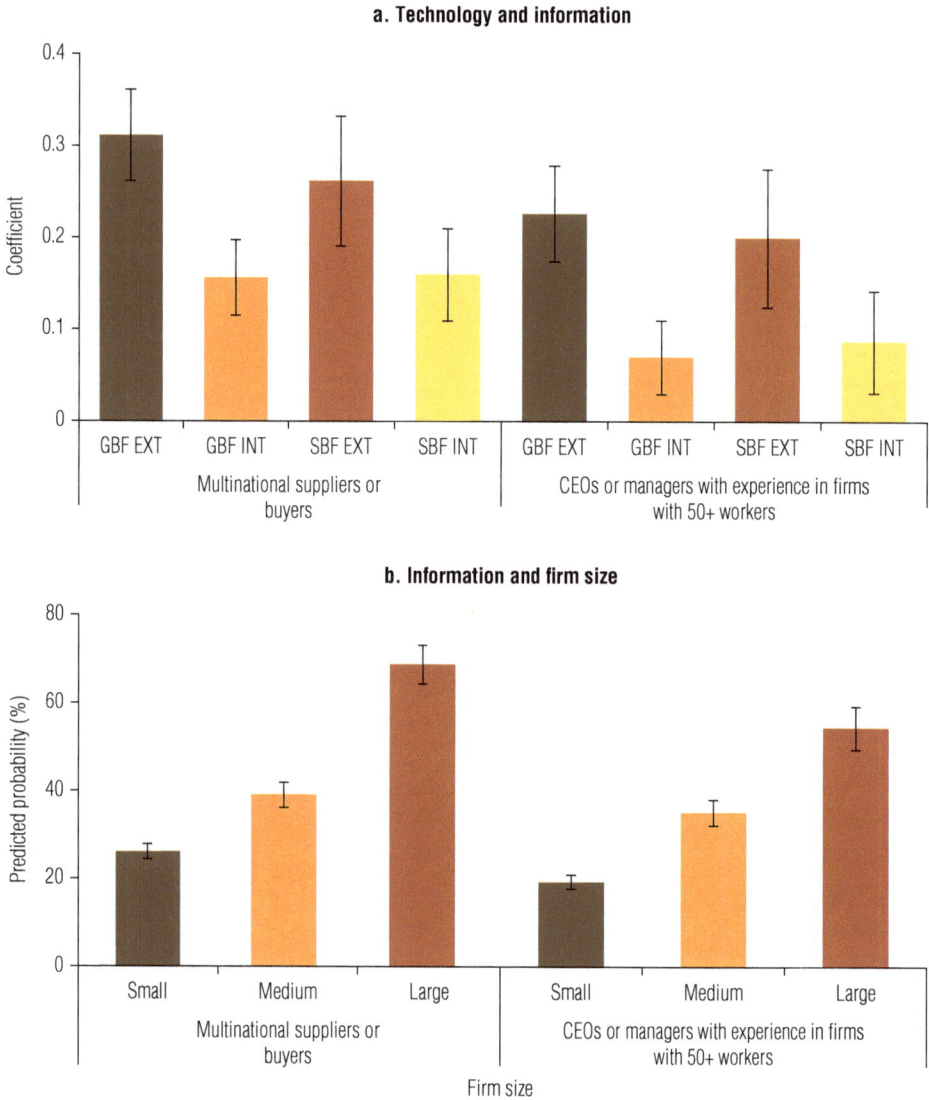

a. Technology and information

b. Information and firm size

Source: Original figure based on Firm-level Adoption of Technology (FAT) survey data.

Note: Panel a provides the coefficients and 95 percent confidence intervals from regressions. Each technology measure is regressed on a dummy for providing formal incentives and performance indicators, respectively, while controlling for country, sector, and firm size. Panel b shows the predicted probability of each awareness variable on firm size from the probit regressions with controlling for other baseline characteristics. All estimates are weighted by sampling and country weights. Firm size refers to the number of workers: small (5–19), medium (20–99), and large (100 or more). CEOs = chief executive officers; EXT = extensive margin; GBF = general business function; INT = intensive margin; SBF = sector-specific business function.

Management Quality and Organization

Firm capabilities can be defined as those elements of the production process that cannot be bought "off the shelf" on the market and hence must be learned and accumulated by the firm (Lall 1992; Sutton 2012). To accumulate these capabilities and manage them, organizational structures (Garicano and Rossi-Hansberg 2006); management practices (Bloom and Van Reenen 2007; Cirera and Maloney 2017); and worker skills are needed. Knowledge is also required to master technologies, and elements that facilitate the accumulation of this knowledge are important drivers of the adoption of new technologies. This process is emphasized in historical accounts of the East Asian miracles, which stress the importance of learning and raising the technological capabilities of firms (Kim and Nelson 2000).

An important source of firm capabilities is, therefore, the quality of management, which starts with the human capital of the main manager. Figure 6.12 shows the correlation between the human capital of managers (panel a) and technology use. The FAT data show that having a manager who has a college degree or who has studied abroad is significantly associated with higher levels of technology across different measures. Panel b shows that large firms are more likely to have managers with greater human capital.

Managerial practices and organizational capabilities have been emphasized as important drivers of technology adoption by the literature. For example, Atkin et al. (2017) conducted an experimental evaluation to demonstrate the importance of organization and incentives in technology adoption. The authors provided producers of leather soccer balls with an off-the-shelf technology to cut leather and produce balls that was more cost-effective. However, many producers did not adopt this new technology due to a misalignment of incentives within firms. Specifically, the key employees (cutters and printers) were typically paid piece rates and had no incentive to reduce waste and adopt the new technology. Given that the new technology slowed them down, at least initially, and there were no incentives to reduce waste, the new technology was not widely adopted.

The FAT survey also allows comparisons of the relationship between a firm's management practices and technology adoption. The questionnaire asks (1) whether firms make use of formal incentives and (2) the number of performance indicators they use as measures of the firm's overall management quality. Our analysis uses these two measures and correlates them with the GBF technology index. Panel c of figure 6.12 shows that firms that use formal incentives with workers have a higher index for both the extensive and intensive margin of technology sophistication. Panel d also suggests that firms with more performance monitoring indicators use more advanced technologies. Although the correlations are not large, the results highlight the importance of management quality as a complement to technology adoption. This positive relationship is also observed in the FAT survey data. Innovation and technology adoption are often driven by workers when they have incentives to do so.

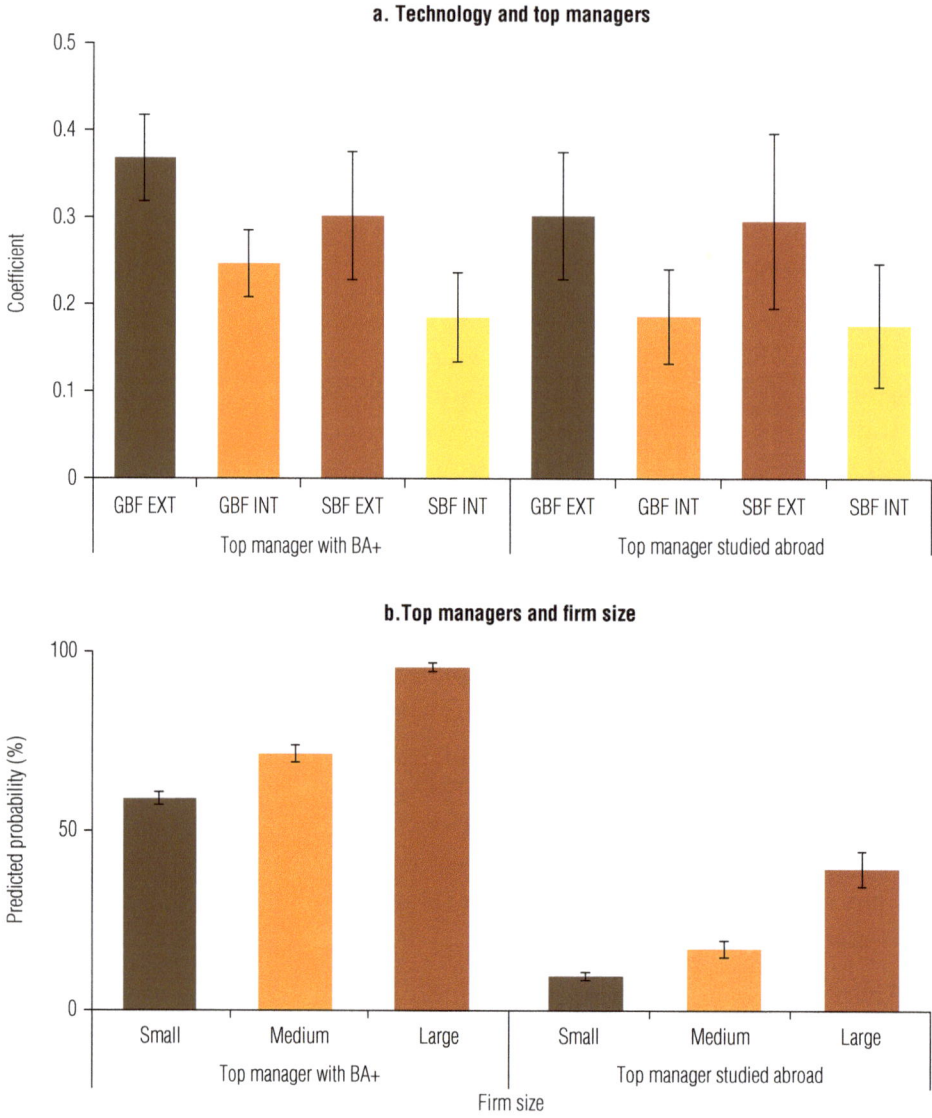

FIGURE 6.12 Firms with Better Management Characteristics, Management Practices, and Organizational Capabilities Have Higher Levels of Technology Sophistication

a. Technology and top managers

b.Top managers and firm size

(Figure continues on the following page.)

FIGURE 6.12 **Firms with Better Management Characteristics, Management Practices, and Organizational Capabilities Have Higher Levels of Technology Sophistication** *(continued)*

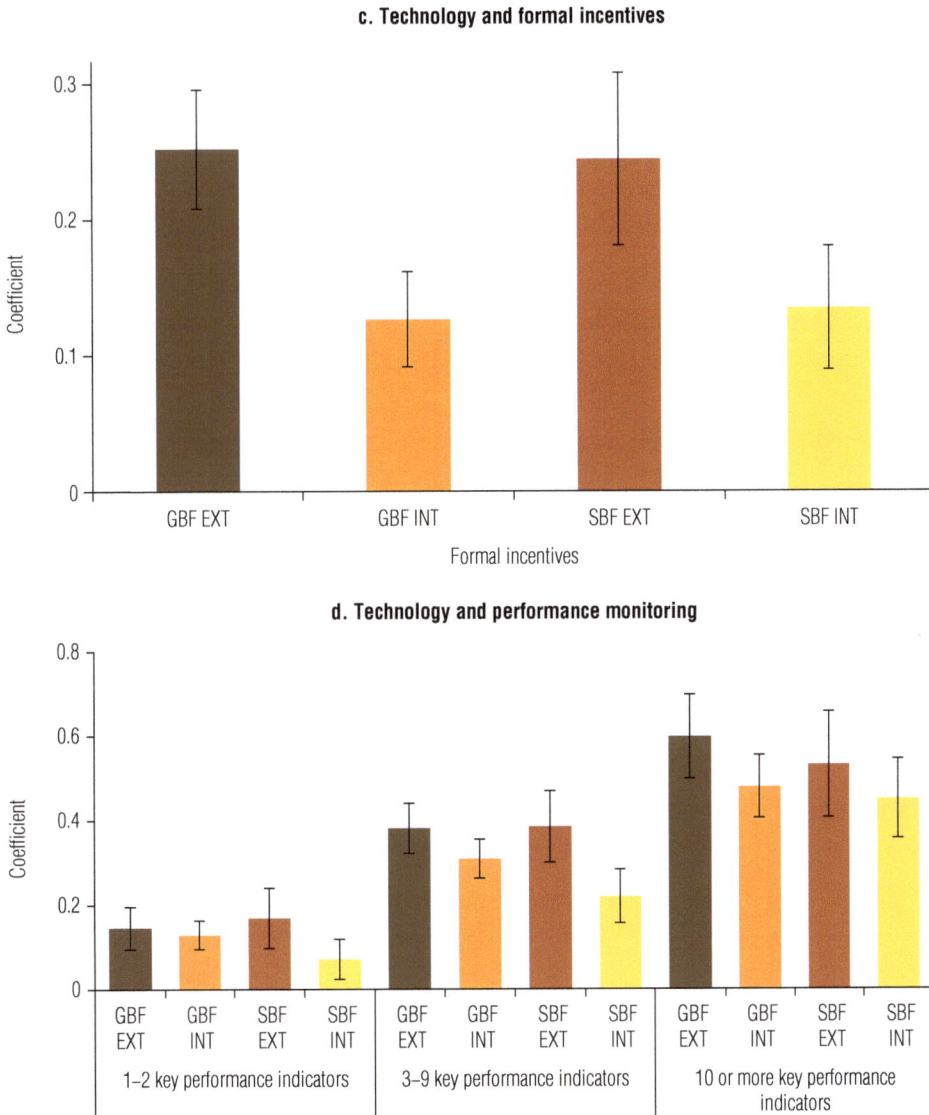

c. Technology and formal incentives

d. Technology and performance monitoring

Source: Original figure based on Firm-level Adoption of Technology (FAT) survey data.

Note: Panel a provides the coefficients and 95 percent confidence intervals from regressions. Each technology measure is regressed on a dummy for the education of the top manager (such as a bachelor's degree or higher degree [BA+] and study abroad), while controlling for country, sector, firm size, and regions. Panel b shows the predicted probability of having top managers with BA+ or studying abroad by firm formality and firm size, with confidence intervals from the probit regressions controlling for other baseline characteristics. Panels c and d provide the coefficients and 95 percent confidence intervals from regressions. Each technology measure is regressed on a dummy for providing formal incentives and performance indicators, respectively, while controlling for country, sector, firm size, and regions. All estimates are weighted by sampling and country weights. BA+ = a bachelor's or higher degree; EXT = extensive margin; GBF = general business function; INT = intensive margin; SBF = sector-specific business function.

What Constrains Firms from Adopting Better Technologies?   161

Know-How and Skills

Know-how and skills capabilities are a key ingredient to adopt more sophisticated technologies. Bartel, Ichniowski, and Shaw (2007), for instance, show how the spread of new capital equipment enhanced by information technology (IT) coincides with increases in the skill requirements of machine operators, notably technical and problem-solving skills, and with the adoption of new human resource practices to support these skills. Harrigan, Reshef, and Toubal (2021) show that increasing investment in ICT adoption—measured by the number of workers who are engineers and technicians with skills and experience in science, technology, engineering, and mathematics—has a positive effect on productivity that goes beyond investment in research and development (R&D).

FAT survey data also demonstrate the importance of know-how and skills capabilities. Figure 6.13 shows that a firm's level of technology sophistication is positively and significantly associated with the fact that these firms were able to develop or customize equipment or software (panel a). This capacity increases with firm size (panel b). But what is the source of these capabilities? Human capital of workers is an important source of know-how and skills capabilities internalized by the firm.

The positive association between human capital and technology sophistication suggests a strong complementary relationship, as highlighted by the literature. The FAT data confirm this. Panel a of figure 6.14 shows that the different measures of technology sophistication—for both GBFs and SBFs at the intensive and extensive margins—are positively and significantly associated with the share of workers with vocational training and the share of workers with a college degree. Panel b also shows that the share of workers with higher levels of human capital increases by firm size.

FIGURE 6.13   **Firms Capable of Developing and Customizing Equipment and Software Are More Sophisticated Technologically**

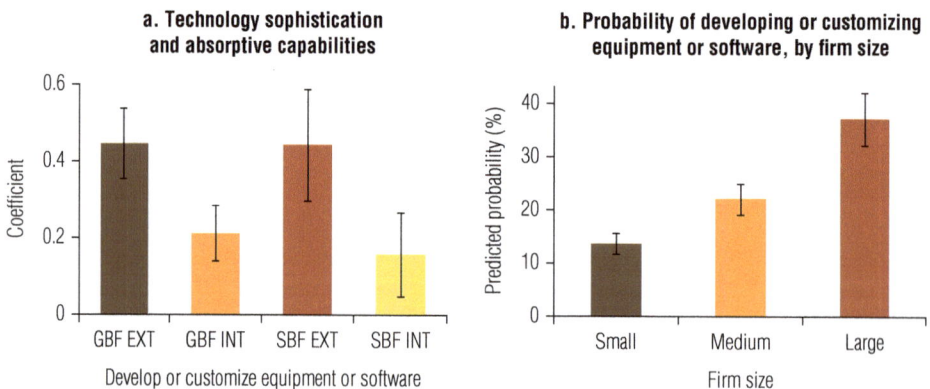

a. Technology sophistication and absorptive capabilities

b. Probability of developing or customizing equipment or software, by firm size

Source: Original figure based on Firm-level Adoption of Technology (FAT) survey data.

Note: Panel a provides the coefficients and 95 percent confidence intervals from regressions. Each technology measure is regressed on dummy variables identifying whether the firm has developed or customized equipment or software, while controlling for country, sector, firm size, and regions. Panel b presents the likelihood of a firm developing and customizing equipment or software by firm size. All estimates are weighted by sampling and country weights. Firm size refers to the number of workers: small (5–19), medium (20–99), and large (100 or more). EXT = extensive margin; GBF = general business function; INT = intensive margin; SBF = sector-specific business function.

FIGURE 6.14 Human Capital Is Higher among Firms with More Sophisticated Technologies

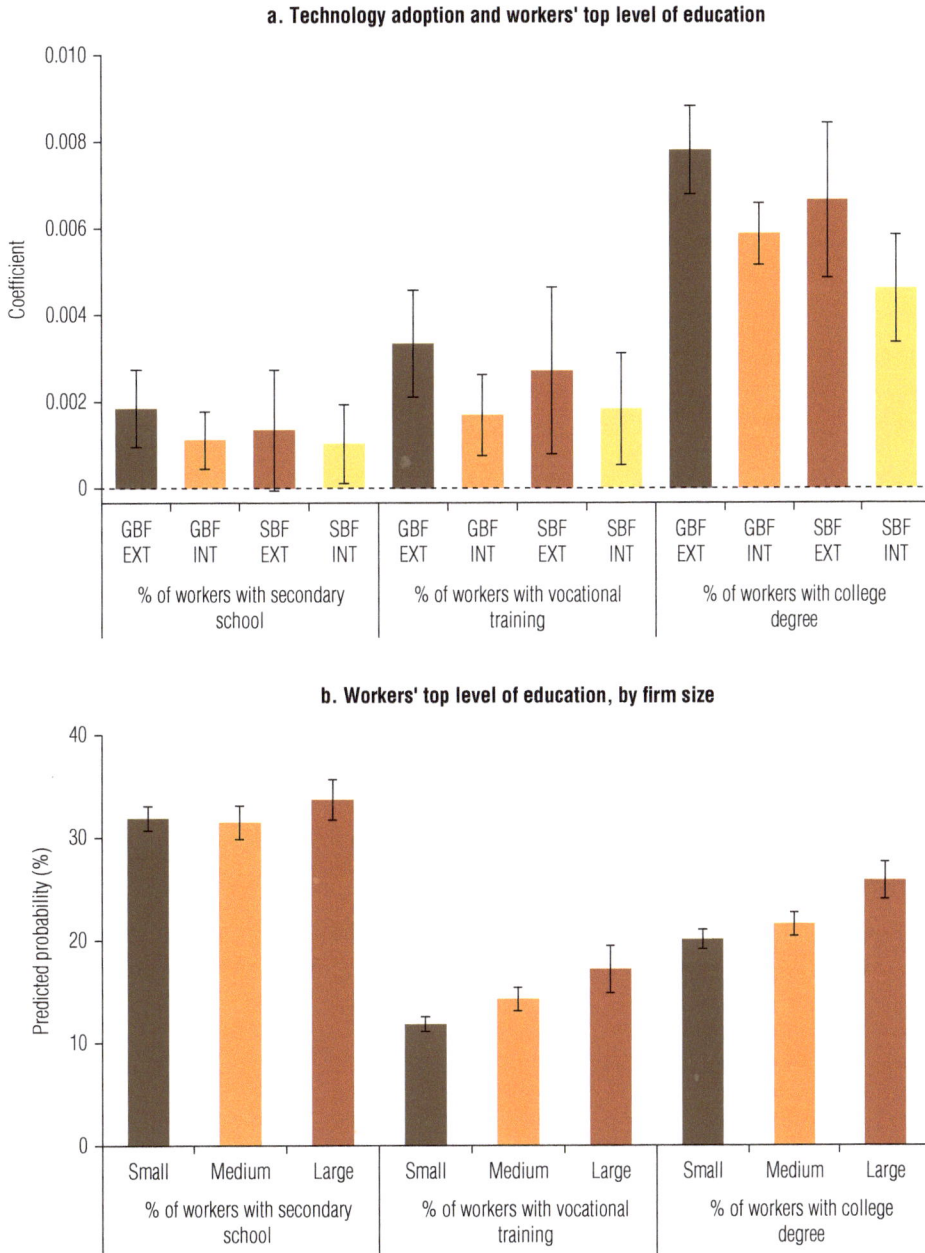

a. Technology adoption and workers' top level of education

b. Workers' top level of education, by firm size

Source: Original figure based on Firm-level Adoption of Technology (FAT) survey data.

Note: Panel a provides the coefficients and 95 percent confidence intervals from regressions. Each technology measure is regressed on the percent of workers with different education levels (such as secondary school, vocational training, and college degree), respectively, while controlling for country, sector, size, and regions. Panel b presents the predicted percent of workers with different education by formality and size from the linear regressions controlling for other baseline characteristics. All estimates are weighted by sampling and country weights. EXT = extensive margin; GBF = general business function; INT = intensive margin; SBF = sector-specific business function.

Summing Up

This chapter shows that a multiplicity of barriers explain the lack of technology adoption by firms. The importance of these factors depends on the context, the type of technology, and the type of firm.

When designing policies it is important to ensure that the key enablers external to the firm are in place, including appropriate infrastructure, a favorable regulatory environment, and a well-functioning financial market. In addition, it is also critical to build the conditions that improve firms' internal capacity to benefit from improvements in infrastructure and market reforms. Firm capabilities to absorb, learn, and accumulate know-how about production and service provision should not be taken for granted. In many developing countries, the lack of human capital and dysfunctional institutions impose constraints on workers' and entrepreneurs' ability to benefit from existing technologies that could potentially lead to economic transformation.

This chapter highlights four key policy lessons. First, firm capabilities are a key driver of technology adoption. Therefore, any technology adoption support program cannot focus only on "hardware" such as infrastructure, machinery, and equipment; it must also focus on how to strengthen the capabilities—such as management, education, and learning—needed to run these machines effectively in the firm. Second, public policies should take into account the fact that very often entrepreneurs do not see any positive value in upgrading because they lack information, the returns are uncertain, or they are overconfident. Providing adequate information about the availability of technologies and the importance of upgrading is key. Third, access to external knowledge—by utilizing knowledge services, knowledge created in universities, or learning from other firms via trade flows or relationships through global value chains—is an important driver of technology adoption. Fourth, policies need to consider that for some technologies, for example digital technologies that use data intensively or create new business models, the main focus should concentrate in designing appropriate regulatory frameworks to enable the adoption of these technologies.

Notes

1. For decades, economists and sociologists have been studying the uptake of technologies involved in production. Going back to the seminal works by Ryan and Gross (1943) and Griliches (1957) on the diffusion of hybrid varieties of corn, the dominant approach in this early work was to measure the process of diffusion of an advanced technology, especially in agriculture (Mansfield 1961). A common pattern observed though the diffusion literature is that the diffusion process across regions resembles an S-shaped function (such as a logistic function). In his seminal work, Griliches (1957) analyzed the technological gap across regions in the use of hybrid seed corn within the United States. Hybrid corn was a new method of breeding superior corn, but it was not immediately adopted everywhere. The differences in S-shaped curves across US states reflect two different problems associated with technology adoption. The first is the acceptance problem, which refers to differences in the rate of adoption of hybrids by farmers in states where the technology was already available. The second

is the availability problem, which refers to the lag in the development of technologies (such as hybrid corn) adapted for specific areas. Several other studies provided some support for the S-shaped curves as a good fit to traditional measures of technology diffusion (Gort and Klepper 1982; Skinner and Staiger 2007). Mansfield (1961) analyzed the factors determining the speed of technology diffusion across firms. Despite some heterogeneity across industries, his findings also suggest that the growth over time in the number of firms having introduced an innovation conforms to a logistic function (S-shape). Mansfield found that the probability of a firm introducing a new technique is an increasing function of the proportion of firms already using it and the profitability of doing so, set against a decreasing function of the size of the investment required: hence, the S-shape.

2. This chapter builds on background papers describing the FAT results for the state of Ceará, Brazil (Cirera et al. 2021b), Senegal (Cirera et al. 2021a), and Vietnam (Cirera et al. 2021c). This chapter extended the analysis on drivers and obstacles for adoption to all 11 countries covered in this volume.

3. Cusolito (2021) provides a comprehensive review of barriers to adoption, including a detailed coverage of the literature specific to accessing digital platforms.

4. The framework becomes more complex in the presence of technology externalities because the decision is conditional to other firms adopting. Different types of externalities are associated with technologies. Direct network externalities arise when the value directly increases with the number of users, such as with automated teller machines (ATMs), credit cards, or some infrastructure. Some other externalities are more indirect. They arise as the result of learning, whereby users teach other users—such as farmers teaching other farmers to use seeds—or by increasing the provision of support and complementary services.

5. For a review of microeconomic approaches to estimating technology adoption, see Foster and Rosenzweig (2010).

6. While Verhoogen focuses the literature review on manufacturing, his conceptual framework can be generalized to other sectors.

7. An extensive literature has focused on the impact of energy prices on the adoption of energy-saving technologies. Popp (2002) shows that energy prices and existing knowledge largely affect the introduction of energy-saving technologies. Pizer et al. (2002) find that both energy prices and the financial situation of plants influence technology adoption among a sample of industrial plants in four heavily polluting sectors in the United States. In a completely different sector, Macher, Miller, and Osborne (2021) show for the cement industry how factor prices are important and how competition and demand change the responsiveness of technology adoption to factor prices.

8. The results in this section are based on Berkes et al. (forthcoming), which is a background paper for this volume.

9. This effect remains stable even after controlling for various firm and managerial characteristics, as well as industry times region fixed effects.

10. Some "placebo" tests were also run. As expected, they found that the quality of internet service does not have any predictive power on other types of connections (such as dial-up or satellite) or infrastructure (such as access to water).

11. As is common in an instrumental variable framework, there are two identifying assumptions. First, distance from the node needs to be a predictor of access to the internet. Second, distance needs to affect technology adoption only through the internet. The first assumption constitutes the first stage and was extensively tested by, for example, showing that distance to the internet node is not correlated with the access to other nondigital-related resources, such as access to water, or access to the internet through satellite or wireless service. The second assumption cannot be tested directly, but the evidence that the location relative to an access node does not seem to be correlated with access to other infrastructure, such as water, suggests that the "only through the internet" assumption is believable in this context.

12. Kugler and Verhoogen (2009) show that importers perform better by using better inputs for production.

13. The self-assessment question is asked before any of the technology adoption questions to prevent any bias in the self-assessment from potential framing.

References

Abate, G. T., S. Rashid, C. Borzaga, and K. Getnet. 2016. "Rural Finance and Agricultural Technology Adoption in Ethiopia: Does the Institutional Design of Lending Organizations Matter?" *World Development* 84 (C): 235–53.

Aghion, P., N. Bloom, R. Blundell, R. Griffith, and P. Howitt. 2005. "Competition and Innovation: An Inverted-U Relationship." *Quarterly Journal of Economics* 120 (2): 701–28.

Alfaro-Serrano, D., T. Balantrapu, R. Chaurey, A. Goicoechea, and E. Verhoogen. 2021. "Interventions to Promote Technology Adoption in Firms: A Systematic Review." *Campbell Systematic Reviews* 17 (4): 1–36.

Alipranti, M., C. Milliou, and E. Petrakis. 2015. "On Vertical Relations and the Timing of Technology Adoption." *Journal of Economic Behavior & Organization* 120 (C): 117–29.

Atkin, D., A. Chaudhry, S. Chaudry, A. K. Khandelwal, and E. Verhoogen. 2017. "Organizational Barriers to Technology Adoption: Evidence from Soccer-Ball Producers in Pakistan." *Quarterly Journal of Economics* 132 (3): 1101–64.

Atkin, D., A. K. Khandelwal, and A. Osman. 2017. "Exporting and Firm Performance: Evidence from a Randomized Experiment." *Quarterly Journal of Economics* 132 (2): 551–615.

Bandiera, O., and I. Rasul. 2006. "Social Networks and Technology Adoption in Northern Mozambique." *Economic Journal* 116 (514): 869–902.

Bartel, A., C. Ichniowski, and K. Shaw. 2007. "How Does Information Technology Affect Productivity? Plant-Level Comparisons of Product Innovation, Process Improvement, and Worker Skills." *Quarterly Journal of Economics* 122 (4): 1721–58.

Beaman, L., A. BenYishay, J. Magruder, and A. M. Mobarak. 2021. "Can Network Theory-Based Targeting Increase Technology Adoption?" *American Economic Review* 111 (6): 1918–43.

Berkes, E., X. Cirera, D. Comin, and M. Cruz. Forthcoming. "Infrastructure, Productivity, and Technology Adoption." Background paper for *Bridging the Technological Divide*. World Bank, Washington, DC.

Besley, T., and A. Case. 1993. "Modeling Technology Adoption in Developing Countries." *American Economic Review* 83 (2): 396–402.

Bircan, C., and R. De Haas. 2019. "The Limits of Lending? Banks and Technology Adoption across Russia." *Review of Financial Studies* 33 (2): 536–609.

Bloom, N., M. Draca, and J. Van Reenen. 2016. "Trade Induced Technical Change? The Impact of Chinese Imports on Innovation, IT and Productivity." *Review of Economic Studies* 83 (1): 87–117.

Bloom, N., and J. Van Reenen. 2007. "Measuring and Explaining Management Practices across Firms and Countries." *Quarterly Journal of Economics* 122 (4): 1351–408.

Bustos, P. 2011. "Trade Liberalization, Exports, and Technology Upgrading: Evidence on the Impact of MERCOSUR on Argentinian Firms." *American Economic Review* 101 (1): 304–40.

Camerer, C., and D. Lovallo. 1999. "Overconfidence and Excess Entry: An Experimental Approach." *American Economic Review* 89 (1): 306–18.

Cirera, X., D. Comin, M. Cruz, and K. M. Lee. 2020. "Technology within and across Firms." Policy Research Working Paper 9476, World Bank, Washington, DC.

Cirera, X., D. Comin, M. Cruz, and K. M. Lee. 2021a. "Firm-Level Adoption of Technologies in Senegal." Policy Research Working Paper 9657, World Bank, Washington, DC.

Cirera, X., D. Comin, M. Cruz, K. M. Lee, and A. Soares Martins-Neto. 2021b. "Firm-Level Technology Adoption in the State of Ceará in Brazil." Policy Research Working Paper 9568, World Bank, Washington, DC.

Cirera, X., D. Comin, M. Cruz, K. M. Lee, and A. Soares Martins-Neto. 2021c. "Firm-Level Technology Adoption in Vietnam." Policy Research Working Paper 9567, World Bank, Washington, DC.

Cirera, X., and W. F. Maloney. 2017. *The Innovation Paradox: Developing-Country Capabilities and the Unrealized Promise of Technological Catch-Up.* World Bank Productivity Project series. Washington, DC: World Bank.

Cole, H. L., J. Greenwood, and J. M. Sanchez. 2016. "Why Doesn't Technology Flow from Rich to Poor Countries?" *Econometrica* 84 (4): 1477–521.

Conley, T. G., and C. R. Udry. 2010. "Learning about a New Technology: Pineapple in Ghana." *American Economic Review* 100 (1): 35–69.

Cusolito, A. P. 2021. "The Economics of Technology Adoption." World Bank, Washington, DC. Unpublished.

Daza Jaller, L., S. Gaillard, and M. Molinuevo. 2020. *The Regulation of Digital Trade: Key Policies and International Trends.* Washington, DC: World Bank.

Duflo, E., M. Kremer, and J. Robinson. 2008. "How High Are Rates of Return to Fertilizer? Evidence from Field Experiments in Kenya." *American Economic Review* 98 (2): 482–88.

Foster, A. D., and M. R. Rosenzweig. 1995. "Learning by Doing and Learning from Others: Human Capital and Technical Change in Agriculture." *Journal of Political Economy* 103 (6): 1176–209.

Foster, A. D., and M. R. Rosenzweig. 2010. "Microeconomics of Technology Adoption." *Annual Review of Economics* 2 (1): 395–424.

Garicano, L., and E. Rossi-Hansberg. 2006. "Organization and Inequality in a Knowledge Economy." *Quarterly Journal of Economics* 121 (4): 1383–435.

Gort, M., and S. Klepper. 1982. "Time Paths in the Diffusion of Product Innovations." *Economic Journal* 92 (367): 630–53.

Griliches, Z. 1957. "Hybrid Corn: An Exploration in the Economics of Technological Change." *Econometrica* 25 (4): 501–22.

Gupta, A., J. Ponticelli, and A. Tesei. 2020. "Information, Technology Adoption and Productivity: The Role of Mobile Phones in Agriculture." NBER Working Paper 27192, National Bureau of Economic Research, Cambridge, MA.

Hannan, T. H., and J. M. McDowell. 1984. "The Determinants of Technology Adoption: The Case of the Banking Firm." *RAND Journal of Economics* 15 (3): 328–35.

Harrigan, J., A. Reshef, and F. Toubal. 2021. "Techies, Trade, and Skill-Biased Productivity." NBER Working Paper 25295, National Bureau of Economic Research, Cambridge, MA.

Hjort, J., and J. Poulsen. 2019. "The Arrival of Fast Internet and Employment in Africa." *American Economic Review* 109 (3): 1032–79.

Jin, Y., and Z. Sun. 2020. "Lifting Growth Barriers for New Firms: Evidence from an Entrepreneurship Training Experiment with Two Million Online Businesses." https://docplayer.net/200049815-Lifting-growth-barriers-for-new-firms.html.

Kim, L., and R. R. Nelson, eds. 2000. *Technology, Learning, and Innovation: Experiences of Newly Industrializing Economies.* Cambridge, UK: Cambridge University Press.

Kugler, M., and E. Verhoogen. 2009. "Plants and Imported Inputs: New Facts and an Interpretation." *American Economic Review* 99 (2): 501–07.

Lall, S. 1992. "Technological Capabilities and Industrialization." *World Development* 20 (2): 165–86.

Lileeva, A., and D. Trefler. 2010. "Improved Access to Foreign Markets Raises Plant-Level Productivity... for Some Plants." *Quarterly Journal of Economics* 125 (3): 1051–99.

Macher, J. T., N. H. Miller, and M. Osborne. 2021. "Finding Mr. Schumpeter: Technology Adoption in the Cement Industry." *RAND Journal of Economics* 52 (1): 78–99.

Maloney, W. F. 2002. "Missed Opportunities: Innovation and Resource-Based Growth in Latin America." Policy Research Working Paper 2935, World Bank, Washington, DC.

Maloney, W. F., and F. Valencia Caicedo. 2022. "Engineering Growth." *Journal of the European Economic Association*. https://doi.org/10.1093/jeea/jvac014.

Mansfield, E. 1961. "Technical Change and the Rate of Imitation." *Econometrica* 29 (4, October): 741–66.

Mansfield, E. 1963. "Intrafirm Rates of Diffusion of an Innovation." *Review of Economics and Statistics* 45 (4, November): 348–59.

Midrigan, V., and D. Y. Xu. 2014. "Finance and Misallocation: Evidence from Plant-Level Data." *American Economic Review* 104 (2): 422–58.

Pizer, W. A., W. Harrington, R. J. Kopp, R. D. Morgenstern, and J. S. Shih. 2002. "Technology Adoption and Aggregate Energy Efficiency." Discussion Paper 10616, Resources for the Future, Washington, DC.

Popp, D. 2002. "Induced Innovation and Energy Prices." *American Economic Review* 92 (1): 160–80.

Ryan, B., and N. Gross. 1943. "The Diffusion of Hybrid Seed Corn in Two Iowa Communities." *Rural Sociology* 8 (1): 15–24.

Skinner, J., and D. Staiger. 2007. "Technology Adoption from Hybrid Corn to Beta-Blockers." In *Hard-to-Measure Goods and Services: Essays in Honor of Zvi Griliches,* edited by Ernst R. Berndt and Charles R. Hulten, 545–70. University of Chicago Press for the National Bureau of Economic Research.

Suri, T. 2011. "Selection and Comparative Advantage in Technology Adoption." *Econometrica* 79 (1): 159–209.

Sutton, J. 2012. *Competing in Capabilities: The Globalization Process.* Oxford, UK: Oxford University Press.

Verhoogen, E. Forthcoming. "Firm-Level Upgrading in Developing Countries." *Journal of Economic Literature.*

Wagner, J. 1995. "Exports, Firm Size, and Firm Dynamics." *Small Business Economics* 7 (1): 29–39.

7. Policies and Instruments to Accelerate Technology Adoption

Introduction

This chapter analyzes what public policies can do to incentivize firms to upgrade their technology and, more important, how to design these policies to deal with the barriers described in the previous chapter. Specifically, it addresses the following questions:

- What are the key principles for designing policies to support technology adoption?
- How can policy instruments to promote technology upgrading be identified, designed, and refined by considering factors that are external and internal to the firm?
- How can the results from the Firm-level Adoption of Technology (FAT) survey inform policy design?
- What are the instruments available to support firm technology upgrading?

The discussion begins by describing some general good practices and processes to formulate policies to promote technology adoption. It follows with general guidance and a framework to prioritize policies. It then reviews some of the key policy instruments to support technology upgrading, showcases some examples, and describes the limited evidence of impact. The chapter concludes with key messages.

A Checklist to Design Technology Upgrading Programs

Policy makers around the world have been trying to directly address the problem of lack of technology adoption with very mixed results. A recent systematic review of impact evaluations of various instruments to promote technology adoption finds that the impact on both adoption and performance outcomes is mixed, at best (Alfaro-Serrano et al. 2021). More important, the results emphasize the importance of context-specific factors and suggest that that there is no one-size-fits-all solution.

Given the complexities that surround the design and implementation of technology adoption policies, the discussion that follows provides some guidance for policy makers on how to structure policy support and minimize the risk of government failure. The section builds on the first volume of the World Bank Productivity Project series,

Cirera and Maloney (2017), as well as Cirera et al. (2020), focusing more narrowly on technology adoption and drawing on the evidence from the FAT survey.

1. Identify Market Failures

Technology adoption, like the process of innovation more broadly, is characterized by market failures that can result in underinvestment in the adoption of new technologies. For example, individual firms' decisions to generate or to adopt technologies can generate positive technological or knowledge externalities or spillovers in other firms in the same cluster or location that the adopter or creator cannot fully appropriate. In addition, some of the investments needed in knowledge are indivisible and may require large up-front investments that firms may not be able to make or afford by themselves (Cirera et al. 2020).

The policy response to these market failures has been a combination of tax incentives, grants, and favorable finance (Bryan and Williams 2021). The recent mechanism design literature has proposed a set of optimal policies that tailor the size of subsidy and the cost of finance depending on the size of spillovers and externalities and the extent of moral hazard or adverse selection (Lach, Neeman, and Schankerman 2021).[1]

In the case of off-the-shelf technologies or digital solutions, a critical question is whether positive externalities or spillovers exist, and if so, how large they are. Adoption of more sophisticated technologies can create positive spillovers across the value chain or the spatial cluster of firms, or to society in general (such as green technologies). Associated knowledge spillovers can be transmitted through the training of workers or the creation of spinoffs.

An important question for policy is how large these positive spillovers need to be to justify subsidies. Many public agencies assume that these spillovers exist. In many developed countries, including Canada, Singapore, and the United Kingdom, government agencies provide small subsidies in the form of vouchers and grants to small and medium enterprises (SMEs) for basic technology upgrading and digitalization projects, in the belief that extensive digitalization of businesses generates positive externalities. Public agencies in developing countries with more constrained resources need to articulate and try to measure these externalities or spillovers, and also make sure that these programs do not indirectly have a negative effect on market structure or consumers (for an analysis of potential indirect negative effects of finance programs, see Cai and Szeidl 2022).

Another relevant market failure, especially for some digital technologies, arises from large network effects (see chapter 6). Some technologies require a sufficient number of adopters for the technology to be profitable and for the development of additional support services. In these cases, it may be optimal to subsidize early adopters, although the uncertainty about the sustainability of the technology is a challenge for public agencies.

Identifying what type of market failure justifies government support and the size of the market failure, as well as articulating why and under what conditions government support could lead to higher adoption and not waste public resources, are critical initial steps for public policy.

2. Ensure High-Quality Infrastructure and Remove Regulatory Bottlenecks

The previous chapter examined several barriers to technology adoption and use, and showed how these depend on the context, the entrepreneur or manager, and the type of technology. Accordingly, policies must take these differences into account and ensure that some key elements (enablers) are in place to foster the adoption of new technologies. Two enablers, in particular, need to be on policy makers' list of priorities: access to high-quality infrastructure and an appropriate regulatory framework.

- *Access to high-quality infrastructure.* A key message of this volume is that infrastructure that provides access to general-purpose technologies is a necessary although not a sufficient condition to promote the adoption of more sophisticated technologies across firms, sectors, and countries. As discussed in chapter 1, developing countries still face significant problems in guaranteeing the quality of electricity infrastructure and the availability of internet services. Access to a reliable electricity network is necessary to facilitate the use of all technologies, and firms will hesitate to invest in sophisticated technologies when they must contend with unreliable networks. Policies that facilitate rolling out internet nodes or 5G infrastructure are also critical to facilitate access to advanced digital technologies, such as the Internet of Things (IoT). Ensuring the minimum quality of and access to these technologies is the first step in fostering adoption of sophisticated technologies.
- *An appropriate and agile regulatory framework.* As the digital economy expands, policy makers are grappling with the challenge of transforming laws and regulations governing trade, taxation, labor, finance, social security, and other spheres that are increasingly inadequate for a digital world (Zhu et al., forthcoming). An agile and appropriate regulatory framework is needed to deal with the regulatory demands of constant technological changes, the frequent offering of new services, and issues related to data management and privacy. Regulatory issues are even more important for digital platforms, including those applied to financial technology. Fintech holds the promise of increasing the financial access of SMEs and underrepresented segments of consumers in low- and middle-income countries. But regulations to minimize investor and financial risks or concerns about data privacy and fraud often prevent the development and growth of firms in the sector. As discussed in chapter 5, two-sided platforms and some data-driven sectors have a tendency toward market dominance, especially though horizontal mergers. This requires strong competition and antitrust measures (see box 7.1).

Digital Platforms Are Prone to Market Concentration and Dominance

Three key features of the digital economy create a tendency for market concentration. The first is returns to scale, driven largely by technologies that have led to a rapid and steep decline in the costs of data storage, computation, and transmission. The second feature is network externalities, which arise from the fact that the convenience (value) of using a product or service increases with the number of users that adopt it. The third feature is the intensive use and accumulation of personal data. Digital technologies allow companies to collect, store, and use large amounts of data that in turn lead to continuous improvements in business intelligence and more profitability.

These features erect barriers to entry and make certain digital markets, such as digital platform markets, prone to market tipping: that is, once a firm gains an initial advantage, it keeps building on that advantage at the expense of its competitors. This in turn creates conditions for a winner-take-most economy, leading to concentration of market power and wealth in a small number of global "big tech" firms and individuals. Although these features are not unique to the digital sectors, they tend to be much more relevant than in most traditional activities.

There is also evidence that firms based in high-income countries have been using anti-competitive practices in overseas markets to gain market dominance. An analysis of publicly available information on 103 finalized antitrust cases around the world, as of January 2020, reveals that most cases concerning abuse of dominance and anticompetitive agreements have been filed in developing countries against firms headquartered abroad. This pattern calls for international cooperation to prevent such abuse, such as a coordinated effort on digital taxes, data interoperability policies, and adoption of standards to allow data flows across firms, industries, and borders so firms in developing countries also have a fair chance to scale.

Source: Zhu et al., forthcoming.

3. Ensure an Open Trade Regime that Supports Access to External Knowledge and Technology

As shown in the previous chapter, participation in international markets and global value chains facilitates the adoption of technologies. While trade and investment policies appear to be beyond the realm of technology policies, they are in fact intertwined. For example, high import tariffs or nontariff barriers on equipment, restrictions on hiring foreign engineers and managers, or restrictions on investors and technology licensing can be critical barriers to technology adoption. Maloney (2002) shows how in addition to lack of investments in knowledge institutions, inward policies focusing on import substitution played a key role in impeding economic growth in Latin American countries. Ensuring access to external knowledge and the diffusion of technologies is key, especially for most developing countries that adopt existing technologies.

4. Facilitate Access to Finance for Technology Upgrading

Financial market imperfections related to information asymmetries and lack of competition in the financial sector make the financing of technology upgrading in developing countries difficult and costly. In many developing countries it is unusual for commercial banks to finance technology upgrading projects. Firms must make these investments with their own resources, which considerably limits their capacity to invest, or they must deal with very high collateral requirements or very high interest rates, which make investing in new technologies unprofitable.

Public agencies need to work with the financial sector to stimulate this type of lending by providing funds that reduce potential liquidity problems and lower the cost of finance, or by providing credit guarantees. In addition, public agencies can support the use of expert consultants and technology mentors to strengthen firms' loan applications. More important, publicly backed finance programs can provide a demonstration effect with commercial banks to show how to screen technology upgrading projects and minimize risks while financing this type of project.

5. Provide Information and Build Institutions to Address Coordination Failures

Flows of specialized information are particularly important for small businesses, which tend to be less informed about the latest technologies available in the market. While it should be in their private interest to join forces to obtain this information, private firms face a common coordination failure that pushes them to act independently. As a result, there is a role for public policy to facilitate information and information flows. However, public institutions are not always best placed to provide this type of specialized information. Public-private partnerships with private sector organizations should be prioritized to ensure information flows. Filling this information gap is important to minimize entrepreneurs' uncertainty about adoption. No information flow can guarantee the returns to investing in such technology, but better information can help entrepreneurs assess these returns and make more informed decisions.

Perhaps the most important role played by public agencies to support technology upgrading is addressing coordination failures. A firm's performance depends on the actions of other firms. Market failures associated with economies of scale, spillovers, or nonexcludability (where other firms can enjoy the benefits without paying for knowledge) in the provisions of these inputs and services can lead to multiple equilibria, which in turn require coordination to move from low to a high equilibrium (Rodríguez-Clare 2006). Moreover, information frictions, irrational behavior, or path dependency, among other factors, can lead also to a low equilibrium (Hoff 2000). Coordination to deal with such failures is not always possible in the market.

Consider the fact that many firms do not upgrade their technologies because of the lack of information or an adequate skilled labor force, as described in chapter 6.

A market solution is to coordinate with other firms in the industry so this information and training are provided. However, industry associations sometimes respond to the rent-seeking behavior of some of their more powerful associates, and participation in those associations is often low, especially among smaller firms. Hoff (2000) provides some examples of coordination failures in different contexts of developing countries. The important takeaway is that private agents may not necessarily coordinate to achieve a second-best outcome.

There is, therefore, a role for public policy in working with the private sector in aligning interests and ensuring an efficient provision of physical infrastructure, information, and skills. Perhaps the most important role is ensuring that firms of all sizes have good information about what technologies and what types of support from technology and digital solutions providers are available, as well as supporting adequate training for the labor force. This should be implemented jointly with private sector associations that know the sectors better. In addition, in countries where there is significant mistrust between the suppliers of technologies and digital solutions and local firms concerning the quality of services provided public agencies can play a role in matching supply and demand and ensuring some minimum quality standards that reduce information asymmetries.

This important coordination role does not guarantee that public agencies will be successful in achieving upgrading. Policy failure remains a risk (Besley and Case 1993), especially when public agencies want to take roles where they have no expertise or when interests diverge due to agency problems—when agents do not necessarily implement the interests of the agency. Public agencies need to take this risk seriously and make sure that there are checks and balances in the design of support policies (see the discussion later in this chapter).

6. Improve the Provision of and Markets for Business Advisory and Technology Extension Services

Access to knowledge through business advisory and technology extension services is an important mechanism to build technological know-how and skills. They can enhance not only the absorption of new technologies but also the capacity for further learning (Cohen and Levinthal 1990). Although these services should not necessarily be provided by government agencies directly, many of them do so, and most important, there is significant room for improving failures related to asymmetric and incomplete information in these markets.

The potential market failure for knowledge has been well described by Arrow (1962) in what is known as Arrow's information paradox, which applies broadly to the production of knowledge used by firms. The development and transfer of a technology involves the production and transfer of information that has three properties:

indivisibility, nonappropriability, and uncertainty. The main idea is that unless the information (such as business advice) is revealed, a potential buyer cannot accurately assess its value, but once the information is known, a buyer may have little incentive to pay the seller. These features present challenges to a well-functioning market for business and technology information. While these issues can be partially addressed by reputation mechanisms and contracts (Anton and Yao 2002), these instruments tend to be challenging, particularly for SMEs in developing countries. Yet evidence suggests potential productivity gains from these services (Bruhn, Karlan, and Schoar 2018). These programs can also be used to prepare firms interested in instruments that require further capabilities to benefit from them, such as export promotion.[2] Thus, there is a role for policy in improving the provision of and markets for business advisory and technology extension services.

7. Enhance Awareness, Improving Targeting Mechanisms for Government Support and Strengthening Government Capabilities

Small firms are much less aware of government support programs and are also less likely to benefit from them, as shown in figure 7.1. FAT survey data reveal that only about 30 percent of small firms are aware of government support programs, compared to about 46 percent of large firms. A very low share of small firms benefits from existing support mechanisms. The gap between awareness and access is also larger in small firms. On average, the probability of a small business receiving public support for technology adoption is around 13 percent versus more than 35 percent for large firms. These results are associated with the fact that large firms have better access to information and have managers and business organizations that are better prepared, as described in chapter 6.

These results underscore the importance of disseminating information about government support programs to facilitate adoption, especially among SMEs. Smaller firms also tend to participate less in industry associations, and their entrepreneurs and managers have less time to participate in association activities. Thus, public agencies need to make more of an effort to reach out to these smaller firms.

Targeting mechanisms also need to be effective. Mistargeting occurs when public policies support unintended beneficiaries, either because they do not need the support or because they are not the targeted group. For example, during the COVID-19 pandemic, around 20 percent of firms that did not experience a drop in sales received support (figure 7.2).[3] Among businesses whose sales dropped, large firms had a much larger probability of getting support. As seen in figure 7.1, larger firms also get more support for technology upgrading. This may be driven by barriers in terms of lack of information and fixed costs to apply, which are more binding for smaller firms, but also raise some potential political economy issues on how support may be implemented

FIGURE 7.1 Large Firms Tend to Be More Aware of and Benefit More from Public Support of Technology Adoption than Small and Medium Firms

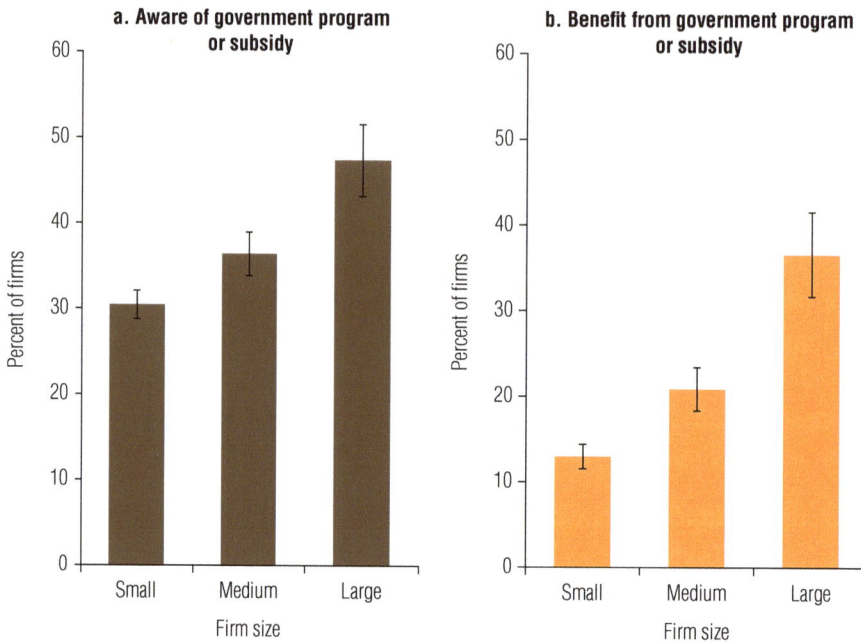

a. Aware of government program or subsidy

b. Benefit from government program or subsidy

Source: Original figure based on Firm-level Adoption of Technology (FAT) survey data.

Note: Estimated share of firms that benefit from government program or subsidy by size from the probit regressions controlling for country, sector, and other baseline characteristics. All estimates consider sampling design variables by country. Firm size refers to the number of workers: small (5–19), medium (20–99), and large (100 or more).

(Besley 2007). Often the costs of targeting can be large, given the difficulties of identifying those in need. This is also why the use of proper diagnostics is critical to inform the program as well as to improve targeting.

Technology upgrading policies can be complex to implement, especially those targeted to specific sectors, which require more specialized knowledge. Thus, it is critical to invest in the capacity of government agencies to design and implement policies.

Cirera and Maloney (2017) and Cirera et al. (2020) provide a general set of principles to improve the quality of policy making in the context of innovation policies. In the case of technology policies, improvements are even more important, given the associated complexities. Strengthening government capabilities goes beyond training and adequate recruitment to include the use of good practices in public management and the implementation of adequate evaluation mechanisms. The costs of not investing in government capacities are high and deficiencies could result in government failure and market distortions.

FIGURE 7.2 **A Considerable Share of Public Support to Businesses to Cope with the COVID-19 Pandemic Went to Firms That Did Not Need It**

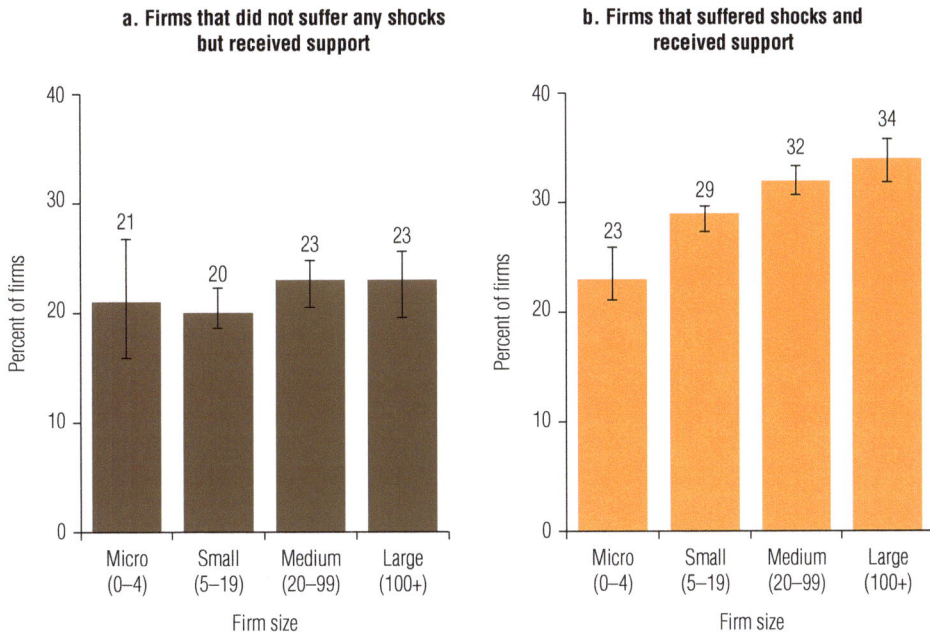

a. Firms that did not suffer any shocks but received support

b. Firms that suffered shocks and received support

Source: Business Pulse Survey (BPS), based on Cirera et al. 2021.

Note: Estimated share of firms controlling for country, sector, and other baseline characteristics. Firm size refers to the number of workers.

In addition, joint implementation with the private sector is crucial. Joint efforts with clusters of firms, platforms, and industry associations can address coordination failures and better inform firms on what technologies are available and what expertise is needed. This is also critical to reduce uncertainty in adoption and minimize preference biases in government agencies that may favor specific local technologies or universities when more efficient technologies are available.

A Policy Design Checklist

Summing up, figure 7.3 presents an initial checklist of questions for policy makers seeking to actively promote technology adoption. The first column highlights some of the key questions that policy makers should ask themselves when designing this type of policy and the considerations related to each question. The second column proposes policy instruments. It is important to undertake these analyses before designing the policy program to avoid policy failure. More important, the analysis is needed to better understand the local context because what has worked in one country will not necessarily work in another country.

FIGURE 7.3 A Checklist for Policy Makers to Upgrade Technologies

Question	Policy instrument(s)
Why are firms not adopting technologies that could enhance productivity and profitablity?	• Use diagnostics and benchmarking to identify existing gaps. • Incorporate factors external to the firm (e.g., regulations and infrastructure) and internal to the firm (e.g., know-how and skills capabilities).
What are the market failures that justify your intervention?	• Identify and quantify the main market failures to be solved and the ability of existing agencies to act on these issues.
What are the main regulatory bottlenecks?	• Undertake regulatory impact assessment to identify whether regulations enable the supply and adoption of technologies.
Is infrastructure adequate?	• Identify the key limitations with infrastructure (e.g., access to and quality of electricity, internet). • Identify a priority plan for key infrastructure projects.
Is the financial sector financing technology upgrading projects?	• Consider the use of loan programs through financial intermediaries or credit guarantees to finance technology upgrading.
Do firms have adequate information and access to skills and knowledge?	• Consider online tools to provide diagnostics and technology information. Work with sector associations on technology road maps and skills training needs. Improve the provision of business advisory and technology extension services.
Will the extensive adoption of technology generate large positive spillovers?	• Consider the use of vouchers for implementation of off-the-shelf digital solutions. • Consider grants or tax incentives for technologies with large spillovers or externalities, for example in green technologies.
Are there large network effects in the adoption of technologies with large externalities?	• Consider subsidies to first adopters.

Source: Original figure for this volume.

Using the FAT Survey to Inform the Design and Implementation of Policies Supporting Technology Upgrading

The multiple dimensions of technology adoption documented in this volume suggest the critical need for policy design to identify technology gaps precisely. For example, while generic digital solutions and sufficient service providers may be available to upgrade general business functions (GBFs), technologies to digitalize sector-specific business functions (SBFs) may be more limited and may require more customization and specificity.

Firm-level diagnostics, such as the FAT survey, can provide valuable information about the technology gap across different dimensions and help identify some of the necessary complementary factors needed for technology upgrading. One of the key factors, as discussed, is the role of management and organizational practices (see Cirera and Maloney 2017). Adopting some advanced technologies necessitates changes in business models and organization. For example, adopting digital technologies for sales requires adjustments in marketing strategies and the organization of the firm to bring about a closer relationship with final consumers. Accordingly, diagnostic tools need to be more holistic, looking beyond the technology in question to assess a firm's "management readiness" to implement and deal with these changes. If management and organization do not adapt, the returns to the investment in technologies are likely to be low. A firm-level diagnostic can measure this readiness to upgrade and suggest complementary interventions to address these additional gaps.

Finally, a firm-level diagnostic can help address the problems of overconfidence and reference group neglect (Camerer and Lovallo 1999) described in chapter 6. By providing an objective benchmark that can pinpoint not only a firm's technology gaps but also its relative technology sophistication with respect to other firms, firm managers can have a more objective basis for decision-making, reducing behavioral biases. This will have the additional benefit of increasing the take-up of technology support programs, which is often low, especially when the firm's financing requirement is high.

Using Results from the FAT Survey to Design, Implement, and Evaluate Policy

Results from the FAT survey can aid policy makers in understanding the reality of the technology gap, identifying key bottlenecks, and providing benchmark information to firms. This potential contribution to inform policy was taken into consideration when designing the FAT questionnaire, in collaboration with industry and policy experts, as described in the previous chapters. The discussion that follows provides practical examples of how information from the FAT survey can be utilized by practitioners through the policy diagnostic and the implementation phases.

Diagnostic Phase

1. *Measuring the distance to the technology frontier at the business function level.* The first contribution from the FAT data is providing granular measures of distance from the technology frontier. As described in chapters 1, 2, and 3, the granular measures of technology from the FAT data can be aggregated through different dimensions (such as country, sector, or size of the firm) at the business function level. This information can provide a clearer picture of the reality of firms in developing countries, which is usually far from the reality observed in advanced economies. For example, FAT data for Senegal show that a large share of firms still rely on predigital technologies to perform GBFs. Cruz, Dutz, and Rodríguez-Castelán (2022) highlight that technology upgrading policies for Senegal need to adjust to this reality, for both formal and informal businesses. Another important contribution from the FAT data is to disentangle the technology gap between GBFs and SBFs.

2. *Identifying key policy priorities for the country, region, or sector.* The FAT survey also provides information on factors that may play a role as barriers to or potential drivers of technology adoption. This information can be disaggregated by type of firm, sector, or region. As described in chapter 6, the data capture both perception-based and actual obstacles. Both measures are important for policy. If there is a misconception about the perceived obstacles, the design of the intervention needs to take this into consideration by providing better information about the problems to be addressed. The data can be combined with additional sources of information (such as census and administrative data), if available. For example, FAT data have been combined with other sources to examine the effect of firms' proximity to internet nodes on their adoption of technology in Senegal (see chapter 6) and the association between wages and technology sophistication in Brazil (see chapter 4).

Implementation Phase

When a program is being implemented, the FAT survey can be used to provide benchmarks and monitor the effects of interventions at the firm level. These measures can help firms understand how they compare to similar firms and can be used to develop a work plan for technology upgrading.

1. *Providing benchmark information to potential beneficiary firms.* The FAT benchmark tool is being prepared to be used in interventions in Cambodia and Senegal supported by the World Bank Group, with the potential to expand globally. It is being piloted by public agencies and could ultimately be used by nongovernmental organizations and private institutions that aim to improve the market for knowledge transfer and business advisory services in developing countries. The tool includes measures of technology, management practices, innovation capabilities, and performance. It allows firms to compare themselves with peer firms in their country and identify the areas where they are lagging. It can also be used by business advisory services, thus reducing the asymmetry of information that firms face regarding the need for and quality of the business services provided. Box 7.2 summarizes how the FAT survey can be used as a diagnostic tool to inform policies.

2. *Evaluating the impact of and learning from interventions.* Information obtained to conduct the firm-level technology diagnostic can also be used for monitoring and evaluation and research purposes. The data can be collected from potential beneficiary firms directly or indirectly, as supported through public programs, and used as a baseline. A follow-up exercise can be implemented to monitor and evaluate the impact at a very granular level, and across different dimensions of technology adoption. This requires building a proper counterfactual group, ideally through the design of the project. On a broader level, and of value to researchers and policy makers, the analysis presented in chapters 4 and 5 suggests the potential for using this information to understand how firms' adoption

The Firm-Level Technology Diagnostic Tool

The first version of the firm-level technology diagnostic was designed to support the implementation of public programs providing information and technical assistance for technology upgrading. Each diagnostic is generated for individual firms and can be comparable with other firms with similar characteristics, such as sector or size, in the same country for which data from the Firm-level Adoption of Technology (FAT) survey are available.

Figure B7.2.1 provides an example of the information covered by the diagnostic. The front page summarizes where the firm stands with respect to other firms in the country along four dimensions: technology adoption, management practices, innovation capabilities, and performance (see panel a).

FIGURE B7.2.1   The Firm-Level Technology Diagnostic

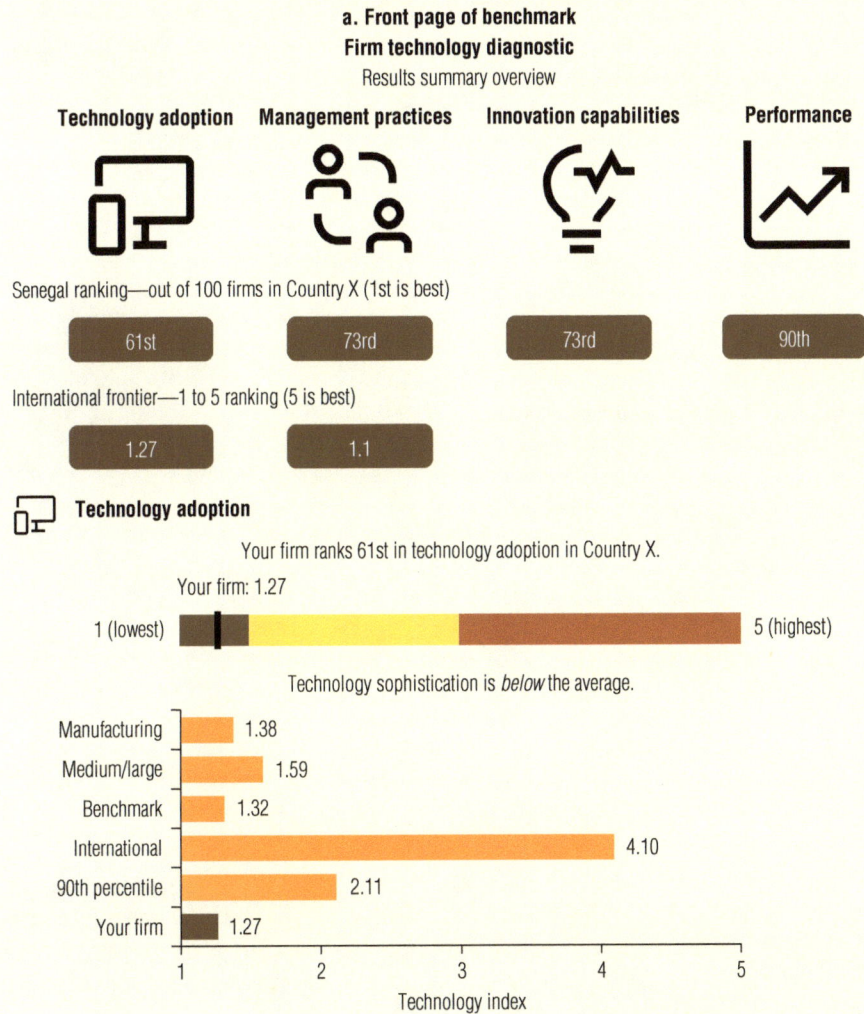

**a. Front page of benchmark
Firm technology diagnostic**
Results summary overview

Technology adoption	Management practices	Innovation capabilities	Performance

Senegal ranking—out of 100 firms in Country X (1st is best)

61st	73rd	73rd	90th

International frontier—1 to 5 ranking (5 is best)

1.27	1.1

Technology adoption

Your firm ranks 61st in technology adoption in Country X.

Your firm: 1.27

1 (lowest) ████████████ 5 (highest)

Technology sophistication is *below* the average.

	Technology index
Manufacturing	1.38
Medium/large	1.59
Benchmark	1.32
International	4.10
90th percentile	2.11
Your firm	1.27

(Figure continues on the following page.)

(Box continues on the following page.)

BOX 7.2

The Firm-Level Technology Diagnostic Tool *(continued)*

FIGURE B7.2.1 The Firm-Level Technology Diagnostic *(continued)*

b. Example of diagnostics for GBFs

Technology sophistication in general business functions (GBFs)

Your firm ranks 87th out of 100 in general technology adoption in Country X.

Your firm: 1.10

1 (lowest) ▮ ▬▬▬▬▬▬▬▬▬▬▬▬▬▬▬ 5 (highest)

Most-used technology, by function (comparison with firms in Senegal)

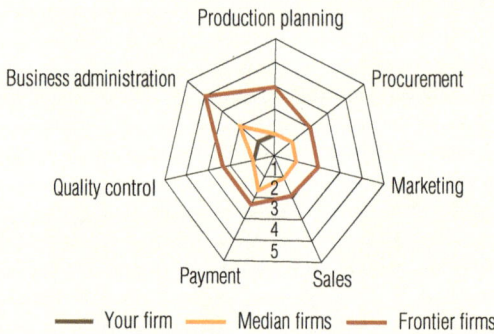

— Your firm   — Median firms   — Frontier firms

Functions above the frontier firms

Functions below the frontier firms
Business administration
Production planning
Procurement
Marketing
Sales
Payment
Quality control

Technology adoption versus usage by function

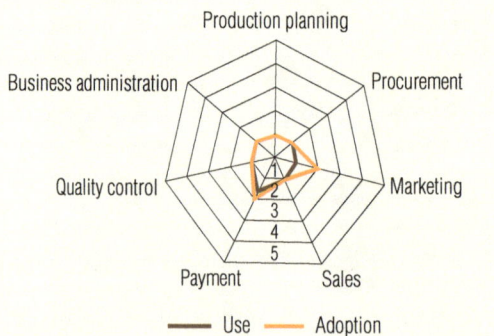

— Use   — Adoption

Functions lacking intensive use
Marketing
Payment

Source: Original figure for this volume.

The technology adoption measure is based on the general business function (GBF) and sector-specific business function (SBF) indexes described in this volume, which also allows for international comparison with respect to the global frontier. The index is calculated for the firm and compared to other firms with similar characteristics, including a reference for international comparison, based on results from top firms in the Republic of Korea (the frontier in the FAT data).

(Box continues on the following page.)

of different types of technologies can lead to significant effects in terms of productivity, employment, and economic resilience. These are key microeconomic drivers of growth and can provide a broad picture of potential interventions.

Instruments to Support Technology Upgrading at the Firm Level

Once the diagnostic is in place and the policy priorities are defined, policy makers need to decide what instrument to use to support technology upgrading. Governments directly support technology adoption and technology generation by providing services, technical assistance, and finance.[4] At one end of the spectrum, governments promote technology upgrading among SMEs, which starts with building firms' absorptive capacity (Cohen and Levinthal 1990) and providing information and know-how on how to adopt new technologies. At the other end is the objective of transfer and commercialization of new technologies from universities and public research institutions. Figure 7.4 presents a typology of instruments.

Different policy instruments can support these technology objectives. Grants, vouchers, and loans can facilitate the purchase and adoption of technologies and digital solutions. Open innovation and other collaborative instruments can also promote the development of new technological solutions, while some research and development (R&D) projects are oriented toward generating new technologies. But the three generic instruments that focus more directly on equipping firms with the capabilities of using technologies, particularly through digitalization programs and Industry 4.0 strategies, are business advisory services (BAS), technology extension services (TES), and technology centers (TCs).[5] These instruments can be implemented free of charge, with different degrees of payment and through the use of grants and vouchers. There is considerable heterogeneity in the models of implementation of these technology

FIGURE 7.4   A Typology of Instruments to Support the Firm-Level Adoption of Technology

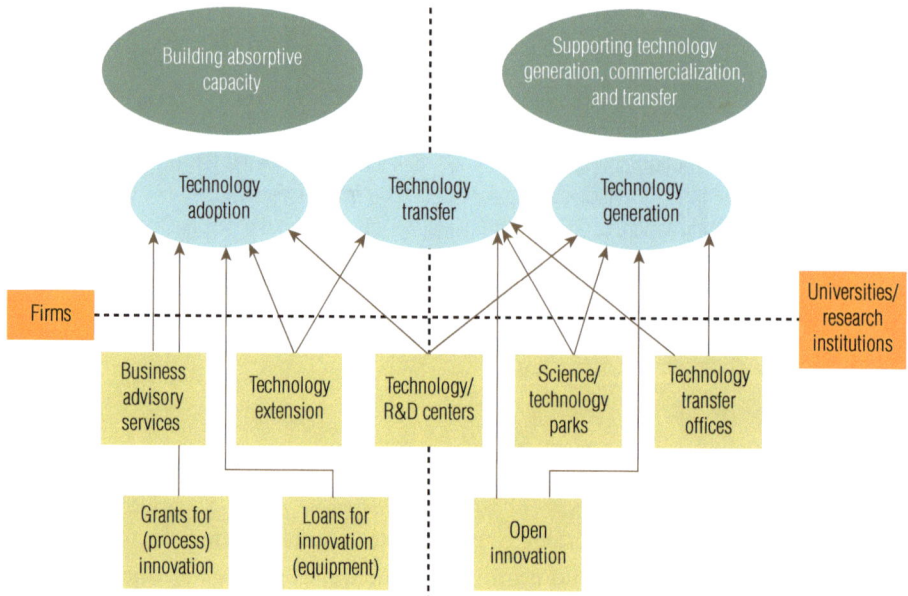

Source: Cirera et al. 2020.
Note: R&D = research and development.

services instruments, especially in the case of BAS and TCs. The subsections that follow describe these instruments in more detail.

But first, it is important to define how the multiple dimensions of technology can be mapped to policies. This can help in the choice of instruments and the program design. To this end, figure 7.5 provides a framework that links technologies to policy instruments.

It is important to split the technology options of the firm into two broad groups: GBFs and SBFs. Although they are complementary, policy instruments that support these two types of business functions are usually different in terms of knowledge, skills, and resources required. Efforts to upgrade the technology for GBFs are usually served by BAS or TES. This includes digitalization programs, and often requires less specialized knowledge because solutions are more readily available.[6] Efforts to upgrade technology for SBFs often require more specialized knowledge and, therefore, demand more specialized institutions such as TES or TCs that tend to focus on particular sectors, such as Embrapa in Brazil (agriculture) and the Fraunhofer Institutes in Germany (manufacturing). These TCs support not only technology adoption but the creation of new technology applications with universities and research centers.

FIGURE 7.5   **Framework for Policy and Instruments to Support the Firm-Level Adoption of Technology**

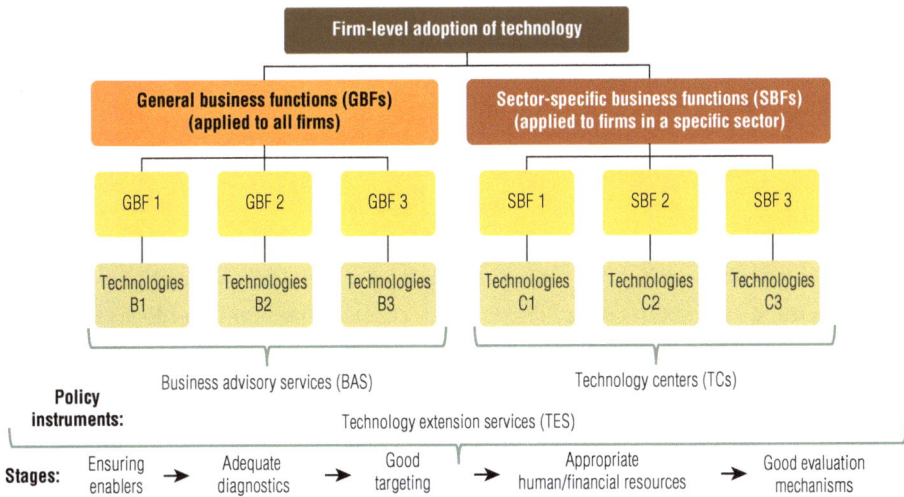

Source: Original figure for this volume.

1. Supporting Basic Technology Upgrading: Business Advisory Services

Business advisory services (BAS) consist of access to or the direct provision of specialist advice in areas such as accounting and financial services, human resources management, legal services, supply chain management, marketing and advertising, or pricing strategies. The delivery model tends to be more centered on demand. It is often structured around physical centers that act as infrastructure to serve SMEs and entrepreneurs, which can find either a suite of available services or referrals to those services. These services are directly linked to the digitalization of GBFs, and the specialist or consultants can act as mentors to SMEs during the digitalization project. These BAS models target smaller firms, although their more demand-driven approach is probably better suited to medium-size firms that may have more specific needs.

BAS are a common type of instrument in many countries but are implemented using different business models and degrees of proactivity in getting firms to engage. BAS were a key policy instrument of some of the "Asian miracles" such as Japan and Singapore (Cirera and Maloney 2017). In addition, some impact evaluations suggest very high returns for this type of intervention in developing countries. In low-income countries, agencies may struggle to find high-quality consultants to implement these services effectively, and willingness to pay for these services is usually low, which makes it difficult to reach out to large numbers of beneficiaries.

The primary target group of advisory services is usually SMEs. Owners and/or managers of SMEs often have a relatively narrow set of skills and competencies and limited networks, and therefore may not be knowledgeable about the skills needed to implement in their business practices. Another important target group is advisory service providers. This group may comprise public, private, and nonprofit organizations involved in the provision of advisory, digital, and extension services, including regional business support centers, chambers of commerce, and small business associations and societies, in addition to private consultancy firms. Various organizations focus on specific types of services, firms, and local areas.

The main strengths of BAS need to be counterbalanced with the potential drawbacks and risks. This instrument has several positive features. First, it can provide an integrated suite of services to SMEs through a one-stop-shop approach, which can substantially reduce advisory costs. Second, it can provide diagnostics that enable programs to be tailored to SMEs. Third, it can support the building blocks of technological capabilities for SMEs. However, the design and implementation need to account for several risks. First, there is risk of overcrowding the market and lack of coordination between service providers, including government and nongovernmental organizations.[7] Second, there might be a poor match between supply and demand for services and weak demand from those that could benefit most from the instrument.

Despite the diversity of BAS programs, there are a few key elements for good policy design that are likely to make them, and the firms they help, more effective. A common model is to have an external expert make an assessment in an initial diagnostic stage. Then, an action or improvement plan is developed, and further advice can be provided to help implement this plan. The advantage of this type of sequenced approach is that SMEs may misdiagnose their key problem, and an up-front assessment can improve the prioritization of subsequent activities. Using a rapid standard diagnostic to quickly benchmark the firm with respect to other firms with similar characteristics (such as the level of technology used by other firms and how this is associated with performance) can demonstrate the value of the information and build a relationship of trust between consultants and the firm.[8]

A key design issue is ensuring the quality and relevance of the business advice. As discussed, one of the main market/system failures in this area is strong information asymmetry that can result in adverse selection, where SMEs cannot determine the value and quality of the consultancy services provider. To address this issue, one option is to develop a vetted list of service providers that are known to provide quality services, and help SMEs negotiate the scope of any work from consultants if they are unfamiliar with the process. Given the severe information asymmetry that exists and lack of willingness to pay, constant outreach and engagement by the program is critical.

Digital Upgrading Programs. One type of BAS instrument that has gained popularity in recent years focuses on supporting the adoption of digital technologies. These programs follow the same general structure as BAS. They address information gaps and provide incentives and finance in different combinations. A difference is that they tend to concentrate on general business functions and tasks, with a large bias toward marketing and sales. The digitization of more specific production processes, as well as the automation and use of Industry 4.0 technologies, tends to be the role of instruments such as TES and TCs, given the need for much more niche technologies and more specialized advice.

A review of 22 digital upgrading programs mainly in member-countries of the Organisation for Economic Co-operation and Development shows that at least 40 percent use BAS as the main instrument (Balbontin, Cusolito, and Cirera 2021).[9] The use of financial incentives is very widespread, with 36 percent using vouchers and 27 percent using grants. At least 41 percent use outsourced expertise, even if combined with in-house expertise. Interestingly, most programs support business functions linked to transactions in marketing and sales as well as the processing of information for administration. Two-thirds of the programs emphasize the need for complementary investments.

Some of the support programs reviewed also aim to increase firms' participation on digital platforms. Support is concentrated in specific elements needed to sell online, such as customer orientation, maintaining a good reputation, pricing, and quality control. As discussed, in most cases policy makers need to first assess why the platform itself is not offering support to small firms to participate and what the appropriate role of public policy is—which often should focus on ensuring compliance, regulating noncompetitive practices, and addressing regulatory bottlenecks.

2. Supporting Technology Upgrading in Sector-Specific Technologies: Technology Extension Services

Technology extension services (TES) provide direct on-site assistance to SMEs through extension staff, field offices, or dispersed technology centers to foster technological and knowledge-based modernization. A key differentiation between TES and BAS relates to the focus of services. TES tend to be more sophisticated, sector specific, and directly focused on supporting production technology and innovation capability and activity. While this type of instrument is a long-established model in agriculture (see box 7.3) and in manufacturing, it is less common in services sectors, although manufacturing extension services have often been utilized in sectors such as health care (for example, in hospitals) where process efficiency is important.[10] TES can also offer skills development training, addressing both the demand for technology in the firm and the needed supply of adequate labor skills.

Some extension centers offer both BAS and TES indistinguishably, as well as skills development services and training. Some public research institutions also offer TES to industry. They are a key instrument to implement Industry 4.0 strategies such as smart manufacturing because they directly address the lack of technological capabilities.

TES and BAS usually address similar types of market and system failures. The potential beneficiaries targeted in TES tend to be larger, given that TES involves more sophisticated advice. TES also focuses on a third target group: knowledge providers, such as research organizations, universities, and public laboratories.

Agriculture Extension: The Case of Embrapa

Embrapa, the Brazilian Agricultural Research Corporation, is a state-owned research corporation affiliated with the Brazilian Ministry of Agriculture. Embrapa generates and transfers new technologies and techniques tailored to Brazil's climate and soil conditions. The use of these technologies by Brazilian farmers for decades has facilitated the expansion of Brazilian agriculture and increased exports at internationally competitive prices: first, by expanding the supply of arable land; and second, by improving the productivity of selected crops. New techniques to improve the quality of the otherwise inhospitable Cerrado soil in the tropical savanna opened a vast tract of newly arable land, keeping marginal agricultural costs down and enabling an increase in agricultural production, while improvements in the cultivars of soybeans and cotton ultimately yielded twice-yearly harvests. Both activities increased the productivity of land.

Why did Embrapa succeed while other research organizations have failed? Embrapa's mission orientation, focusing from the outset on the improvement of agricultural productivity rather than the production of scientific work, has been a key driver of its success. Integration into the international flow of knowledge has increased research efficiency and accelerated training. An open intellectual property rights policy—and a network of offices spread throughout the country—has facilitated the dissemination of Embrapa's discoveries. Funding has been kept at adequate levels for more than two decades. Investments in human capital have been highly prioritized. The organization has actively promoted a meritocratic culture. Research has dealt with the practical problems of agriculture, and farmers have quickly deployed technology and innovations sourced through Embrapa. By reacting to market signals and focusing on activities for which demand was increasing in international markets, Embrapa has avoided the usual challenges of purely "supply-push" technology transfer policies.

Sources: Cirera and Maloney 2017, based on Correa and Schmidt 2014.

TES and BAS share similar strengths, drawbacks, and risks. Among the strengths, TES provide the opportunity for creating a clear and centralized offer of services, supplying tailored services based on diagnostics, building core competencies in production and managerial operation, and addressing the skill gaps for specific technologies. On the other hand, TES also face the risks of overcrowding the market, firms' lack of willingness to pay for upgrading, and wrongly prioritizing some services if they are not fully integrated and coordinated with the private sector.

TES interventions can be delivered to groups of SMEs, which allows SMEs to learn from and support one another in the change process. However, some individual advice and coaching should also be involved. TES also often provide "one-to-many" services such as awareness-raising events (for instance on new technological developments, business digitalization, or Industry 4.0).

TES and BAS can operate with each other and with other policies aimed at supporting SMEs. BAS are generally relevant to a broader market (which includes firms that are not innovators). These services often take a sequential approach that reflects the need for SMEs to develop and build their absorptive capacities. A firm may first focus on improving its basic managerial skills and technologies applied to GBFs before moving into sector technology upgrading.

Most TES develop standardized assessment and benchmarking tools, and standardized approaches to common SME upgrading problems (such as business planning, production, and efficiency-lean manufacturing), but tailor the implementation and sequencing to the specific circumstances of the client. There is evidence that TES schemes (as well as BAS schemes) are often more effective when they are combined with market development initiatives such as supplier linkages programs to large firms or multinationals or new export markets, as these provide the motivation and incentives to invest in internal improvements. They can also be accompanied by financial support to companies to support implementation, usually through matching grants. Such support can address the financial risk of implementing new technologies and business models within SMEs.

3. Supporting More Sophisticated Technologies: Technology Centers

Technology centers (TCs) are a broad category of institutions that provide a range of technological services to businesses, from the provision of basic or customized technological services to more sophisticated R&D projects and technological development. TCs are often supported by government and implemented as public-private partnerships with industry or sector associations. They tend to be sector specific, often helping to develop new technological solutions or adapting existing market technologies to the needs of the private sector. TCs are an important actor in regional innovation systems, given their location and proximity to industry clusters (for more on innovation systems, see Cirera and Maloney 2017).

TCs can have very different functions in developing countries than in developed countries. In developing countries, technology centers can serve as a policy vehicle to house support measures such as provision of modern manufacturing equipment and related training, testing, product design, development, and demonstration. They might not have a strong focus on R&D. Instead, they tend to focus on the diffusion of technologies to SMEs. Typically, they offer workforce training (often for a fee) for the target group. TCs address cross-cutting issues such as design and fabrication, as well as skills gaps in new production technologies and processes. They also frequently involve BAS and TES, as well as certification services. By contrast, in developed countries, TCs tend to have less focus on mainstream workforce training and have moved up the value chain, often providing practical advice on how to innovate and adopt new technologies, brokering applied R&D and providing technology awareness. In Japan, local public technology centers not only provide small local firms with various technological services, but also conduct their own research and patent inventions (Fukugawa 2009).

TCs may be stand-alone entities or part of a larger network. One of the best-known networks globally is the Fraunhofer Society in Germany, a network of 72 applied research centers that work closely with industry and other parts of the research sector.[11] An example of a network of technology centers in developing countries is the Indian Technology Centers Network, which aimed to provide access to advanced manufacturing technologies and offer young workers opportunities for technical skills development. The World Bank–funded initiative ran from 2015 to 2021. More recently, TCs worldwide have been focusing on supporting smart manufacturing and Industry 4.0 technologies.

TCs are also an attempt to address coordination failures and asymmetric information about existing technologies. While TCs target SMEs, other potential target groups include large firms and other stakeholders such as industry associations, given that the focus is usually more specific and geared toward more sophisticated technologies. Some key strengths of this instrument are the provision of targeted training and services close to industry and the creation and diffusion of technologies. Some potential drawbacks and risks include the potential of being captured or rent seeking; the challenge to remain close and relevant to industry; and the lack of proper governance structure, leadership, staff, and service mix to deliver effective services, which risk turning these centers into dysfunctional physical infrastructure.

To lay the foundation for good policy design for TCs, policy makers need to make appropriate decisions on a few crucial issues. First, the ownership of the program needs strong engagement from industry and the private sector, rather than being run as a fully government-owned scheme. Second, TCs require a sustainable business model. Typical revenue sources include fees charged for training services, testing, certification services, and use of equipment. Third, a strategic focus needs to be decided in collaboration with the private sector. Most centers have a focus on specific industry sectors or types of technology (such as subsectors of manufacturing), which need to match with the demand coming from the private sector. Finally, it is critical to define a strategic location to ensure that it is close to main industry customers.

4. Finance Instruments to Support Technology

Financial imperfections are pervasive in many developing countries and are particularly severe for technology upgrading projects, especially for smaller firms, as discussed. Many public and development banks, such as Brazil's development bank (BNDES) and Chile's Production Development Corporation (CORFO), provide credit lines or loan guarantees to businesses to finance the purchase of technologies. This is an extensive practice in some countries, and should be a focus for policy makers, especially when the potential externalities and spillovers are low and financial imperfections are obvious. When externalities in an innovation project such as upgrading a technology are low and public finance is costly, loans should be preferred to grants to induce innovation efforts, as Lach, Neeman, and Schankerman (2021) show. However, depending on whether the financial problem regarding information asymmetries centers on screening and identifying good projects from bad ones, or successful upgrading, the preferred policy should be an interest rate that is higher or lower than the market rate. This contrasts with many public programs that finance technology acquisition, which almost always provide a lower-than-market interest rate.

Credit guarantees provide a mechanism for lenders to mitigate risk and work as an insurance scheme to cover some portion of the losses to lenders associated with extending credit to firms investing in risky technologies. For instance, the Korea Technology Finance Corporation (KOTEC) provides an innovative policy instrument to finance technology (see box 7.4). It offers credit guarantees based on a technology appraisal to provide clear signaling to banks to finance the development and acquisition of new technologies. While the model has been exported to other countries, the capacities required to appraise the technologies suggest that this type of instrument is more likely to be effective in upper-middle-income and high-income countries.

Policy makers should keep in mind some key elements in implementing finance instruments (Cirera et al. 2020):

- *The need to leverage the broader commercial environment.* While government loans are often justified in the context of a weak financial market, policy makers should bear in mind that the ultimate objective is to create a competitive financial market that finances technology. Before launching a loan scheme, policy makers need to consider the alternatives underpinned by commercial initiatives, and work with the financial sector to reduce information asymmetries and ensure future availability of finance from commercial banks for technology upgrading.
- *Complementary policy measures.* Firms that face financing problems can also be subject to weaknesses such as low capacity to exploit technology. In such cases,

BOX 7.4

Credit Guarantees for Technology through the Korea Technology Finance Corporation (KOTEC) *(continued)*

FIGURE B7.4.1   KOTEC's Credit Guarantee Scheme

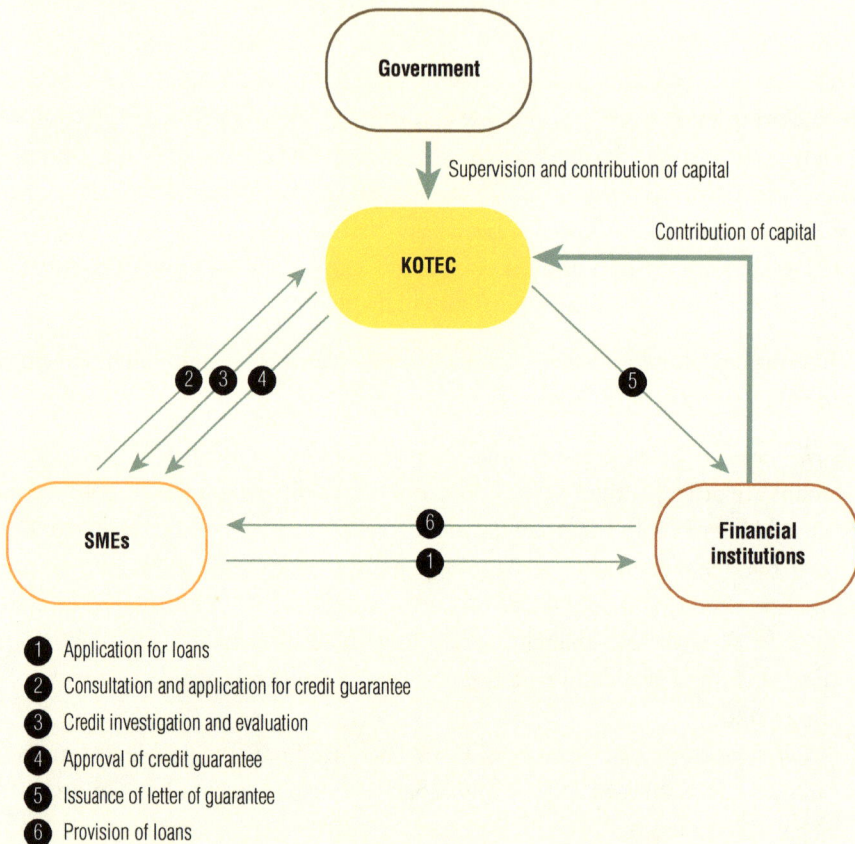

1. Application for loans
2. Consultation and application for credit guarantee
3. Credit investigation and evaluation
4. Approval of credit guarantee
5. Issuance of letter of guarantee
6. Provision of loans

Source: KOTEC, https://www.kibo.or.kr/english/work/work010100.do.

Note: KOTEC = Korea Technology Finance Corporation; SMEs = small and medium enterprises.

technologies, the SME's commercialization capacity risks, and macroeconomic risks. Since its first iteration in 2005, KTRS has diversified to operate 65 models differentiated by a firm's growth stages, size, and sectors. As of 2019, KOTEC has produced about 714,000 technology appraisals and provided credit guarantees totaling ₩22 trillion (KOTEC 2020).

Firms that received KOTEC's credit guarantees in the 1990s and 2000s increased sales, assets, and debt in the medium to long term (Kwon 2012). A self-evaluation by KOTEC (2019) noted that beneficiaries that received credit ratings in 2016 recorded a higher operating profit-to-sales ratio, greater value added per employee, and higher expenditure on research and development in 2017 and 2018.

Source: Lee, Shin, and Frias 2020.

complementary policy measures such as advisory services can step in to maximize the effects of financing provided by the loan scheme.

- *A strong legal framework for upholding creditor rights.* The feasibility of establishing and maintaining a credit guarantee scheme depends on sound processes for collection and recovery of assets in case of default and effective contract enforcement. These are preconditions for the effective design, implementation, and evaluation of a credit guarantee scheme.

5. Grants and Vouchers

Two common instruments to support technology upgrading are grants and vouchers (see box 7.5). *Grants* are a direct allocation of funding from public agencies to finance all or part of a technology project. In the case of matching grants, public agencies match a percentage of the contribution made by the applicant to ensure the applicant's commitment to the activity. *Vouchers* are small, entitlement-based grants that do not need to be repaid. They are used to incentivize firms to digitalize with simple projects that require ready-made digital solutions, and to push firms to collaborate with technology providers. With effective auditing, vouchers require only light management. The simplicity of administration is a key attraction of voucher schemes; however, they require

---

BOX 7.5

The Difference between Vouchers and Grants

A voucher is a type of grant with specifically defined characteristics regarding the selection process, implementation mechanisms, and value of the grant. When choosing one instrument over the other, policy makers need to consider the following important features of vouchers compared to regular (matching) grants:

- Vouchers are entitlement based rather than competition or merit based; that is, applicants can get vouchers if they fulfill the selection criteria set in advance.
- Vouchers are small in value. Typically, the face value of vouchers is no more than a few thousand dollars, while regular grants can be much larger.
- Vouchers focus on behavior change: inducing small and medium enterprises and technology providers to collaborate and begin a process of technology upgrading, often of digital technologies. By contrast, regular grants typically focus on input additionality—implementing the adoption of a technology or digital solution—and are intended to crowd in private investment in technology projects.
- Vouchers rely heavily on brokers, which perform the functions of advertising, selecting technological solutions, vetting technology providers, monitoring, and ex post verification.
- Vouchers are simple to administer. Disbursement occurs when technology providers redeem vouchers, and firms often do not receive any value except the technical assistance.

Source: Cirera et al. 2020.

an established brokerage system to link recipients with digital solution providers and ensure compliance through random audits or other mechanisms.

Both grants and vouchers are based on the idea that inducing more firms to upgrade their technologies generates positive spillovers or externalities. One channel of spillovers is through the know-how embedded in workers and managers who use these more sophisticated technologies that can spill over to other firms. It is important that policy makers have in mind the idea of demonstrating such spillovers or externalities when justifying this type of intervention.

Grants and vouchers are often used to subsidize part of the costs of the services of extension services (BAS, TES, TCs). The government usually provides a voucher or grant to the SMEs to purchase the services from a third party. When the government provides the service directly, they generally have centers with advisers at the regional and local levels that deliver the services to SMEs, as described. In this direct provision model, it is critical that the advisers have knowledge and credibility and can quickly add value to SMEs. This is often the critical failure for implementing this type of instrument in developing countries.[12] Therefore, a realistic assessment of the quality and depth of the supply of these services is needed before deciding on the scope of the delivery model.[13] When implemented externally through the grants or vouchers, it is important that public agencies maintain a list of technology and knowledge providers that is monitored to guarantee the quality of services. In the case of vouchers, often these lists are connected to a list of preapproved providers of technology solutions, software licenses, customization services, and training.

An extensive description of how to design these types of instruments can be found in Cirera et al. (2020). One important element in the case of grants is the matching component. When matching rates by firms are high, they may not provide sufficient incentive to compensate for the spillovers generated and take-up may be low. When matching rates are too low, they may substitute for private funding and create low additionality. One good practice is to ask applicants to disclose in advance what percentage of the project they require to be financed and without which they will not engage in the technology upgrading project. That can help reveal beneficiaries' willingness to pay and maximize additionality.

6. Other Instruments to Support Technology

Other policy instruments to support technology tend to be more oriented toward the generation and commercialization of technologies and the links to universities. Ideally, public agencies should have mechanisms to link both supply and demand instruments, so the supply of technologies targets the needs of the private sector.

Recently, there has been a proliferation of regulatory sandboxes, which aim to create a regulation-free environment to develop and test certain digital technologies and business models that may not comply with current regulatory frameworks. In practice, they temporarily suspend some regulations until the technology and business model have been deemed to be fully tested.

Evidence of Impact

There is little evidence of the impact of policies that aim to promote technology upgrading. More evidence is needed, especially in relation to programs that seek to increase digitalization among SMEs. Much of the existing evidence has concentrated on smallholder agriculture in developing countries, especially Africa and India. Fewer studies have focused on manufacturing technology services, and these tend to be more qualitative studies.

Recently, Alfaro-Serrano et al. (2021) systematically reviewed 80 studies, of which 79 are from developing countries, drawn from a universe of 42,462 candidates, and covering about 4.8 million firms. Their definition of technology is broad and includes management and organizational processes. The study also explores different types of interventions, including direct and indirect financial support, regulatory measures, and other kinds of support such as information. Of the 33 studies they analyze for manufacturing and services, 19 show a positive and statistically significant effect on technology adoption. Of the 47 studies for agriculture, they find positive and statistically significant effects for 20, and no significant effect on adoption in the other 27. Some of the studies with positive impacts concentrate on management and organization processes and do not focus much, if at all, on upgrading technologies and equipment. The results are even more mixed regarding the impact of these interventions on performance outcomes, such as sales growth or productivity. The large variation in context makes it difficult to generalize recommendations to guide policy.

Cirera et al. (2020) and McKenzie et al. (2021) also summarize some of the evidence about the impact of several of the instruments discussed. Starting with BAS, most of the evidence suggests positive impacts on business performance. In perhaps one of the most influential studies, Bloom et al. (2013) find in a randomized experiment with large textile plants in India that intensive consulting intervention significantly increased output per worker and total factor productivity, reduced inventory levels and the rate of quality defects, and improved management practices. A follow-up study (Bloom et al. 2020) nine years later shows the interventions in management quality and productivity had long-lasting effects. Other studies identifying positive effects on BAS include Wren and Storey (2002) for the United Kingdom; Cruz, Bussolo, and Iacovone (2018) for Brazil; Bruhn, Karlan, and Schoar (2018) for Mexico; and Iacovone, Maloney, and McKenzie (2022) for Colombia. These studies also do not directly explore the implementation of technology upgrading.

Evidence from interventions providing management training and equipment directly suggest a complementary effect. Giorcelli (2019) compares the effects of management training trips for Italian managers to US firms that provided technologically advanced machines to Italian companies.[14] The results show that those firms that sent their managers to the United States increased sales growth for at least 15 years after the program. The effect was even larger for those firms that benefited from new machines that were provided, suggesting these were complementary interventions. Firms that only received new machines also improved the performance, but these gains flattened out over time.

An alternative to consulting services emphasized by Anderson and McKenzie (2022) is to provide businesses with support to insource or outsource knowledge by finding specialized professionals to help perform general business functions, such as marketing and business administration. Based on an experiment in Nigeria, the authors find that this option led to more effective outcomes than consulting services. BAS can also be used from a broader perspective, such as providing firms with diagnostics and advice to find solutions in the market.

The other two instruments, TES and TCs, are more directly linked to the process of technology upgrading, but evidence is even scarcer for them than for BAS, except in the area of agriculture. An extensive body of studies provides evidence of the positive impact of extension services for agriculture. A large share of this literature focuses on small business in agriculture in developing countries (Owens, Hoddinott, and Kinsey 2003; Kondylis, Mueller, and Zhu 2017; Maertens, Michelson, and Nourani 2021), suggesting positive effects for these interventions, which range from providing information to training to showcasing the use of new technologies.

For manufacturing and services, there is some evidence, such as Jarmin (1999) and Shapira, Youtie, and Kay (2011), but the use of randomized control trials or quasi-experimental approaches is less common. The same applies for TCs. In terms of historical experience, Japan has had a long history of utilizing TCs as a policy instrument to boost regional innovation and competitiveness, dating back to the 1880s or so (Fukugawa 2009). These technology centers have long served as the cornerstone of local technology service provision in Japan (Shapira 1992).

Most of the existing studies evaluating TCs focus on design features, with little emphasis on their impact, because it is difficult to randomize services within centers and to find counterfactual firms. An exception is a recent study focusing on the Fraunhofer Society, which suggests a positive effect of their interventions on firm performance (see box 7.6).[15]

Overall, the evidence, although scarce, suggests that policy instruments to promote technology tend to have a positive impact on technology upgrading and firm growth. However, caution is warranted in interpreting this evidence. Most of the evidence

Fraunhofer Institutes

The Fraunhofer Society (FhG), comprising 72 research institutes across Germany, is considered to be the world's largest public organization for applied research. It is dedicated to applied research and technological co-development with firms, rather than basic research, addressing searching and matching frictions to build technological knowledge. The research institutes employ approximately 24,500 workers, who conduct applied research in all fields of science, leading to around 500 patents per year.

A relatively new initiative is the Industry 4.0 Competence Centers, which are intended to address cutting-edge technologies and to bring digitalization and networking technologies to German manufacturing small and medium enterprises.

A recent study suggests that a 1 percent increase in FhG expenditures results in 1.4 percentage points of higher growth in turnover, and 0.7 percentage point in productivity for the German firms supported. German institutions are leading several initiatives to support adoption of new technologies, especially digital technologies, by manufacturing firms.

Source: Comin et al. 2019.

outside agriculture is concentrated in high-income countries, which suggests that some of these policy instruments are more demanding in terms of human and financial resources. Technology centers and extension services like Fraunhofer in Germany and abroad, or the manufacturing extension partnerships in the United States, are also the outgrowth of a more advanced productive sector that needs more specialized support on sector-specific business functions. While these can be out of reach for most low-income countries, creating the infrastructure to support some of the more general business functions and their digitalization can play a critical role in increasing productivity in these countries.

Summing Up

This chapter has described a variety of policy options to support technology upgrading. These instruments can play an important role in addressing some of the barriers highlighted in the previous chapter to promote technology diffusion and the digital transformation of businesses. Public agencies have an important role to play to address coordination and information failures. The starting point for policy makers should be to make sure that the enabling conditions to adopt technologies are in place in terms of access to infrastructure and information, the removal of regulatory bottlenecks and to ensure access to external knowledge. When considering more direct support, public agencies should identify and measure the type of market failure they are trying to address and ponder whether their planned support can address these failures effectively. To this end, implementing good diagnostics to identify key technology gaps and better target firms, investing in adequate human and financial resources to implement the programs, and implementing good evaluation mechanisms are necessary conditions.

The chapter also has reviewed some of the key policy instruments to support technology upgrading. While there is some evidence that some instruments are effective in some contexts and countries, there are still large gaps in the evidence, and positive results are very specific to a particular context, which makes it difficult to guide the choice of instrument. A critical objective of direct support instruments is to address information and capability failures. The design and implementation of this type of policy instrument increase in complexity when moving from general to sector-specific business functions, as these require more specialized knowledge support.

A critical type of support is related to the financing of technology upgrading projects, given that financial markets in many developing countries suffer from large market imperfections. Working with commercial banks to address this lack of finance can help facilitate technology upgrading, especially for firms that have higher capabilities to adopt but are financially constrained. However, these finance instruments may not work in cases of firms with very low capabilities.

Finally, the COVID-19 crisis has been a wake-up call for many businesses around the world about the need to upgrade their technologies, digital and nondigital. The pandemic has increased the incentives of businesses to upgrade, reducing some of the earlier overconfidence about their technological capabilities and making it more likely that they will undertake upgrading programs. Policy makers should seize this opportunity to minimize the risk of an increase in the technological divide across countries and firms, and bring more sustained growth and prosperity to their economies.

Notes

1. In the context of financing a technology project, adverse selection is related to the difficulties the financier faces in screening and identifying good projects, while moral hazard is associated with the difficulties in monitoring the implementation of the technology upgrading project, thus transferring the risk of failure to the financier (Cirera et al. 2020).

2. Cruz, Bussolo, and Iacovone (2018) examine an exporting program in Brazil that advances funds to a business based on historic orders from buyers. They find that the program, which provided a detailed diagnostic and consulting services, had a positive impact on the reorganization of participating firms. This program was designed in response to the fact that many SMEs were not ready to benefit from more traditional export promotion instruments.

3. Targeting has been an important challenge for government programs supporting businesses during the pandemic. Emerging evidence highlights two main factors associated with mistargeting: (1) barriers to access to policy support, such as information and application costs, which are particularly large for smaller firms; and (2) the inability of public agencies to target the right beneficiaries (Cirera et al. 2021). This difficulty in targeting and the urgency to provide rapid support resulted in universal targeting.

4. This section draws heavily on Cirera et al. (2020); for a full description of these activities, readers should refer to that publication.

5. Some BAS are oriented to the adoption of digital technologies in key management functions. TCs can be entirely dedicated to facilitating adoption of technologies in production and tend to be sector based. These and other technology-generation instruments are described in detail in Cirera et al. (2020). On the technology transfer side, science and technology parks aim at attracting technology-intensive firms with the objective of generating spillovers with local universities and industries. Technology transfer offices support the generation and commercialization of technologies from universities and public research institutions. In some cases, they are used to help entrepreneurs address knowledge gaps in the commercialization process. In other cases, they target established SMEs so these firms can enter a market and then start climbing the capabilities escalator, as discussed Cirera and Maloney (2017).

6. Programs targeting technology upgrading in GBFs can apply to all firms, but are especially common supporting micro, small and medium enterprises. These instruments involve upgrading the methods applied to perform functions that are common across all firms, such as business administration, planning, sourcing, marketing, sales, or payment. Rather than differentiating by sector, these interventions can be customized by the level of overall capability, including management practices, firm size, or formal status.

7. The provision of BAS should be considered carefully to avoid distorting the existing advisory market. For example, there are plenty of private providers to support implementation of enterprise resource planning and other digital solutions.

8. In some cases having a mandatory assessment as an entry criterion can be counterproductive because SMEs can be suspicious of external advisers until they experience tangible benefits from interacting with them (particularly when the service is perceived to be linked to the government). Given these circumstances, a holistic assessment should be implemented once SMEs have engaged and are more trusting.

9. The digital upgrading programs reviewed are available in Spain, Denmark, Chile, the Republic of Korea, Malaysia, Singapore, and the United Kingdom. They are (in order by countries listed): Acelera pyme, cloud Computing, Digital Advisors, SMV:Digital, Sprint:Digital, Digitalization Boost, Digitaliza tu Pyme, Smart Factory Korea, Support for Remote Work within SMEs, SME Business Digitalization Grant, SMART Automation Grant, Global Tech Fund, Industry4WRD Readiness Assessment, SMEs Go Digital, A*STAR Collaborative Commerce Marketplace, Tech Access, Made Smarter, konfer, SPRINT SPace Research and Innovation Network for Technology, Gigabit Broadband Voucher Scheme, Business Growth Hub, and Global Business Innovation Programme (GBIP).

10. Some of the most common TES services include: quality management and process efficiency (such as lean manufacturing); management of environmental impacts and energy use; advice on the purchase and installation of new technologies; advice on optimizing the use of existing technologies; development of new business models; R&D and commercialization; accreditation for International Organization for Standardization (ISO) and technical standards; and more generally, digitalization. TES can also involve longer-term and more systematic engagements with SMEs, such as through formal continuous improvement programs. Given this focus, they are typically delivered by technical experts.

11. For more details on Fraunhofer Institutes, see box 7.6.

12. These advisers generally need to have a business background and be recruited and remunerated accordingly. This is sometimes a challenge for government organizations.

13. This government delivery business model may also restrict the potential growth of the private market given that supply is limited to the amount of program funding. Ideally, a program outcome is that SMEs continue to utilize BAS, in which case having a viable private BAS market is important. The optimal delivery model will involve private sector providers and may also involve capacity building (such as training) for those consultants if capability gaps are identified.

14. The analysis is based on a quasi-experimental approach under the United States Technical Assistance and Productivity Program (1952–58).

15. Some centers associated with Fraunhofer are multinational and have locations on all continents, focusing on specific technologies and sectors that are of key importance for the host country.

References

Alfaro-Serrano, D., T. Balantrapu, R. Chaurey, A. Goicoechea, and E. Verhoogen. 2021. "Interventions to Promote Technology Adoption in Firms: A Systematic Review." *Campbell Systematic Reviews* 17 (4): e1181.

Anderson, S. J., and D. McKenzie. 2022. "Improving Business Practices and the Boundary of the Entrepreneur: A Randomized Experiment Comparing Training, Consulting, Insourcing, and Outsourcing." *Journal of Political Economy* 130 (1): 157–209.

Anton, J. J., and D. A. Yao. 2002. "The Sale of Ideas: Strategic Disclosure, Property Rights, and Contracting." *Review of Economic Studies* 69 (3): 513–31.

Arrow, K. 1962. "Economic Welfare and the Allocation of Resources for Invention." In *The Rate and Direction of Inventive Activity: Economic and Social Factors,* compiled by the Universities–National Bureau Committee for Economic Research and the Committee on Economic Growth of the Social Science Research Council, 609–26. Princeton, NJ: Princeton University Press.

Balbontin, R., A. Cusolito, and X. Cirera. 2021. "A Review of Digital Upgrading Programs." Unpublished.

Besley, T. 2007. *Principled Agents? The Political Economy of Good Government.* Oxford, UK: Oxford University Press.

Besley, T., and A. Case. 1993. "Modeling Technology Adoption in Developing Countries." *American Economic Review* 83 (2): 396–402.

Bloom, N., B. Eifert, A. Mahajan, D. McKenzie, and J. Roberts. 2013. "Does Management Matter? Evidence from India." *Quarterly Journal of Economics* 128 (1): 1–51.

Bloom, N., A. Mahajan, D. McKenzie, and J. Roberts. 2020. "Do Management Interventions Last? Evidence from India." *American Economic Journal: Applied Economics* 12 (2): 198–219.

Bruhn, M., D. Karlan, and A. Schoar. 2018. "The Impact of Consulting Services on Small and Medium Enterprises: Evidence from a Randomized Trial in Mexico." *Journal of Political Economy* 126 (2): 635–87.

Bryan, K. A., and H. L. Williams. 2021. "Innovation: Market Failures and Public Policies." NBER Working Paper 29173, National Bureau of Economic Research, Cambridge, MA.

Cai, J., and A. Szeidl. 2022. "Indirect Effects of Access to Finance." NBER Working Paper 29813, National Bureau of Economic Research, Cambridge, MA.

Camerer, C., and Davies, Lovallo. 1999. "Overconfidence and Excess Entry: An Experimental Approach." *American Economic Review* 89 (1): 306–18.

Cirera, X., M. Cruz, E. Davies, A. Grover, L. Iacovone, J. E. Lopez Cordova, D. Medvedev, F. O. Maduko, G. Nayyar, S. R. Ortega, and J. Torres. 2021. "Policies to Support Businesses through the COVID-19 Shock: A Firm-Level Perspective." *World Bank Research Observer* 36 (1): 41–66.

Cirera, X., J. Frias, J. Hill, and Y. Li. 2020. *A Practitioner's Guide to Innovation Policy: Instruments to Build Firm Capabilities and Accelerate Technological Catch-Up in Developing Countries.* Washington, DC: World Bank.

Cirera, X., and W. F. Maloney. 2017. *The Innovation Paradox: Developing-Country Capabilities and the Unrealized Promise of Technological Catch-Up.* World Bank Productivity Project series. Washington, DC: World Bank.

Cohen, W. M., and D. A. Levinthal. 1990. "Absorptive Capacity: A New Perspective on Learning and Innovation." *Administrative Science Quarterly* 35 (1): 128–52.

Comin, D., G. Licht, M. Pellens, and T. Schubert. 2019. "Do Companies Benefit from Public Research Organizations? The Impact of the Fraunhofer Society in Germany." Discussion Paper 19–006, ZEW–Leibnitz Center for European Economic Research, Mannheim, Germany.

Correa, P., and C. Schmidt. 2014. "Public Research Organizations and Agricultural Development in Brazil: How Did Embrapa Get It Right?" *Economic Premise* 145: 1–10.

Cruz, M., M. Bussolo, and L. Iacovone. 2018. "Organizing Knowledge to Compete: Impacts of Capacity Building Programs on Firm Organization." *Journal of International Economics* 111 (March): 1–20.

Cruz, M., X. Cirera, N. Dalvit, and K. Lee. Forthcoming. "Implementing the Firm-Level Diagnostic Tool: Operation Manual." World Bank, Washington, DC.

Cruz, M., M. A. Dutz, and C. Rodríguez-Castelán. 2022. *Digital Senegal for Inclusive Growth: Technological Transformation for Better and More Jobs.* International Development in Focus series. Washington, DC: World Bank.

Fukugawa, N. 2009. "Determinants of Licensing Activities of Local Public Technology Centers in Japan." *Technovation* 29 (12): 885–92.

Giorcelli, M. 2019. "The Long-Term Effects of Management and Technology Transfers." *American Economic Review* 109 (1): 121–52.

Hoff, K. 2000. "Beyond Rosenstein-Rodan: The Modern Theory of Underdevelopment Traps." *Proceedings of the World Bank Annual Conference on Development Economics.* Washington, DC: World Bank.

Iacovone, L., W. F. Maloney, and D. McKenzie. 2022. "Improving Management with Individual and Group-Based Consulting: Results from a Randomized Experiment in Colombia." *Review of Economic Studies* 89 (1): 346–71.

Jarmin, R. S. 1999. "Evaluating the Impact of Manufacturing Extension on Productivity Growth." *Journal of Policy Analysis and Management* 18 (1): 99–119.

Kondylis, F., V. Mueller, and J. Zhu. 2017. "Seeing Is Believing? Evidence from an Extension Network Experiment." *Journal of Development Economics* 125 (C): 1–20.

KOTEC (Korea Technology Finance Corporation). 2019. *2019 Evaluation of Microeconomic Impact of 2019 Technology Finance Support Program.* Busan: KOTEC.

KOTEC (Korea Technology Finance Corporation). 2020. *KOTEC 2019 Annual Report.* Busan: KOTEC.

Kwon, S. 2012. "A Study on the Characteristics and the Performances of the Technology-Based Guaranteed SMEs." *Journal of Industrial Economics* 25 (3): 2069–87.

Lach, S., Z. Neeman, and M. Schankerman. 2021. "Government Financing of R&D: A Mechanism Design Approach." *American Economic Journal: Microeconomics* 13 (3): 238–72.

Lee, H., K. Shin, and J. Frias. 2020. "An Overview of KOTEC's Credit Guarantee Scheme." Unpublished.

Maertens, A., H. Michelson, and V. Nourani. 2021. "How Do Farmers Learn from Extension Services? Evidence from Malawi." *American Journal of Agricultural Economics* 103 (2): 569–95.

Maloney, W. F. 2002. "Missed Opportunities: Innovation and Resource-Based Growth in Latin America." Policy Research Working Paper 2935. World Bank, Washington, DC.

McKenzie, D., C. Woodruff, K. Bjorvatn, M. Bruhn, J. Cai, J. Gonzalez-Uribe, S. Quinn, T. Sonobe, and M. Valdivia. 2021. "Training Entrepreneurs: Issue 2." *VoxDevLit* 1 (1): 3.

Owens, T., J. Hoddinott, and B. Kinsey. 2003. "The Impact of Agricultural Extension on Farm Production in Resettlement Areas of Zimbabwe." *Economic Development and Cultural Change* 51 (2): 337–57.

Rodríguez-Clare, A. 2006. "Coordination Failure, Clusters, and Microeconomic Interventions." *Economia* 6 (1): 1–42.

Shapira, P. 1992. "Modernizing Small Manufacturers in Japan: The Role of Local Public Technology Centers." *Journal of Technology Transfer* 17 (1): 40–57.

Shapira, P., J. Youtie, and L. Kay. 2011. "Building Capabilities for Innovation in SMEs: A Cross-Country Comparison of Technology Extension Policies and Programmes." *International Journal of Innovation and Regional Development* 3 (3–4): 254–72.

Wren, C., and D. J. Storey. 2002. "Evaluating the Effect of Soft Business Support upon Small Firm Performance." *Oxford Economic Papers* 54 (2): 334–65.

Zhu, T. J., P. Grinsted, H. Song, and M. Velamuri. Forthcoming. "Digital Businesses in Developing Countries: New Insights for a Digital Development Pathway."

Appendix A. The Firm-level Adoption of Technology (FAT) Survey, Implementation, and Data Set

The Firm-level Adoption of Technology (FAT) data set is based on multicountry, multisector, representative firm-level surveys. The data set provides information about the technologies used by firms in particular general business functions (GBFs) and sector-specific business functions (SBFs) that encompass the key activities that each firm conducts. The survey measures four dimensions of technology adoption: which technologies firms use; what business functions firms use them for; how intensively firms use them; and how sophisticated those technologies are. More detailed information on data collection, implementation, and robustness is provided by Cirera et al. (2020).

Business Functions and Relevant Technologies

To identify business functions and relevant technologies associated with them, the team developed a methodology that follows three steps, involving more than 50 industry experts. First, the team reviewed journal articles and technical reports. Based on this initial research, the team implemented several internal review processes with sector specialists at the World Bank Group to confirm these business functions and technologies for each sector. Then, the team conducted a thorough external review process with senior private sector technology experts outside of the World Bank. These experts had experience in production processes in each specific sector of both advanced economies and developing countries, so they could easily map the variety, scope and complexity of different technologies.

The series of figures that follow focus on SBFs and associated technologies covered by the FAT survey for various sectors. One sector in agriculture is covered: livestock (figure A.1). For manufacturing, four sectors are included: wearing apparel (figure A.2); leather and footwear (figure A.3); motor vehicles (figure A.4); and pharmaceuticals (figure A.5); along with the business functions and associated technologies common across fabrication (figure A.6). For services, four sectors are featured: land transport (figure A.7); financial services (figure A.8); accommodation (figure A.9); and health services (figure A.10). Additional sectors in agriculture (crops), manufacturing (food processing), and services (retail and wholesale), as well as the GBFs and their respective technologies are shown in figure 1.5 in chapter 1.

FIGURE A.1 Livestock: Sector-Specific Business Functions and Technologies

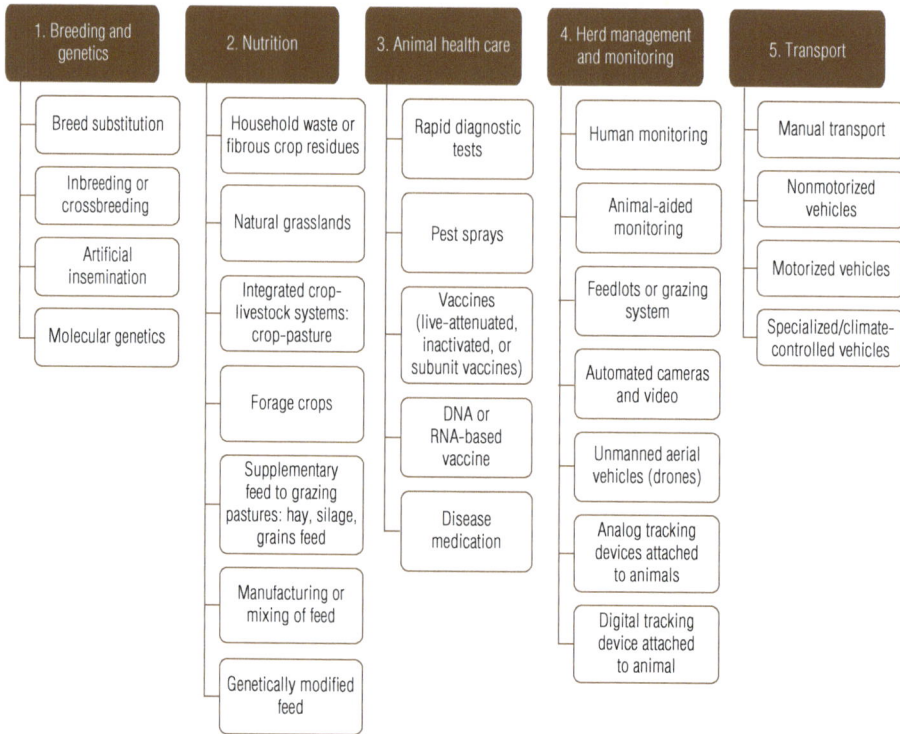

1. Breeding and genetics	2. Nutrition	3. Animal health care	4. Herd management and monitoring	5. Transport
Breed substitution	Household waste or fibrous crop residues	Rapid diagnostic tests	Human monitoring	Manual transport
Inbreeding or crossbreeding	Natural grasslands	Pest sprays	Animal-aided monitoring	Nonmotorized vehicles
Artificial insemination	Integrated crop-livestock systems: crop-pasture	Vaccines (live-attenuated, inactivated, or subunit vaccines)	Feedlots or grazing system	Motorized vehicles
Molecular genetics	Forage crops	DNA or RNA-based vaccine	Automated cameras and video	Specialized/climate-controlled vehicles
	Supplementary feed to grazing pastures: hay, silage, grains feed	Disease medication	Unmanned aerial vehicles (drones)	
	Manufacturing or mixing of feed		Analog tracking devices attached to animals	
	Genetically modified feed		Digital tracking device attached to animal	

Source: Original figure based on the Firm-level Adoption of Technology (FAT) survey.

FIGURE A.2 Wearing Apparel: Sector-Specific Business Functions and Technologies

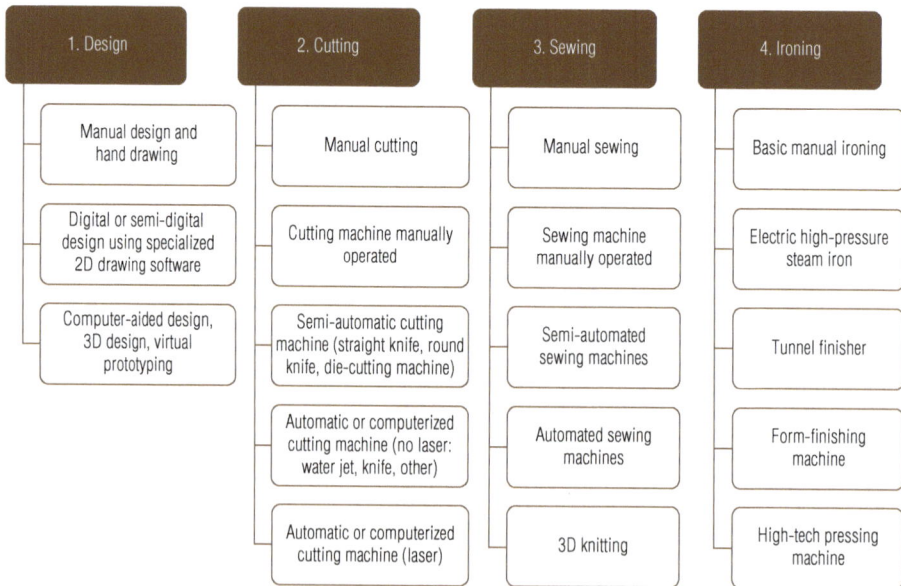

1. Design	2. Cutting	3. Sewing	4. Ironing
Manual design and hand drawing	Manual cutting	Manual sewing	Basic manual ironing
Digital or semi-digital design using specialized 2D drawing software	Cutting machine manually operated	Sewing machine manually operated	Electric high-pressure steam iron
Computer-aided design, 3D design, virtual prototyping	Semi-automatic cutting machine (straight knife, round knife, die-cutting machine)	Semi-automated sewing machines	Tunnel finisher
	Automatic or computerized cutting machine (no laser: water jet, knife, other)	Automated sewing machines	Form-finishing machine
	Automatic or computerized cutting machine (laser)	3D knitting	High-tech pressing machine

Source: Original figure based on the Firm-level Adoption of Technology (FAT) survey.
Note: 2D = two-dimensional; 3D = three-dimensional.

Bridging the Technological Divide

FIGURE A.3 Leather and Footwear: Sector-Specific Business Functions and Technologies

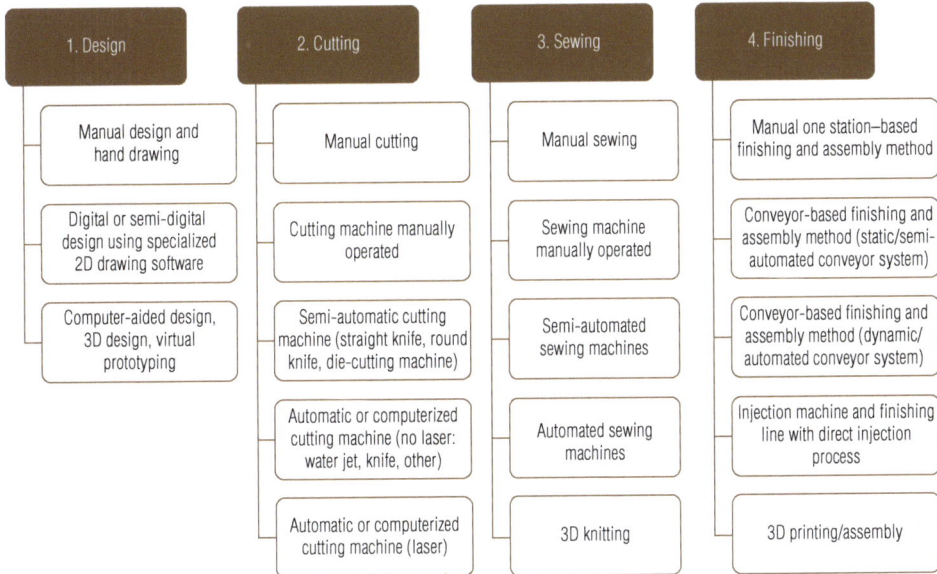

1. Design	2. Cutting	3. Sewing	4. Finishing
Manual design and hand drawing	Manual cutting	Manual sewing	Manual one station–based finishing and assembly method
Digital or semi-digital design using specialized 2D drawing software	Cutting machine manually operated	Sewing machine manually operated	Conveyor-based finishing and assembly method (static/semi-automated conveyor system)
Computer-aided design, 3D design, virtual prototyping	Semi-automatic cutting machine (straight knife, round knife, die-cutting machine)	Semi-automated sewing machines	Conveyor-based finishing and assembly method (dynamic/automated conveyor system)
	Automatic or computerized cutting machine (no laser: water jet, knife, other)	Automated sewing machines	Injection machine and finishing line with direct injection process
	Automatic or computerized cutting machine (laser)	3D knitting	3D printing/assembly

Source: Original figure based on the Firm-level Adoption of Technology (FAT) survey.
Note: 2D = two-dimensional; 3D = three-dimensional.

FIGURE A.4 Motor Vehicles: Sector-Specific Business Functions and Technologies

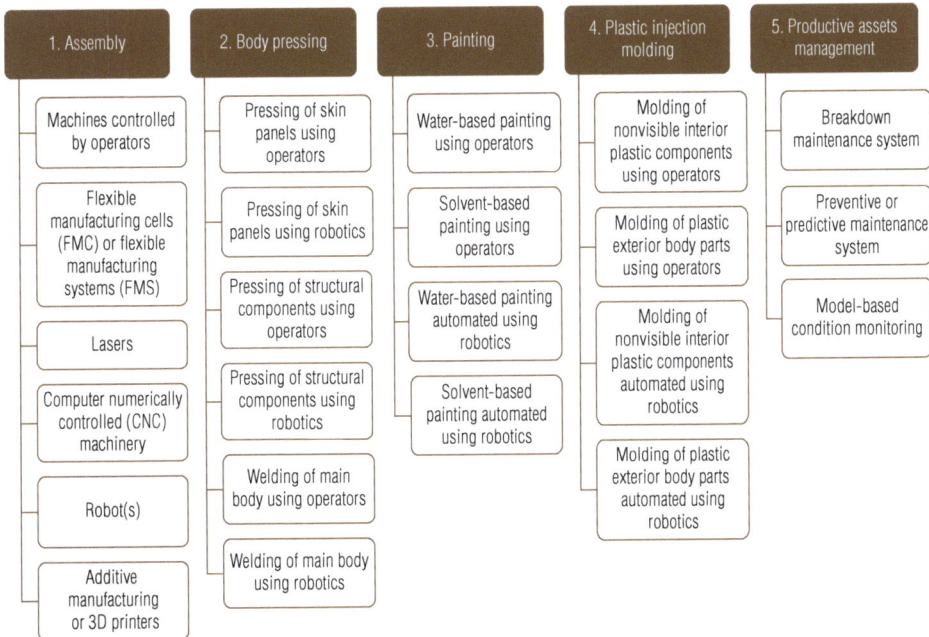

1. Assembly	2. Body pressing	3. Painting	4. Plastic injection molding	5. Productive assets management
Machines controlled by operators	Pressing of skin panels using operators	Water-based painting using operators	Molding of nonvisible interior plastic components using operators	Breakdown maintenance system
Flexible manufacturing cells (FMC) or flexible manufacturing systems (FMS)	Pressing of skin panels using robotics	Solvent-based painting using operators	Molding of plastic exterior body parts using operators	Preventive or predictive maintenance system
Lasers	Pressing of structural components using operators	Water-based painting automated using robotics	Molding of nonvisible interior plastic components automated using robotics	Model-based condition monitoring
Computer numerically controlled (CNC) machinery	Pressing of structural components using robotics	Solvent-based painting automated using robotics	Molding of plastic exterior body parts automated using robotics	
Robot(s)	Welding of main body using operators			
Additive manufacturing or 3D printers	Welding of main body using robotics			

Source: Original figure based on the Firm-level Adoption of Technology (FAT) survey.
Note: 3D = three-dimensional.

FIGURE A.5   Pharmaceuticals: Sector-Specific Business Functions and Technologies

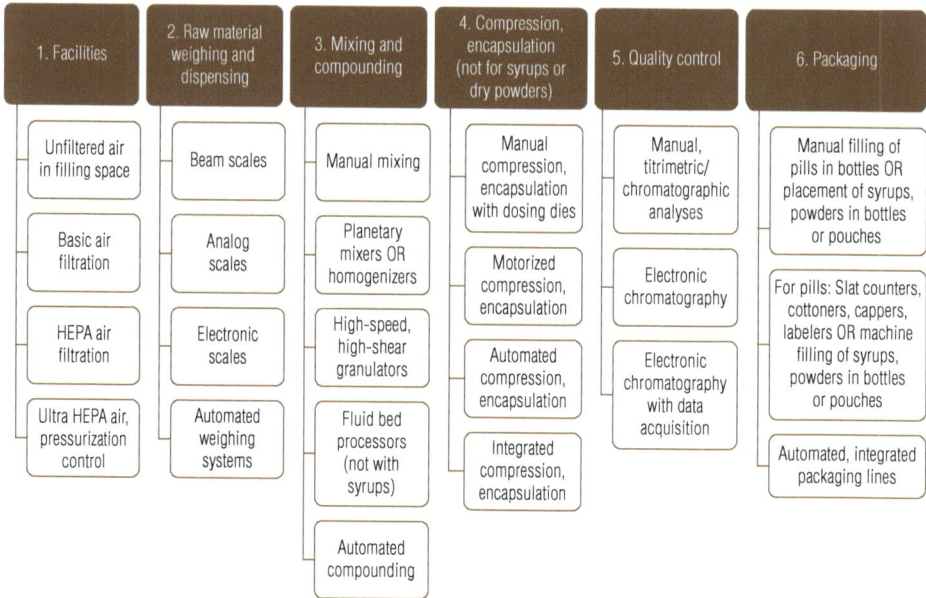

1. Facilities	2. Raw material weighing and dispensing	3. Mixing and compounding	4. Compression, encapsulation (not for syrups or dry powders)	5. Quality control	6. Packaging
Unfiltered air in filling space	Beam scales	Manual mixing	Manual compression, encapsulation with dosing dies	Manual, titrimetric/ chromatographic analyses	Manual filling of pills in bottles OR placement of syrups, powders in bottles or pouches
Basic air filtration	Analog scales	Planetary mixers OR homogenizers	Motorized compression, encapsulation	Electronic chromatography	For pills: Slat counters, cottoners, cappers, labelers OR machine filling of syrups, powders in bottles or pouches
HEPA air filtration	Electronic scales	High-speed, high-shear granulators	Automated compression, encapsulation	Electronic chromatography with data acquisition	Automated, integrated packaging lines
Ultra HEPA air, pressurization control	Automated weighing systems	Fluid bed processors (not with syrups)	Integrated compression, encapsulation		
		Automated compounding			

Source: Original figure based on the Firm-level Adoption of Technology (FAT) survey.
Note: HEPA = high-efficiency particulate air filter.

FIGURE A.6   Manufacturing (Fabrication): Sector-Specific Business Functions and Technologies

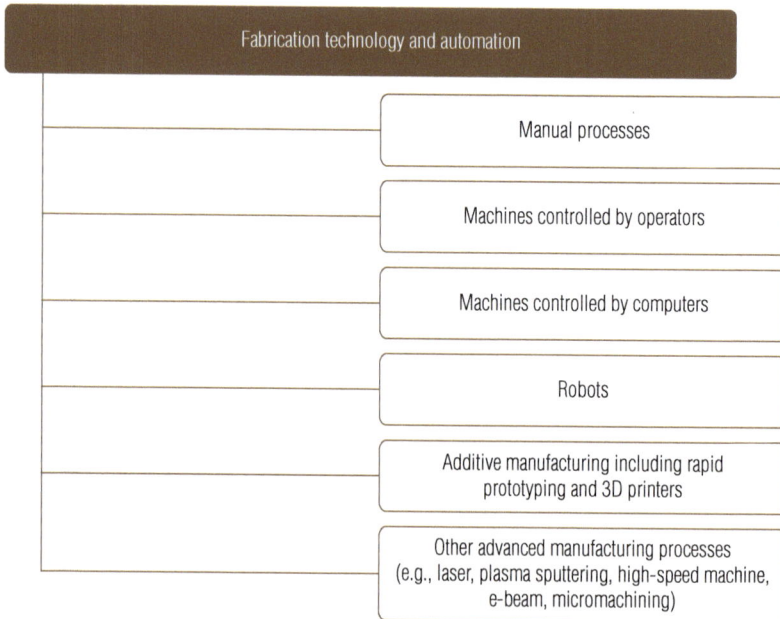

Fabrication technology and automation

- Manual processes
- Machines controlled by operators
- Machines controlled by computers
- Robots
- Additive manufacturing including rapid prototyping and 3D printers
- Other advanced manufacturing processes (e.g., laser, plasma sputtering, high-speed machine, e-beam, micromachining)

Source: Original figure based on the Firm-level Adoption of Technology (FAT) survey.
Note: "Manufacturing" here excludes the food-processing and wearing apparel sectors. 3D = three-dimensional.

Bridging the Technological Divide

FIGURE A.7 Land Transport: Sector-Specific Business Functions and Technologies

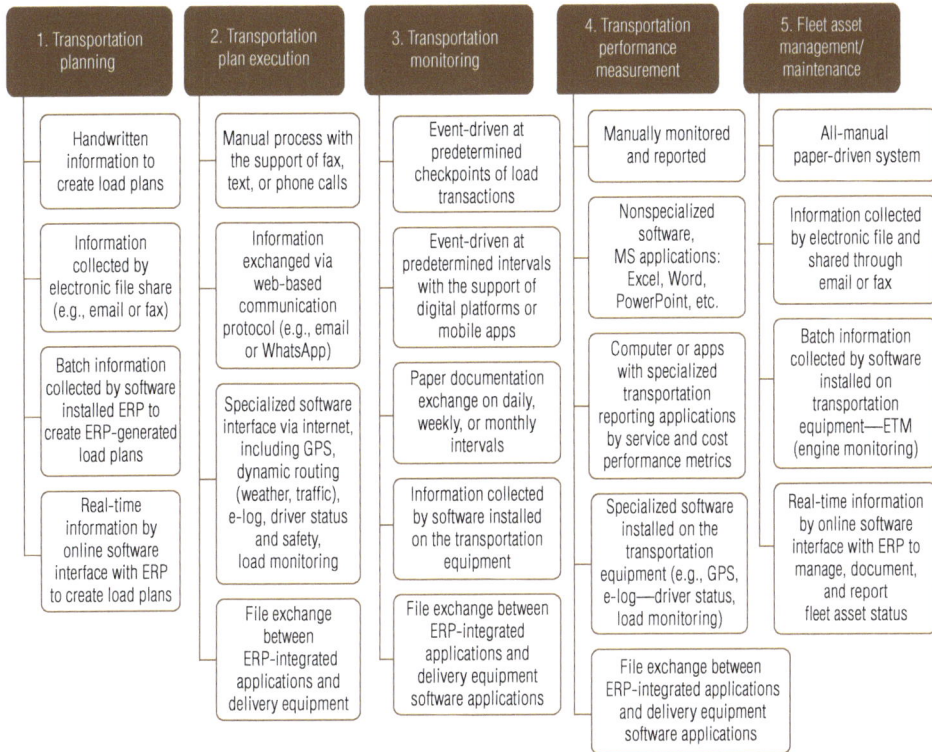

1. Transportation planning	2. Transportation plan execution	3. Transportation monitoring	4. Transportation performance measurement	5. Fleet asset management/ maintenance
Handwritten information to create load plans	Manual process with the support of fax, text, or phone calls	Event-driven at predetermined checkpoints of load transactions	Manually monitored and reported	All-manual paper-driven system
Information collected by electronic file share (e.g., email or fax)	Information exchanged via web-based communication protocol (e.g., email or WhatsApp)	Event-driven at predetermined intervals with the support of digital platforms or mobile apps	Nonspecialized software, MS applications: Excel, Word, PowerPoint, etc.	Information collected by electronic file and shared through email or fax
Batch information collected by software installed ERP to create ERP-generated load plans	Specialized software interface via internet, including GPS, dynamic routing (weather, traffic), e-log, driver status and safety, load monitoring	Paper documentation exchange on daily, weekly, or monthly intervals	Computer or apps with specialized transportation reporting applications by service and cost performance metrics	Batch information collected by software installed on transportation equipment—ETM (engine monitoring)
Real-time information by online software interface with ERP to create load plans		Information collected by software installed on the transportation equipment	Specialized software installed on the transportation equipment (e.g., GPS, e-log—driver status, load monitoring)	Real-time information by online software interface with ERP to manage, document, and report fleet asset status
	File exchange between ERP-integrated applications and delivery equipment	File exchange between ERP-integrated applications and delivery equipment software applications	File exchange between ERP-integrated applications and delivery equipment software applications	

Source: Original figure based on the Firm-level Adoption of Technology (FAT) survey.
Note: ERP = enterprise resource planning; ETM = equipment and tool management; GPS = global positioning system; MS = Microsoft.

FIGURE A.8 Financial Services: Sector-Specific Business Functions and Technologies

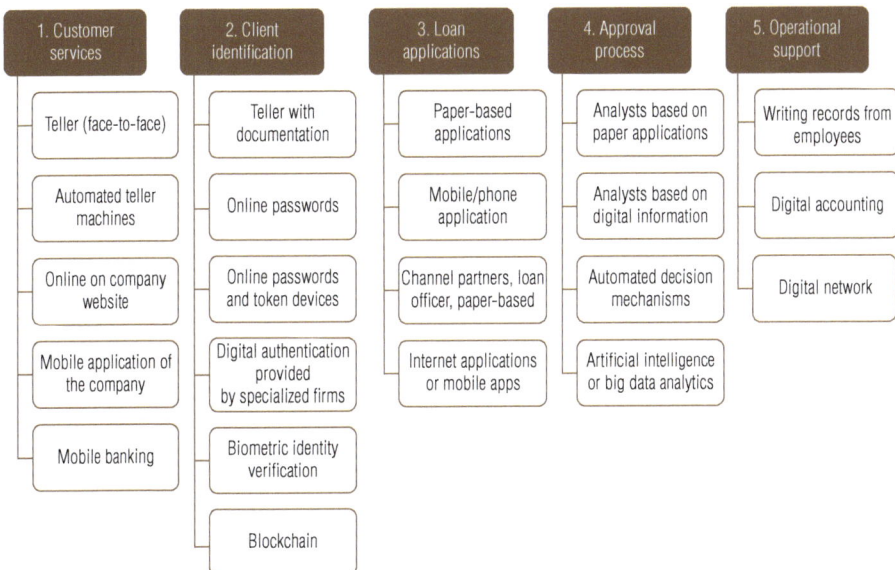

1. Customer services	2. Client identification	3. Loan applications	4. Approval process	5. Operational support
Teller (face-to-face)	Teller with documentation	Paper-based applications	Analysts based on paper applications	Writing records from employees
Automated teller machines	Online passwords	Mobile/phone application	Analysts based on digital information	Digital accounting
Online on company website	Online passwords and token devices	Channel partners, loan officer, paper-based	Automated decision mechanisms	Digital network
Mobile application of the company	Digital authentication provided by specialized firms	Internet applications or mobile apps	Artificial intelligence or big data analytics	
Mobile banking	Biometric identity verification			
	Blockchain			

Source: Original figure based on the Firm-level Adoption of Technology (FAT) survey.

FIGURE A.9   Accommodation: Sector-Specific Business Functions and Technologies

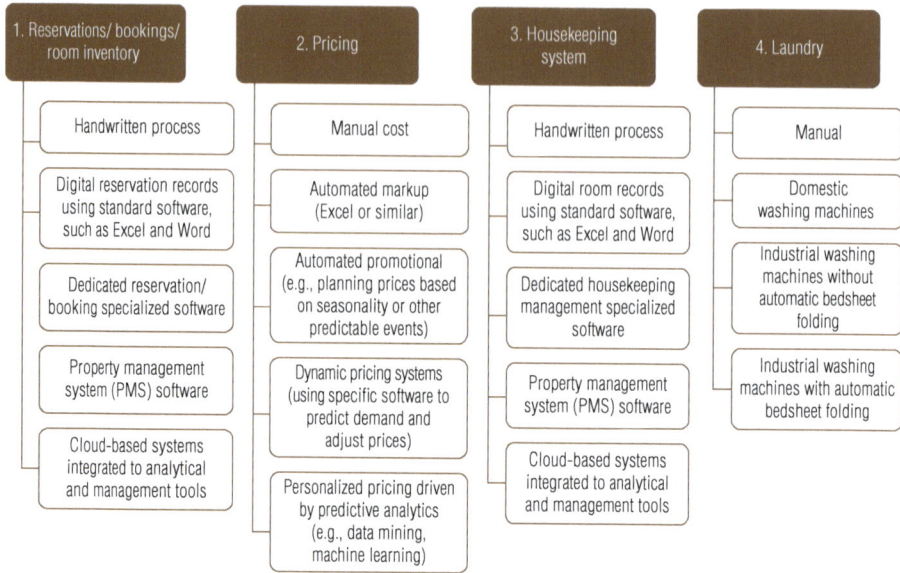

1. Reservations/ bookings/ room inventory	2. Pricing	3. Housekeeping system	4. Laundry
Handwritten process	Manual cost	Handwritten process	Manual
Digital reservation records using standard software, such as Excel and Word	Automated markup (Excel or similar)	Digital room records using standard software, such as Excel and Word	Domestic washing machines
Dedicated reservation/ booking specialized software	Automated promotional (e.g., planning prices based on seasonality or other predictable events)	Dedicated housekeeping management specialized software	Industrial washing machines without automatic bedsheet folding
Property management system (PMS) software	Dynamic pricing systems (using specific software to predict demand and adjust prices)	Property management system (PMS) software	Industrial washing machines with automatic bedsheet folding
Cloud-based systems integrated to analytical and management tools	Personalized pricing driven by predictive analytics (e.g., data mining, machine learning)	Cloud-based systems integrated to analytical and management tools	

Source: Original figure based on the Firm-level Adoption of Technology (FAT) survey.

FIGURE A.10   Health Services: Sector-Specific Business Functions and Technologies

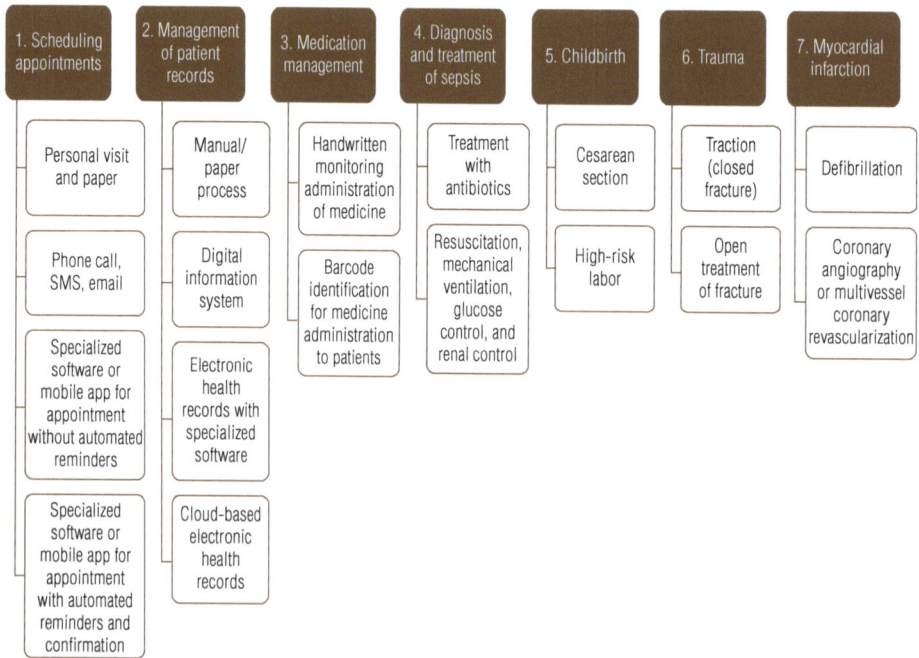

1. Scheduling appointments	2. Management of patient records	3. Medication management	4. Diagnosis and treatment of sepsis	5. Childbirth	6. Trauma	7. Myocardial infarction
Personal visit and paper	Manual/ paper process	Handwritten monitoring administration of medicine	Treatment with antibiotics	Cesarean section	Traction (closed fracture)	Defibrillation
Phone call, SMS, email	Digital information system	Barcode identification for medicine administration to patients	Resuscitation, mechanical ventilation, glucose control, and renal control	High-risk labor	Open treatment of fracture	Coronary angiography or multivessel coronary revascularization
Specialized software or mobile app for appointment without automated reminders	Electronic health records with specialized software					
Specialized software or mobile app for appointment with automated reminders and confirmation	Cloud-based electronic health records					

Source: Original figure based on the Firm-level Adoption of Technology (FAT) survey.

Note: The intensive margin of technology for business functions 4–7 for health is based on the level of availability of these technologies for patients. SMS = short message service (text message).

The Firm Adoption of Technology Index

The FAT survey asks two types of questions about the technologies used to perform a business function. The first type of question regards the use of each of the technologies listed by the experts as relevant in a given business function (corresponding to whether or not firms adopt technology). The answer to this question characterizes the full array of technologies that the firm uses. The second type of question gathers information about which of the technologies used is employed more intensively (corresponding to *what* and *how* firms use technology). The answer to this question is used to construct technology measures that reflect the nature of the most frequently used technology in the business function (the intensive margin) as opposed to the array of technologies used by the firm (the extensive margin). This distinction is relevant because firms do not use all the technologies available to perform a business function with the same intensity, and the impact of a technology on the firm's productivity may depend on the importance of the technology used most intensively.

To measure technology sophistication, the technology options are combined into an index, following the methodology proposed by Cirera et al. (2020), capturing the proximity to the technology frontier for each business function. The technology indexes are defined as

$$EXT_{f,j} = 1 + 4 \times \hat{r}_{f,j}^{EXT}$$

$$INT_{f,j} = 1 + 4 \times \hat{r}_{f,j}^{INT}$$

$EXT_{f,j}$ is the most advanced technology (extensive margin) used in a business function f within a firm j. $INT_{f,j}$ is the index for most widely used technology (intensive margin). $\hat{r}_f$ is a relative rank of technology defined as $\dfrac{r_{f-1}}{R_{f-1}}$, where r_f is a rank of technology and R_f is the maximum rank in a business function. The technology index ranges from 1 to 5, where 1 stands for the most basic level of technology and 5 reflects the most sophisticated. With the help of experts for each industry, a rank was assigned to the technologies in each business function according to their sophistication. The analysis presented in this volume relies mostly on the INT index, except if the use of EXT is explicitly specified. More details about the index and robustness checks are available in Cirera et al. (2020).

Sampling Frame

The sampling frames for the FAT survey were based on the most comprehensive and latest establishment census available from national statistical agencies or the administrative business register in each country. Table A.1 describes the main source of data, the sampling frame, and the year and mode of data collection.

The universe of study includes establishments with 5 or more workers in agriculture, manufacturing, and services. The sector classification is based on the International

TABLE A.1   **Number of Establishments Surveyed, by Strata**

Country	Source	Sampling frame	Year and mode of data collection
Bangladesh	Bangladesh Bureau of Statistics	Establishment census, 2013[a]	2019, face-to-face
Brazil	Ministry of Labor	Establishment census, RAIS, 2018[b]	2019, face-to-face
Burkina Faso	Business Registry	Business Registry in Commerce and Industry Chamber	2021, telephone
Ghana	Ghana Statistical Service	Economic Census (IBES Phase 1 and Phase 2), 2013	2021, telephone
India	Central Statistics Office of India	Economic Census, 2013 Annual Survey of Industries (ASI), 2017–18[c]	2020, face-to-face
Kenya	Kenya National Bureau of Statistics	Establishment census, 2017	2020, telephone
Korea, Rep.	Statistics Korea	Establishment census, 2018	2020–21, telephone
Malawi	National Statistical Office of Malawi	Establishment census, 2018	2019–20, face-to-face
Poland	Statistics Poland	Establishment census, 2020	2021, telephone
Senegal	National Agency for Statistics and Demography	Establishment census, 2016	2019, face-to-face
Vietnam	General Statistics Office of Vietnam	Establishment census, 2018	2019, face-to-face

Source: Original table based on the Firm-level Adoption of Technology (FAT) survey.

a. For Bangladesh, the sampling frame was based on the latest establishment census available complemented with an updated list from the business registry.

b. For Brazil, the information came from *Relação Anual de Informações Sociais* (RAIS), a matched employer-employee database covering all formal firms. Data for Brazil are only for the state of Ceará.

c. For India, the sampling frame included firms with 10 or more workers and combines the latest establishment census (2013) for services and the ASI (2017–18) for manufacturing. Data for India are only for the states of Tamil Nadu and Uttar Pradesh.

Standard Industrial Classification of All Economic Activities (ISIC), Rev. 4. More specifically, the sample includes firms from the following ISIC Rev. 4 sectors: agriculture (ISIC 01, from Group A); all manufacturing sectors (Group C); construction (Group F); wholesale and retail trade (Group G); transportation and storage (Group G); accommodation and food service activities (Group I); information and communication (Group J); financial services (ISIC 64) (from Group K, financial and insurance activities); travel agency (ISIC 79, from Group N); health services (ISIC 86, from Group Q); and repair services (ISIC 95, from Group S).

The survey was stratified according to the universe of establishments by sector of activity, firm size, and geographic regions. The sample is representative across these dimensions. For sectors, for all countries, the sample was stratified at least for agriculture (ISIC 01); food processing (ISIC 10); wearing apparel (ISIC 14); retail and wholesale (ISIC 45, 46, and 47); other manufacturing (Group C, excluding food processing and apparel); and other services (including all other firms, excluding retail). This sector structure of the data was used for most of the analysis in this volume. Additional sector stratification that was country specific included: motor vehicles (ISIC 29); leather (ISIC 15); pharmaceuticals (ISIC 21); land transport (ISIC 49); financial services (ISIC 64); and health services (ISIC 86). For the firm size stratification, there are three strata: small firms (5–19 workers); medium firms (20–99 workers); and large firms

(100 or more workers). Table A.2 shows the distribution of the universe of establishments by sector (agriculture, manufacturing, and services) and firm size (small, medium, and large). In the geographic stratification, subnational regions are used. To calculate the optimal distribution of the sample, the team followed a methodology described in World Bank (2022). The sample size for each country was aligned with the degree of stratification of the sample. Table A.3 presents the number of firms surveyed by aggregated sector and by firm size.

Survey Weights

FAT surveys are cross-sectional surveys and rely on probability samples. Before starting the survey in each country, an independent and entirely new sample was randomly selected from the most recent and comprehensive sampling frame available. Therefore, for any FAT survey, the initial weights to be attached to sampled units (which are establishments) are design weights: they are equivalent to unit inclusion probabilities. For any given country, the target population of the FAT survey is the population of establishments that (1) exist at the reference time of the survey; (2) are located within a specific set of regions; (3) operate within a specific set of sectors; and (4) have at least 5 workers.

All FAT surveys adopt a stratified one-stage element sampling design. Establishments are randomly selected with equal probabilities within strata, by sector, region, and firm size groups. Because the sample is not proportionally allocated to the strata, inclusion probabilities differ between strata. The statistical analysis of FAT survey data presented in this volume is performed using the weights to properly account for the selection of sample units with unequal probabilities. FAT weights were adjusted for nonresponse by means of a simple Response Homogeneity Groups (RHG) model (Särndal, Swensson, and Wretman 1992), with groups determined by sampling strata.

Because of the different number of establishments in each country, when computing global statistics for the data, weights were rescaled so that all countries are equally weighted. This means that for results between strata presented in this volume that are not country specific, the weights represent the cross-country average, such that each country has similar weights. Technical details about the weights used in the FAT data are described by Zardetto (forthcoming). In addition, given the significant differences in economic structure, formality, and other economic characteristics of the samples included in the FAT survey, regression tools with controls (e.g., size, sector, and country) are used to adjust some of the statistics shown for the whole sample with different countries and sectors, and to facilitate the comparisons.

Implementation, Quality Control, and Validation

A critical objective of the data collection effort is to obtain robust and comparable measures of the sophistication of technologies used across countries, sectors, firms, and business functions. This requires fully harmonized implementation processes across countries that minimize potential nonresponse, enumerator, and respondent biases.

TABLE A.2   Total Number of Establishments (Population Distribution by Sector and Firm Size)

Country	Total	Sector			Firm size		
		Agriculture	Manufacturing	Services	Small	Medium	Large
Bangladesh	15,363	—	15,363	—	2,154	6,030	7,179
Brazil[a]	23,364	407	4,420	18,537	17,875	4,680	809
Burkina Faso	3,328	93	223	3,012	2,335	770	223
Ghana	44,561	1,077	11,515	31,969	36,016	7,606	939
India[b]	92,061	—	46,655	45,406	56,381	30,610	5,070
Kenya	74,255	4,174	4,102	65,979	50,584	16,676	6,995
Korea, Rep.	461,556	1,424	168,410	291,722	386,796	64,911	9,849
Malawi	2,218	—	365	1,853	1,111	644	463
Poland	244,999	3,826	58,674	182,499	198,112	37,803	9,084
Senegal	9,631	1,026	4,337	4,268	8,196	1,134	301
Vietnam	179,725	1,087	45,810	132,828	140,889	29,070	9,766
Total	**1,151,061**	**13,114**	**359,874**	**778,073**	**900,449**	**199,934**	**50,678**

Source: Original table based on representative sampling frames used by the Firm-level Adoption of Technology (FAT) survey.

Note: For regional stratification, subnational regions are used. Firm size refers to the number of workers: small (5–19), medium (20–99), and large (100 or more). — = not available.

a. Data for Brazil are only for the state of Ceará.

b. Data for India are only for the states of Tamil Nadu and Uttar Pradesh.

TABLE A.3   Number of Establishments Surveyed, by Sector and Firm Size

Country	Total	Sector			Firm size		
		Agriculture	Manufacturing	Services	Small	Medium	Large
Bangladesh	903	—	903	—	361	232	310
Brazil[a]	711	72	387	252	205	322	184
Burkina Faso	600	80	140	380	335	187	78
Ghana	1,262	85	275	902	774	382	106
India[b]	1,519	—	791	728	629	598	292
Kenya	1,305	155	335	815	499	421	385
Korea, Rep.	1,551	129	652	770	656	569	326
Malawi	482	—	137	345	284	122	76
Poland	1,500	90	607	803	779	394	327
Senegal	1,786	204	679	903	1,219	395	172
Vietnam	1,499	110	806	583	774	426	299
Total	**13,118**	**925**	**5,712**	**6,481**	**6,515**	**4,048**	**2,555**

Source: Original table based on the Firm-level Adoption of Technology (FAT) survey.

Note: Firm size refers to the number of workers: small (5–19), medium (20–99), and large (100 or more).

— = not available.

a. Data for Brazil are only for the state of Ceará.

b. Data for India are only for the states of Tamil Nadu and Uttar Pradesh.

The survey was initially implemented face to face. After 2020, with the start of the COVID-19 pandemic, phone interviews were used. To ensure the accuracy of the responses and the comparability of the data collected across countries, a standardized process for implementation was used across all countries. The same terms of reference across all countries were used for the organizations that implemented the survey. These include the requirement that both the organizations, as well as the main team of interviewers, supervisors, and managers, have ample experience in collecting firm-level data in their respective country and follow similar procedures for implementing the survey. Enumerators, supervisors, and managers leading the data implementation in each country received a standard training. The same questionnaire was administered through face-to-face or telephone interviews with Computer Assisted Personal Interviewing (CAPI)/Computer Assisted Telephone Interviewing (CATI) in all countries. The questionnaire was implemented at the establishment level. In the sample, 86 percent of the observations refer to single-establishment firms. In the case of multi-establishment firms, the questionnaire was applied to the specific unit of production that was randomly selected.

Minimizing Potential Nonresponse Bias

Survey implementation was designed to minimize nonresponse through the use of well-prepared agencies and institutions to administer the survey and the presentation of adequate supporting letters to encourage participation. Response rates varied between 24 percent and 80 percent. The response rates were higher when the survey was implemented by national statistical agencies.

The sampling weights were adjusted to minimize response bias. To check the possibility that variation in response rates could lead to biases in the analyses, the team implemented a series of ex post tests in countries with additional data available. For example, the team investigated whether, in the sample of contacted firms, there were significant differences between firms that responded and firms that declined participating or could not be reached. The team also checked whether common variables were similar on average to other available surveys. For details on the overall protocol for sampling weights of the FAT data and several robustness checks implemented by the team, see Zardetto (forthcoming) and Cirera et al. (2020).

References

Cirera, X., C. Comin, M. Cruz, and K. M. Lee. 2020. "Anatomy of Technology in the Firm." NBER Working Paper 28080, National Bureau of Economic Research, Cambridge, MA.

Särndal, C. E., B. Swensson, and J. Wretman. 1992. *Model Assisted Survey Sampling*. New York: Springer Verlag.

World Bank. 2022. "Enterprise Surveys: Sampling Methodology." World Bank, Washington, DC.

Zardetto, D. Forthcoming. "Firm-level Adoption of Technology (FAT) Survey Program: Proposal of a Standardized Weights Calculation Procedure." World Bank, Washington, DC.

www.ingramcontent.com/pod-product-compliance
Lightning Source LLC
Chambersburg PA
CBHW050832220326
41598CB00006B/355